# The New Public Organization

D1343279

Kenneth Kernaghan
Brian Marson
Sandford Borins

Monographs on Canadian Public Administration – No. 24
Monographies sur l'administration publique canadienne – No. 24

IPAC
The Institute of
Public Administration of Canada

IAPC
L'Institut d'administration
publique du Canada

Third Printing: January 2005

**Canadian Cataloguing in Publication Data**

Kernaghan, Kenneth, 1940–
    The new public organization

    (Monographs on Canadian public administration; 24 = Monographies
    sur l'administration publique canadienne; 24)
    Issued also in French under title: L'administration publique de l'avenir.
    ISBN 0-920715-95-8

    1. Public administration – Canada.   I. Marson, Brian.   II. Borins,
    Sandford F., 1949– .   III. Institute of Public Administration of Canada.
    IV. Title.   V. Series: Monographs on Canadian public administration; 24.

    JL75.K47 2000      351.71      C00-932116-0

*PUBLISHED BY / PUBLIÉ PAR*

L'INSTITUT D'ADMINISTRATION PUBLIQUE DU CANADA
THE INSTITUTE OF PUBLIC ADMINISTRATION OF CANADA
1075, rue Bay St., Suite/Bureau 401
Toronto, Ontario, CANADA M5S 2B1
Tel./Tél.: (416) 924-8787 Fax/Bél.: (416) 924-4992
e-mail/courriél.: ntl@ipaciapc.ca

*To public servants who innovate with integrity*

# Table of Contents

# Foreword

Government practices have evolved so dramatically over the past twenty years that innovation hardly qualifies as an unusual practice. The citizenry expects public-service reform and innovation: it wants a wide range of services that are delivered promptly, efficiently, effectively and with integrity. What may surprise some citizens is the degree to which public servants not only demand innovation of themselves and their colleagues but actively pursue it as well – in our towns, cities and provinces and in our federal government.

The Institute of Public Administration of Canada and the Canadian Centre for Management Development are proud to support what must become a definitive reference not only for students of public administration but for students of reform and innovation in all enterprises. Kenneth Kernaghan, Brian Marson and Sandford Borins have delved deeply into the real experience of practitioners and into the scholarly literature to unearth the secrets of reform and innovation that are the hallmark of the new public organization. Their reflections are valuable guides to the challenges facing public servants: serving the public in a manner that champions the "learning public service," adapts to the new environment of digital technology and respects the democratic will.

The book sets a wide range of performance-enhancing measures into an integrated framework that describes the ten dimensions of the new public organization. This framework is an important new tool for government in that it can help public managers to develop a strategic plan to improve their performance.

Reform and innovation are not easy. Whether it is in establishing smarter policy processes or choosing a technology that will better serve public ends, the urge to bring in new thinking and new practices relies heavily on the encouragement of public servants at every level – from front-line workers to deputy ministers and chief administrative officers. We hope that this book will go a long way in convincing its readers that seeking high performance is not merely an ambition: it is – and must continue to be – a daily reality.

Mary Gusella
President, Institute of Public Administration of Canada

Jocelyne Bourgon
President, Canadian Centre for Management Development

# Preface

This book explains concepts and practices that are changing dramatically the structure and culture of public organizations. It also describes innovations that public-service managers may adapt to their own organizations and that may prompt them to take a more innovative approach to managing. While this book discusses reforms in general, particular emphasis is placed on reforms in the sense of *innovations*.

Our experience in writing this book reinforced our view that the study of public administration is very much a multidisciplinary enterprise, with scholars from different disciplines bringing different perspectives to bear. Political scientists, for example, tend to focus on such matters as the senior public service, accountability, law, public policy and the public interest. However, management scholars tend to focus on such matters as leadership, organizational culture, service quality, performance measurement and innovation. Another important perspective for scholarly research in public administration is provided by the ideas and insights of public-service *practitioners*. The co-authors of this book represent these various perspectives. Kenneth Kernaghan, the principal author of the book, is a political scientist from Brock University who specializes in public administration; Brian Marson is a senior public servant at the Treasury Board Secretariat (formerly at the Canadian Centre for Management Development); and Sandford Borins is a management scholar at the University of Toronto. Our cross-disciplinary collaboration has helped us to provide a more balanced and more complete view of the virtues and limitations of the new public organization.

The data for the book are drawn from a wide range of theoretical and case materials on reform in public-sector organizations. A valuable source of data was the submissions to the Institute of Public Administration of Canada (IPAC) Award for Innovative Management competition. Since 1990,

IPAC has publicized, celebrated and documented hundreds of public-sector management innovations. At our invitation, thirty-three of these organizations completed long questionnaires that provided detailed information on their innovations, including information on the major obstacles they faced and updates on their experience since they applied to the IPAC competition. Data are drawn also from the large volume of scholarly writings on public-service reform and on interviews with public servants in all spheres of Canadian government.

Two features of this book distinguish it from most writings on reform in public organizations. The first is that an effort is made to identify and illustrate barriers to successful reform. The second distinguishing feature is that the book deals not only with the political and managerial dimensions of reform but with its often-neglected value and ethical dimensions as well.

Chapter 1 discusses the major forces driving public-service reform, the forms and functions of public organizations, and the characteristics of the bureaucratic and post-bureaucratic models of public organization. Chapter 2 explains the scholarly literature and practical experience on which the post-bureaucratic model is based and illustrates the characteristics of the model by reference to public organizations that have been significantly transformed through innovation. Chapter 3 examines shared values as an integrating and energizing force that can serve as an alternative, or at least a complement, to structural change and reliance on rules. The traditional and new public-service values identified in this chapter are related throughout the book to the movement from the bureaucratic to the post-bureaucratic model of organization.

Chapter 4 provides an overview of the determinants and process of innovation in Canadian governments as a basis for a discussion of specific areas of innovation in the following chapters. Chapter 5 focuses on reforms in the structures and processes of public organizations, and Chapter 6 examines reforms designed to promote improved service to the public, including the setting and implementing of service standards. Chapter 7 explains the concept and practice of empowerment, with special reference to employee participation in decision-making, and Chapter 8 examines the related topic of consultation and partnership involving public organizations and other policy actors. Chapter 9 discusses the extent to which innovation can be sustained and fostered by creating a culture of continuous learning in the organization. Chapter 10 examines the innovative use of information technology, and Chapter 11 examines the need for reforms in the management of the policy-making process, with particular reference to policy capacity and horizontal coordination.

Finally, Chapter 12 examines the lessons learned about making and sustaining reforms in these several areas and assesses the role of leadership in promoting successful innovation.

The content of chapters 5 through 11 is organized in a similar way. Each chapter begins with a discussion of the meaning, origins and evolution of the main concept (e.g., empowerment) or concepts (e.g., consultation and partnership). This is followed by an explanation of the purposes and benefits of putting the concept(s) into practice, the lessons learned from practical experience about how to do this successfully, and the managerial, organizational, political, value and ethical implications involved.

We are indebted to public servants in all spheres of Canadian government for the information and insights they have contributed to this work. We are especially indebted to those public servants who gave so generously of their time in granting us interviews and completing our lengthy questionnaire. A debt of gratitude is owed to the Canadian Centre for Management Development for its financial support for research and publication and in particular for the assistance of Jocelyne Bourgon, Ralph Heintzman and Maurice Demers. We express warm appreciation also to Joe Galimberti, Geoff McIlroy and Patrice Dutil of the Institute of Public Administration of Canada for giving us access to the submissions to its innovative management competition and for managing the publication of the book, including the French version. Finally, we acknowledge the important contribution to our work of anonymous reviewers and of Peter Aucoin (editor of IPAC's Monographs on Canadian Public Administration series). Of course, we are responsible for any errors that remain.

# 1

# Towards the New Public Organization

## BEYOND BUREAUCRACY

Since the mid-1980s in particular, the traditional bureaucratic model of public organization has been subjected to considerable criticism. It is notable, for example, that the impetus for innovation in the award-winning Office of the Registrar General in Ontario was the realization that the office

> reflected a typical bureaucratic structure; where the layers of management are too deep (6 layers from Director to front line), functionality is too specialized (12 separate units), jobs are too detailed and responsibilities over-controlled (147 staff with 41 job descriptions reflecting 23 different job classifications).[1]

Historically, many public servants and public organizations, operating within the traditional bureaucratic model, have played a vital role in fostering economic and social development and sustaining our democratic institutions. However, the environment within which public servants now work is changing rapidly and dramatically. This new environment calls for new approaches to organizing and managing public organizations. Several characteristics of the bureaucratic model seem inadequate to meet the new and anticipated challenges facing the public sector. Thus, public organizations need to take careful account of new theories, practices and technologies that can help them to improve their performance. At the same time, it is important to note the staying power of the bureaucratic model and to avoid blaming this model for what is really poor design and bad management.[2]

This introductory chapter examines briefly the several forces that are driving public-sector reform in the direction of a new model of public organization – the *post-bureaucratic* model. What are the characteristics of this post-bureaucratic model? What is the connection between this model and high-performance organizations? How can high-performance organizations be created? How can high performance be sustained? What is the role of innovation in creating and sustaining high-performance organizations? These are some of the major questions addressed in this book. Particular attention is paid in this first chapter to the contrasting characteristics of the bureaucratic and post-bureaucratic models of organization.

Most of the other chapters focus on the means by which public organizations can move towards the post-bureaucratic model. These means include new organizational forms and processes, new approaches to service delivery, the use of technology, employee empowerment, consultation, partnership, continuous learning and strengthened policy capacity. The *new public organization* discussed in this book has two main features. First, it has moved along the continua between the bureaucratic and the post-bureaucratic models to the extent that is appropriate to the *type* of organization it is and the *functions* it performs. Second, it has learned to sustain the progress it has made and to improve continuously.

## LEARNING FROM OTHERS

This chapter lays the foundation for an analysis in subsequent chapters of the means by which public organizations can, when it is in the public interest, move from the traditional bureaucratic model towards the post-bureaucratic model of public organization.[3] The two models are depicted in Table 1.1. Many public organizations have primarily the characteristics of the bureaucratic model. However, many other public organizations have moved towards the post-bureaucratic model by making reforms to improve their performance and to adjust to changing circumstances. Consider, for example, a departmental unit that becomes a revenue-dependent special-operating agency and must, therefore, become more service-oriented.

We do not suggest that every public organization should – or can – adopt all the characteristics of the post-bureaucratic model. Some organizations can be substantially transformed through extensive reform, but in other organizations and in the public sector as a whole the cumulative impact of relatively small changes can also be impressive. Each organization can learn how to improve its performance by examining the experience of other organizations that have sought or achieved improvement through change, especially through innovation The term innovation is defined broadly here as "an idea, a technique, or a device that was new to the adopting body, no matter whether it was something completely new

Table 1.1. *From the Bureaucratic to the Post-Bureaucratic Organization*

| Characteristics of the bureaucratic organization | Characteristics of the post-bureaucratic organization |
| --- | --- |
| *POLICY AND MANAGEMENT CULTURE* | |
| ORGANIZATION-CENTRED<br>Emphasis on needs of the organization itself | CITIZEN-CENTRED<br>Quality service to citizens (and clients/stakeholders) |
| POSITION POWER<br>Control, command and compliance | PARTICIPATIVE LEADERSHIP<br>Shared values and participative decision-making |
| RULE-CENTRED<br>Rules, procedures and constraints | PEOPLE-CENTRED<br>An empowering and caring milieu for employees |
| INDEPENDENT ACTION<br>Little consultation, cooperation or coordination | COLLECTIVE ACTION<br>Consultation, cooperation and coordination |
| STATUS-QUO-ORIENTED<br>Avoiding risks and mistakes | CHANGE-ORIENTED<br>Innovation, risk-taking and continuous improvement |
| PROCESS-ORIENTED<br>Accountability for process | RESULTS-ORIENTED<br>Accountability for results |
| *STRUCTURE* | |
| CENTRALIZED<br>Hierarchy and central controls | DECENTRALIZED<br>Decentralization of authority and control |
| DEPARTMENTAL FORM<br>Most programs delivered by operating departments | NON-DEPARTMENTAL FORM<br>Programs delivered by wide variety of mechanisms |
| *MARKET ORIENTATION* | |
| BUDGET-DRIVEN<br>Programs financed largely from appropriations | REVENUE-DRIVEN<br>Programs financed as far as possible on cost-recovery basis |
| MONOPOLISTIC<br>Government has monopoly on program delivery | COMPETITIVE<br>Competition with private-sector program delivery |

to the world or something borrowed in whole or in part."[4] We encourage readers to consider whether public organizations can be improved by adopting or adapting some of the innovative practices of high-performance organizations – and by avoiding unsuccessful practices and overcoming obstacles to change.

## NO MAGIC PILL

We are writing this book at a time when some of the bloom is off the "reinvention" rose. The literature on reinventing, re-shaping, re-thinking and re-engineering government has stimulated a remarkable amount of innovative activity in public organizations; it has also, however, provoked a vigorous debate among academics and practitioners of public administration as to its relevance and utility. We have aimed to present in this book a balanced, realistic picture of public-sector reform. We have noted the criticisms levelled at the reinvention writings,[5] and we have included in our own research an examination of the problems as well as the benefits associated with reform. In particular, we have drawn attention to the political, constitutional, legal and ethical constraints that can present significant barriers to innovative management in the public sector.

We are sensitive also to the *panacea phenomenon*, that is, the pattern in which a particular approach to reform is heralded as a cure-all, fails to deliver on over-hyped promises, leads to frustration, and then gives way to the search for a new panacea.[6] This phenomenon is all too familiar in the field of public management. Consider, for example, the fate of management by objectives (MBO) and the Planning Programming Budgeting System (PPBS) in the 1970s, and zero-base budgeting (ZBB) and the Policy and Expenditure Management System (PEMS) in the 1980s.

## FORCES DRIVING PUBLIC-SERVICE REFORM

The reform of public organizations in Canada, as elsewhere, is being driven by a variety of domestic and external forces. These forces are discussed briefly here because they are already well known not only in the public administration community but in society generally. The next chapter explains the ways in which public organizations have responded to these forces through reforms in their structure, management and culture.

For analytical purposes, the environmental forces stimulating reform in public organizations can be grouped into "external" and "domestic" forces. External forces (e.g., globalization) are those that affect governments largely from outside the country whereas "domestic" forces (e.g., public demands, public debts) arise largely from a country's unique political, social and economic circumstances.

### External Forces

Increasingly, most policy issues facing governments have an transnational

4

dimension. The globalization phenomenon, combined with the technologically driven information and communications revolution, means that
public managers must think and act on a transnational basis.

## Globalization

Nancy Adler captures the importance of globalization for governments in
her assertion that the challenge to compete globally is as compelling for
government leaders as for business executives: "In today's interdependent
world, no leader – whether government or corporate ... has the luxury of
narrowing the scope of his or her thinking to within predefined political,
economic, or cultural boundaries. Expanding beyond historic boundaries
requires that we learn to manage and to think very differently."[7]

The interdependence of national economies involves not only business
organizations but most government organizations as well. It also requires
effective management of interaction *between* business and government, if
only to match high levels of business–government cooperation in other
countries. Governments must help business to cope with the impact of
global forces, especially the impact of highly competitive international
markets.

Governments can also provide advice to business on economic and
political structures in other countries and on how to establish strategic
alliances with foreign businesses and governments. However, a management challenge arises from the need for governments to coordinate the
international activities and linkages of departments and agencies that are
pursuing their particular functional concerns, so that governments can
present a united front on the international scene. There is the prospect
here of an enhanced coordinating role for departments of foreign affairs.

Globalization challenges public managers to engage in innovative management, continuous learning and creative thinking, both to increase the
nation's productivity and competitiveness and to protect industries and
individuals from the adverse effects of the global economy. A recent study
concludes that public-sector innovation can enhance Canada's competitiveness "by improved public sector productivity, by raising the morale of
public servants, by increasing service quality, by lowering the cost of
producing public sector outputs, and by lowering the private sector's cost
of doing business."[8]

## The Technological Revolution

Globalization has been facilitated by technological advance. Modern tele-
communication and computer technologies permit rapid transmission of
information across national borders by governments, businesses, non-
profit organizations, and individuals. Sophisticated information technolo-

gies enable governments to deal more successfully with the increasing number of policy issues (e.g., competitiveness) that transcend national boundaries. These technologies also enable governments to deal with domestic policy issues (e.g., environmental protection) that cross departmental boundaries. As explained in Chapter 10, technological innovation, especially in the area of information technology, has made possible many of the reforms leading to improved organizational performance. A common characteristic of such issues "is that no one department has the mandate and resources to address them adequately ... [I]t is vital to find better ways of pulling together resources from across departments to address" these issues.[9]

The management of information and technology is a large and complicated task that requires – and enables – public managers to adopt new management approaches and new forms of organization. Restructuring and re-engineering, improving service quality, empowering employees and citizens, continuous learning, and creating partnerships all rely to a significant extent on the use of sophisticated information technology. Such measures as providing direct public access to government databases and converting government records from paper forms to computer images promote the public-service values of efficiency, effectiveness and responsiveness. Information exchange within a single workplace as well as between organizations has been greatly transformed through the use of computer networks, faxes, conference calls and electronic mail.

## Domestic Forces

Reducing costs and improving services are widely viewed as the primary domestic forces underpinning public-service reform. We shall see, however, that changes in political culture and demographics and the legacy of earlier reform initiatives are also important influences.

### Financial Constraint

The pervasive influence on government operations of debts and deficits underlies much of the present emphasis on public-service reform and, indeed, government reform more generally. Reforms designed to promote efficiency and effectiveness are extremely important; they are, however, more difficult to achieve in a milieu perceived by some public servants to be suffering from an excess of reforms. The heavy and increasing workload borne by public servants as a result of program and staff reductions harms morale. Moreover, the recent downsizing frenzy, including the privatization and contracting-out of government services, may result in Canada sharing the experience forecast for the United States – a "hollowing out" of government, both in programs and employees, to the point where it can no longer perform effectively its essential service and regulatory roles.[10] John Manion, a former federal deputy minister, worried about this possibility for Canada several years ago. He called for the identification of the core group of functions that can be "performed only by government and warned that [the] continued devolution, decentralization, deregulation and contracting out of government functions may ... create risks to the identity, coherence and values that make up a public service and ensure its integrity, but, more important, may undermine the ability to govern."[11]

## Public Demand for Quality Service

For sheer repetition, it is hard to beat the assertion that Canadians want governments to provide more services of a quality higher than in the past. Combined with the financial constraints noted above, the demands for more and better service will severely strain public servants' personal and organizational resources. Yet, improved service delivery seems most likely to improve the public's perception of, and confidence in, government. We shall see later, especially in Chapter 6, that the emergence of service as perhaps the most high-profile public-service value has had an enormous impact on the structures and management of the public service. We shall see also that the quality of many public-sector services, compared to the private sector, has been considerably underestimated.

## The Changing Political Culture

Over the past decade, the Canadian political culture has become a much more participative one. Canadians not only want government to provide more and better services with fewer resources but also to consult widely on policy development and on what services should be provided and how. Several forces have combined to give consultation a central place in the governance of Canadian society. The "rights-oriented" nature of this society, legitimized and fostered by the Charter of Rights and Freedoms, encourages citizens to demand involvement in the public policy process. Unhappiness about the perceived inadequacy of public participation in the constitutional negotiations reinforced this demand. The public's negative perception of governments and of their ability to resolve society's problems further increased the public's insistence that governments become more responsive to the public's needs and demands. The impact of the emphasis on consultation will be seen in Chapter 4, on service to the public, and in Chapter 8, on consulting and partnering. We shall see also, notably in Chapter 7, that public servants themselves increasingly expect to participate in decision-making and problem-solving with respect to matters affecting their responsibilities and their working conditions.

*Demographic Change*

Several demographic changes in Canadian society have particular relevance for public-service reform. The rapid aging of the population means, among other things, that the current demand for health care will increase, leading to widespread concern about its availability, cost and quality and to demands for new and better ways of delivering it. Another consequence of an aging population is an aging workforce. It is anticipated that in the early years of the new century the smaller labour force resulting from a large number of retirements will lead to vigorous competition between government and business for skilled workers.

A related factor is that changing immigration patterns have created a highly multicultural society and, therefore, a culturally diverse population and workforce. An increasingly large portion of the skilled workforce mentioned above will be composed of members of visible minority groups. The success of public organizations in attracting a reasonable share of these workers will depend significantly on the ability of public organizations to provide an attractive workplace through innovative approaches to managing diversity.

*The Legacy of Earlier Reforms*

A final, and often-neglected, force driving public-service reform is the inadequacy of previous reform efforts. The evolution of public administration in Canada has been marked by several periods of significant reform, including such watershed events as the introduction of the merit system and the job classification system in the early decades of the century and the introduction of collective bargaining and the movement towards a bilingual public service in the late 1960s. These latter events came in the midst of efforts to implement significant management reforms growing out of the Royal Commission on Government Organization (the Glassco Commission) which reported in 1962–63. As a result, in the mid- to late-1960s, the pace and scope of public-service reform became so overwhelming that the incapacity of the system to absorb this "excessive administrative innovation" was described as a state of "saturation psychosis."[12] Provincial and local governments have experienced similar periods of major reform.

Public-service reform was a constant feature on the federal landscape during the 1970s and 1980s. Among the central reforms in the 1970s were the introduction of the Program Planning and Budgeting System (PPBS), management by objectives (MBO), the Operational Performance Measurement System (OPMS), and value-for-money auditing. In addition, expanded powers for the auditor general were accompanied by the creation of the Office of the Comptroller General, and further reforms were stimulated by the reports of the Royal Commission on Financial Management and Accountability (the Lambert Commission) and of the (D'Avignon) Committee on Personnel Management and the Merit Principle. These events were followed in the 1980s by the creation of the Policy and Expenditure Management System (PEMS) in 1980, the Increased Ministerial Authority and Accountability (IMAA) program in 1986, and by the creation of Public Service 2000 in late 1989. Moreover, these many reform initiatives since 1970 were accompanied by major – and continuous – changes in the structures and processes of the cabinet decision-making system.

In the late 1980s, the spectre of saturation psychosis re-emerged with full force. The need for reforms during this period was in large part the result of the several environmental factors discussed above, but it was also the result of the inadequacy, or failure, of reform efforts during the 1980s, especially in the sphere of human resource management. An influential study in 1986, based on an extensive survey of senior managers in both the public and private sectors, concluded that there was a "vertical solitude" in the senior ranks of the federal public service. The values of the top managers were not shared by middle- and lower-level managers; there was no shared corporate culture: "[A]s one moves down the bureaucratic hierarchy, managers are less satisfied and less positive about managerial practices in their organization."[13] Moreover, private-sector managers were found to have a much more positive perception of managerial practices and were much more likely to have a shared corporate culture.

The government subsequently took several measures[14] to improve the morale of senior public servants, but another survey in 1988 found that there had been no improvement.[15] In addition, a survey of *all* employees in one department – the Department of Communications – showed that morale was low at *every* level of the organization, and a very senior official at this time suggested later that a similar result would likely have been found in most other departments.[16] Further studies led the government to the view that the problem was not simply high stress and low morale; rather, the conclusion was drawn that "the entire management philosophy and the systems, policies and structures of the federal government needed fundamental re-examination and reform, not only to improve morale, but also to improve the quality, effectiveness and productivity of the public service in meeting the challenges of the future."[17] By the early 1990s, there was considerable support within all spheres of Canadian government for major public-sector reform.

The 1990s did not, however, provide a working environment conducive to successful reform. The pressures on the public service included major cutbacks in expenditures, programs and staff; public criticism of public servants; lack of political support for the public service; and wage freezes. A federal study published in January 1999 found that knowledge workers in the public service "enjoy their work, are keen to learn new skills, [and] take great pride and personal satisfaction in making a contribution to Canadian society," but they are "frustrated by a perceived lack of recognition for the work they do (both within the Public Service and from the Canadian public), the human resource practices within the Public Service, and by various aspects of the bureaucracy."[18]

## THE POST-BUREAUCRATIC MODEL

A striking variety of reforms has been proposed to help governments cope effectively with the several challenges explained above. Table 1.1, set out earlier in this chapter, provides a summary of these proposed reforms within an analytical framework that compares the characteristics of the traditional bureaucratic model with the post-bureaucratic model of public organization. This framework also provides a basis for assessing the performance of individual organizations. The intellectual and empirical foundations of the post-bureaucratic model are explained in the next chapter.

### Fit to Be Tried

Given the substantial differences among various *types* of public organizations and, indeed, among individual organizations within each type, it is risky to generalize about the applicability of the Table 1.1 reforms to all public organizations. Reforms must be adapted to the needs – and peculiarities – of individual organizations. Figure 1.1 depicts several types of both public and private organizations along a public sector–private sector continuum. The organizations range from departments and agencies (including central agencies, regulatory agencies and special operating agencies) to arm's-length service agencies, Crown corporations, not-for-profit organizations, and private-sector organizations.

It is often argued that private-sector organizations are easier to reform than public organizations and that certain types of public organizations – for example, Crown corporations – are easier to reform than operating departments. An important determinant of ease of reform, however, is the size of an organization, irrespective of whether it is in the public or private sphere. We will provide evidence of impressive reforms in a variety of public organizations, both large and small.

The *functions* being performed by an organization are also an important influence on the likelihood of successful reform. For example, employee empowerment is likely to be simpler to accomplish in a department of health than in a department of defence, where, especially in wartime, such characteristics as command, control and hierarchy are so important. Yet, in

Figure 1.1. *Public Sector – Private Sector Continuum*

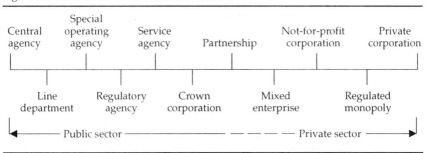

Figure 1.2. *The Government Service Model*

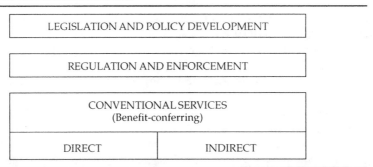

Source: Adapted from Joan A. Barton and D. Brian Marson, *Service Quality: An Introduction* (Victoria: Service Quality B.C., 1991), p. 13.

day-to-day management, even in a defence department, there are opportunities to improve performance, especially in the area of support services.[19] It is common to divide the great mass of government activities into service and regulatory functions supported by research. An alternative three-fold classification, which puts the *provision of services* as *the* major purpose of government, is shown in Figure 1.2.[20]

The first function, which involves *providing benefits*, is performed both directly and indirectly. Direct service involves providing benefits by transferring resources to the public (e.g., unemployment insurance) or operating various facilities (e.g., consular offices abroad). Indirect service involves such activities as scientific research and such departments as public works that serve those departments that serve the public directly. Still other indirect services are those delivered through intermediaries (e.g., weather forecasts developed by public servants but delivered through the news media) and services funded by one order of government but delivered by another (e.g., federal funding of social services delivered by provincial

11

agencies).[21] The second function – *providing regulatory services* – refers to the public service's responsibility to serve the public interest by developing, interpreting and enforcing regulations under delegated legislative authority. The third function – supporting ministers by *developing policy proposals and legislation* – reminds us that the objectives of the elected government must receive top priority and that management reformers must be highly sensitive to the political and policy implications of change.

By depicting private- as well as public-sector organizations, Figure 1.1 demonstrates the wide range of options available for the delivery of government services, including their privatization. Nevertheless, most of the organizations discussed in this book are *public* organizations performing one or more of the types of government services shown in Figure 1.2. In the next chapter, we examine several organizations that have undergone extensive transformation in their structure and culture. Taken together, they represent different types of organizations of varying sizes and they perform different functions.

### The Post-Bureaucratic Model and the Organizational Profile

Public organizations differ considerably in the extent to which they adhere to the bureaucratic or the post-bureaucratic model, both in an overall sense and in relation to each set of contrasting characteristics outlined in Table 1.1. Each organization can be conceptualized as having an *organizational profile*, as shown in figures 1.3 and 1.4. This profile is a composite of the locations of the organization along each of the continua running from the bureaucratic to the post-bureaucratic model (e.g., from a process-oriented organization to a results-oriented one). A high-performing public organization is one that has adopted or adapted the characteristics of the post-bureaucratic model *to the extent that doing so has enhanced the organization's performance.* Thus, striving for high performance should not be equated with movement towards the post-bureaucratic pole of the framework. Some organizations, or parts of them, will perform best by adhering to certain features of the bureaucratic model. For example, a rule-centred, risk-averse and process-oriented culture makes good sense for the central function of air-traffic controllers. Similarly, a heavy emphasis on control, rules and accountability for process is essential for the performance of certain immigration and environmental functions.

An organizational profile can be developed for any public organization, and organizations can be compared in terms of their profile. Figure 1.3 depicts two organizations. The first is a department of defence, which for obvious reasons tends towards the bureaucratic pole on most continua (e.g., monopolistic), but which has moved towards the post-bureaucratic

Figure 1.3. *Organizational Profile of Two Public Organizations*

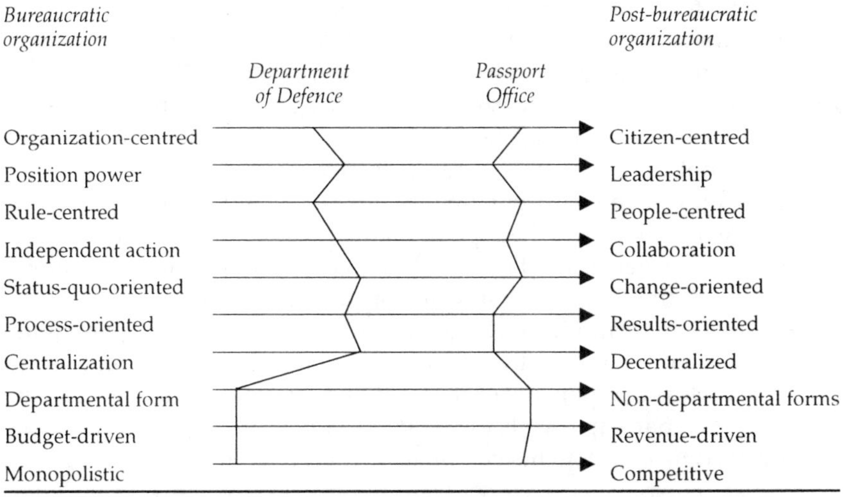

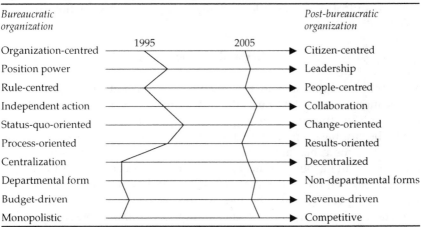

Figure 1.4. *Organizational Profile of One Organization Over Time*

pole on other continua (e.g., change-oriented). The second organization is a passport office, which may not be performing at a very high level but which will still be closer to the post-bureaucratic pole compared to a high-performing department of defence.

An organizational profile can also depict change over time. Figure 1.4 shows the change over a ten-year period in an organization that has significantly transformed its management and structure. It is conceivable also that over time an organization may, either for good reasons or because of slippage, move towards the bureaucratic pole on one or more continua.

Determining an organization's precise location is easier for some continua than for others. For example, data on the extent to which the organization is revenue-driven are easier to quantify than data on the extent to which it is people-centred. The organizational profile is intended, however, as a tool for assessing where organizations stand in relation to the characteristics of the post-bureaucratic model – and in relation to one another. As noted above, the type of public organization (Figure 1.1) and the functions it performs (Figure 1.2) are central factors in determining how far along the several continua the organization will go.

The post-bureaucratic model is not portrayed here as a new "paradigm" in the sense of an internally coherent and mutually dependent set of principles. Most components of the post-bureaucratic model are complementary (e.g., participative leadership and a people-centred workplace). However, some components can be in tension (e.g., revenue-driven programs versus citizen-centred service). Reformers need to keep in mind that in moving along the continua of the post-bureaucratic model they can sometimes only have more of certain features (e.g., decentralized authority and control) by having less of others (e.g., collective action through coordination).

## Policy and Management

Much of the discussion in this chapter has centred on the *managerial* implications of a shift towards the post-bureaucratic model. It is notable, however, that this shift has important implications for *policy-making* as well. The emphasis on improved management in government is still quite recent, but there has already been a reaction to this emphasis in some quarters on the grounds that policy-making has been comparatively neglected and that the policy-making skills of public servants have become rusty. Some proponents of this view swing too far in the other direction by overstating the relative importance of policy-making. It seems necessary to assert that successful governance requires high performance of the interrelated skills of policy-making and management and on an appropriate balance between them. Consider, for example, the implications for policy-making of increased emphasis on such post-bureaucratic characteristics as citizen-centred service, consultation, collaboration, innovation, cost-recovery and competition. We return to this issue in Chapter 11. We move now, however, to an examination of intellectual influences on the composition of the post-bureaucratic model and of public organizations that have made a substantial shift towards this model.

# 2

# Reforming Public Organizations

Chapter 1 explained the major factors driving public-sector reform and the characteristics of a new model of public organization towards which many organizations are moving. This chapter explains ideas and practices underpinning this new model and describes the experience of several public organizations that have moved a considerable distance towards it.

## SIGNIFICANT WRITINGS AND PRACTICES

### Influential Publications

From the large volume of literature relevant to public-service reform, we examine here several influential works that, directly or indirectly, encourage movement towards a post-bureaucratic model of public organization:

*Management: Tasks, Responsibilities, Practices*
This 1974 book by Peter Drucker makes an important contribution to an enduring debate in public-sector reform that has heated up considerably in recent years.[22] This is the debate over whether public organizations can improve their performance by adopting or adapting private-sector practices so as to operate in a more "business-like" fashion. This is certainly not a new debate; in the early 1960s, for example, the Royal Commission on Government Organization (Glassco) urged government organizations to be more business-like.

Drucker takes issue with this popular panacea. He describes as *alibis* the three most common explanations for the inadequate performance of "public-service institutions,"[23] namely, that their managers are not business-like, they need better people, and their objectives and results are not easily quantified. He contends that the most significant difference between a service institution (e.g., a public organization) and a business is that the former is budget-driven and is not, therefore, being paid according to its performance or results. This factor, combined with the monopoly powers typically wielded by service institutions, reduces concern about efficiency and about doing the wrong things: "An institution which is financed by a budget – or which enjoys a monopoly which the customer cannot escape – is rewarded for what it deserves rather than what it earns. It is paid for good intentions and for 'programs.'"[24]

Drucker recognizes that service institutions differ from business organizations in their values and objectives and their contribution to society. He recognizes also that different types of service institutions (natural monopolies, quasi-governmental institutions like universities and hospitals, and operating departments) differ in the way they are structured and in the functions they perform. Still, he contends that all service institutions need "a system and structure that directs them toward performance – wherever possible."[25] In particular, they need to define what their business is, set clear objectives and goals, establish their priorities, define measurements of performance, use these measurements for feedback on their efforts, and audit objectives and results to provide a basis for abandoning obsolete and unproductive activities.[26]

Thus, public organizations do not have to emulate private-sector organizations, but they do need to be managed for performance. Whatever works in the private sector should not necessarily be tried in the public sector; but public-sector organizations can benefit considerably from writings and practices in business and general management. Similarly, business organizations can learn much from innovative practices in public organizations, including practices in such areas as comprehensive auditing and managing diversity. In this context, it is important to note the argument that public-service reform should aim to make government more "government-like" rather than more business-like. This argument is based on a recognition of the significant differences between public- and private-sector organizations: "The purpose of public sector renewal ... is not to make government more like the private sector but to make it more true to itself, better able to serve the people and to provide the public goods they expect and need from it."[27]

### In Search of Excellence

This influential book by Thomas J. Peters and Robert H. Waterman was published in 1982.[28] While the lessons in the book are based on a study of high-performance business organizations and are directed primarily to business readers, they have had a significant impact on the public sector as well. Indeed, excellence became not just a buzz-word but a cherished public-service value. In a survey of Canada's public administration community conducted in the late 1980s,[29] this book ranked first among books that every public administrator should read, and in a 1994 study, *excellence* was ranked eighth on a list of the twenty-top values of public organizations across Canada.[30]

Among the lessons that Peters and Waterman derived from their study of excellent business organizations are several lessons that have influenced recent public-sector management practices and writings. These include

– *autonomy and entrepreneurship* – insulate creative people from the deadening effects of bureaucracy so they can remain creative;

– *productivity through people* – trust your employees and treat them like they are competent human beings; and

– *simultaneous loose–tight properties* – give employees a great deal of operating autonomy as long as they do not violate certain strongly held central tenets of the organization.

## Reinventing Government

David Osborne and Ted Gaebler's book focused on *public* management and stimulated considerable controversy among public servants and academic scholars.[31] Its arguments underpin a large portion of the report of the National Performance Review, supported by President Bill Clinton and led by Vice-President Al Gore, which has been the basis of much public-service reform in the United States government.[32]

Having seen many public organizations transformed from "staid bureaucracies to innovative, flexible, responsive organizations," Osborne and Gaebler call for a new paradigm of "entrepreneurial government."[33] Among the ten principles of entrepreneurial government are the following:

– separate policy decisions ("steering") from service delivery ("rowing") so that managers are freed up to choose such alternatives to in-house delivery as contracting-out and partnerships;

– measure the performance of organizations and focus on results or outcomes rather than on inputs;

– treat clients as customers by such means as customers surveys ... and quality guarantees;

- decentralize government by moving from hierarchy to participation and teamwork; [and]

- minimize bureaucratic mechanisms and public programs by emphasizing such market mechanisms as managing demand through user fees and creating market institutions to fill gaps in the market.

The authors argue that these principles offer a potent conceptual tool; applying the principles to any organization or system or, in fact, to "any of society's problems" will suggest approaches to public managers that are radical departures from their traditional approaches.

In a 1997 book entitled *Banishing Bureaucracy* and co-authored with Peter Plastrik, Osborne reiterated the validity of the reinvention principles, based on experience drawn not only from the United States but from Australia, Britain, Canada and New Zealand as well.[34] As a basis for the successful reinvention of public organizations, the authors set out five strategies called the "Five Cs": the *core strategy* – to help organizations create clarity of purpose; the *consequences strategy* – to provide incentives for high performance; the *customer strategy* – to make organizations accountable to their customers; the *control strategy* – to empower organizations and their employees; and the *culture strategy* – to bring about change in the organizational culture.[35]

*Breaking Through Bureaucracy*
In this 1992 book, Michael Barzelay bases his analysis on a case study of Minnesota's celebrated STEP (Striving Toward Excellence in Performance) Program.[36] He calls for public organizations to move from the bureaucratic to the post-bureaucratic paradigm. In particular, he calls for the use of innovative strategies to move from a bureaucratic agency to a "customer-driven agency." Moving from the bureaucratic to the post-bureaucratic paradigm involves, for example, shifts such as the following[37]:

| Bureaucratic paradigm | Post-Bureaucratic Paradigm |
| --- | --- |
| Public interest | Results citizens value |
| Control | Winning adherence to norms |
| Specify functions, authority and structure | Identify mission, services, customers, and outcomes |
| Follow rules and procedures | Understand and apply norms Identify and solve problems Continuously improve processes |

The characteristics of the post-bureaucratic paradigm are similar to the principles of entrepreneurial government contained in *Reinventing Government*. One especially notable addition, however, is the replacement of the concept of "the public interest" by the concept of "results citizens value." Barzelay argues that use of the latter concept will lead to "more deliberation about what results citizens collectively value" and will create a mental image of the interrelated ideas of service to the customer, emphasis on results rather than on process, and determination by citizens, not professional public servants, of what should be valued. This emphasis on results citizens value does not capture adequately the ethical implications contained in the notion of public interest.

Barzelay pays special attention to the role of central agencies. He urges them to move from a focus on efficiency, administration and control, which has led to many of the constraints and incentives faced by line agencies, to a focus on delivering results citizens value. Central agencies, like line agencies, should transform their organizational strategies so as to pursue the characteristics of the post-bureaucratic paradigm.

Some of Barzelay's ideas are reflected in the "new public administration paradigm" developed by Sandford Borins as a framework for explaining public-service reform in Commonwealth countries: "*Despite the diversity of the Commonwealth countries, there was a common pattern in their responses [to environmental forces]. So strong is this common pattern that it could be labelled a new paradigm in public administration.*"[38] The five components of this paradigm are

- the provision of high-quality services that citizens value;
- increased autonomy, particularly from central-agency controls;
- the measurement and rewarding of organizations and individuals on the basis of whether they meet demanding performance targets;
- the provision of the human and technological resources that managers need to meet their performance targets; and
- the maintenance of receptiveness to competition and an open-minded attitude about which public purposes should be performed by the public sector as opposed to the private sector.

### The Pursuit of Significance

Unlike the Osborne/Gaebler and Barzelay books, which draw solely on experience in the United States, *The Pursuit of Significance*, by Robert Denhardt, celebrates cases of successful organizational change not only in the United States but also in Australia, Great Britain and Canada.[39] Unlike these other books, Denhardt's analysis is based on a participative rather than on a market model of public organization. Aside from emphasis on serving clients and citizens, he steers clear of business-like and market-like mechanisms; indeed, he emphasizes the differences between public- and private-sector management. He emphasizes also the value and ethical dimensions of public management; his version of the post-bureaucratic organization is one that is "creative, responsive and imbued with a new spirit of responsibility."[40] The five interrelated strategies for bringing this about are as follows:

1. *A Commitment to Values.* The manager seeks organizational change less by attention to structure than by developing a pervasive commitment to the mission and values of the organization. ...

2. *Serving the Public.* The manager gives priority to service to both clients and citizens. ...

3. *Empowerment and Shared Leadership.* The manager encourages a high level of participation and involvement on the part of all members of the organization. ...

4. *Pragmatic Incrementalism.* Change occurs through a free-flowing process in which the manager pursues a wide variety of often unexpected opportunities to move the organization in the desired direction. ...

5. *A Dedication to Public Service.* ... The manager insists that members ... maintain high ethical standards."[41]

Denhardt calls for the pursuit of significance, that is, showing concern for others, promoting the public interest and *making a difference* – a sharp contrast to the bottom-line concerns of the private sector.

### Well-Performing Organizations
The importance of values in public-sector reform is also recognized in Otto Brodtrick's study for the auditor general of eight federal organizations in Canada that were reputed to be well-performing organizations.[42] He noted that these organizations have shifted from control to commitment: "Their leaders envision goals, describe values and articulate purposes in such a way that people can support and commit themselves to the overall direction of the organization. Managers focus on vision, purpose and goals instead of on mindless compliance with rules and controls."[43] Brodtrick identified twelve common attributes of well-performing organizations, which were grouped into the four major categories of emphasis on people, participative leadership, innovative work styles, and strong client orientation:

The most striking attribute of the well-performing organizations is the emphasis they place on their people. People are challenged, encouraged and developed. They are given power to act and to use their judgement.

Leadership ... is not authoritarian or coercive, but participative. The leaders envision an ideal organization, define purpose and goals, then articulate these and foster commitment in their people.

Staff ... are innovative, flexible and creative. They maintain strong monitoring, feedback and control systems, but only as useful tools.

People in these organizations focus strongly on the needs and preferences of their clients. They derive satisfaction from serving the client rather than the bureaucracy. There is an alignment of values and purpose between the well-performing organizations and their political and central agency masters with a view to strong performance and high achievement.

In another study written for the auditor general and entitled "Values, Service and Performance,"[44] Brodtrick noted that managers have neglected the role of values despite the fact that the improvement of organizational performance depends not only on systems and structures but on people and values as well.

### The Three Pillars of Public Management

Many of Brodtrick's arguments are reinforced in *The Three Pillars of Public Management*, by Ole Ingstrup and Paul Crookall, which examines well-performing organizations in fourteen countries.[45] The authors conclude that the following three pillars support successful management in these organizations:

1. Aim: The top agencies know clearly the direction they are headed in. Their mission is deeply ingrained in the daily actions and long-term planning of the organization. ...

2. Character: These agencies have a strong sense of who they are and what is important. That organizational character, fueled by a high degree of trust, is communicated internally and externally through principle-centred activities. ...

3. Execution: These organizations get things done, achieving their aim and demonstrating their character through the use of a broad range of management tools.

Each of these pillars is composed of three management elements:

– Aim – mission, leadership, accountability;

– Character – people, communication, trust; and

– Execution – management tools, teamwork, change management.

Taken together, these nine elements constitute the major attributes of well-performing organizations.

### Re-engineering the Corporation

Table 1.1 also reflects the influence of arguments for "re-engineering" organizations, contained in *Reengineering the Corporation*, by Michael Hammer and James Champy.[46] While the focus of this book is on business organizations, its message has had a substantial impact on public organizations as well.

Re-engineering is "the fundamental rethinking and radical redesign of business processes to achieve dramatic improvements in critical, contemporary measures of performance, such as cost, quality, service and speed."[47] In short, it involves "starting over." The authors emphasize the importance of discontinuous thinking, that is, "identifying and abandoning rules and fundamental assumptions that underlie current business operations."[48] Managers are exhorted to ask, not how they can do better with less – a common theme in public-sector innovation – but *why* they are doing *what* they are doing in the first place.

Hammer and Champy contend that the fundamental organizing principles of business organizations are now obsolete as a result of what they call the three Cs, that is, customers taking charge, competition intensifying, and change becoming constant. Among the changes resulting from the re-engineering process are work units changing from functional departments to process teams; jobs changing from simple tasks to multidimensional work; people's roles changing from controlled to empowered; and managers changing from supervisors to coaches.

Some of these principles are similar to those put forward in the books described above, but Hammer and Champy stress that compared to such approaches as "total quality management" (TQM), for example, re-engineering is not an incremental approach to change. It is a radical approach that is accompanied by considerable organizational disruption.

Champy soon recognized that in many organizations the benefits of re-engineering were not as significant as they could have been. In a second book, *Reengineering Management*, he argues that the first book, with its emphasis on re-engineering work processes, neglected the critical role of effective management.[49] The elements of his proposed solution have much in common with other books considered in this chapter, especially Denhardt's. Like Denhardt, Champy puts considerable emphasis on organizational culture in general and on values in particular. What Denhardt argues for public organizations, Champy argues for business enterprises: "The rules of governance (and self-governance) for effective business enterprises today are being determined by their culture, not their organizational structure."[50]

Each of the books discussed above has outlined the desirable characteristics of a well-performing public organization. While the post-bureaucratic model set out in Chapter 1 is informed by all of these books, it is also informed by many other scholarly writings. This model is more inclusive than either the market model or the participatory model alone in that it contains ideas drawn from both models and from other models of public organization as well. The books examined here have had a substantial impact on recent public-service reforms in Canada and elsewhere, but many reforms preceded the publication of these books, and many subsequent reforms have proceeded without apparent reference to them.

The Osborne/Gaebler and Barzelay books are often treated as integral parts of a considerable body of writings on what is called new public management (NPM). Note that these two books came after NPM was well established outside North America; they were, therefore, able to draw on experience elsewhere. The intellectual roots of NPM are found in two different sets of ideas that came together as "a marriage of opposites," namely, public choice theory, transactional economics and principal–agent theory, on the one hand, and business-type managerialism, on the other.[51] Peter Aucoin has explained that the spirit of the public choice approach is best represented by William Niskanen's *Bureaucracy and Representative Government*,[52] "because it pits representative government against bureaucracy in the struggle over ... the public purse. In doing so, it seeks to demonstrate why bureaucrats have been able to pursue their own interests ... in their relations with elected representatives."[53] Business-type managerialism, exemplifed well by Peters and Waterman's *In Search of Excellence*, draws its ideas largely from writings on business administration. Its appeal lies in the fact that it "represents a critique of 'bureaucracy' as a mode of organizational design and management," and it regards private-sector management "as superior to public sector management."[54]

### Influential Practices

The term NPM is also used to cover a wide range of actual public-sector reforms. There is vigorous debate as to whether the application of NPM has improved, or is likely to improve, public-sector management. Moreover, there is much uncertainty as to what ideas and practices are covered by NPM. The term is often used narrowly to refer to the application of business principles and market mechanisms to public organizations. But it is frequently used also to embrace a wide range of approaches to public-sector governance. These approaches can be grouped into three related categories: 1) those concerned with reducing the role of the state (e.g., privatization and contracting-out); 2) those concerned with reforming the machinery of government (e.g., restructuring, new forms of organization); and 3) those concerned with improving management (e.g., empowerment, collaboration). An important political motivation behind these approaches is the desire to reduce and control the influence of career public servants in the development and management of public policy. The model of the post-bureaucratic organization contains several ideas commonly associated with NPM. However, some of the ideas lumped under NPM have their origins not in business practices alone but in theories of organization and management applicable to all types of organizations.

The third category, that of management improvement, has close links with the TQM movement, which was initially adopted by private-sector organizations and then extended to many public organizations. As explained in Chapter 6, TQM requires that all aspects of the organization focus on serving the customer or client, that the service provided be of the highest possible quality, and that all employees be involved, often through empowered work teams, in decisions as to how the objective of quality service can best be achieved. It is widely acknowledged that it is more difficult to implement TQM in public than in private organizations, but there is considerable agreement also that TQM can be successfully implemented in public organizations.[55]

The ideas associated with NPM, TQM and other reform models have had an enormous impact on governance in general and public-sector management in particular. These ideas have greatly influenced management thinking and practices in such countries as Australia, Britain and New Zealand, and reforms carried out in these countries have in turn stimulated public-sector reform in Canada. Increasingly during the 1980s, these ideas and practices were adopted or adapted by public organizations across the country. Earlier trends towards privatization, deregulation and contracting-out were complemented by new organizational structures such as special operating agencies and by new approaches to management, including emphasis on service to the public, empowerment and partnerships. Several provincial governments were especially active in the sphere of management innovation.

24

The influence of public management writings and reforms was evident in the content and recommendations of the federal government's 1990 white paper on public-service renewal, commonly referred to as the PS 2000 report.[56] This report was intended to provide a basis for coping with the forces described in Chapter 1, including the dismal legacy of previous reform efforts. The centrepiece of the report was improved service to the public, complemented by support for innovation, improved human resource management, and accountability for results rather than for process. While the report led to improvements in the management of the public service, the general lack of effective implementation has been attributed to a variety of obstacles, including a major public-service strike that put into question the extent of the government's commitment to its employees and the activities of a "control lobby" that was able to focus attention on the risks rather than the benefits of public-service reform.[57]

Some observers have argued that the obstacles were more fundamental than labour unrest and an anti-reform lobby. When Canada's reform initiatives during this period are placed in comparative perspective, they pale by comparison. It has been other Westminster systems – Britain, New Zealand and Australia – that have led the world in devising and implementing reforms in public management.[58] The Office of the Auditor General of Canada reported in 1993 that, compared to Canada's reforms, the reforms in these three countries had "a more strategic focus and greater coherence and consistency" and that "the Canadian federal public service could benefit from the adoption of a more strategic approach to public management and public service reform."[59] According to Peter Aucoin, "it is difficult to disagree with the implied conclusion" of this report "that the relative lack of success in the Canadian experience to 1993 was due, in some large measure, to shortcomings in political leadership." Moreover, among the public-service leadership, "there was little support for the major initiatives that were beginning to emerge in the other three Westminster systems. A gradualist, experimental approach was deemed more appropriate."[60] A similar cautious, incremental approach has been followed by the federal political and public-service leadership since 1993.

The prominence of PS 2000's centrepiece – improved service – was restored and enhanced by the federal cabinet's approval in May 1995 of the Quality Services Initiative – a government-wide strategy for improving client satisfaction and the quality of service delivered to Canadians. This initiative, and similar subsequent ones, fostered the use of an array of mechanisms for delivering government services. As explained in Chapter 6, the terms "alternative delivery mechanisms" and "program delivery alternatives" are used to encompass an increasing number of instruments, ranging from traditional ones such as departments, Crown corporations and mixed enterprises to newer ones such as special operating agencies, privatized public organizations, single-window service-delivery units, and partnerships. Several characteristics of the post-bureaucratic model reflect this trend towards new forms of organization and new approaches to service delivery.

## INNOVATION IN PUBLIC ORGANIZATIONS

Across Canada and in other Westminster democracies, many public organizations have improved their performance for both clients and citizens by moving towards the post-bureaucratic model of public organization. Improved performance includes becoming more efficient, effective and adaptive for citizens as taxpayers and more innovative and service-oriented for clients. Our research suggests that very few organizations have moved simultaneously along all ten dimensions of the bureaucratic/ post-bureaucratic framework. For example, in some organizations, because of the program they are delivering, it is not appropriate to introduce a new organizational form or to become revenue-driven. However, many of the organizations examined in subsequent chapters have moved along several dimensions of the framework.

In this chapter, we focus on organizations that are especially notable for the holistic way in which they are being transformed. The purpose of focusing on these organizations is not to suggest that all public organizations can or should be similarly transformed; we recognize that such extensive reforms are rare compared to the more limited, but still very important, reforms undertaken by many other organizations. We selected these organizations to demonstrate the variety and magnitude of change that is possible, the different kinds of organizations and business lines that can be involved, and the fact that organizational transformation is occurring at all levels of Canadian government.

### The Manitoba Fleet Vehicles Agency: SOA Status Leads to Improved Performance

The Manitoba Fleet Vehicles Agency (MFVA) is an organization that provides *internal services* to public-sector clients. It also provides an outstanding example of an agency that dramatically improved its performance and developed an entrepreneurial corporate culture by moving from a departmental structure to a special operating agency (SOA) structure. In the process, the organization moved to being revenue-driven, market-dependent (through competition), and more client-centred and people-focused.

The MFVA "was established in 1994 as a branch of the Government of Manitoba to provide centralized fleet management and related services to provincial departments and agencies. It was created to maximize efficiencies in vehicle acquisitions, maintenance and use, and to lower overall vehicle operating costs to government."[61] In 1992, in an attempt to foster a higher level of organizational performance, the Government of Manitoba made MFVA its first special operating agency, and the first provincial SOA in Canada. An SOA is an operational unit within a department that receives greater managerial autonomy in return for being held accountable for results. According to the 1996–97 annual report of the MFVA, "[o]perating as an SOA has increased initiative and innovation, led to increased customer service and service quality, provided better use of information technology, and increased training and development for staff."[62]

In its new organizational form, which involves operating more like a business, the MFVA has achieved impressive results. It has paid off its debt to the Department of Finance, and, in fiscal 1997 it made a profit of $2.4 million on revenues of $17.4 million. This was achieved in a new climate of competition. Departments are now permitted to lease their vehicles from the private sector, so the MFVA operates in a marketplace environment. Not only has it retained its market share, but it is also extending its services to public organizations across Manitoba at other levels of government. Recent analysis suggests that the MFVA's leasing rates are approximately five per cent below private-sector rates for the same services.

Operating in an entrepreneurial business mode, the MFVA has developed an award-winning track record. Not surprisingly, the agency's core values reflect many dimensions of the post-bureaucratic organization:

- "satisfy and exceed customer expectations;
- provide dependable and responsive service at competitive prices;
- promote open communication and teamwork;
- encourage individual learning, growth and achievement;
- provide a safe work environment for employees; and,
- eliminate or minimize risks to the environment."[63]

The management philosophy at MFVA is client-centred, people-centred, and results-oriented, all driven by a new organizational form and a competitive environment for its services. The results that the agency has achieved since 1992 suggest that citizens, clients and staff have all benefited from its transformation.

In Chapter 1, we introduced the concept of performance profiles (figures 1.3 and 1.4). By way of illustrating the extent to which public organizations have moved towards the post-bureaucratic model, we have shown

Figure 2.1. *Performance Profile of the Manitoba Fleet Vehicles Agency*

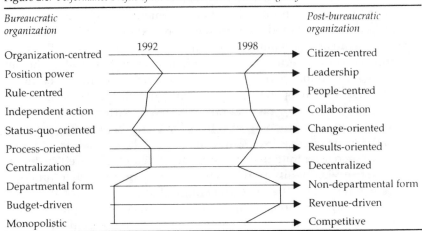

| Bureaucratic organization | | | Post-bureaucratic organization |
|---|---|---|---|
| | 1992 | 1998 | |
| Organization-centred | | | Citizen-centred |
| Position power | | | Leadership |
| Rule-centred | | | People-centred |
| Independent action | | | Collaboration |
| Status-quo-oriented | | | Change-oriented |
| Process-oriented | | | Results-oriented |
| Centralization | | | Decentralized |
| Departmental form | | | Non-departmental form |
| Budget-driven | | | Revenue-driven |
| Monopolistic | | | Competitive |

in Figure 2.1 the change in the performance profile for the MFVA over a six-year period. Similar profiles can be designed for the other organizations examined in this chapter.

### Human Resources Development Canada, Quebec Region: Building a Client Focus

Human Resources Development Canada (HRDC) is the federal department responsible for delivering employment insurance, job training, job market, labour standards, and social security services to Canadians. These programs touch eleven million Canadians each year. The department has been on a path of organizational transformation since the mid-1980s to become more people-centred, more innovative, and more client-focused. According to the assistant deputy minister of the Quebec region, "In the mid-1980's, Gaétan Lussier, then Deputy Minister Employment and Immigration Canada (EIC), announced a new management philosophy which stated very clearly that the client is our focus."[64] This new management philosophy began to permeate the department, encouraging managers to place stronger emphasis on both people management and client service. This was particularly true in the Quebec region of the department, which over the past ten years has become known for its innovative approaches to public management.

In 1991, the executive director of the region invited union leaders to join in a partnership to improve client service and the quality of working life for staff. By the next year, the partnership had been cemented, and, in a

28

joint management–union publication, the executive director wrote, "We are quite convinced that our organization is unanimously behind improving the quality of services to clients. This is a point we will never neglect, if only out of respect for the human dignity of our clients. Management and the union have decided to join forces to give concrete expression to their common interest in this cause, and thereby make a lasting contribution." In the same publication the union leader wrote, "An organization's survival depends directly on the quality of the products or services it provides, and this principle applies to the public and private sectors alike. In our case Service Quality is essential."[65]

After using the Malcolm Baldridge Award framework to undertake an assessment of the organization's strengths and weaknesses, union and management agreed to focus their quality improvement efforts in three areas: leadership, as regards strategic orientations for quality service; improvement of life at work, especially by means of empowerment; and knowing the service needs of the organization's clientele and of the general public. The organization then developed a three-year strategic plan with specific targets for improvement in these three areas. Quality service was defined in the strategic plan as "a set of effective, innovative, proactive actions and gestures that would enable us to go beyond the clientele's expectations. ... At HRDC Quebec, empowerment was defined as the delegation of decision making to those who are closest to the clientele, in order to maximize and develop the skills of the entire personnel."[66] The organization also moved substantially to extend its service-delivery partnerships with other governments and with the non-profit sector.

Has the movement towards the post-bureaucratic model made a difference to the organization's performance in the eyes of clients and staff? Regular surveys of client satisfaction and of staff indicate that this is the case. In a 1996 client survey, 97.9 per cent of the HRDC region's clients indicated they were very or somewhat satisfied with the services they received. In that same year, the staff survey indicated that staff are especially satisfied with the power they have to organize their work, with communications with their supervisors, workplace tools, and with their ability to serve their clients. Areas still requiring improvement included the management of change and post-training monitoring.

These innovations at HRDC Quebec demonstrate many aspects of the post-bureaucratic model: a focus on clients and citizens; a people-focus; collective action; a change orientation; a results orientation; leadership; collective action; empowerment; and decentralization. On the other hand, HRDC Quebec's organizational form has not changed significantly, and there has been no significant move to competition or revenue generation. The results achieved suggest that, over a period of several years, adopting key features of the post-bureaucratic model can help organizations to improve their performance significantly, even during times of great turbulence and change.

## Prince Edward Island's Department of Agriculture and Forestry: Improving Organizational Peformance through Results-Based Management

The PEI Department of Agriculture and Forestry is one of several innovative organizations at the provincial level that have adopted many elements of the post-bureaucratic model during the 1990s. The mandate of the department is "[t]o contribute to economic and community development throughout PEI by promoting the continued growth and operation of successful, sustainable farming and forestry businesses, and promoting quality in the Island's primary products."[67] The department is organized into four divisions: the Agriculture Division; the Forestry Division; the Planning and Development Division; and the Income Support Division. The Forestry Division is responsible for the management of Crown land forests as well as forest fire control; the Agriculture Division delivers services to farmers, including production, extension services, farm management and disease control.

In its approach to continuous improvement and results-based management, the department has established the following six major corporate goals:

- increased public satisfaction with the department;
- improved quality of service offered to clients;
- increased client satisfaction;
- increased catalytic influence on clients' results and on the results of other departments and agencies that affect the department's clients;
- improved quality of legislation and enforcement; and
- improved staff morale.

Each goal has a performance measure attached to it, and a system is in place to measure progress towards the goal, including the annual citizen, client and staff satisfaction surveys. The surveys are administered by an independent organization. Accountability for results is achieved through formal role and responsibility statements for staff, directors, and the deputy minister.

As part of its ambitious results-based performance measurement initiative, the department has set a target of achieving a ninety-per-cent client satisfaction rating and a ninety-per-cent staff satisfaction rating by the year 2000. So far, it has moved client satisfaction levels up from sixty-eight per cent in 1995 to eighty-two per cent in 1997; at the same time, cost effectiveness has been maintained, and staff satisfaction has gone from seventy per cent in 1994 to eighty-one per cent in 1997. These are extraordinary results for a public organization over a very short time, and they demonstrate the power of the post-bureaucratic model to enhance organizational performance in the public sector.

The department is especially notable because of its adoption of a results-based approach to management, but it also illustrates many other features of the post-bureaucratic model, including citizen focus, people focus, participative leadership, decentralization, change orientation, continuous improvement, and collective action. For example, the leadership of the department has implemented a participative approach to the process of building a high-performance organization, by involving all staff in the strategic planning process and in the implementation of the system of results-based performance: "Teaching employees how to develop their own organizational plan and measurement instruments rather than hiring someone to do this for them was key to building support for this initiative."[68]

The department is a typical budget-driven public-sector organization, but, in recent years, it has become entrepreneurial in seeking off-budget revenue from other sources to allow it to extend its operations and meet its goals. It has also sought partnerships with other organizations that can help it achieve its objectives. For example, it has worked with Statistics Canada and its experts to develop internal staff competence in performance measurement. With its progress on so many of the dimensions of the post-bureaucratic model (with changes in departmental structure being a notable exception), the PEI Department of Agriculture and Forestry is an excellent example of modern approaches for improving public management and for enhancing organizational performance in the public sector.

### Ontario Ministry of Consumer and Commercial Relations

The Ontario Ministry of Consumer and Commercial Relations (MCCR) has four responsibilities: commercial registries; marketplace standards; public safety standards; and vital statistics. During the 1980s, its culture emphasized advocating for the consumer and hands-on regulation of the marketplace. During the late 1980s, its leadership thought strategically about the impact that the external forces identified in Chapter 1 (e.g., information technology, financial constraint, public demand for quality service) would have on its operations. Senior management felt that information technology had great potential for transforming MCCR's operations and that its customers, both businesses and individuals, would be demanding that it realize this potential by using up-to-date technology. It was also expected that, as a line operation, MCCR would be expected to produce substantial savings. Thus, its culture would have to shift away from social control and detailed regulation of the marketplace.[69]

In response to these challenges, by 1992, MCCR had developed the following vision: *to promote a fair, safe, and informed marketplace which supports a competitive economy in Ontario*. Then-deputy minister Judith Wolfson explained the evolution in organizational culture that would be needed to achieve the vision in terms of the following dichotomies:[70]

| From | To |
| --- | --- |
| organization-based service delivery | client-based service delivery |
| process | results |
| command and control | shared responsibility |
| consumer service | consumer self-reliance |
| doing it all | ensuring it gets done |
| we serve | self-service |
| consultation | power-sharing partnerships |
| equal treatment | targeting greatest risks |
| staff training programs | continuous learning |

It is notable that these dichotomies correspond very closely with the characteristics of bureaucratic and post-bureaucratic organizations identified in Chapter 1. One unique aspect of MCCR's vision is a recognition of the limitations of its resources and its attempt to deal with those limitations both by focusing its activities (targeting greatest risks) and by involving the public in co-production (self-reliance and self-service).

What has MCCR done to achieve this vision? First, it has a strong planning culture and has worked through the implications of this vision for the entire organization. Part of the planning process was to survey its customers; its business customers made clear their preference for remote electronic access. In May 1995, the ministry surveyed all staff about their understanding of the new vision, and, as a result of this survey, the different divisions undertook to translate the vision into their own operations. Subsequently, the divisions have defined their objectives and established performance measures. Another indication of MCCR's planning culture is that its innovations have been marked by careful planning, as will be discussed in Chapter 4.

Second, MCCR has made major investments in information technology, for example by instituting electronic access for its personal property security registry and single-window new business registration and by automating the province's vital statistics registration.[71]

Third, MCCR has established many partnerships with the private sector and with other government organizations. For example, the land registration system is being automated by the Teranet Partnership between MCCR and a consortium of private-sector technology and management consulting firms.[72] In this partnership, the private sector has provided capital, expertise and technology, while MCCR retains ownership of the database and regulates terms of service. Teranet is one year ahead of schedule and is producing an annual profit of $6 million. One of the virtues of its organizational structure is that it has been able to establish terms and conditions of employment that attract and retain information technology workers, something that has been a problem in core government departments (see Chapter 10). Teranet has also begun to market its technology abroad. An example of an interdepartmental partnership is the Used Vehicle Information Program, designed to improve marketplace performance and increase sales-tax revenue in transfers of used vehicles and developed in conjunction with the ministries of Transport and Finance.[73]

Fourth, MCCR is restructuring its organization, for example by reducing the number of levels of management from eight to four. When it moved the Office of the Registrar General (responsible for vital statistics) from Toronto to Thunder Bay, the new organization, as a pilot project, established multifunctional work teams.[74] This successful pilot project is now being emulated throughout MCCR. To support organizational change, MCCR has emphasized learning, for example by developing necessary skills for working with new technology, by helping staff manage their own careers, and by encouraging staff to learn from one another.

Fifth, MCCR has implemented its vision in ways that are consistent with broader government priorities. For example, it established teams of people from employment-equity target groups to automate its companies records (the Night Shift Project) and to video-image the vital events statistics that were to be moved from Toronto to Thunder Bay (Partners in Goodwill), and it was successful at increasing the representation of employment-equity target groups in the new Thunder Bay office.[75]

Sixth, MCCR has begun the transition from a regulator of industry to a partner in industry self-management. It has developed a framework for self-management, involving the establishment of not-for-profit corporations with representation from government, business, and consumers on their boards. Government maintains control of the legislation governing these corporations. Self-management initiatives are under way in the real estate, motor vehicle, and travel industries, and in the monitoring

33

of technical standards and safety for elevators, boilers, and pressure vessels.[76]

Seventh, MCCR has been innovative and willing to take risks – with new technology, with new types of partnerships, and with programs that enfranchise the disadvantaged. Indicative of this is that the ministry has often entered and frequently won IPAC's Award for Innovative Management: third prize in 1990 for its Night Shift Project; first prize in 1994 for its re-shaping of the Office of the Registrar General when it moved to Thunder Bay; and third prize in 1996 for Clearing the Path for Business Success, its single-window new business registration initiative. It also took first prize in the 1998 Commonwealth Association for Public Administration and Management International Innovations awards.

This willingness to innovate is in large measure the achievement of its senior management team. While MCCR has had four deputy ministers in the last ten years, its cadre of assistant deputy ministers has stayed in place. The deputy ministers have been supportive of the ADM's initiatives, and the ADMs themselves have been supportive of one another. Art Daniels, who was assistant deputy minister of the Business Division for most of this period, is a well-known public-sector innovator. He has long been interested in learning about management outside his organization and in introducing innovative practices to it. For example, he had studied private-sector multifunctional work teams and championed that concept in MCCR. Daniels was also on a committee of public servants that convinced the government to establish the Amethyst Award for distinguished service by members of the Ontario Public Service, and he has been president of the Institute of Public Administration of Canada.

As a result of all these initiatives, MCCR can show significant achievements. In the last ten years, as a result of automation and the industry self-management program, its staffing has decreased by fifty-three per cent, from 2,800 to 1,700. It is becoming a "steering," rather than a "rowing" organization. Its annual expenditures have decreased from $150 million to $100 million. Its net revenues are holding constant at $50 million. As will be discussed in Chapter 10, its electronic registration initiatives have improved service dramatically, by reducing service time and increasing convenience. As a result, most personal property security and business registrations are being done electronically. To get a picture of employee reaction, Mohga Badran and Sandford Borins surveyed the forty-five non-managerial staff in the personal property security registry about their attitudes regarding the change process.[77] The results, based on thirty-eight completed questionnaires, show that staff strongly agreed with management about the need for change and understood the new vision and agreed, though somewhat less strongly, that management communicates well with them. They also responded positively to job redesign, feeling that it has given them more understanding of the organization as a whole and has upgraded their skills, and, finally, they expressed a high level of commitment to the organization.

## Town of Ajax

The Town of Ajax is a rapidly growing community of 67,000 people just east of Toronto, on the shores of Lake Ontario. As Canada's first municipality to become ISO 9000 certified, the town is now managed in a way consistent with the ten dimensions of the post-bureaucratic model.

You may have seen ISO 9000 banners proudly displayed on the buildings of some of Canada's most famous multinational corporations. These banners indicate that the organization has met the International Standards Organization's high standards for quality management. According to the Standards Council of Canada, ISO 9000 certification is "the formal recognition of a company's (or organization's) quality management system by an independent third party known as a quality system registrar. ... [Q]uality systems registrars perform initial assessments and on-going audits to verify compliance with ISO 9000 quality management system standards."[78] Moreover, the benefits of achieving the ISO 9000 standard for an organization's management systems are that

- performance and quality improve;
- customer satisfaction, productivity and efficiency increase; and
- quality improvements continue.

Besides achieving fame as Canada's first municipality to have all departments certified as meeting international ISO 9000 management standards, the Town of Ajax provides an excellent example at the local government level of the holistic transformation of a public organization towards the post-bureaucratic model. During the 1990s, successive chief administrative officers, including Barry Malmsten and Richard Parisotto, have actively transformed the management of the Town of Ajax and its 500 employees along every one of the ten dimensions of the model. Ajax is now recognized not only for meeting international ISO 9000 standards of quality management but also for its innovative approaches to employee involvement, partnerships, and cost reduction.

During the budget squeezes of 1994 and 1995, Ajax introduced a nationally recognized program called STARS: "Saving the Town of Ajax Real Dollars." To balance the town's budget in an era of major cutbacks in provincial transfer payments, the town's chief administrative officer (CAO) challenged each employee to come up with at least two ideas for reducing costs or increasing revenues as part of the STARS program. The 500 employees suggested over 3,000 ways in which savings could be made and revenues expanded – an average of six ideas per employee. Employees were assured that no lay-offs would occur as a result of the town's implementation of their ideas.

Over the course of eighteen months, the implementation of the suggestions contributed $1,600,000 towards balancing the town's budget. For example, by implementing a staff idea to increase the ice temperature in the town's arena by one degree centigrade, the town saved $2,000 in cooling costs; and by re-surfacing the ice in the morning rather than at the end of the day, further annual savings of $750 in power costs were achieved. In another department, staff proposed to take over grass-cutting, which had been contracted-out to the private sector: the town saved $50,000 per annum. Another employee idea was to let staff sell dog tags by going door to door after regular working hours, and council authorized the volunteers to be awarded a portion of every dog license they sold to owners of unlicensed dogs. Tens of thousands of additional dog-tag revenues were generated, and the staff who participated earned themselves extra dollars during a time of salary freezes. To provide an additional incentive for all staff to participate in the STARS program, the town council agreed that a portion of all savings generated by the staff would be paid back as bonuses; as a result, full-time employees each received a STARS bonus of $400 when the $1,600,000 savings were achieved. According to Ajax's CAO, both the council and citizens were strongly supportive of the STARS program – as were the staff sharing in the savings they had generated for taxpayers.

The STARS program and ISO 9000 certification are the management initiatives for which Ajax has become famous; but Ajax's managers have also implemented many other management innovations that have propelled it forward from the bureaucratic to the post-bureaucratic model. For example, Ajax has moved consistently towards a client focus in the provision of its services to both citizens and to the business community. When Ajax was internally focused, citizens who came to visit town facilities found that the best parking spaces were already taken by staff; citizens, including elderly members of the community, had to park in the outer reaches of the parking lots. In Ajax, things have changed; the customer is now king. These days, staff park their cars in the outer reaches of the parking lot when they arrive at work, and the best parking slots now have clear signs designating them as "customer parking." Similarly, customer complaints used to be dealt with in an ad hoc manner; now Ajax has a sophisticated management system for investigating and tracking all customer complaints. Departments are held accountable for responding expeditiously to all complaints, which are centrally recorded and reported quarterly to the senior management meeting, along with recommendations to deal with recurring customer problems.

A 1996 survey of customers of Ajax's planning services showed that citizens and the development industry were frustrated by the red tape and lack of interdepartmental coordination in providing development approvals. Clients had to deal with three different departments: planning, engineering, and building inspection, and, for commercial projects, approval took two or three years. The CAO created an interdepartmental task force to undertake a review of existing processes, in consultation with citizens and the development community. The review led to the implementation of a "single-window" approach that involved merging the staff from three departments into a single, new planning and development department. Forms and processes were streamlined, while ensuring that all legislative requirements were still met by the integrated approval process. As a result, approval times have been cut in half, and staff are able to handle a larger volume of approval requests within existing resources. Again, senior management assured staff that there would be no lay-offs as a result of their proposals for streamlining the approval process.

The STARS program and the redesign of the planning approval process at Ajax also illustrate the town's move from position power towards participative leadership – a feature of the post-bureaucratic model. The same approach was taken for the implementation of the ISO 9000 certification process. Instead of using outside consultants to document the town's 500 service-delivery processes, management asked teams of staff to review and document existing processes and to bring them up to ISO 9000 standards.

These examples also demonstrate the transition by Ajax towards a more people-centred management culture, particularly through the commitments to a no-lay-off policy for permanent staff, and the strong recognition and reward systems. During the STARS implementation process, employees were empowered to "Just Do It" if a suggestion could be implemented within an employee's own work area. According to CAO Richard Parisotto, "this program created a cultural change unlike anything I have ever seen – changes in attitude, thinking and approach to work. Before, management just told staff to do the job and not to think – now we ask staff not to check their brains at the door but to contribute their innovative ideas for improving the way things are done."[79] The town has now reinforced incentives for staff to generate innovative ideas through awarding "Ajax Booster Bucks," which are coupons given out to staff for good ideas or for outstanding performance. These "Booster Bucks" can be redeemed for T-shirts, caps, pens and other merchandise carrying the Town of Ajax logo.

The Town of Ajax also demonstrates the trend from independent action to collective action in the post-bureaucratic model, in such forms as greater consultation, cooperation and collaboration. For example, the town now routinely consults citizens and clients about both policy and service delivery, as we saw in the restructuring of the planning department. The town has also developed a range of innovative partnerships with nearby municipalities for the joint delivery of services, such as handicapped transit and fire department dispatch services. Consistent with the post-bureaucratic model, the town has moved from a culture of avoiding mistakes towards an innovative, risk-taking, continuous improvement culture. This transition is illustrated by the commitment to innovation and continuous improvement embedded in the town's ISO 9000 quality management system, through systems to encourage innovation, and a culture of "Just do it." Similarly, the municipality moved from a process orientation to a strong results orientation, illustrated by its systematic approach to accountability for results within the ISO 9000 management system.

Movement towards the post-bureaucratic model involves a decentralization of authority and control and the delivery of programs via a wider variety of organizational mechanisms. In this respect, Ajax implemented a "de-layering" of its bureaucratic hierarchy in 1996, moving from five or six layers of hierarchy to three layers. Moreover, more authority has been delegated to front-line staff to enable them to meet clients' needs. Alternative approaches to organizational form have included the contracting-out of Ajax's garbage services to the private sector (again, without job loss to long-term staff), as well as co-location of staff with neighbouring municipalities for the joint delivery of specialized services such as handicapped transit.

Ajax has also demonstrated a trend towards a market orientation in its approach to management, especially in adopting the "user-pay" philosophy for the provision of services that benefit specific citizens. For example, soccer and baseball fields used to be provided without cost to the sports clubs that used them. Since introducing modest user fees, the town has not only generated revenue to cover maintenance costs, but the sports clubs have also become more judicious in booking field times only when they really need them, thereby opening up the sports fields to a much wider range of groups in the community that could not get access to community sports facilities before.

It is clear that the Town of Ajax has in recent years implemented reforms within every dimension of the post-bureaucratic model. While it is a recognized leader in implementing new approaches to public management, it is only one of many Canadian municipalities that have responded to fiscal and public pressures by implementing the post-bureaucratic model. Like Ajax, these municipalities have achieved higher levels of organizational performance for taxpayers, as well as higher levels of satisfaction for their staff and their clients.

## Canada Post: Improving Performance as a Crown Corporation

In 1980–81, Canada Post had a loss of $487 million; in 1996–97 it recorded a profit of $112 million. In 1980–81, most Canadians thought that Canada Post's service left a lot to be desired; in 1996 an Angus Reid poll showed that sixty-one per cent of Canadians thought that Canada Post had improved its operations in recent years, and almost eighty per cent said they were satisfied with their postal services.[80] During this same period, service outlets grew by thirty-one per cent, mail volume by sixty-four per cent, mail processed per hour by sixty-six per cent, and revenue per employee by 137 per cent. This transformation of Canada Post to much higher levels of performance illustrates three elements of the post-bureaucratic model that did not emerge in the transformation of HRDC Quebec discussed above, namely a transition to a non-departmental structure, to revenue dependency, and to greater use of competition. We have singled out Canada Post for special consideration here not simply because it has moved from departmental to Crown corporation status; that is an old story. What is especially notable about Canada Post is how it has, during the 1990s in particular, taken advantage of its increased autonomy to improve its performance.

Prior to 1981, Canada Post was a department of government and was therefore subject to all of the complex administrative controls imposed by central agencies. It was also highly subsidized by tax revenues and was therefore partly budget-driven rather than revenue-driven, even though it was one of Canada's largest commercial enterprises. In 1981, the Government of Canada passed legislation to make Canada Post a Crown corporation, thereby creating a new organizational form that gave Canada Post more autonomy to manage its resources. At the same time, the government gave the corporation the challenge of becoming financially independent and of actually making a profit. With a corporate organizational structure, and with an outside board of directors, Canada Post embarked on a multi-year journey to reinvent itself as a high-performance public organization. Having to move towards revenue dependency meant that the incentives had changed: Canada Post had to become a more customer-focused, more people-focused, and more efficient organization to achieve its fiscal and marketplace objectives. As a Crown corporation rather than a department, it had more tools available to accomplish these tasks, including greater flex-ibility to manage its human, financial and technological resources.

Another element in the Canada Post strategy of transformation was greater use of competition. The corporation embarked on an ambitious program of extending its points of service through franchising its post offices to the private sector. Approximately forty per cent of its 7000 postal outlets across Canada are now franchised. This process illustrates two aspects of the post-bureaucratic model: the introduction of competition (since franchised postal outlets can compete for clients) and alternative organizational forms for service delivery.

Becoming more competitive in the marketplace was also a key strategy for Canada Post's high performance in a revenue-dependent world: "As large corporate customers have come to play an expanding role in the Corporation's future, the impetus behind developing new market strate-gies has grown. To implement such strategies, the Corporation has had to enter the competitive sector where customers must be won and retained. To do so the Corporation must satisfy the customer."[81] The purchase of Purolator Courier was one strategy that allowed Canada Post to become more competitive in its own industry, a move applauded by most Canadi-ans according to the 1996 Angus Reid survey.

While Canada Post is particularly interesting as an example of achiev-ing higher levels of performance through more appropriate organizational structures and revenue dependency, the corporation has also put stronger emphasis on becoming client- and people-centred. In recent years, Canada Post has begun routinely to measure client and staff satisfaction levels and to use the feedback as part of its continuous improvement process. Simi-larly, Canada Post has become a results-based organization that holds its managers accountable for specific business results, as part of the perform-ance appraisal and compensation system.

## The Canadian Passport Office

One of the most important features of the post-bureaucratic model is the re-thinking of organizational structures and the adoption of non-departmental forms that will allow organizations to conduct operations more efficiently and effectively while continuing to protect the public interest. In this context, the Canadian Passport Office is of particular interest because of its transformation from a traditional operational divi-sion within a government department to a more independent, revenue dependent special operating agency.

The Passport Office was one of the first five special operating agencies designated by the Treasury Board in 1989. For two decades prior to 1989, the office had already been a self-supporting (revenue dependent) unit within the Department of Foreign Affairs and International Trade, where it was subject to the same bureaucratic rules and constraints governing the non-commercial programs of the department. When it became an SOA in 1990, it moved to a more independent status, reporting directly to the deputy minister and having a greater degree of financial and program management freedom. In exchange for this increased authority to manage on a commercial-like basis, the Treasury Board required the Passport Office to improve its service and productivity. According to the office's 1995–96 annual report, "[t]he Office places great emphasis on the use of sound business practices in the delivery of its services. While the Office operates like a private enterprise, it is a government institution, an agency of the Department of Foreign Affairs and International Trade."[82]

The Passport Office finances its operations from the fees charged for the issue of passports and operates under a revolving fund that allows it to incur deficits of up to $4 million and to carry forward surpluses into future years. This financing scheme allows it to work to a financial "bottom line," like a private-sector company. The office is still a monopoly service provider, however, and the fees it charges have to be approved by Treasury Board. What are some of the elements of this more business-like approach to the provision of service? According to one academic observer,

[q]uality of service in the Passport Office is described as "quality of service that meets or exceeds the expectations of the Canadian public." This in turn is linked in Passport Office statements and practices to the provision of a "positive working environment" for all the agency's employees. Vastly increased resources compared to the past have been put into training personnel who deal directly with the public. Much more concerted attention is also being given to how clients perceive the services, particularly the location of offices, hours of operation, turnaround times and so on.[83]

The Passport Office also puts a great deal of emphasis on strategic planning and on reporting results. Within its framework document – its agreement with Treasury Board on its authorities and performance accountabilities – the office produces a rolling three-year strategic plan and an annual business plan to guide its operations. The office's public accountability document is its annual report, which contains both financial and performance data.

Is there concrete evidence that this new organizational form has achieved improved performance in terms of service and efficiency in the use of resources? One indicator of the office's efficiency is the $32-million surplus that it had accumulated by the end of 1996. However, the office also increased its fees during this period, so measures of productivity may be a more reliable indicator of success. In this respect, in 1995–96 the Passport Office achieved a productivity improvement (documents issued per person year) of almost nine per cent. This was the third year in a row that the agency achieved a productivity increase year-over-year. In 1995–96 the agency produced over 2,900 travel documents for every person-year of resources employed. Revenues during the year were $53 million and expenditures were $44 million, for an operating surplus of $9 million.

From 1990 to 1997, the Passport Office increased its staff by twenty per cent, while most other federal departments experienced budget and staff cuts. This increase in staff was a response to increased demand for the office's services as well as to the need to improve security over the passport approval system. The increase illustrates the advantages of operating as an agency that finances itself through fees for its services.

The move to SOA status has resulted in a greatly enhanced emphasis on service. For example, the office has been one of the leaders inside the federal government in setting and monitoring service standards: "To personalize its service, the Passport Office has carefully selected the locations of its 31 points of service. Because offices are located in urban locations, the Agency can serve 85 per cent of its clients in person. The average turnaround time to process an application is five working days if submitted in person, ten working days if submitted by mail. ... Emergency services are available after normal working hours, on weekends, and on statutory holidays."[84] The agency undertakes client satisfaction surveys to assess the level of satisfaction with the service and with the fees charged. According to the 1995–96 survey, "clients rate highly the quality of service provided by the Passport Office service staff with regards to courteousness, promptness, knowledge of service staff, as well as understanding of their specific needs."[85] Clients were also generally satisfied with the timeliness of the service, whether they submitted their application in person or by mail. On the question of cost (an important factor to address in a monopoly service), the $60 passport processing fee includes a $25 consulate fee and a $35 fee for the passport itself. Clients considered the passport fee to be a fair price. Moreover, they were prepared to pay up to $30 extra for a forty-eight-hour express-service by mail. In response to these survey results, the Passport Office began a partnership in 1997 with Canada Post to accept passport applications at post offices and to offer an extra-premium express-delivery service through Canada Post.

The Passport Office and its clients have benefited from the move to SOA status: productivity has improved, a greater investment has been made in staff and technology, and an increased emphasis on service appears to be paying off for those Canadians who use the service. The downside is that passport fees have been increased substantially in order to improve the service. However, market research shows that customers feel that the passport fees are reasonable.

Overall, the Passport Office is a good example of the post-bureaucratic organization in action. It has levered its new SOA organizational form and its revenue dependency to implement other elements of the post-bureaucratic model. It has become far more client-centred, while continuing to balance better service with its regulatory and public interest objectives; it has introduced a culture of shared values, including "quality service, quality people, integrity, security, cost effectiveness, efficiency, research, development, and recognition of achievement"; it has empowered employees and invested in their development through systematic three-week training programs and ten-week apprenticeship programs; it has developed a more collaborative approach to its service-delivery through service delivery partnerships with Canada Post and with Citizenship and Immigration Canada; it has developed a multi-year strategic-planning process to promote continuous improvement and a results orientation; and it has decentralized authority through a regional structure of service-delivery outlets across the country. Thus, the Passport Office demonstrates a very significant transformation along the dimensions of the high-performance model of public organization embodied in the post-bureaucratic model, and this transformation appears to be paying off for both clients and taxpayers.

## CONCLUSIONS

The organizations examined in this chapter can be distinguished from most other public organizations, not simply because they have moved considerably towards the post-bureaucratic model, but because they have adopted so many of the model's ten components. The reforms that these organizations have implemented have been stimulated and shaped in part by the scholarly writings examined earlier in this chapter. They have also been significantly influenced by practices that have been implemented in other public organizations, both in Canada and elsewhere. We noted above the increased emphasis on the importance of values in public-service reform. Our agreement with this emphasis is reflected in our focus in the next chapter on sharing and managing values.

# 3

# Sharing and Managing Values

Efficiency. Effectiveness. Integrity. Accountability. Service. Innovation. These are some of the most prominent values associated with public service. Brief reference to such public-service values has already been made in the first two chapters of this book. More frequent reference will be made to them in subsequent chapters, because a focus on values provides a useful basis for explaining past, current and emerging developments in public administration. We shall see that the values currently espoused by public organizations in all spheres of government are in tune with ongoing and anticipated public-service reforms. Among the most prominent of the *new* public-service values that have emerged over the past decade are service, quality, teamwork and innovation.[86] There is a striking congruence between these new values and the characteristics of the post-bureaucratic organization shown in Table 1.1 in Chapter 1. We shall see, however, that there is a significant difference between the values espoused by public organizations and the values actually in use and that it is the espoused values that are most in tune with the characteristics of the post-bureaucratic model.

While the *analytical* benefits of a focus on values will be evident throughout the book, this chapter centres on the utility of values as a *management* tool, especially in the area of organizational change. A central feature of the reform of many public organizations is a concern about values: "An approach to organizational change based on a reassessment and realignment of values that guide the work of those in the organization has proven successful in a surprising variety of public organizations."[87] Several studies show that *business* organizations that identify and live their core values perform at a much higher level because, among other things, "[t]here's a sharp focal point for culture change or renewal. ... Everyone makes more consistent choices according to a shared hierarchy of values. ... Trust, toleration and forgiveness levels increase. Morale, pride and team identity are enhanced."[88] And the value statement of a *public* organization asserts that

[v]alues form the core of our identity, both as individuals and as an organization. ... Values can be used to harness the human energy of an organization and to create an atmosphere of vitality, loyalty and pride. ... [Our] values are our ideals and we can take pride in them while recognizing the challenge they represent. ... Through our values, we are challenging ourselves to achieve excellent quality service to the public, [to] recognize our employees as a critical resource, and to strive for excellence in management. ... By aligning our actions to these values, in everything we do, we will affirm, through our behaviour, a continuing commitment to them.[89]

The first part of this chapter explains the meaning and types of public-service values.[90] The second part examines the importance of shared values for the successful management of public organizations, and the third part discusses traditional and new values in public organizations. The fourth part examines what has been learned about managing values, and the final part considers benefits and limitations of focusing on shared values as a means of effecting organizational change.

## THE MEANING AND TYPES OF PUBLIC-SERVICE VALUES

Values have been defined in various ways, but in essence they are enduring beliefs that influence our attitudes and actions. One of the most widely cited definitions is that by Milton Rokeach, who defines a value as "an enduring belief that a specific mode of conduct or end-state of existence is personally or socially preferable to an opposite or converse mode of conduct or end-state of existence."[91] Values influence the choices we make from among available means and ends. They "influence which tasks people will do with care, which they will do superficially, and which they will try to avoid."[92] They are central, therefore, to our decisions and actions, both within and outside the workplace.

The large number of values associated with public service can be divided into the three categories of *ethical* values such as accountability, loyalty and excellence; *democratic* values such as accountability, loyalty and responsiveness; and *professional* values such as effectiveness, excellence and leadership.[93] The importance of a small number of values (e.g., accountability, loyalty and excellence) is enhanced by the fact that they belong to more than one category of values. An argument can be made for including accountability in all three categories. It is notable that the new values that have come to the fore in recent years (e.g., innovation and quality) tend to fall primarily into the category of professional values.

Another helpful distinction is between public-service values and organizational values. Throughout this book, the term *public-service values* refers broadly to the values associated with the attitudes and actions of the public service as a whole. The term *organizational values* refers, more narrowly, to the values of particular public organizations.[94] Most public organizations include some traditional values in their value statements, together with values that are especially relevant to the purposes of the organization (e.g., *reliability* for Statistics Canada).

Historically, certain public-service values have permeated the study and practice of Canadian public administration.[95] Among these *traditional* values are integrity, accountability, efficiency, effectiveness, responsiveness, representativeness, neutrality, fairness and equity.[96] These are the values that have been discussed most frequently in academic writings and government reports on the public service since Confederation.[97] These values have been central to discussions of *service-wide* issues such as merit, patronage, classification, organizational design, and accountability.

The relative importance of these traditional values has changed over time, and new values have emerged that complement or challenge these older values. Thus, it is appropriate occasionally to re-examine the traditional values and, in particular, to assess the extent to which current organizational values, both of individual organizations and of all organizations taken together, are in tune with the traditional service-wide values.

## SHARED VALUES AND ORGANIZATIONAL CULTURE

Values have been increasingly recognized, especially over the past decade, as providing a foundation and framework for guiding individual and organizational behaviour. A persuasive case has been made for the role of *shared* values as an integrative and energizing force in organizations: "Values are always the unifying force of organizations which have a strong identity; in these cases, it is a value system to which employees can relate and commit and thus, the by-product is pride in, and loyalty to, the organization."[98]

Many organizations that have gone through the exercise of clarifying their values have used the results to develop, revise or renew a statement of their core values. For some of these organizations, the results have provided a basis for beginning to make substantial change in their organizational culture. But getting agreement on a list of core values is much easier than getting all members of the organization to *share* a commitment to them and to demonstrate this commitment in the day-to-day operations of the organization. An organization's culture is defined not by the values it espouses but by those it practices.[99]

The very process of developing a list of core values can have a beneficial impact on an organization. It has been argued that

The articulation of a set of common values can be used to develop a shared sense of context, goals and means within an organization, as well as to promote integrity and accountability. Furthermore, formulating these values can be a positive exercise in itself – one that can lift employee morale, facilitate teamwork, and provide guidance in setting priorities in decision-making and resource allocation.[100]

Still, an organization in which employees, at the end of the value-setting process, *share* an enthusiastic commitment to the core values is more likely to be a high-performing one. The concept of shared values usually refers to a joint commitment to a limited number of values by most of the organization's members and across all of its levels. To the greatest extent possible, the core values should be compatible with the personal values of individual members. Thus, for example, an employee whose primary personal value is risk-avoidance will be uncomfortable in an organization where innovation is highly regarded.

The notion of *shared* values is central to the concept of *organizational culture* (often described as corporate culture): "Defining organizational culture as a system of shared values and viewing it as the social glue that holds the organization together comes close to an anthropological definition of culture."[101] The organizational culture of the public service as a whole must, however, be distinguished from that of its individual organizations. The public-service culture is made up of a large number of different organizational cultures. There can even be subcultures within a single organization, for example, between the managerial and other levels of the hierarchy or between head offices and field offices.

Barbara Wake Carroll and David Siegel, on the basis of their study of field-headquarters relationships, concluded that "[m]ost organizations do not seem to have a unifying organizational culture which extends throughout the organization. In many cases, field staff do not feel as though there is any sort of culture permeating the organization."[102] They do note some exceptions, however, where strong organizational cultures exist, or have existed, and they conclude that the factors leading to a strong organizational culture are small size, a clear stable mandate, shared professional background, an extensive communication system, and promotion from within.[103]

## THE VALUE OF SHARED VALUES

Given the rapid changes in the political, social and economic environment within which public servants work and the large size and complexity of government, it cannot be assumed that public servants share fundamental values, even within a single department or agency, much less across an entire government. Yet, there is considerable agreement that this very size and complexity make the cooperative pursuit of these values essential to high levels of performance in the public service and, as a result, to public confidence in government.

The significance of the value dimension of public-service decision-making has, until recently, been unduly minimized. In recent years, however, a substantial number of public organizations have acknowledged the importance of shared values to organizational success by developing a statement of their core values, often as part of a strategic planning exercise but sometimes as a separate exercise. Figures 3.4 and 3.5 (later in this chapter) show how the development of a value statement is an integral part of a strategic planning process. Written commitment to core values, such as service or quality, is likely to enhance these values in an organization's day-to-day operations: "Experience shows that in a value-based and results-driven organization projects can be carried out more quickly and at a higher level of quality than in organizations where such is not the case."[104] Most public organizations in Canada, however, do not have a formal value statement.

It is often argued that shared values should be pursued in the light of the public service's ultimate objective of promoting the public interest. Pursuit of the public interest over private, narrow or personal interests is a major feature distinguishing public servants from their private-sector counterparts. Ideally, concern for the public interest is a unifying and motivating force that pervades the practice of public administration. A shared commitment to core values can facilitate among public servants a sense of belonging to a community devoted to values that are commonly associated with the public interest and that transcend lesser values, especially those based on self-interest.

Some experts argue that a focus on values can serve as a preferable alternative, or at the very least as a prelude, to restructuring. Denhardt argues that "today, it is far less likely that an organizational 'turn around' will begin with a change in the structure of the organization or its patterns of authority and control. Progressive public managers are much more likely to focus on values. In doing so, these managers are seeking a basic transformation of their organizations, one far beyond what a change in structure could bring about."[105] Thus, it is argued, it is a change in culture that is required. This view is in keeping with the conclusion of a federal task force concerned with public-service renewal, which concluded that the "fundamental change in corporate culture and management attitudes" that is required should be pursued by developing "a set of values and operating principles to guide the actions of public service managers, both within departments and at the service-wide level. These should encourage creativity and initiative, trust and teamwork, and excellence in the delivery of government services."[106] This conclusion was endorsed by a federal task force that concluded that "a statement of principles ... could help to provide not only a new foundation for public service values, but could establish a new contract between the public service, the Government and the Parliament of Canada."[107]

Values have also been proposed as an alternative to rules as an instrument for internal management of the public service. Management instruments can be conceptualized, according to the extent of their intrusiveness, along a continuum from values, through incentives and guidelines, to directives: "The least intrusive instrument is shared values. Values shared across government can serve to align the actions of individuals so that they achieve the desired result without detailed policies or rules. ... Values, incentives and guidelines are the greatest influence on decision-making behaviour of people trying to achieve program objectives with limited resources."[108] Clearly, the choice of management instruments, like the choice of budgetary styles, is determined in large part by the economic conditions of the time. However, the current emphasis on less intrusive instruments in general and on values in particular is also based on organization theories supporting greater reliance on personal responsibility and less reliance on overhead controls.

We shall explain in the final section of this chapter that opinion is divided as to whether a focus on values can serve the purposes noted above.

## CHANGING AND CONFLICTING VALUES

As explained earlier, certain values have been central in the evolution of Canadian public administration, namely integrity, accountability, efficiency, effectiveness, responsiveness, representativeness, neutrality, fairness and equity. The values recently identified by a federal task force on service to the public "as part of the fabric of the public service in Canada" overlap considerably with this list; in addition to economy, efficiency and effectiveness, the task force included "equity or fairness, entitlement and neutrality. Another less explicit value, or tradition, is risk avoidance or prudence. And, finally, there is responsiveness: a traditional value, at times in conflict with the overemphasis on the three Es."[109] While all of these traditional values are of enduring significance, their relative importance rises and falls over time.

In addition to these traditional values, value statements may contain values related to the organization's particular functions (for example, *cost-consciousness* for the auditor general's office and *safety* for the NWT Department of Safety and Public Services). Value statements are also increasingly likely to include "new values." An analysis of the value statements of public organizations at all levels of government found that the traditional values are being challenged by the emergence of new values, especially those of service, innovation, teamwork and quality.[110] Other new values of increasing prominence are commitment, openness, communications, recognition, trust and leadership. Most of these new values are closely associated with public-service reforms, including emphases on strategic planning, serving clients, employee empowerment and teamwork, quality assurance, measurement of processes and outputs, commitment to training and recognition, and top-management leadership and support.

The presence of new values in the value statements of so many public organizations indicates the impact that new approaches to management have already had, both on individual organizations and across the public service as a whole. The prominence of these new values is especially striking in that many of the strategic plans in which they appear were completed in the late 1980s and reflect values that were highly regarded even earlier. This helps to explain the high ranking of *excellence*, a value that was extremely popular in the mid-1980s but that is now less prominent.

Some of the new values reinforce certain traditional values. For example, the emphasis on quality complements the traditional value of effectiveness. However, some of the new values conflict with traditional values, in the same way as the traditional values sometimes conflict with one another. For example, the emphasis on innovation may tempt some public servants to be more concerned about creativity and less concerned about accountability. It is important to remember that value conflict is commonplace and to be expected. The federal Deputy Ministers' Task Force on Public Service Values and Ethics noted that

[e]ven our most cherished values are regularly in tension, and we are constantly having to make trade-offs between them. This is true of our personal life. It is equally true, perhaps especially true, of public service and public administration whose very essence lies in the balancing of conflicting values and purposes. Yet ... we are sometimes inclined to think that some value or principle is being betrayed when it is only being subordinated or accommodated, in a specific instance, to some other important value.[111]

As already suggested, there can be considerable difference between the

Figure 3.1. *Public Service Culture (Future vs Current). Values to Enhance to Achieve an Effective Future Public Service*

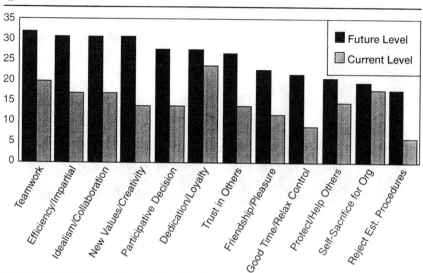

Source: CCMD-SYMLOG Survey of 216 Federal Executives/Managers, 1996. Scoring: 21–34 = "Often"; 11–20 = "Sometimes"; 0–10 = "Rarely"

values espoused by public organizations and the values that are actually practiced. A 1996 survey of 216 federal managers found that the primary types of behaviour rewarded in the public service were compliance and obedience to the chain of command, doing things in the established ways, reinforcing rules, putting self-interest first, and being tough and assertive (Figure 3.1).[112] These types of behaviour are much more congruent with the traditional bureaucratic organization than with the post-bureaucratic one. The survey also showed that managers did not value these current types of behaviour and that, in the optimum future public-service culture, emphasis should be placed on teamwork, efficiency, impartiality, idealism, collaboration, new values, creativity, dedication, loyalty, and trust in others (Figure 3.2). These desired types of behaviour are clearly attuned to the characteristics of the post-bureaucratic model.

## MANAGING VALUES

### Leadership and Values

Leadership involves "attracting and mobilizing energies and talents to work towards a shared purpose in the best interests of the organization,

51

Figure 3.2. *Public Service Culture (Future vs Current). Aspects of Current Culture that Should be De-Emphasized*

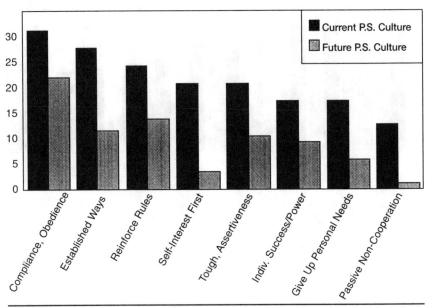

Source: CCMD-SYMLOG Survey of 216 Federal Executives/Managers, 1996. Scoring: 21–34 = "Often"; 11–20 = "Sometimes"; 0–10 = "Rarely"

the people comprising it and the people it serves."[113] The critical importance of effective leadership to high organizational and individual performance is well documented in the huge volume of scholarly writings on this subject. We focus here on one of these writings, because the principles of effective leadership it provides are strikingly similar to characteristics of the post-bureaucratic model of public organization provided in Chapter 1 of this book. James Kouzes and Barry Posner, in their book *The Leadership Challenge*, set out five fundamental practices of exemplary leadership and ten related commitments that are imbedded in these practices.[114] (See Figure 3.3). Note in particular the practice of inspiring a shared vision by appealing to values, interests, hopes and dreams and the practice of modelling the way by behaving in a manner that is consistent with shared values.

*Leadership and Participation in the Values Process*
The vigorous and unwavering support of an organization's leadership is critical to the systematic and sensitive management of values. The integral

Figure 3.3. *Ten Commitments of Leadership*

| PRACTICES | COMMITMENTS |
|---|---|
| Challenging the Process | 1. *Search out* challenging opportunities to change, grow, innovate, and improve.<br>2. *Experiment*, take risks, and learn from the accompanying mistakes. |
| Inspiring a Shared Vision | 3. *Envision* an uplifting and ennobling future.<br>4. *Enlist* others in a common vision by appealing to their values, interests, hopes, and dreams. |
| Enabling Others to Act | 5. *Foster* collaboration by promoting cooperative goals and building trust.<br>6. *Strengthen* people by giving power away, providing choice, developing competence, assigning critical tasks, and offering visible support. |
| Modeling the Way | 7. *Set* the example by behaving in ways that are consistent with shared values.<br>8. *Achieve* small wins that promote consistent progress and build commitment. |
| Encouraging the Heart | 9. *Recognize* individual contributions to the success of every project.<br>10. *Celebrate* team accomplishments regularly. |

*Source: The Leadership Challenge* by James M. Kouzes and Barry Z. Posner. Copyright © 1995. Reprinted with permission from Jossey–Bass Inc., San Francisco, California.

link between values and successful leadership was identified early on by Phillip Selznick, who argued that the organizational leader is "primarily an expert in the promotion and protection of values. ... The art of creative leadership is the art of reworking human and technological materials to fashion an organism that embodies new and enduring values."[115] Ultimately, the leadership – those who are responsible for providing direction and who are accountable for results – must decide what the content of the value statement will be. They must also decide on the extent and the means of participation in the statement's formulation and implementation.

*The Development Phase.* A variety of approaches for the development of value statements may be taken. Some of them "are developed through strategic planning processes, some through organization development efforts, and some through extended dialogue within the management team. All these statements provide an opportunity for the manager to help articulate a vision and a way for the manager to begin to change the organization's culture."[116] It is important to place the value-setting exercise in its organizational context. Figure 3.4 provides a framework for doing this through a strategic planning process in which the organization's value statement is tightly linked to its mission, vision, goals and

53

Figure 3.4. *Organizational Framework for Values*

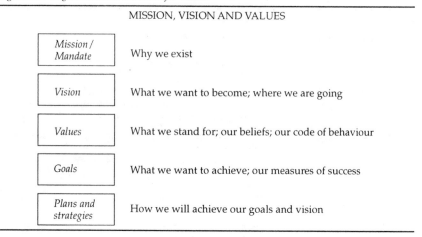

MISSION, VISION AND VALUES

| | |
|---|---|
| Mission / Mandate | Why we exist |
| Vision | What we want to become; where we are going |
| Values | What we stand for; our beliefs; our code of behaviour |
| Goals | What we want to achieve; our measures of success |
| Plans and strategies | How we will achieve our goals and vision |

strategies.[117] A mission statement sets out the reason(s) for the organization's existence, and a vision statement describes its future "ideal state." The inclusion of a statement on values is widely considered central to the success of a strategic plan: "The organization's values and its strategic plan must be congruent. Strategic plans that do not take values into account will ... probably fail."[118] It is notable, however, that many organizations have successfully formulated mission, vision and value statements separately from a strategic planning process. (Appendices A-1 to A-3 contain examples of value statements that have emerged from various approaches.[119]) Figure 3.5 provides a real-life example of a statement of the Alberta Department of Labour's vision, mission and values.[120]

A *participative leadership* style is, in general, the best approach for bringing about shared commitment to an organization's core values. The organization's leadership should encourage widespread participation in both the development and implementation of its value statement. Active involvement by employees is especially important, because it fosters a sense of ownership in the content of the statement and a commitment to its successful implementation. Employees are less likely to cherish a value statement that is handed down from on high – in the tradition of "command-and-compliance" management. This consideration is especially important in the light of findings, for the federal sphere at least, that the values of the most senior managers were not even shared by managers a few levels down in the hierarchy.[121]

While many value statements are developed by the organization's top

Figure 3.5. *Department of Labour, Government of Alberta*

---

*Vision, Mission and Values*

Our Vision

Quality Service Through Partnerships

Our Mission

At Alberta Labour we work in partnership with Albertans
to promote safe and healthy workplaces,
quality working life, and comprehensive safety systems.

Our Values

We are committed to quality
service through innovation and
creativity. Quality means achieving standards of
excellence in everything we do.

We are accountable and
responsible for actions and results.

We respect and value each and
every staff member. All staff are
encouraged to reach their full potential.

We respect individuals, groups
and organizations. We treat them
fairly and respect their views.

---

leader or its senior management group, it is desirable to involve employees down and across the organization. This is often accomplished by creating a group that is representative of the various segments of a department or that is composed of officials predisposed to support change and innovation, or both. A federal deputy minister has explained that her department's mission and values statement was created "as part of our strategic planning process" based *"on employee participation, the key to achieving lasting positive results"*:

First, we created a Strategic Planning Working Group made up of managers representing a cross-section of the Department, with help from a consultant in team building. This group developed an initial mission statement and guiding principles [*values*]. Then, I sent all staff a confidential questionnaire about this statement and principles. All staff received a synthesis of responses. The results formed the basis of discussions by managers on the mission and guiding principles. An equitable representation of regional, headquarters and common services managers took part in a planning meeting and a three-day strategic planning forum. More suggestions came from employee focus groups. After each of these phases, the working group revised the mission statement to reflect the feedback

55

from staff. Once the Executive Committee had approved the statement and principles, I sent a copy to all staff. ... We are now integrating the mission into the daily life of the Department. Managers and employees are discussing its impact on their work.[122]

Although management and staff are usually the major participants in the value-setting process, the leadership must decide what other stakeholders (e.g., clients, citizens), if any, should be involved and to what extent. The extent of involvement can vary considerably from one group of stakeholders to another and this involvement can include one or more of such activities as articulating the organization's values, commenting on them, indicating the level of agreement with them, and assessing their congruence with policies and actions. Widespread participation in the process helps to ensure that different perspectives on the relative significance of various values can be considered.

The value system of Tandem Computers, a business firm, provides a noteworthy example of concern that the organization's values meet the needs of a broad range of stakeholders. This company lists eleven values and provides one paragraph of elaboration on the meaning and implications of each value. It then explains how these values are to be applied in *relationships,* not only between employees but also between employees and their families, the community, investors, partners, customers and suppliers. The company's value system "is composed of an interconnected set of core values and the business relationships in which they are applied."[123]

In most public organizations, the strategic planning process in general and the value-setting exercise in particular are management driven; elected politicians do not usually play an active role. It is advisable, however, to involve political superiors in the process so as to ensure their support, especially if such values as innovation, empowerment and risk-taking are included among the organization's core values.

A variety of *means* can be used to involve stakeholders not only in the value-setting process but also in the broader process of developing all four components shown in Figure 3.4. These can include workshops, employee and client focus groups, employee and client surveys, workshops, interviews, or any combination of these techniques. More specifically,

you can ask people to mentally project themselves into the future and describe the organization to a publication. There are several other workshop exercises based on writing scenarios. You can ask your staff to take a hard look at the culture of your organization: what works, what has been memorable and what motivates people?

You can ask people outside the organization for their honest opinion. Or you can convene a group to identify the top-ten best experiences in the organization and the most common irritants.[124]

Regardless of the techniques used, a strong argument can be made for clarifying the organization's values (often described as conducting a "values audit"[125]) at an early point in the process, usually following the development of the organization's vision statement.

*The Implementation Phase.* For effective implementation of a value statement, the leadership must *communicate* the organization's values openly and frequently: "The problem is not the absence of values among senior managers, but rather that managers at lower levels do not appear to share the values of their superiors."[126] Employees who have participated in the value-setting process will be more receptive to the leadership's effort to diffuse and reinforce the organization's values, but the leaders must be seen to *live* the values as well. They must demonstrate that their decisions, especially in the human resource area, are based on the values. A federal task force argued that

[t]op management is the most important influence on the growth of values and culture of an organization. ... Some executives believe that the way to shape corporate values is through improved communication. While communication helps, employees look for cues in executive *actions* rather than in *pronouncements*. If actions are inconsistent with pronouncements, management loses credibility. No one places stock in the proclamations.[127]

Communicating the values to stakeholders, both within and outside the organization, will facilitate an assessment of the extent to which there is congruence between stated values and actual decisions. Even if employees become emotionally attached to a values statement through participation in its development, their support for it will diminish if the organization's leadership does not live the values – if they do not "walk their talk": "Numerous managers have 'done their values thing' and produced pretty parchment papers filled with inspiring words. However, many are frustrated because they feel that people throughout their organization or team 'aren't getting the message.' But the people do get management's message. They see it loud and clear."[128] Another effective means by which leaders can communicate and reinforce the organization's values is to recognize and reward employees whose actions are in tune with these values.

Since the organization's policies and activities should reflect its values, it is important to audit the extent of its commitment to the values. The techniques for involving stakeholders in implementing the values are similar to those for their development. A useful technique for involving large numbers of stakeholders is the use of periodic employee and customer surveys. The approach adopted by B.C. Parks is especially noteworthy. This organization not only adopted a value statement – in the form of a set of "management principles" – but it also made a commitment to an annual review of how well these principles were being applied throughout the organization. Each year a questionnaire is sent to all employees; the results of this survey, including suggestions for improvement, are published; and, to help assess progress, comparisons are made with the previous year's results.

## FORM AND CONTENT OF VALUE STATEMENTS

Virtually all organizations with formal value statements (sometimes called management principles or organizational philosophy) include them as part of a multi-part strategic plan or mission statement (See appendices A-1 to A-3 for examples). There is, however, enormous variety in the statements' form and content. To provide guidance on developing a value statement, the federal Committee on Governing Values recommended that the values should be

- few in number;
- mutually reinforcing (i.e., interrelated at least, perhaps even overlapping);
- words, not statements (although the words may later be converted to statements);
- easy to communicate (i.e., in the sense of being able to explain to others or have them interpreted correctly);
- easy to understand (i.e., no fog, static, or stilted language);
- easy to remember (i.e., eventually every employee should know them, be able to name them, be able to explain them);
- easy to adapt (i.e., applicable to any situation, any job, any role, any department, division, etc.); and
- easy to identify with (i.e., compatible with the personal values of the majority of employees).

The Committee on Governing Values noted two other critical conditions. The statements must appeal to employees at a visceral, not just an intellectual, level, and they must account for the values of those outside the organization (Parliament, the public) as well as government's objectives.[129]

The rest of this section elaborates briefly on each of the committee's suggestions.

The committee concluded that a long list of possible values might be reduced to as few as three "governing" values – respect, responsibility and responsiveness.[130] The federal Department of Transport lists three values – service, respect and professionalism. The City of Saskatoon lists four values – pride, quality, responsive[ness], and caring. Some statements list so many values that the probability that employees will *remember* them is remote, and the usefulness of the statement is questionable. It has been argued that "[m]ore than three to four values aren't values, they're a wish list. As with so many issues of strategy and culture, executives need to set priorities about what's really important to the organization. Core values are those few single words or short statements that act as central 'hooks' on which to hang the key behavioural guidelines that shape everyone's actions."[131] Very few value statements meet this strict standard. Nevertheless, to keep the number of values at a reasonable level, public organizations need to dig deeply to the core of their values rather than to choose the easier, but ultimately ineffective, option of providing a long list.

Most public organizations with carefully crafted value statements identify between five and ten values. There is considerable variety, however, in the manner in which the values are expressed. Some organizations express their values in a few words. For example, the Saskatchewan Department of Economic Development's statement of core values is as follows:

In dealing with our colleagues and stakeholders we value and demonstrate:
− effective communication
− respect for others
− personal and professional development
− quality service
− honesty and integrity
− innovation and improvement
− leadership and initiative
− teamwork and partnership

New Brunswick's Office of the Comptroller uses short *statements* rather than just *words*:

− We work in a consultative, constructive manner sharing ideas, knowledge, and experience with our clients and colleagues.
− We are accountable for adding value to the work we undertake.
− We act with integrity, independence and objectivity.
− We are committed to excellence.

Other organizations provide more elaboration on each value. The Ontario Ministry of Natural Resources' statement, "Organizational Beliefs and Values," contains two or three sentences on each value. For example,

*Caring*: Everyone is ultimately responsible for his or her own career. But as we make decisions that affect staff we treat others as we ourselves would like to be treated: with dignity, honesty, openness, and as much fairness and support as possible.

This example illustrates a popular approach to dealing with the pressure to choose only a few values from among many possible ones, namely, listing additional values in the elaboration on each core value. This enables the drafters to highlight a few core values while at the same time satisfying those who would have selected slightly different ones. This approach helps to make the value statement as a whole *easier to identify with* (i.e., more compatible with the personal values of the majority of employees). Moreover, the additional values tend to *reinforce* the core values (i.e., they are at least closely related and are sometimes overlapping). Still another benefit of this approach is that a small number of values is *easier to remember* and the elaboration makes them *easier to communicate* (in the sense of being able to explain them to others or have them interpreted correctly).

The tension between having enough values in a value statement and having too many to remember can be illustrated well by reference to the experience of Tandem Computers, which lists eleven values in its corporate philosophy. Four years after the values were decided upon, employees were asked for suggestions on how to make the list shorter and thereby easier to remember. Among the flood of responses, opinions ranged from "Don't you dare touch those values" to "Great idea, maybe I can remember them."[132]

Value statements vary considerably not only in their content but also in their inspirational tone. It is no easy task to develop a statement that is attractive to all employees *on the visceral as well as the intellectual level*. The examples noted above – and additional examples in appendices A-1 to A-3 – illustrate several options. The suggestion by the Committee on Governing Values that a values statement should take account of *the values of those outside the organization* has been fulfilled by many organizations that emphasize such values as accountability, service and responsiveness.

The federal Deputy Ministers' Task Force on Public Service Values and Ethics has called for the adoption of a service-wide statement of principles or code of conduct that will "anchor the public service in its primordial values, those that we have called the 'democratic values.'" In recognition of the importance of the considerations outlined above, "[t]he ideal statement would be succinct, dignified in tone and diction, focused on the great principles of public service, and intended to endure."[133]

## CONCLUSIONS

It is widely argued that shared values are centrally important for organizational success. A survey of federal public servants in the United States led to the conclusion that "clarifying, communicating and reinforcing value systems is the most important function of management."[134] The same conclusion was drawn by Thomas Peters and Robert Waterman about the management of business organizations.[135] We have seen that in many public organizations the formulation and implementation of value statements provide the vehicle for clarifying and diffusing an organization's core values. As explained earlier, even the analytical and consultative exercise involved in drafting a statement can be very beneficial.

It follows that public organizations without a value statement should seriously consider developing one. Moreover, those organizations that already have value statements should re-examine them regularly with a view to improving their content and format, reinforcing their importance, and assessing the extent to which the organization is "living" its values. The quality of the value statements of many public organizations is inadequate. It is hard to imagine, for example, how employees' behaviour can be successfully guided, much less inspired, by statements containing fifteen to twenty "core" values.

Another argument for developing a value statement is that it can provide a strong ethical underpinning for the organization. A nation-wide survey of American managers led to the conclusion that as the compatibility of personal and organizational values increased, "so did the extent to which respondents agreed that their organizations were guided by highly ethical standards. ... [A] low congruence manager would be a more likely candidate to take a bribe, falsely report earnings, steal company secrets and the like."[136]

*Ethical* values, that is, values related to questions of right and wrong, appear frequently in value statements. Indeed, the ethical values of integrity, accountability and fairness/equity are among the top-five values contained in the value statements of Canadian public organizations.[137] While value statements cannot serve as codes of ethics, they can, and should, be explicitly tied to the organization's ethics code or other ethics rules. For example, ethics rules on such matters as conflict of interest, confidentiality, harassment and discrimination can be based on such core values as integrity and fairness.

Despite the benefits claimed for a focus on values as a means of changing an organization's culture and improving its performance, this approach has its limitations – and its critics. We have already mentioned such issues as the disparity between an organization's espoused values and its values in practice, the existence of subcultures within a single organization, and the critical importance of effective and dedicated leadership. An important additional consideration is that experts disagree as to the utility of a change in culture as a means of transforming an organization. We noted earlier the argument that progressive public managers are increasingly inclined to focus on values as a means of bringing about a more substantial transformation than restructuring could[138]: "Culture has replaced structure as the most popular variable in the organizational change process. Change the culture, the message goes, and the majority of organizational problems will be solved."[139]

However, other experts contend that cultural change and structural change must go hand-in-hand. Francine Séguin contends that to effect an organizational transformation, a change in *culture* must be complemented by a change of *structure*.[140] And Frank Swift notes that "to be successful, restructuring towards transformation needs to be accompanied by ... a renewal of the organization's value systems."[141] Séguin argues also that "any genuine cultural change, which implies that new ways of doing things result from a changing mentality, is very difficult to bring about."[142] Both academics and practitioners agree on this point – that changing an organization's culture is a challenging and lengthy process requiring sustained commitment from all members of the organization, but especially from its leadership.

A related concern is that, even if an organization is successful in fostering shared commitment to a core set of values, performance may not be significantly enhanced as a result. According to Paul Thomas,

Despite a growing empirical research base that testifies to the difficulty in defining, let alone managing, organizational culture, the use of cultural change to achieve renewal of public services is being strongly recommended. ... However, the assumption of a simple linear connection between the existence of a strong shared culture based on vision statements and goals and excellence in organizational performance is not supported by the available research.[143]

Yet Zussman and Jabes concluded, on the basis of their extensive survey of public- and private-sector managers, that "culture makes a difference in the degree of work satisfaction ... it is an important predictor of work satisfaction."[144] And Vijay Sathe contends, at least for private-sector organizations, that "it is possible to determine what is needed to influence culture change," and he outlines approaches by which management can understand and change the culture so as to promote both organizational efficiency and effectiveness.[145] Finally, Posner et al. conclude from their national survey of private-sector managers that "strong shared values provide individuals with a sense of success and fulfillment, a healthy (less cynical) assessment of the values and ethics of their colleagues, subordinates and bosses, and a greater regard for organizational objectives and significant organizational constituents."[146]

There is considerable support among academics and practitioners for the view that shared commitment to a set of core organizational values can significantly enhance organizational performance. As a result, many public organizations are implementing a value statement, often as part of a strategic planning process, under the leadership of deputy ministers or chief administrative officers. A federal deputy minister has noted that

incorporating the [mission/values] statement into the corporate culture and involving all employees in the implementation of the statement initially met with some apathy and opposition. However, we have had considerable success, and are continuing to work at implementing the statement at all levels of the department. ... The exercise has also enabled us to involve employees more fully in decision making, and we have learned that consulting with employees and giving them feedback on their ideas and concerns are essential to providing good service to our clients.[147]

Providing good service is only one of several major public-service values to be discussed in subsequent chapters. We focus in the next chapter on a new public-service value – innovation.

# 4

# Innovating for High Performance

## INTRODUCTION

Innovation is an important theme of our study. In Chapter 1, we identified change-orientation, the willingness to innovate and take risks, as a key characteristic of the post-bureaucratic organization. We also discussed opportunities, such as the technological revolution, and pressures, such as financial constraints, that are compelling public-sector organizations to innovate. In Chapter 2, we described a number of particularly innovative public-sector organizations. And Chapter 3 identified innovation as one of the most prominent new public-service values.

This chapter expands the discussion of public-service innovation by presenting evidence regarding innovative programs or policies. In defining innovation, we follow the academic literature, which distinguishes between invention, the creation of a new idea or a better way of performing an existing function, and innovation, which is the adoption of an existing idea for the first time by an organization.[148] Innovation in organizations is often characterized by the re-shuffling of known elements to create new programs or policies and adaptations of general ideas to particular circumstances.

One of the best places to find accounts of public-sector innovation is in the applications to innovation awards. The largest and best-known competition of this kind in Canada is the Institute of Public Administration of Canada's (IPAC) Award for Innovative Management in the public sector. It has been in operation since 1990 and receives an average of 100 applications per year. In the U.S., the largest and best-known award of this kind is the Innovations in American Government Award program, which is funded by the Ford Foundation and managed by Harvard University's Kennedy School of Government. This award began in 1986 at the state and local government level and included the federal government for the first time in 1995. It receives an average of 1500 applications per year.

The Innovations in American Government Award program requires its semi-finalists to complete a very detailed questionnaire that asks about the nature of the innovation, its target population, budget, organizational structure, history, supporters and opponents, results and replication. Sandford Borins has used these semi-finalist applications as the basis of a book about public-sector innovation in state and local government in the U.S.[149] We sent out a similar questionnaire to the best applicants to the IPAC award between 1990 and 1994. This chapter will therefore be able to draw comparisons between public management innovation in Canada and the U.S. The chapter will discuss the following topics: the characteristics of innovations (as identified by the applicants) and their congruence with the characteristics of post-bureaucratic organizations that we have identified; the innovations' target populations; the initiators of the innovations; and the conditions leading to the innovations. It will also address the mode of analysis used; the obstacles faced by innovators and the tactics most frequently used to overcome them; the results of innovations; media attention and awards received; and replication of the innovations.

## RESEARCH METHODOLOGY

In his earlier research Borins used a sample of 217 of 350 semi-finalist applications between 1990 and 1994 to the Ford Foundation–Kennedy School of Government (Ford–KSG) state and local government innovations awards, as the program was then called. He argued that this sample was representative of best practice, the essence of the argument being as follows. The Ford–KSG awards are well known, the organizers make strenuous efforts to encourage as many public-sector innovators as possible to apply, and the initial application form is not hard to complete. From the approximately 1500 initial applications that come in each year, expert juries choose seventy-five semi-finalists that represent each policy area (e.g., policing, housing, economic development) in the same proportion as in the 1500 applications.[150]

For this study, we sent out a similar questionnaire to the best applications to the IPAC award between 1990 and 1994. The IPAC award is also well known and easy to apply for, and IPAC also works hard to maximize the number of initial applications. The institute uses a panel of experts to do a preliminary triage, and in 1995 we sent our questionnaire to the ninety applicants deemed by the panel to have been the best between 1990 and 1994. The questionnaire was accompanied by a letter from the project's sponsor, the Canadian Centre for Management Development, urging co-operation; a persistent research assistant followed up the mailing with telephone calls. Ultimately, we received thirty-three completed question-naires, a completion rate of thirty-seven per cent. Answering this long and detailed questionnaire was voluntary and, unlike an innovation competi-tion, there were no awards. In almost every case, the research assistant was able to find the organization or unit that had submitted the applica-tion; the innovative programs had rarely been terminated. Sometimes, however, the person who filed the original application had moved on, and his or her successor did not have enough information to complete the questionnaire.

We checked the representativeness of this sample relative to the entire population of applications to the IPAC award between 1990 and 1996, in the following way. During that period, of a total of 647 applications, thirty per cent were from the federal government, fifty-four per cent from the provinces, and fifteen per cent from municipalities. Of the thirty-three questionnaires we received, eighteen per cent were from the federal government, seventy per cent from the provinces, and twelve per cent from municipal governments. The over-representation of provincial governments is to be expected, because their applications were consist-ently ranked higher by the juries; of the twenty-one first-, second-, and third-prize winners between 1990 and 1996, seventeen were from pro-vincial governments, two from federal departments, and two from municipal governments.

The questionnaire we sent to applicants to the IPAC awards is in Ap-pendix B. This questionnaire differs from the one we sent the Ford–KSG semi-finalists, in three places. Because the questionnaire was sent to some applicants several years after they had applied to the IPAC awards, we asked them to complete their historical narrative by discussing how their implementation strategy had evolved since their original applica-tion. Much discussion among students of public management has fo-cused on whether innovators follow a process of "groping along" by trial and error towards loosely defined goals or whether they use clear and comprehensive plans. In addition to analysing the applicants' narra-tives, as Borins did in his study of the American innovations, we have explicitly asked applicants for their views about whether they were groping or planning. Finally, we asked applicants, whom we expected would be more reflective when completing an *ex post* questionnaire than when applying for an award, to discuss what they learned from initiat-ing and implementing an innovation and what advice they would give to would-be innovators.

Table 4.1. *Innovations' Target Populations*
(Entries are in percentages)

| Target Population | Group | |
| --- | --- | --- |
| | Canada | U.S. |
| General population | 64 | 29 |
| Businesses | 36 | 15 |
| Government bodies | 24 | 9 |
| Non-profit institutions | 6 | 4 |
| At-risk individuals | 3 | 17 |
| Low-income individuals | 9 | 23 |
| Young people | 3 | 21 |
| Old people | 3 | 3 |
| People with disabilities | 12 | 3 |
| People with dysfunctions | 0 | 5 |
| Other | 3 | 13 |
| Total (%) | 163 | 141 |
| N | 33 | 217 |

N = number of observations.
General population includes groups that form a large proportion of population (e.g., drivers); business includes professionals; non-profit institutions include hospitals and schools.
r = .53; t = 1.88 with 9 degrees of freedom, not significant at .05

## Differences between Canada and the U.S.

Several researchers who have undertaken comparative studies of public-management reform in the four Commonwealth OECD countries have been reluctant to extend their work to include the U.S. because of its congressional, as opposed to parliamentary, institutions.[151] In addition, Canada and the U.S. are different societies. From a public policy viewpoint, the most visible difference is that Canada's social safety net (for example, its regional income transfers and its system of universal health insurance) is more highly developed. Its income distribution is somewhat more egalitarian and its underclass is smaller. This is illustrated in Table 4.1, which classifies the innovations by their target populations.[152]

In the Canadian sample, most of the programs are targeted at the general population (or large groups within it), businesses, or government bodies. An example of a program aimed at the entire population is Environment Canada's Ultraviolet Index, now incorporated routinely in weather forecasts during the summer.[153] The U.S. sample is quite different, with a much greater frequency of programs aimed at high-risk individuals, low-income individuals, and the young. Innovative programs in the U.S. are often designed to help those who slip through the social safety net. Thus, the U.S. sample includes many programs intended to provide health care for the uninsured, improve safety and public services in urban ghettoes, and prevent young people at risk of joining gangs and taking drugs from doing so.

These differences in political institutions and public policies between Canada and the U.S. would lead us to expect that the nature and process of public-sector innovation would differ as well. If, however, we were to find that the characteristics and processes of public-sector innovation were similar in the two countries, this might be evidence that public-sector innovation is a more universal phenomenon.

## Characteristics of the Innovations

Table 4.2 shows what applicants said made their program or policy initiative innovative. The statistical test indicates that the pattern of responses in both countries is similar. The most common response, in both Canada and the U.S., was that programs are holistic. Applicants stressed one or more of the following three senses of that term: taking a systems approach to a problem, coordinating the activities of a number of organizations, or providing multiple services to a target population. "Holistic" is therefore defined as the union of these three characteristics; that is, one or more of these characteristics appeared in fifty-five per cent of the Canadian applications and sixty-one per cent of the U.S. applications. (Because some applications had more than one of these three characteristics, the frequency for "total holistic" is less than the sum for each of its three components.) The frequent citing of holism is consistent with our describing the post-bureaucratic organization as favouring collective action – consultation, cooperation and coordination – rather than independent action, as is the case in the bureaucratic organization.[154]

An example of a holistic program coordinating the activities of several organizations is the Ontario Used Vehicle Information Program.[155] The objective of the information package, required for the sale of used cars, is to ensure that the cars have been certified as roadworthy and that the province collects sales tax on the fair market value of the car. It was developed collaboratively by the Ministry of Transport, which is responsible for vehicle licensing, the Ministry of Finance, which is responsible for taxation, and the Ministry of Consumer and Commercial Relations, which is responsible for consumer protection and for registering automobile loans.

This theme of holism is also evident in the literature on private-sector innovation. For example, in her review article, Rosabeth Kanter concludes

Table 4.2. *Self-identified Characteristics of Innovations*
(Entries are in percentages)

| Characteristic | Group | |
| --- | --- | --- |
| | Canada | U.S. |
| Systems approach | 3 | 26 |
| Coordinates organizations | 48 | 29 |
| Multiple services | 9 | 28 |
| *Total Holistic* | 55 | 61 |
| New technology | 21 | 28 |
| Simplified technology | 0 | 2 |
| *Total Technology* | 21 | 29 |
| Faster process | 21 | 31 |
| Simpler process | 3 | 7 |
| *Total process improvement* | 24 | 34 |
| Empowerment | 21 | 34 |
| Prevention | 0 | 16 |
| Uses incentives, not regulation | 3 | 8 |
| Use of private sector | 45 | 17 |
| Use of volunteers | 3 | 7 |
| New management philosophy | 27 | 15 |
| Attitude change | 6 | 13 |
| Groundwork for others | 0 | 6 |
| Spillover benefits | 0 | 8 |
| Pilot program | 0 | 1 |
| *Total (%)* | 205 | 249 |
| *N* | 33 | 217 |

$N$ = number of observations.
Systems approach (takes a systems approach to a problem); coordinates (activities of various) organizations; multiple services (makes available a wide range of services to target population); new technology (introduces or increases use of a new or existing technology); faster process (makes a process faster, more accessible, friendlier, etc.); simpler process (for dealing with problems); empowerment (of citizens and/or communities); prevention (rather than remediation); uses incentives, not regulation (program voluntary, uses incentives in addition to or in place of regulation); use of private sector (to achieve public purposes)
$r$ = .80; $t$ = 3.77 with 8 degrees of freedom, significant at .01

that one of the distinctive characteristics of private-sector innovation is that

[t]he innovation process crosses boundaries. An innovation process is rarely if ever contained solely within one unit. First, there is evidence that many of the best ideas are interdisciplinary or interfunctional in origin – as connoted by the root meaning of entrepreneurship as the development of "new combinations" – or they benefit from broader perspective and information from outside the area primarily

responsible for the innovation. Second, regardless of the origin of innovations, they inevitably send out ripples and reverberations to other organization units, whose behavior may be required to change in the light of the needs of innovations, or whose cooperation is necessary if an innovation is to be fully developed or exploited.[156]

The second-most frequent theme in the Canadian responses to the questionnaire is that an innovation uses the private sector in some way to deliver a program. This phenomenon includes partnerships, such as programs in both Ontario and Saskatchewan to involve industry, interest groups and associations, aboriginal bands, and municipalities in environmental management and a program in Alberta to involve the private sector in the management of occupational health and safety.[157] It also includes instances where the private sector is a contractor, such as IBM's role in supplying electronic kiosks to the Ontario Ministry of Transportation, or where a service has been contracted-out to the private sector, such as road maintenance in Alberta and British Columbia.[158] The recurring incidence of partnerships and private-sector service delivery is consistent with the willingness of post-bureaucratic organizations to use nondepartmental forms of program delivery.

Other themes occurring frequently are the use of new technology (twenty-one per cent of applications), process improvement (twenty-four per cent), the use of new management philosophies (twenty-seven per cent), and empowerment (twenty-one per cent). New information technologies are discussed at length in Chapter 10. In addition, some applications cited other types of technologies such as the implementation in Ontario of no-till agriculture, which involves the use of drills that enable farmers to plant without removing or ploughing under existing crop residue, thereby using much less fuel than conventional technology.[159] While information technology often facilitates process improvement, there were cases of process improvements achieved without its use. An example is the Alberta Workers' Compensation Board's introduction of work hardening, an approach to rehabilitation that had been developed in the United States. Instead of dealing with injuries to certain parts of the body, treatment teams now deal with injuries incurred in certain industries. In addition, they give injured workers real or simulated work activities as part of the rehabilitation process.[160] The process improvement theme is consistent with another characteristic of the post-bureaucratic organization, namely its citizen-centred focus on delivering quality service.

The use of new management philosophies and empowerment often overlapped, since the philosophies generally involved giving more responsibility to front-line workers. The Township of Pittsburgh, Ontario,

Table 4.3. *Initiators of Innovations*
(Entries are in percentages)

| Initiator | Group | |
|---|---|---|
| | Canada | U.S. |
| Politician | 30 | 18 |
| Agency head | 27 | 23 |
| Other public servant | 55 | 48 |
| Interest group, non-profit org'n | 6 | 13 |
| Individual citizen | 0 | 6 |
| Clients of program | 6 | 2 |
| Other | 6 | 4 |
| Total initiators | 130 | 114 |
| N | 33 | 217 |

N = number of observations
r = .95; t = 6.8 with 5 degrees of freedom, significant at .01

established a gainsharing program in which staff were given a target goal for cost-savings, encouraged to come up with ideas for cost-sharing, and rewarded by receiving a share of the cost-savings as bonuses.[161] The Ontario Region of Human Resources Development Canada undertook a major team-building exercise, intended to improve the quality of its work, by encouraging initiative and risk-taking on the part of front-line workers.[162] Here, too, are several points of contact with the characteristics of the post-bureaucratic organization, in that it emphasizes participative leadership, attempts to be an empowering and caring milieu for employees, and decentralizes authority and control.

Applicants' descriptions of the nature of their innovations, in both Canada and the U.S., demonstrate that many of the characteristics of the post-bureaucratic model appear frequently in their narratives. However, we should not expect that every innovation would display every characteristic. These innovations usually represent individual initiatives set in the context of larger organizations, so that an initiative would be the appropriate response to a specific problem or opportunity. Initiatives involving the transformation of entire organizations are more likely to display more elements of the set of characteristics of the post-bureaucratic organization.

## Local Heroes

Table 4.3 identifies the main initiator(s) of the innovations. Once again, the pattern of responses is correlated in the two countries. Still more interesting is the distribution of the responses in both countries. By a wide margin, the most frequent initiators were not politicians or agency heads. In fifty-five per cent of the Canadian sample and forty-eight per cent of the U.S. sample they were career public servants below the agency-head level, that is, middle managers and front-line workers. This result seems to contradict one of the basic tenets of both parliamentary and presidential democracy. Voters elect politicians to enact policies. Deputy ministers are cabinet appointments and agency heads in the U.S. are political appointments – the objective in both cases being to make the bureaucracy responsive to politicians. In addition, the standard model of public bureaucracy emphasizes the existence of stringent central agency controls on entrepreneurship and innovativeness to minimize corruption and ensure due process.[163] The media's interest in exposing public-sector failings (management in a fishbowl) is yet another impediment to innovation. Parliamentary Question Period provides an opportunity for the Opposition to pose embarrassing questions to ministers; because ministers are accountable for their departments, these questions often deal with bureaucratic mismanagement. For all these reasons, public servants, it is assumed, will not be rewarded for successful innovation and may well be punished for unsuccessful innovation. A further consequence of these incentives would be that intrinsically innovative people would select against careers in the public sector. Yet, in spite of controls and disincentives, there are people in the public sector who innovate.

This result also differs from James Iain Gow's empirical work on public-sector innovation in Canada.[164] Gow asked a sample of 607 practitioners and academics to identify the major source of innovative ideas in government. Using a closed list, his results were as follows: senior public servants (thirty-nine per cent), commissions of inquiry (seventeen per cent), scientific and professional meetings (twelve per cent), interest groups (eleven per cent), books and journals (eight per cent), consultants (six per cent), and cabinet ministers (five per cent). It is unfortunate that he did not include middle-level and front-line public servants as an option for this question. It may well be that they are the ones who adapt ideas from books, journals, and professional meetings to their organizations. In addition, their innovations may be the result of their own problem-solving.

The following is a clear example of innovation introduced by a local hero. Parks Canada's accessibility program for seniors and people with disabilities was initiated by Robert Fern, himself a person with a disability. Fern moved from the field to a staff position in Ottawa because of vision problems. He began by developing some low-budget pilot projects for people with disabilities; for example, he taught a course at the University of Waterloo School of Architecture in which students developed designs to make the boyhood home of former Prime Minister Mackenzie King wheelchair accessible. The Canadian Parks Association then took the best student design and completed the project. Through such projects, and with the support of interest groups for the disabled, Fern convinced both his assistant deputy minister and Parks Canada field staff that increasing accessibility was both desirable in itself and a good way to increase visits. When the Treasury Board Secretariat put in place a policy of increased accessibility and funding for pilot projects, Fern had built momentum. In completing our questionnaire, Fern commented that people at the top don't have time for new ideas and that many other staff members are afraid to experiment or take risks.[165]

The literature on private-sector innovation supports this finding on the importance of local heroes. Peters and Waterman argued that innovation came about through the efforts of mavericks at "skunkworks" far from central offices, often operating without a clear mandate from above and using bootlegged resources. It is a view that has now become conventional wisdom in the private sector.[166] The frequency of public-sector innovation coming from the front lines or middle management, as demonstrated by these results, suggests that the traditional model of public-sector bureaucracy may be inappropriate and that, with respect to the origins of innovation, public-sector organizations may actually be closer to their private- and voluntary-sector counterparts.

The IPAC questionnaire concluded by asking applicants to identify lessons they had learned and to give advice to would-be innovators. While the answers were not coded, the most frequently cited lessons concerned entrepreneurship, and the most frequently given advice was an exhortation to take risks, for example, "'rebels,' idea people, and employees involved in a leadership capacity outside [the organization] came to the fore," "senior executives were predisposed to entrepreneurship," "most people involved were entrepreneurial, results-oriented, not process-oriented," "it's easier to seek forgiveness than ask permission," "dare to be creative," "don't be bureaucratic," "break the rules," "occasionally go over people's heads," and "just do it. If it makes sense, no one will criticize it."

## Why Innovate?

In their narratives, innovators described the different conditions or challenges that led to their innovations. The conditions fell into five groups: initiatives coming from the political system, due to an election mandate, legislation or pressure by politicians; new leadership, whether from outside or within the organization; a crisis, defined as a publicly visible failure or problem, either current or anticipated; a variety of internal problems (failing to respond to a changing environment, inability to reach

Table 4.4 *Conditions Leading to Innovations*
(Entries are in percentages)

| | Group | | |
| | Canada | | |
| Condition | Large sample | Small sample | U.S. |
|---|---|---|---|
| Election | n.a. | 12 | 2 |
| Legislation | n.a. | 12 | 11 |
| Pressure, lobbying | n.a. | 24 | 6 |
| *Total political* | 21 | 49 | 19 |
| New leader (outside) | n.a. | 3 | 6 |
| New leader (inside) | n.a. | 0 | 4 |
| *Total new leader* | 6 | 3 | 9 |
| *Crisis* | 13 | 27 | 30 |
| Environment changing | 19 | 18 | 8 |
| Unable to reach market | 11 | 6 | 27 |
| Unable to meet demand | 11 | 15 | 11 |
| Resource constraint | 23 | 15 | 10 |
| No policy coordination | 10 | 0 | 4 |
| *Total internal* | n.a. | 49 | 49 |
| Technology opportunity | 6 | 12 | 18 |
| Other new opportunity | n.a. | 18 | 16 |
| *Total opportunities* | 6 | 27 | 33 |
| Stakeholder dissatisfaction | 20 | n.a. | n.a. |
| *Total conditions* | 146 | 155 | 154 |
| Number of observations | 339 | 33 | 217 |

r = .98; t = 8.5 with 3 degrees of freedom, significant at .01

a target population, inability to meet demand for a program, resource constraints, or an inability to coordinate policies); and new opportunities, created either by technology or other causes. Four of the five groups (the exception being crises) had multiple components, and Table 4.4 reports the union of the components of each group. The frequency of both individual conditions and the five groups of conditions is shown. In addition to the thirty-three applicants to the IPAC award between 1990 and 1994 who completed our questionnaire, Borins also coded in earlier research a much larger sample of all 339 applications to the IPAC award between 1990 and 1993, based on their responses to the questionnaire IPAC used.[167] In this case as well, the pattern of responses in the two countries is closely correlated.

The most frequent catalyst for innovation, occurring in half the cases in both the small Canadian and American samples (and also, it would appear, the large Canadian sample, even though the union of the five internal problems was not calculated), was internal problems. For example, the Township of Pittsburgh is the location of a number of federal government facilities. As part of a strategic planning exercise, it forecasted revenue shortfalls due to a likely reduction in federal government grants in lieu of taxes. This was the impetus for its cost-management initiative.[168] Crises feature in the narratives in approximately thirty per cent of the applications in both the small Canadian and the U.S. samples. In the large Canadian sample, the category "stakeholder dissatisfaction" likely covers what were coded in the small Canadian and U.S. samples as crises.[169] Environment Canada's Ultraviolet Index Program is an example of a crisis-driven program. It was initiated in response to NASA's prediction in February 1992 of a severe thinning of the ozone layer over North America that spring.

Political initiatives appear in twenty per cent of both the American and the large Canadian sample, but with a much higher frequency for the small Canadian sample. Putting one's trust in large numbers suggests that the small Canadian sample overstated their frequency. Examples of political initiatives include decisions by the governments of both British Columbia and Alberta to privatize road maintenance and by Alberta's government to sharply reduce funding for its labour ministry, which led to the delegation of occupational health and safety to the private sector.[170]

There were many examples of information technology creating opportunities for innovation. Both Ontario and British Columbia redesigned their personal property security registries around remote electronic access.[171] An instance of a new opportunity of a non-technological nature was the Ontario government's decision to move the Office of the Registrar General from Toronto to Thunder Bay. This provided an opportunity to redesign the organization by creating more flexible front-line positions and by increasing opportunities for non-traditional groups.[172] In all three samples, fewer than ten per cent of the innovations were the result of new leadership (i.e., a new deputy minister in Canada or agency head in the U.S.) for the organization.

The responses for all three samples regarding the conditions leading to the innovations call into question the conventional wisdom that innovation in the public sector occurs primarily in response to a major crisis.[173] The argument underlying this view would be that many public-sector agencies, because they are monopolies and because they lack performance measures, could perform poorly for a long time without improvement until they encounter a publicly visible crisis. The relative infrequency of crisis-driven innovation, however, suggests that crises are not a necessary condition for innovation. Research based on private-sector organizations has also differentiated between innovations that respond to problems and innovations stimulated by opportunities such as the availability of resources.[174] (Once again, the frequencies with which the five conditions were identified in Canada and the U.S. were very similar.[175])

## Planning or Groping?

Two competing hypotheses for describing how innovations occur are 1) that they are the result of careful planning based on a preconceived vision, or 2) that they are reached largely spontaneously by a groping process. In his seminal article on this subject, Robert Behn describes "groping along" and argues on the basis of the small number of cases, with which he was very familiar, that innovative public managers often improve their organizations through an experimental process of groping towards goals that are initially loosely defined. He advocates that would-be innovators follow this process. Behn's original work was amplified by Olivia Golden and by Martin Levin and Mary Bryna Sanger.[176] Both used relatively small samples – Golden analysed seventeen cases and Levin and Sanger twenty-nine cases – of the successful applications to the Ford–KSG awards in its initial years (1986 to 1990).

In his U.S. study, Borins used the narrative responses describing the initiation and evolution of the innovations to determine how frequently they displayed Behn's groping, as opposed to comprehensive planning (see Table 4.5). Two types of comprehensive planning were coded: a strategic plan for the organization behind the innovation and a comprehensive plan for the innovation itself.[177] Behn's groping process was also coded – along with the use of pilot studies, consultants, public consultation, the replication of the program by other public-sector and non-profit organizations, policy or legislative analyses, and client surveys. The total incidence of all modes of analysis is 167 per cent in the Canadian sample and 177 per cent in the U.S. sample, indicating that most of the innovations involved more than one mode. In attempting to differentiate between "groping along" and comprehensive planning, attention was paid to whether the applicant indicated that a comprehensive plan was followed or that the innovation began with a broad idea that was implemented in an evolutionary manner. Milestones were also used to help determine how long it takes an innovation to take hold and how the original conception was modified.

Both the Canadian and U.S. samples indicate that planning was used more frequently than groping. Our IPAC questionnaire, by asking the innovators whether they were groping or planning, provided a more subtle result. While comprehensive planning (forty per cent) was more popular than groping (twenty-four per cent), as it was in the U.S. sample, a surprising thirty per cent of the Canadian sample said they were both planning and groping.[178] The following are some examples of pure groping, pure planning, and combinations of the two.

The Township of Pittsburgh started with the goal of achieving cost-savings. Cost-savings were achieved not by a comprehensive plan by the

Table 4.5. *Mode of Analysis for Innovations*
(Entries are in percentages)

| Mode | Group Canada | U.S. |
|---|---|---|
| Comprehensive planning alone | 42 | 56 |
| "Groping along" alone | 24 | 27 |
| Planning and groping | 30 | 3 |
| Pilot study | 15 | 35 |
| Replicate public-sector practice | 3 | 12 |
| Public consultation | 3 | 11 |
| Consultant | 0 | 7 |
| Legislative process | 2 | 8 |
| Strategic plan for organization | 9 | 7 |
| Client survey | 0 | 4 |
| Replicate non-profit org'n practice | 0 | 4 |
| *Total modes* | 167 | 177 |
| *N* | 33 | 217 |

$N$ = number of observations
$r = .72$; $t = 3.11$ with 9 degrees of freedom, significant at .01 when
"planning and groping" included
$r = .94$; $t = 7.8$ with 8 degrees of freedom, significant at .01 when
"planning and groping" excluded

chief financial officer but on the basis of suggestions from staff and a good deal of experimentation. Staff response to the questionnaire describes one such experiment:

[We responded] to a suggestion by a local resident (who is a shepherd) that we use sheep to cut the grass in parks, rather than hiring summer students. As a demonstration project, Council agreed to have 100 sheep graze on the vacant land next to the municipal office for a week. The experiment was a mixed success. The sheep were a drawing card for the residents of a nearby senior's home, local children, staff, and visitors to the municipal office. On the other hand, some neighbours complained about the odour, and the sheep proved to be quite particular about the weeds that they actually consumed! However, this experiment sent a valuable message that it is alright to take a risk because, even if you fail, you know more at the end of the experience than you knew when you started.[179]

Environment Canada's development of the ultraviolet index was the result of groping in a different context. When NASA predicted a severe thinning of the ozone layer in February 1992, then-environment minister Jean Charest gave his officials four months to design a program to respond to the problem. At that point, the questionnaire recounts, "we had a clear goal of informing the public, [but] initially we had no idea of how best to accomplish it." The department began a process of rapid experimentation and consultation with stakeholders.[180]

On the other hand, the Ontario Ministry of Consumer and Commercial Relations' programs usually followed a planning process. Moving the Office of the Registrar General from Toronto to Thunder Bay required detailed physical and human logistics:

Between 1987 [when the government announced the re-location] and opening up in April 1991, in Thunder Bay, a number of interdependent activities had to be planned, finalized, and implemented. Layout in the new building was dependent on the new organizational structure, the new business process, and the new information and communications technology to be used. New technology had to be identified, selected, tested, and in place sufficiently in advance of opening to permit the training of new staff. New staff had to be recruited, trained, and ready to start production in April 1991. The complexity of the planning required was such that a groping along model simply would not achieve what was needed.[181]

The ministry told a similar story about the establishment of electronic access to the Personal Property Security Registry:

The system was completely redesigned from the ground up in 1988/89. Although electronic access was not offered then, the designers of the systems upgrade positioned the system's capabilities so that electronic access could play a key role in the Branch's future. ... However, it was not a matter of simply throwing a switch to let electronic access start. Advance planning was necessary to create training content for clients, to identify and train persons in the registry who would help clients get set up technically, and then to provide the initial training. A help/hot line with procedures, staffing, and trained staff had to be in place when the first electronic client started.

The application did attribute a small role to groping, described as follows:

Although there was a clear plan in place and the destination was determined well in advance, some groping along did occur. Every contingency was not thought of and some mistakes were made. Constant interaction with the users highlighted areas of weakness and resulted in enhancements to the system that were not originally planned. If one were to break the program down among the two models, you could probably say that it was 80% planning and 20% groping. To respond to this, a small amount of money was set aside to use for systems improvements each year, as needed changes were identified.[182]

The applications that combined planning and groping did so in two different ways. In some cases, a comprehensive plan was developed but had to be modified under changing circumstances. An example of this was the Saskatchewan government's ten-year economic development plan that was announced in November 1992. It had a number of components, including consultation and partnerships with industry, single-window service for business programs, and management reform within the economic development department. When new labour legislation was proposed one year into the plan, the business community threatened to withdraw from any and all partnerships if the legislation wasn't changed. The resulting negotiations affected both the labour legislation and the economic development plan.[183]

On other occasions, individuals or organizations started by groping but, after a certain point, put a plan together. This happened either because greater clarity about the problem and its solution had been achieved or because the process of seeking cabinet approval for the program and/or Treasury Board approval for its funding required a plan. For example, Robert Fern started with the goal of making national parks and historic sites accessible to persons with disabilities but had to experiment and find ways to gain support from his superiors in Ottawa and his colleagues in the field. He reported that "trust was given to a peon" while he was experimenting. To win Treasury Board approval for $22 million in funding over five years, however, the peon then had to present a plan.[184]

A second example of groping followed by planning is the Ontario Used Vehicle Information Program. Initially, the Ministry of Consumer and Commercial Relations and the Ministry of Transport saw it as a form of consumer protection. They had difficulty getting approval, however, because the program required expenditures on improved customer service and start-up expenditures to link their databases. The Used Car Dealers' Association then released a study showing significant retail sales-tax evasion in the private sale of used vehicles. This enabled the two initiating ministries to recast their proposal to include revenue generation, which brought the Ministry of Finance on board. In addition, the proposal won the endorsement of the Non-Tax Revenue Committee, a government-wide committee seeking ways to increase non-tax revenues. With the bureaucratic coalition in place, the departments shifted to a comprehensive planning model with an exceedingly fast implementation schedule involving changes to legislation, the introduction of technology to link the three departments' databases, and marketing the Used Vehicle Information Program.[185]

Once again, there is great similarity between the frequencies of responses to the question about modes of analysis in the U.S. and Canada, regardless of whether the category of "planning and groping," which was specifically asked about only in the Canadian questionnaire, is or is not included.

In his study of state and local government innovation in the U.S., by virtue of the large database, Borins was able to test statistically hypotheses about the circumstances under which an initiator will follow either model. In general, comprehensive planning is more likely for innovations involving large capital budgets, innovations in which a theory is being operationalized, and innovations involving the coordination of numerous partners. Conversely, groping is less likely under each of these three situations. In addition, groping is more likely for new programs and for programs initiated by civil servants. The Canadian cases described above include a number of these factors, sometimes acting in opposite directions. Parks Canada's accessibility program was a new program initiated by a public servant, and it was characterized by groping. When a large capital budget was involved, however, the mode shifted to planning. Similarly, the Ontario Ministry of Consumer and Commercial Relations' initiatives to establish electronic access and to reinvent – by re-location – the Office of the Registrar General involved large capital budgets and were characterized by planning. The Used Vehicle Information Program, when it became a multi-party collaboration, moved to a comprehensive planning mode.

The data show that both planning and groping have a place in management innovation and that innovators may have to shift from one mode of operation to another as circumstances change. The value of this finding to innovators is that it may first enable them to recognize circumstances that favour one approach or the other and then use the approach that experience has shown is most appropriate.

## Winning Hearts and Minds

We asked about obstacles to the program or policy initiative, how the initiator attempted to overcome them, and whether they were in fact overcome. Table 4.6 outlines the obstacles that were identified. It compares the relative frequency of occurrence for each in the sample of thirty-three Canadian programs with the sample of 217 semi-finalists to the state and local government innovations awards in the U.S. The obstacles were broken into three groups. The first consisted of those arising primarily in the bureaucracy: attitudes in the bureaucracy, turf fights, other bureaucratic resistance, difficulty coordinating organizations, logistic problems, difficulty maintaining the enthusiasm of program staff, difficulty implementing a new technology, opposition by unions, opposition by middle management, and opposition to acting entrepreneurially within the public sector. The second identified obstacles arising in the political environment, for example inadequate funding or other resources, legislative or

Table 4.6. *Obstacles to Innovation*

| Obstacles | Canada | | U.S. | |
|---|---|---|---|---|
| | *Occurrences* | *% of total* | *Occurrences* | *% of total* |
| *Internal obstacles* | | | | |
| Bureaucratic attitudes | 10 | 14.5 | 48 | 9.4 |
| Turf fights | 0 | 0 | 9 | 1.8 |
| Other bureaucratic resistance | 8 | 11.6 | 35 | 6.8 |
| *Total bureaucratic* | 18 | 26.1 | 92 | 18.0 |
| Difficulty coordinating | 9 | 13.0 | 52 | 10.2 |
| Logistics | 3 | 4.3 | 51 | 10.0 |
| Maintaining enthusiasm, burnout | 1 | 1.5 | 33 | 6.4 |
| Implementing technology | 3 | 4.3 | 30 | 5.9 |
| Union opposition | 3 | 4.3 | 7 | 1.4 |
| Middle-management opposition | 3 | 4.3 | 7 | 1.4 |
| Opposition to entrepreneurs | 2 | 2.9 | 4 | .8 |
| *Total internal* | 42 | 60.9 | 276 | 53.9 |
| *Political environment* | | | | |
| Inadequate resources | 7 | 10.1 | 89 | 17.4 |
| Legislative, regulatory constraints | 5 | 7.2 | 34 | 6.6 |
| Political opposition | 2 | 2.9 | 8 | 1.6 |
| *Total political* | 14 | 20.3 | 131 | 25.6 |
| *External obstacles* | | | | |
| External doubts | 2 | 2.9 | 48 | 9.4 |
| Reaching target group | 7 | 10.1 | 30 | 5.9 |
| Affected private-sector interests | 2 | 2.9 | 14 | 2.8 |
| Public opposition | 2 | 2.9 | 7 | 1.4 |
| Private-sector competitors | 0 | 0 | 6 | 1.2 |
| *Total external* | 13 | 18.8 | 105 | 20.5 |
| *Total* | 69 | 100 | 512 | 100 |

$r = .62$; $t = 3.16$ with 16 degrees of freedom, significant at .01

regulatory constraints, and political opposition. The third addressed obstacles in the environment outside the public sector such as public doubts about the effectiveness of the program, difficulty reaching the target group, opposition by affected private-sector interests, public opposition, and opposition from private-sector entities who, as a result of the innovation, are being required to compete with the public sector. One obstacle with both bureaucratic and political aspects is inadequate resources, since that can result from funding decisions made at either the bureaucratic or political levels.

Initially, what is most striking is the very similar distribution of the different obstacles in both Canada and the U.S. The majority of obstacles arise within the public sector rather than at the political level or in the environment outside. This is consistent with the finding that middle managers and front-line workers are responsible for so many public-sector innovations. The infrequency of political obstacles could mean either that bureaucratic innovators are working far enough from the political level that their work isn't very noticeable to politicians or, if their work is noticeable, that they are savvy enough to understand what is and is not politically feasible. For those cases in the U.S. sample for which there was political opposition, it was overcome seventy per cent of the time.[186] The infrequency of external obstacles and the substantial frequency with which any that did arise were overcome suggests that the public recognizes that the performance of the public sector can be enhanced and that policy outcomes in many areas can be improved. The public is not wedded to the traditional bureaucratic organization, with its emphasis on the avoidance of risks and mistakes, but is increasingly receptive to public-sector innovation if it can improve performance.

Obstacles that arose in the bureaucracy are of particular interest. They reflect the ways in which innovations can change occupational patterns, standard operating procedures, and power structures. Some examples should make this clear. Environment Canada's ultraviolet index was opposed by meteorologists, who did not regard it as meteorology, because it did not use traditional procedures for forecasting, and who felt that it would be of little scientific value to the public. Literacy New Brunswick, which delivers literacy courses on an outreach basis, was criticized by education professionals because of its use of non-professional teachers.[187] The U.S. sample encountered many instances of such attitudes, particularly on the part of occupational or professional groups. For example, police officers were sometimes opposed to community policing initiatives, because it required them to do what they considered to be "social work." Health professionals opposed initiatives that employed community health workers or advocates in outreach programs. Put more generally, programs that require professions normally having little contact to work together; programs that require professions to do something that traditionally has not been viewed within the scope of their work; and programs that use volunteers, community workers, or para-professionals have often been opposed by professional groups. Bureaucratic resistance was also encountered when a new program threatened to reduce demand for the services of another part of the bureaucracy. For example, the ServiceOntario kiosks were opposed by the managers of walk-in license offices.[188]

Middle managers sometimes opposed initiatives designed to empower front-line workers, such as those in Revenue Canada, the Ontario Region of Human Resources Development Canada, and the Township of Pittsburgh. The managers who seemed most uncomfortable were those who supervised closely and exhibited a "command-and-control" management style. The Township of Pittsburgh wrote, "Overcoming the fears of middle and senior management was/is the most enduring problem encountered. These fears include: fear of losing control, fear of losing status, losing a job, uncertainty, change, challenge from subordinates."[189] Public-service unions resisted programs, such as Alberta and British Columbia's privatization of highway maintenance, they felt would reduce their membership.

Obstacles at the political level were encountered when an organization was introducing an innovation that was widely visible to the public, with the result that concerns were expressed to politicians. For example, when the Ontario Ministry of Consumer and Commercial Relations introduced electronic personal property registration, it had to convince the politicians that the system could be operated as securely as a paper-based system. Similarly, an inevitable consequence of the Office of the Registrar General moving to Thunder Bay and training a new workforce was that, in the transition period, turnaround times for the production of birth and death certificates increased. This led individuals to approach the constituency staff of MLAS, and hence to political criticism.

The most frequent external obstacle was difficulty reaching a program's target group. A good example of a program that faced, and worked hard to overcome, that obstacle was the Ontario Ministry of Consumer and Commercial Relations' Night Shift Project. The project's objective was to hire a nightshift of workers from employment-equity target groups to handle backlogs of clerical work in the companies branch until the technology there could be modernized.[190]

We also asked respondents if the obstacles they identified had been overcome or if they remained. The responses indicated that seventy per cent of the obstacles had been overcome. Given this relatively high success rate, the next question to consider is the means by which they were overcome.

Table 4.7 shows the different tactics that were used and the number of times each was cited, for both the Canadian and U.S. samples. The tactics most commonly used in both Canada and the United States could be described broadly as persuasion – demonstrating benefits, demonstration projects and marketing – and accommodation – consultation, training, cooptation, compensating losers, and making a program culturally or linguistically sensitive. This table shows a similar pattern of tactics was used in both countries.

It is instructive that the tactic that was used least frequently in both Canada and the United States was changing the manager responsible for program implementation. The innovators usually attempted to persuade or accommodate their opponents rather than appealing to their superiors to use their authority to overcome opponents. Their approach to implementing innovations was democratic in spirit, not authoritarian. One of

Table 4.7. *Tactics to Overcome Obstacles to Innovation, Total Frequency Used*

| | Canada | | U.S. | |
| Tactic | Times cited | Percent of total | Times cited | Percent of total |
|---|---|---|---|---|
| Demonstrate to opponents that program really advances their interests, provides benefits to them | 2 | 2 | 56 | 11 |
| Marketing | 7 | 7 | 29 | 5 |
| Demonstration project | 9 | 9 | 28 | 5 |
| *Total persuasion* | 18 | 18 | 113 | 21 |
| Training | 5 | 5 | 51 | 10 |
| Consultation | 13 | 13 | 50 | 9 |
| Cooptation/buy-in (opponents or sceptics become participants) | 4 | 4 | 40 | 8 |
| Program design made linguistically, culturally sensitive | 2 | 2 | 14 | 3 |
| Compensation for losers, design so that losers won't be worse off | 3 | 3 | 5 | 1 |
| *Total accommodation* | 27 | 26 | 160 | 30 |
| Finding additional resources of any kind | 6 | 6 | 55 | 10 |
| Persistence, effort | 18 | 18 | 49 | 9 |
| Logistical problems were resolved | 2 | 2 | 41 | 8 |
| Other | 15 | 15 | 28 | 5 |
| Gaining political support, building alliances | 5 | 5 | 25 | 5 |
| Focus on most important aspects of innovation, develop a clear vision | 3 | 3 | 21 | 4 |
| Technology was modified | 1 | 1 | 20 | 4 |
| Legislation or regulations were changed | 3 | 3 | 10 | 2 |
| Provide recognition for program participants or supporters | 3 | 3 | 7 | 1 |
| Changing managers responsible for program implementation | 1 | 1 | 4 | 1 |
| *Total use of tactics* | 102 | 100 | 533 | 100 |

$r = .83$; $t = 4.7$ with 10 degrees of freedom, significant at .01

the ways we judge the value of an innovation is by its replications; by definition, those who replicate an innovation are in another jurisdiction than the one where the innovation was introduced and are therefore free to choose it or reject it. We conclude that an innovation is valuable if many people or organizations choose to adopt it. If this logic applies to replication, it would apply to introduction as well.

The following are examples of the tactics most frequently used:

*Persistence*: In the Township of Pittsburgh, the CAO made clear to middle managers that the cost-management initiative was not temporary but would remain a permanent feature of their responsibilities.

*Consultation*: As part of their introduction of electronic filing, the staff of the British Columbia Personal Property Registry met regularly with major client groups, involved them in pilot testing, and used their suggestions to improve the system.

*Demonstration projects*: Robert Fern used Mackenzie King's boyhood home as a demonstration project for an accessible facility.

*Marketing*: The Ontario government used marketing techniques such as media advertising to inform the public of the Used Vehicle Information Program, starting the marketing campaign six months before use of the package was made mandatory.

*Finding additional resources*: Literacy New Brunswick has leveraged limited public-sector resources by appealing for support to employers, unions, foundations and individuals.

*Building alliances*: Literacy New Brunswick responded to the professionals in the adult education field who were critical of its use of non-professional teachers by forming alliances with business leaders, who then spoke out in support of its non-traditional approach.

*Training*: The Ontario Ministry of Consumer and Commercial Relations undertook substantial training for its new workforce in Thunder Bay, both at the time of the move and on an ongoing basis, to increase the flexibility of front-line staff.

*Cooptation*: The Atmospheric Environment Service involved the sceptical meteorologists in the design of the ultraviolet index from the outset.

*Providing recognition for participants*: In addition to the bonuses in its cost-reduction program, the Township of Pittsburgh gave small monthly incentive prizes to staff and held year-end celebrations.

*Compensation for losers*: The British Columbia Personal Property Registry downsized from thirty-nine to twelve positions in four years. This was accomplished by giving staff opportunities to transfer and leaving vacancies unfilled, with the result that there were no lay-offs.

*Program design made culturally sensitive*: To recruit members of disadvantaged employment groups into its nightshift project, the Ontario Ministry of Consumer and Commercial Relations made special efforts to reach them through a network of community organizations. They invited individuals in these groups to self-identify on the application form and used a more informal interview format than that used by standard civil-service boards.[191] Similarly, Literacy New Brunswick discovered that learners felt more comfortable taking classes in non-institutional settings, such as church basements and community centres, than in academic institutions and designed the program accordingly.

## Results and Replication

Table 4.8 shows the results when applicants were asked to provide the three most important quantitative measures by which their programs were evaluated. While the overall pattern of results in the two countries is

Table 4.8. *Results of Innovations*
(Entries are in percentages)

| Result | Canada Large sample | Canada Small sample | U.S. |
|---|---|---|---|
| Goals for program met | 34 | 42 | 70 |
| Clients using program, demand growing | | 30 | 52 |
| Improved service or operations | 39 | 21 | 32 |
| Formal client survey | 10 | 24 | 22 |
| Reduced cost of providing service | 27 | 24 | 19 |
| Informal expressions of stakeholder support | 22 | 6 | 19 |
| Improved morale | 14 | 9 | 8 |
| Increased revenue | 3 | 12 | 6 |
| Quasi-experimental design | n.a. | 0 | 6 |
| Other | 14 | 9 | 5 |
| Improved productivity | n.a. | 12 | 5 |
| Too early to tell | 5 | 15 | 2 |
| Total (%) | 154 | 204 | 246 |
| N | 339 | 33 | 217 |

*N* = number of observations
r = .87; t = 5.6 with 10 degrees of freedom, significant at .01

statistically similar, the major difference between them is that the U.S. had a much higher percentage of responses indicating that a program was meeting its goals or that demand was increasing. The reason for this is that, as discussed above in terms of target populations, a much higher proportion of the U.S. applications were from health, social service, or educational programs that tended to measure performance in terms of meeting goals (for example, to reduce the infant mortality rate among a target population to a certain level) or in increasing demand (for example, to increase the percentage of a target population receiving a certain type of training).

The following are examples of the different types of results. The Township of Pittsburgh set specific *goals* for cost reductions: ten per cent of the operating budget in 1993 and a further five per cent in 1994.[192] Performance was measured, and both targets were exceeded. The British Columbia Pregnancy Outreach Program, which provides education and support for women at risk of giving birth to a low-birth-weight baby, set its goals in terms of client-health indicators during pregnancy (improved diet, reducing smoking, decreased alcohol and drug use) and reported that clients of the program told health clinic staff they were doing better in terms of the goals during pregnancy than they had been before.[193]

Programs introducing new technologies often measured their achievements in terms of *whether demand was increasing* for the new technology.

For example, the personal property registries in British Columbia and Ontario both reported that by their third year of operations, over eighty per cent of transactions were being done electronically.[194] Similarly, the Ontario Soil and Crop Improvement Association reported that fifteen per cent of the province's farms had adopted no-till technology.[195] *Improved service or operations* was sometimes measured in the time required to complete a process; for example, electronic access made turnaround times for transactions with personal property registries almost instantaneous. ServiceOntario's electronic kiosks improved service by expanding the number of locations for and hours of service. An example of an innovation reporting *reduced cost* of providing service is the Alberta Workers' Compensation Board's finding that through work hardening it was able to decrease the average stay in its rehabilitation centre from sixty days in 1990 to thirty-one days in 1995, resulting in a cost reduction of $6000 per patient.[196]

Revenue Canada's initiative to increase teamwork and empower front-line workers was evaluated by staff surveys, which indicated increased participation and *improved morale*.[197] Manitoba's first special operating agency, the Fleet Vehicles Agency, was established in 1992, to manage the government's automobile fleet. The agency undertook several steps to reduce costs, including working with clients to improve vehicle utilization and thus reduce the size of the fleet. As a result, its *net revenue increased*.[198] The Alberta Workers' Compensation Board reported *improved productivity* (clients seen per staff member) as a result of work hardening, and the British Columbia and Ontario personal property registries reported improved productivity (transactions per worker) as a result of the adoption of electronic access.

In addition to identifying the results of these programs, we recorded the use of various assessment methodologies. These include formal client surveys, experimental designs, and informal expressions of stakeholder support. Examples of *formal client surveys* are the Ontario Personal Property Registry finding satisfaction had improved as more customers used electronic access and the Township of Pittsburgh finding that, even though it had reduced costs, high levels of client satisfaction were still being maintained. Although no Canadian programs reported that quasi-experimental designs were used, they were used occasionally in the U.S., particularly in the social services area. An example of this approach would have been if British Columbia Pregnancy Outreach Program had compared health indicators such as average birth weight or the incidence of low birth weight for children of women who had participated in the program with those for women of similar socio-economic and educational backgrounds who had not participated in the program. Finally, some

Table 4.9. *Awards, Media Attention Received*
*by Innovations*
(Entries are in percentages)

| Awards or attention | Group | |
| --- | --- | --- |
| | Canada | U.S. |
| Any award | 33 | 63 |
| Media attention | 88 | 46 |
| None | 12 | 21 |
| N | 33 | 217 |

N = number of observations

programs, such as Revenue Canada's organizational change initiative, reported that it was too early to provide a complete reporting of results.

It was quite common for programs to report a number of different results. In some cases, a program will necessarily have multiple results. For example, a new technology, if implemented well, would be expected to improve service, reduce cost, improve satisfaction, and increase productivity. In other cases, a program will want to track several indicators. For example, a program that reduces cost through process redesign (for example, the Township of Pittsburgh's cost-management program or the Alberta Workers' Compensation Board's work-hardening initiative) will want to measure customer satisfaction to ensure that quality is being maintained.

Table 4.9 shows that many of the programs in the Canadian and U.S. samples have won other awards and have received media attention. (There are too few observations to derive a meaningful correlation coefficient.) It is particularly impressive that eighty-eight per cent of the programs in the Canadian sample have received some media coverage. One of the concerns often expressed by academics and practitioners alike is that, for the last twenty years at least, the public sector has been the victim of negative press. As a consequence of this bureaucrat-bashing, the public service is no longer held in high regard. The amount of media attention that innovative programs have been receiving is, however, a promising sign. Initially, the public reaction to these stories might be to dismiss these programs as islands of excellence in a sea of incompetence, or, at best, mediocrity. As more and more evidence accumulates about high quality and innovative public services, however, the public's overall impression of the public sector may begin to change.

Table 4.10 shows the extent of interest in, and actual replication of, innovations for both the Canadian and U.S. samples. Clearly, actual replication is more important than expressions of interest in replication.[199] In this regard, it is impressive that sixty-one per cent of the Canadian sample has been replicated, as compared with forty-two per cent of the American.

Table 4.10. *Replication of Innovations*
(Entries are in percentages)

| Extent of replication | Group | |
|---|---|---|
| | Canada | U.S. |
| Nearby interest | 18 | 27 |
| National interest | 15 | 54 |
| International interest | 15 | 14 |
| Any interest | 33 | 65 |
| Nearby replication | 33 | 27 |
| National replication | 27 | 24 |
| International replication | 21 | 1 |
| Any replication | 61 | 42 |
| No interest or replication | 12 | 18 |
| *Total* | 141 | 165 |
| *N* | 33 | 217 |

*N* = number of observations

It is also impressive that twenty-one per cent of the sample of Canadian applications was replicated internationally, particularly in comparison to the minimal one per cent international replication for U.S. programs. Some of the following programs or components of programs replicated internationally: the Ontario Office of Seniors' Issues program, which sensitizes people to the difficulties of the aged has been adopted in the United Kingdom, United States, Japan and New Zealand; the Canadian ultraviolet index has been adopted in the U.S., United Kingdom, Denmark and Germany and became the model for an ultraviolet index being developed by the World Meteorological Organization. Many American states followed the lead of British Columbia and Ontario in introducing electronic registration and searches; and the United Nations has adopted Parks Canada's accessibility program as the basis of its international standard. These replications of public management innovations illustrate a major theme running through this book, namely, that the post-bureaucratic model has become truly international.[200]

## CONCLUSION

This study yields conclusions regarding the nature of the innovation process and the surprising similarity in the process in both Canada and the U.S. Conclusions regarding the nature of the process include the following:

– innovative programs are often holistic, in that they require different organizations to cooperate and provide a variety of services to users, increasingly make use of the private sector for service delivery, and often involve the introduction of new technology, process improvement, and new management philosophies, particularly the empowerment of front-line workers – all characteristics of the post-bureaucratic organization;

- the most frequent initiators of public management innovations are "local heroes," visionary middle-level and front-line public servants who are willing to take risks;

- innovations can be triggered independently by internal problems, crises, political mandates, or new opportunities, each of which occurs reasonably often;

- innovations are a result of both comprehensive planning and incremental groping, and sometimes the process will include both;

- the most frequent obstacles to innovations are internal to the bureaucracy, including such factors as the attitudes of professionals whose jobs may have to change, difficulty in coordinating partner organizations, and middle-management and union opposition;

- obstacles to change are most frequently overcome by persuasion (demonstration projects, marketing, sheer persistence, building alliances) or accommodation (consultation, cooptation, compensation for the losers from change);

- innovative programs produce results such as increased demand, reduced cost, improved service, morale, and productivity; and

- innovative programs have received substantial media attention and are being widely replicated.

The similarity between Canada and the U.S. with respect to all these characteristics was unexpected. One explanation for it might be that the data for both countries are based on bottom–up innovation, that is, initiatives that came from particular departments. During the period of the study, neither the federal government of Canada nor the U.S. state and local governments were mandating top–down reform initiatives, such as the U.K.'s Next Steps and Citizen's Charter programs or the U.S. government's post-1993 National Performance Review.

A second, more sweeping explanation is that these characteristics represent the intrinsic structure of public management innovation, at least in the economically more advanced countries. If such an argument were to be constructed, it would rest on common characteristics of society, government and technology. For example, we could argue that all public-sector bureaucracies are excessively differentiated, thus requiring them to integrate across the numerous programs that are applicable to any citizen. We could also argue that these societies share common information technology, so that innovations such as the electronic kiosks, electronic data interchange, smart cards, and the Internet are available to all. Next, we could propose that while some governments are motivated to innovate by budgetary pressure and occasional publicly visible crises, there are many innovative public servants who take action either to overcome problems before they become crises or to take advantage of opportunities. Additionally, we could argue that, in many areas of public management, expertise rests with front-line workers and middle managers, so it is they, rather than politicians or agency heads, who see problems and opportunities first. Finally, we could suggest that planning and groping are sometimes alternative and sometimes complementary ways to innovate and that certain situational imperatives drive innovators to one or the other, or one then the other in sequence.

This chapter has dealt in a general way with a wide variety of different types of public-sector innovations, such as organizational restructuring, empowerment of front-line staff, partnerships, and applications of information technology. Subsequent chapters will deal with each of these more intensively. In addition, some of the cases mentioned in the chapter that illustrate ideas about the process of innovation will be visited in more detail to explain the form these innovations take.

# 5

# Restructuring and Re-engineering

One of the major categories of change from the bureaucratic to the post-bureaucratic model of public organization (Table 1.1) is that of *structure*. This category includes change from traditional departmental structures to a wide variety of organizational mechanisms such as Crown corporations, executive agencies, special operating agencies, shared common services, employee takeovers, and contracting-out. As explained in the next chapter, these and other mechanisms are commonly described as alternative service-delivery mechanisms. Also included in the *structure* category of change is a shift towards decentralized authority and control – a major departure from the central controls of the traditional bureaucratic model.

Another major category of the post-bureaucratic model is *market orientation*. One of the distinguishing features of public organizations is that they are monopolies and budget-driven. To be budget-driven means that the agencies rely on budget funding for their financial resources rather than having to earn revenues from clients, as in the market sector. The post-bureaucratic model addresses both of these structural issues by emphasizing revenue generation (where appropriate) and more competition in the delivery of services (where possible).

The post-bureaucratic model also stresses the importance of finding innovative ways of designing and delivering public-sector programs. One of the major tools being used by innovative public organizations has been adapted from the private sector and is known as *business process re-engineering*. As noted in Chapter 2, business process re-engineering is "the fundamental rethinking and radical design of business processes to achieve dramatic improvements in critical, contemporary measures of performance, such as cost, quality, service and speed."[201] Whereas "total quality management" techniques focus on continuous improvement by small increments, re-engineering focuses on achieving major leaps forward in performance through the total redesign of delivery systems.

How frequent are restructuring and re-engineering? According to an IPAC survey of deputy ministers, restructuring of service delivery and management of change are two of the five major challenges that faced DMs in the second half of the 1990s.[202] It is not surprising, then, that another survey of eighty-four federal, provincial and municipal managers undertaken in 1997 showed that during a recent five-year period, this group of public managers had collectively experienced

- sixty-seven reorganizations, or de-layering initiatives;
- sixty-three downsizing initiatives;
- fifty organizational mergers;
- thirty-seven partnership creations;
- twenty-nine examples of program devolution; .
- twenty-three examples of privatization or contracting-out of service; and
- twenty-eight re-engineering initiatives.[203]

These figures suggest that innovation and change in organizational structure and delivery systems were commonplace in public organizations at all levels of government. Public managers aligned organizational structures more closely to organizational function, and they moved revenue-dependent programs to commercial models of delivery or moved more service delivery to the private sector in the pursuit of improved efficiency and service. The first part of this chapter discusses organizational restructuring; this is followed by an examination of re-engineering in public organizations.

## WHY RESTRUCTURE?

Two federal deputy ministers provided the following reasons for experimenting with different organizational structures.

[N]ew structural approaches are needed to manage four critical and growing pressures. First, there is a need to deal with demands for increased service to the public, as well as the demands of stakeholders to be more involved. Second, there are the pressures for greater involvement and participation of staff at all levels. Third, there is a need to adjust to the changes arising from the arrival of new technologies. Fourth, there is the necessity to provide essential public goods and services at lower costs. ... As a final consideration, as public servants become more aware of the structural diversity taking place ... they will be stimulated to think of new and better ways of structuring their organizations.[204]

The capacity of the *traditional* bureaucratic organization to deal success-fully with these pressures is limited. Consider its limitations in circum-stances where the government operates services of a quasi-commercial nature. For example, several years ago, British Columbia's Department of Lands, Parks and Housing (now the Ministry of the Environment) owned and operated Manning Park Lodge in a provincial park near the town of Hope. Like other programs of the ministry, the lodge was budget-funded, that is, an expenditure budget was set each year as part of the ministry's Estimates, and revenues from lodge sales went back into the govern-ment's Consolidated Revenue Fund. A Treasury Board official* who was setting the budget for the lodge was told by ministry officials that "the budget is fine as long as it doesn't snow." Since the lodge was in the ski business, this was not a reassuring statement. Sure enough, it snowed heavily before Christmas, the lodge had a surge of customers and it spent its whole annual budget after only nine months. The lodge could not, therefore, afford to buy food and liquor to sell to its guests for a profit, because all revenues went back to government coffers rather than to the business. The more business the managers generated, the worse the budget situation became. The Treasury Board official had to ask the provincial Liquor Control Board to extend credit to the lodge for the purchase of food and liquor until a Treasury Board submission could be processed the next week to provide an expanded budget.

Another example can be drawn from the training unit of British Colum-bia's Department of the Comptroller General when it began to charge back to departments for its training programs. Although the revenue went back into the program budget, Treasury Board would not agree to increasing the number of training staff to accommodate an increased demand for training. (The political incentive, when the public sector is under public scrutiny, is to restrict the number of public servants.) The comptroller general's training staff saw a market opportunity and ultimately negoti-ated an employee buy-out of the training function. In essence, they priva-tized themselves and the training service. Once in the private sector, they delivered their former services under contract, while expanding their client base throughout the public sector. Freed from the operational re-strictions of government, the new training company has prospered.

These two examples demonstrate the inappropriateness of budget-funding commercial operations in the public sector. They also show why governments in the 1990s are seeking innovative ways of restructuring so as to reduce costs and improve service. Among the approaches being used

*Brian Marson, a co-author of this book.

Figure 5.1. *The Emerging Public Service: The Diamond Model*

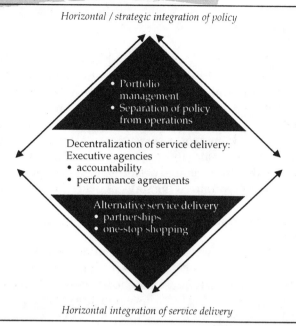

*Horizontal / strategic integration of policy*

*Horizontal integration of service delivery*

are the creation of special operating agencies and the privatization or contracting-out of government functions.

## MEANINGS AND FRAMEWORKS

Figure 5.1 provides a conceptual framework to explain the forces behind the current restructuring and re-engineering of government organizations. This "diamond model" of public-sector reform, developed by Peter Aucoin, Ralph Heintzman and Brian Marson, illustrates three of the most powerful forces in recent public-sector reform:

1. The top of the diamond demonstrates the trend towards integrating policy development across departments and across governments (see Chapter 11).

2. The middle of the diamond depicts the trend towards decentralization of service delivery through such means as executive agencies and the devolution of responsibilities to other levels of government, with service delivery being uncoupled from policy making.

3. The bottom of the diamond shows the trend towards horizontal integration in service delivery across departments and governments to achieve citizen-centred service delivery.

Decentralization of service delivery and its horizontal integration are attempts to improve service delivery along entirely different dimensions – one dimension is vertical (e.g., decentralized delivery) and the other horizontal (e.g., one-stop shopping). This suggests some natural tensions in the two strategies for improving performance: one strategy works within the organization and one works across organizations. The strategies are not mutually exclusive, since there are examples of both of them working together to provide citizen-centred performance. For example, in the 1980s, British Columbia decentralized the services of several departments to the regions, then agreed to co-locate some of their offices in one-stop B.C. Access Centres, associated with the government agents system described in Chapter 6.

Perhaps the best framework for understanding the government restructuring that is taking place is Figure 5.2, which is an elaboration of Figure 1.1 in Chapter 1. This chart shows that the trend in restructuring operates along two dimensions. Along one dimension, organizations are moving to a lower level of central control: some are moving towards a greater degree of independence within the public service and some are moving to other levels of government. Along the second dimension, the trend is for organizations to move towards a market-driven environment – and towards the private sector.

Traditionally, governments have used three basic organizational forms: departments, agencies and tribunals, and Crown corporations. There are now many more organizational structures in use, and there is a trend away from the departmental form towards greater autonomy and market dependency:

Governments implementing alternative program delivery try to select the best way to deliver programs ... including: establishing more service oriented and businesslike special operating agencies (soas) and other flexible service delivery arrangements; establishing new forms of cooperation among departments such as sharing the provision of administrative services; setting up crown corporations; negotiating partnering arrangements with other levels of government and the private and voluntary sectors; devolving programs and services to the provinces; commercializing government services to improve efficiency while protecting the public interest; and privatizing government programs and services that no longer serve a public policy purpose.[205]

Figure 5.2. *Opportunities for Program Delivery Alternatives*

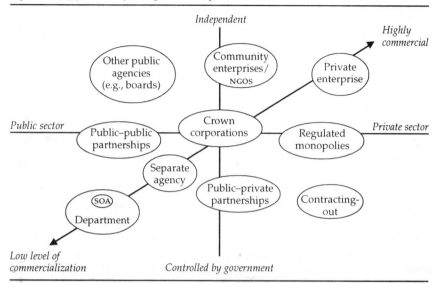

Source: Adapted from Canada, Treasury Board Secretariat, *Framework for Alternative Program Delivery* (Ottawa: Treasury Board Secretariat, 1996)  <http://www.tbs-sct.gc.ca/pubs_pol/opepubs>.

## Traditional and New Forms of Program Delivery

This section provides a brief description of the major structures available for the development and implementation of government policies and programs. It is important to note here that each of these structures is involved, in varying degrees, in service delivery and, therefore, constitutes one of the alternative-delivery mechanisms discussed in the next chapter. We begin here with the structures on the public-sector side of Figure 5.2 and move towards the private-sector side. We also describe some structures that are innovative variations of the structures contained in Figure 5.2 (e.g., citizen-centred departmental structures).

### Departments

Departments have always been the dominant organizing structure of government. Each department is established by a separate enabling statute, is headed by a minister (the political head) and a deputy minister (the administrative head), and is generally funded through annual appropriations approved by Parliament. Among federal departments are Transport

Canada and Environment Canada, which provide external government services to and for Canadians. Typical provincial departments include departments of highways and departments of health. Departments like Public Works and Government Services Canada provide internal services to other government departments rather than to individuals and organizations outside government.

### Special Operating Agencies (soas)

Special operating agencies are "discrete operational units within departments that have been given increased managerial autonomy in exchange for greater accountability for results."[206] The expectation is that this will lead to greater efficiency and better service. In the federal sphere, Treasury Board and an soa negotiate a framework document and a business plan to clarify the soa's delegated authorities and its accountabilities for results achieved. Candidates for soa status are usually those units that provide internal services to other departments (e.g., internal government printing services) or services to the public (e.g., Passport Office) that are revenue generating and that could become commercially self-sustaining from program revenues. They continue to operate as part of a department reporting through the deputy minister.

### Separate Agencies

Separate agencies like Statistics Canada and the Canadian Space Agency have their own legislation and report directly to a minister who usually has a government department as his or her main responsibility. The head of an agency has deputy minister status and operates within a policy framework established by the minister. An agency's employees, like those in departments, are subject to the Financial Administration Act, the Public Service Employment Act, and Treasury Board policies. *Service agencies* (e.g., Parks Canada, the Canadian Food Inspection Agency [CFIA]) are a new type of separate agency; they are given considerable autonomy from departmental control so as to enable them to provide more efficient, effective and responsive service delivery. These agencies are examined in more detail later in this chapter.

### Public Partnerships

As explained in Chapter 8, partnerships are one of the most popular new forms of public-sector innovation. They involve a collaborative pooling of resources such as money and information among two or more parties to meet complementary or compatible objectives. *Public* partnerships, such as the Canada Business Service centres and the Canadian Tourism Commission, are formed when different levels of government develop partnerships around a common objective. They are usually governed by a formal intergovernmental agreement describing the roles and responsibilities of each government and each participating department. *Public–private* partnerships are discussed below.

### Departmental Corporations

The National Research Council, the Atomic Energy Control Board, and the Canadian Centre for Management Development are federal departmental corporations. Generally, this type of organizational structure is used for government's research and regulatory functions. Compared to departments, they have greater decision-making autonomy and may receive special powers to manage their financial and human resources with greater flexibility. The corporation's head normally reports to a minister whose main responsibility is for a government department.

### Crown Corporations

Crown corporations such as the Canada Post Corporation and the Canadian Broadcasting Corporation are well known to Canadians. These organizations operate along commercial lines, delivering goods and services under a broad policy framework established by the government. They are accountable to Parliament through a minister. Some Crown corporations obtain an annual subsidy voted by Parliament, usually in support of a non-commercial social or cultural purpose (e.g., the CBC). Others operate in a competitive environment and are expected to earn a profit (e.g., Canada Post). Crown corporations act more like private-sector corporations and, unlike departments, have direct control over their financial and human resources. At the provincial level, organizations like Ontario Hydro and Quebec Hydro are examples of very large Crown corporations owned by government but operating on a commercial basis as regulated utilities. *Mixed enterprises* are simply organizations such as Petro-Canada and B.C. Rail that are jointly owned by the government and private-sector investors.

### Regulated Monopolies

"A natural monopoly exists when the lowest cost for a good or service is obtained when there is only one producer of that good or service, i.e., certain technical aspects of production mean that competition would increase its costs."[207] Traditional examples include private-sector utilities such as cable, pipeline and telephone companies. Governments regulate these natural monopolies to ensure that they do not take advantage of their monopoly position and that they operate in the public interest by, for example, charging fair prices and providing adequate service to customers. For example, the National Energy Board regulates oil and natural gas companies such as TransCanada Pipeline Corporation, and the Canadian Radio-television and Telecommunications Commission regulates the prices and service standards of cable companies. And when government services such as Nav Canada are privatized and move into the private sector as a monopoly service, the government must have appropriate regulatory mechanisms to ensure that such a natural monopoly operates in the public interest.

### Not-For-Profit or Community Enterprises

Governments may enter into contractual arrangements with non-profit agencies for the devolution of services. For example, the federal government has turned over the management of several airports to local airport authorities. The Vancouver Airport Authority is managed by a board of directors composed, among others, of representatives from various professions in the community, from the private sector, and from the nearby cities. The expectation is that the local airport authorities will operate the airports on a business-like basis and be more sensitive to local interests and needs.

### Public–Private Partnerships

This organizational form, which is discussed at length in Chapter 8, involves collaborative arrangements between government, on the one hand, and business firms, community organizations and other parties outside government, on the other hand. Although many of these partnerships occur through contractual arrangements, sometimes separate entities are created by the organizational partners. For example, the Canadian Tourism Commission (CTC) is a public–private partnership that is structured as an SOA within Industry Canada. The CTC's mandate is "to plan, direct, manage and implement programs that generate and promote tourism in Canada."[208] Through the CTC, the federal and provincial governments and the tourism industry pool their resources and jointly plan and execute tourism marketing and development programs for Canada.

### Contracting-out, Contracting for Services and Employee Takeovers

Contracting-out is a traditional but rapidly growing mechanism that involves transferring the operation of a function to a private contractor for a specific period of time; government retains responsibility for the effective performance of the function. A newer form of contracting-out is *employee takeovers*, whereby the government contracts with an employee (or employees) to deliver a service formerly provided by the government. For example, a group of employees in the National Capital Commission, who previously were responsible for maintaining the Rideau Canal in winter, privatized themselves and now offer as a private company the same service under contract to the commission. *Contracting for services* previously delivered by public servants is a common form of restructuring within government departments. For example, many departments have contracted-out the computer services function. Contracting for services simply involves the competitive purchase of services from the private sector. In prisons and hospitals, internal services such as food and laundry are often provided in this way.

*Government Owned and Contractor Operated (GOCO) Arrangements*
This involves a contractual arrangement that shifts responsibility for operating a facility to a contractor, while the facility remains in the hands of government. For example, the Burlington Waste Water Technology Centre is owned by the federal government but is operated by a private contractor.

*Franchise and Licensing Arrangements*
As public organizations move towards revenue generation and commercialization, they increasingly make use of licensing or franchising. For example, Canada Post sells franchises to the private sector for the creation of postal outlets in designated stores and shopping malls. Similarly, a government department may provide a private-sector company with a license to use or sell government intellectual property. For example, the B.C. government licensed the rights to its BC Online software to a U.S. company for sale to other governments under a royalty arrangement, and the RCMP sold the rights to market certain likenesses of RCMP uniforms to the private sector.

*Privatization (Commercial Enterprise)*
Many governments have undertaken privatization, that is, the transfer of government ownership of parts of departments or of Crown corporations to the private sector. Examples include Nav Canada, the air-navigation system, which was part of the federal Department of Transport but which is now owned by the airline industry, and Air Canada, which was a Crown corporation. Nav Canada is discussed in detail below.

This brief description of the major structures involved in the development and implementation of government programs provides the foundation for an examination of new forms of structural innovation and of movement from one type of structure to another.

## NEW FORMS OF ORGANIZATION:
## SPECIAL OPERATING AGENCIES AND SERVICE AGENCIES

### Special Operating Agencies

In December 1989, the Government of Canada announced the formation of the first five special operating agencies. These were the Canada Communications Group, Consulting and Audit Canada, Training and Development Canada, Government Telecommunications and Informatics Services, and the Passport Office. All but the Passport Office provided services within government to other government departments and charged for their services. The Passport Office has already received a detailed treatment in Chapter 2 as an example of a public organization that has been substantially transformed and that has moved a considerable distance towards the post-bureaucratic model of organization. By the end of 1995, another ten organizations had received Treasury Board approval to become soas, while the Canada Communications Group and the Transport Canada Training Institute had graduated from soa status to become candidates for privatization.

The provinces of Manitoba, Quebec and British Columbia have been especially active in experimenting with soas. As explained in Chapter 2, Manitoba's first soa – the Fleet Vehicles Agency (mfva) – is a notable example of a successful soa (winner of an ipac Award for Innovative Management). The mfva is part of the Department of Government Services and provides fleet management services to government departments, boards, agencies and commissions. In 1995, its chief operating officer predicted that the prospects within five years are for a self-sustaining operation, free of its start-up debt and leveraging new revenues and economies of scale through market development across the Manitoba public sector.[209] In other words, the agency planned to offer its services to other levels of government and to other government institutions in Manitoba – a very innovative and entrepreneurial approach for an internal service provider. The mfva's experience has led other governments (e.g., the Yukon, B.C. and New Brunswick) to follow its example.

New organizational forms such as the mfva require a restructuring of roles and responsibilities within government. According to one of the architects of the Quebec soas (called autonomous service units, or asus),

[t]he new approach of management by results, leading to the development of autonomous service units, is not easy to implement. It implies fundamental changes for managers, ministries and central agencies. With this approach, managers are given more autonomy. However, they must manage with efficiency and transpar-

ency. They have to develop appropriate means of action to respond to the needs of citizens and their clientele. They also are publicly accountable for results achieved. Ministries have to establish new relationships with ASUS, follow-up more on results and control less ... in order to achieve targeted objectives. ... Central agencies, on their end, have to refocus on their strategic role and develop corporate accountability mechanisms.[210]

The federal government's early experience with SOAS demonstrated the importance of such changes. A 1995 report on SOAS concluded that desired outcomes were sometimes not achieved because of a lack of clarity in mandate, authority and accountability.[211]

### Service Agencies

The United Kingdom has transformed large elements of its public service into "executive agencies" that report directly to the minister; are responsible for program delivery, not policy; and operate with considerable autonomy in the management of their resources while being held accountable for specifically agreed-upon results. Unlike Canada's service agencies described below, these executive agencies were not established by legislation. In the 1996 budget, the Canadian government announced its intention to explore the use of a similar agency model by creating through legislation three "service agencies": Revenue Canada, Parks Canada, and the Canadian Food Inspection Agency. Revenue Canada, a department, was to be transformed into an agency; Parks Canada, a section of a department, was to become an agency; and parts of four departments were to be melded together to create the CFIA. According to the budget documents, "the essence of these changes is to give service delivery organizations greater autonomy to provide their services in ways that are more responsive to the needs of their clients and that are more cost-effective."[212] The CFIA exemplifies these purposes.

The genesis of the CFIA is found in the 1994 Program Review and the 1994 auditor general's report, both of which identified the need for a more coordinated approach to food inspection. The 1995 federal budget announced that departments involved in food inspection would "work cooperatively on measures, including possible changes in organizational structure, to improve the effectiveness and cost-efficiency of the federal component of the Canadian food inspection system."[213] Subsequently, the 1996 budget announced the government's decision to consolidate all federal food inspection and quarantine services previously provided by several separate departments into a single service agency. Specifically, food and quarantine services from the departments of Agriculture and Agrifood,

Health, Industry, and Fisheries and Oceans were amalgamated into the new agency. Bill C-60 was introduced into Parliament in 1996 to provide the necessary statutory basis for the creation of the CFIA.

A senior CFIA official has explained five specific benefits of moving from departmental status to agency status: the clarification of roles and responsibilities; reduction of overlap and duplication; improved service delivery; improved federal–provincial harmonization; and better reporting and accountability to Parliament.[214] As in the case of the British executive agencies, CFIA policy-making remained in the departments (e.g., Health Canada remains responsible for setting health and safety standards), while CFIA became responsible for program delivery: "By retaining health and safety standard setting within the departmental system (the 'steering' function) and by moving the inspections system (the 'rowing' function) to a more arm's length agency, the agency can be given a range of flexibilities that will permit it to be more entrepreneurial in its modus operandi."[215]

By reducing overlap and duplication through the consolidation of inspection programs from four different programs, the agency expects to save $44 million per year beginning in 1998–99. Service-delivery improvements flow from the establishment of "single-window" access by industrial clients and consumers and through the greater management flexibilities available to the agency. The agency also plans to "re-engineer" the delivery system by transforming its role from a hands-on inspector to that of monitor and auditor of the industry's own risk-assessment systems. The CFIA also has the legislative power to enter into agreements with provincial governments to promote a harmonized approach to regulation of the industry, both in terms of an agreed framework of national standards and in terms of cooperative delivery. This feature is expected to promote improved service and efficiency. For example, the CFIA has initiated partnership agreements with the Government of Alberta to harmonize dairy plant inspection, livestock slaughter inspection, and the inspection of cattle imports and transportation.[216] In the future, under the CFIA legislation, it will be possible to establish joint federal–provincial corporations to carry out cooperative inspection activities.

Improved accountability to Parliament is also anchored in the agency's legislation – an annual corporate business plan must be submitted to the minister for approval, and tabled by the minister in Parliament. This plan must contain the following elements: the agency's objectives for the plan period; the strategies the CFIA plans to use to achieve these objectives; the agency's expected performance during the plan period; and the proposed annual operating and capital budget for each year of the plan. At the end of each fiscal year, the agency must also prepare an annual report to the minister and Parliament on its performance, which must include a review by the auditor general of the organization's actual financial and operational performance compared to its corporate business plan targets. According to the manager responsible for implementing these accountability systems at the CFIA, "these planning and performance measures will enhance reporting to the Minister and Parliament and lead to greater accountability."[217]

The CFIA is a particularly notable new model for program delivery, because it contains all three of the major thrusts in the "diamond model" described at the beginning of this chapter (Figure 5.1). First, policy is more horizontally integrated for quarantine and food inspection within the federal government; second, operations are separated from policy through the creation of a more decentralized, more autonomous delivery agency; and third, an integrated "single-window" approach is taken in delivery to clients, by consolidating within the agency programs from several departments and by establishing cooperative delivery mechanisms with the provinces. Through this new organizational form, the potential exists for substantial cost-savings to taxpayers, greater efficiency and improved service for clients, better food inspection for consumers, and increased accountability to Parliament.

## CHANGING ORGANIZATIONAL FORMS

In addition to the creation of new organizational forms, there has been substantial movement from traditional forms of organization, notably operating departments, towards Crown corporations and privatization.

### From Department to Crown Corporation:
### B.C. Buildings Corporation and Canada Post

In the late 1970s, the Government of British Columbia created two "internal services" Crown corporations to deliver services that had been previously been supplied through a departmental structure. The first was the B.C. Systems Corporation and, the second, the B.C. Buildings Corporation (BCBC). Moving parts of a department into a Crown corporation structure was innovative at that time, since Crown corporation status is normally reserved for public organizations like the CBC and Ontario Hydro that provide commercial services to citizens (but that are expected to serve the public interest at the same time). In the case of the B.C. Buildings Corporation, parts of the former Department of Public Works were transferred to create the new corporation, which was established with an external board of directors and private-sector accounting principles, including "bottom-line" profitability (the corporation was expected to operate profitably based on the revenues it generated from providing accommodation services to government departments).

Over the past two decades, BCBC has won national recognition for being one of the best managed public organizations in the country and one of the best for which to work. By being independent of normal bureaucratic controls, and having responsibility for managing its own financial and human resources, BCBC has been free to innovate while being driven to improve its services to clients, being revenue dependent, and being in a competitive market place for the provision of some of its services to departmental clients. Reporting to a minister, BCBC is subject to the annual audit of the provincial auditor general and is accountable through the minister to the legislature for its performance. Treasury Board, on behalf of the government as shareholder, still plays a monitoring role with the corporation through examination of its strategic plan and approval of its rate schedule and capital plan.

We noted in Chapter 2 that Canada Post is an excellent example of the use of the Crown corporation structure by governments wishing to create a more market-responsive, more efficient, and more financially independent service. As a department, Canada Post was subject to all of the rules and regulations governing operating departments, even though it had a different character as a revenue-generating commercial service (while also serving the public interest through such means as the internal subsidization of mail service to small and remote communities). Since it became a Crown corporation in 1981, Canada Post has assumed responsibility for the management of its own financial and human resources and has gradually moved towards financial self-sufficiency through a combination of rate increases and efficiency measures. Those who benefit from the postal service now largely pay for its costs rather than having taxpayers in general subsidize the service through annual operating subsidies. As with SOAS and service agencies, Crown corporations like Canada Post have the freedom to concentrate on achieving results in the marketplace, without the bureaucratic burdens and controls that come with being part of the core departmental system of government.

## From Department to the Regulated Private Sector: Nav Canada

To this point we have looked at examples of SOAS (like the Passport Office), service agencies (like the Canadian Food Inspection Agency) and Crown corporations (like Canada Post). By referring again to Figure 5.2, you can see that we have been gradually moving along a continuum towards organizational structures that are less controlled by government and more like the private sector in their nature. The three organizational forms we have examined so far, however, are part of the *public* sector (although Crown corporations like Canada Post and Ontario Hydro do operate a lot like private-sector companies and may operate largely in competition with them). If we move further along the dotted line in Figure 5.2, we move into the private sector, where organizations may be highly regulated by government (e.g., monopoly services such as pipelines and utilities) or may be only subject to the normal government regulation of the market-place (e.g., highly commercialized, competitive private companies). We will now add to our framework of alternative organizational forms by looking at three examples of government departments, or parts of them, that were transferred to the private sector – one is highly regulated, but the other two are not.

The first case is the creation in 1996 of Nav Canada, which involved the commercialization and privatization of Transport Canada's Air Navigation System (ANS). In the context of Figure 5.2, this is an example of a public-sector function moving from government department status (bottom left of the matrix) to private enterprise (regulated sectors) (in the top right). Prior to 1996, Nav Canada was part of the Department of Transport, with responsibility for both the regulation and the delivery of air-traffic control and air-navigation systems (such as airport radar systems) across the country: "Canada's Air Navigation System, one of the world's largest, permits the safe, efficient movement of aircraft from take-off, along in flight paths to landing. It is comprised of: an air traffic control system for domestic and international airspace, which controls timing and space for airport take-off and landing operations and for in-flight pathways; a flight information system providing service such as weather briefings for pilots and airport advisories; and hundreds of coast-to-coast electronic navigation aids."[218]

With the creation of Nav Canada, a private non-share-capital corporation owned by the airline industry, the government retains the responsibility for regulatory policy, while Nav Canada has responsibility for program delivery. As a non-share-capital corporation, Nav Canada retains any financial surplus (profits) inside the corporation rather than having to distribute them to shareholders, as would be the case for a normal share-capital corporate structure.

Why did Transport Canada decide to transfer 6,500 staff and all of the infrastructure and navigational equipment to a private corporation? What were the perceived advantages to this new structure for service delivery? And, under this privatized delivery structure, how can Transport Canada ensure that Nav Canada continues to operate the air-navigation system safely and in the public interest? The reasons why government began looking at alternative delivery mechanisms for the ANS are similar to those described for Manning Park Ski Lodge at the beginning of this chapter. In the mid-1980s, fiscal pressures caused the federal government to initiate a hiring freeze and, in the early 1990s, to cut back the size of the public service. In addition, a forty-per-cent increase in commercial air traffic led to a shortage of air-traffic controllers to manage the increased workload, resulting in a concern for air safety and a major increase in costs for the airline industry due to flight delays. Also, the airline industry was frustrated by the bureaucratic delays caused by inadequate staffing and the department's unresponsiveness in meeting the commercial and operating needs of the industry.

In 1992, the Ministerial Task Force on the Air Navigation System concluded that as long as the system operated within the bureaucratic and fiscal constraints of a government department, it would continue to fall short of user needs. It is especially notable that the task force determined that "this is not the fault of the people who manage and operate the system, for we have been most impressed with their effort and dedication in providing a safe and effective air navigation system."[219] In other words, it was the inappropriate service-delivery structure rather than poor management that was perceived to be at the heart of the problem. The industry was interested in promoting a user-pay approach to the ANS through increased user fees for the industry to pay for the necessary upgrades to the system. This provided a fiscal incentive for government to move the system to the private sector and to make it self-supporting from industry fees. The ANS expenditures exceeded revenues by $200 million in 1994–95. Thus, by privatizing the ANS, the federal government could reduce its own expenditures by that amount and, in addition, receive the revenue from the sale of the ANS assets to help meet its deficit-reduction targets. According to one study of the privatization of the ANS, the unions saw benefits to the new organizational structure as well – mainly in the form of increased job security, improved salaries, and higher morale.

There was some debate among stakeholders as to the preferred new organizational form for Nav Canada. Some unions and Transport Canada preferred the Crown corporation model, whereas the industry and the air-traffic controllers preferred the non-share-capital model, which finally won the day, clearly moving the ANS into the regulated private sector. Under the new structure, the ANS board of directors comprises representatives from the airline industry, the unions, and the federal government. Nav Canada agreed to pay the government $1.5 billion for the transfer of the ANS assets to Nav Canada, this money going to the Consolidated Revenue Fund. The new organization planned to recover all of its costs by charging the industry the full cost of its services and by charging new fees for planes "overflying" Canada to other destinations.

Moving the ANS into the private sector required Transport Canada to establish a new regulation and accountability regime to ensure that Nav Canada operates safely and in the public interest. This will be accomplished by Transport Canada establishing safety standards and by inspecting and auditing Nav Canada for compliance with safety and operating regulations. If Nav Canada proposes service reductions it will have to convince regulators that safety will not be jeopardized. In addition, the federal regulators can direct Nav Canada to pay for whatever improvements are required to meet Transport Canada safety standards. Through this accountability regime, the government "will also ensure transparency of information, mandatory consultation, a notice period for changes to user fees or services, and an appeal process for redress of complaints about charges."[220]

The privatization of the ANS is an example of using more appropriate organizational forms for the quasi-commercial operations of government, including private-sector corporate structures to deliver programs, which can then be regulated by government according to performance standards. What are the potential pay-offs? – increased responsiveness to industry needs; a less bureaucratic management framework; improved efficiency; and, potentially, higher staff morale. On the other hand, the industry and the travelling public pay more for air-navigation services through higher user charges. For the government and for taxpayers, the pay-off includes an end to the $200-million annual subsidy to the ANS, revenue from the sale of government assets, and the potential for a more efficient transportation system. On a cautionary note, it still remains to be seen whether the public will be sanguine about private-sector delivery of essential services such as the ANS should the safety of the travelling public be compromised under the new organizational arrangements.

### From Department to SOA to Privatization: the Canada Communications Group

The Canada Communications Group (CCG), within the Department of Public Works and Government Services, was one of the first federal SOAs. The CCG was formerly known as the Queen's Printer, which had been established in 1869 as the internal provider of federal government printing services for departments and for Parliament. The CCG was privatized in 1997; it was purchased through a competitive bidding process by the St. Joseph Corporation, Canada's third-largest commercial printer.[221] In six years, the CCG and its 600 employees "travelled" along the dotted line in Figure 5.2, from departmental status all the way to competitive commercial status in the private sector, with SOA status being only a five-year station-stop along the way. As a division of the privately held St. Joseph Corporation, will the newly privatized CCG contribute to the objective of providing government departments with better services at lower cost? According to the CCG's vice president of sales: "[c]o-located with government across the country, and comprised of associates who have an extensive knowledge of government, CCG, in tandem with the St. Joseph Corporation, is uniquely positioned to bring value-added solutions to the federal government. As we commit to being the best full-service provider to the federal government, we treasure the values that have shaped our history and that will take us into the future. Quality and service at competitive prices. State of the art technology. And today, more than ever, a virtual service window to meet every client need."[222]

### From Department to Crown Corporation to Privatized Delivery: B.C. Systems Corporation

In the late 1970s, British Columbia's computer services were housed in each government department. In 1977, B.C. Systems Corporation (BCSC), a centralized computer services agency, was established. It was organized as a Crown corporation with a board of directors and operated, within government, along private-sector lines and worked to a bottom line. Despite its commercial structure, BCSC had a virtual monopoly on the provision of computer services, since departments were required by Treasury Board to buy these services from the corporation. This situation changed in two ways in the mid-1980s. First, the corporation privatized a large portion of the organization through an employee buy-out of the computer operations. Second, the Treasury Board removed BCSC's monopoly position, and the Crown corporation had to re-position itself as a competitive service provider to government.[223] More recently, in 1996, the government disbanded the BCSC; some of the remaining pieces were privatized, and some were reintegrated into individual departments.

In addition to the diverse group of structures explained to this point, there are some notable variations of these structures that deserve special mention, namely, de-layered organizations, locally shared services, and citizen-centred departmental structures.

### De-layering

One of the elements of the post-bureaucratic model is decentralization, including "de-layering," that is, reducing the number of levels within the organizational hierarchy. A good example of organizational restructuring and de-layering without changing the departmental form of the organization is found in the Office of the Registrar General (ORG) located within Ontario's Ministry of Consumer and Commercial Relations (and the 1994 winner of the IPAC Award for Innovative Management). The ORG is responsible for registering vital statistics and for records such as birth and death certificates: "It serves the interests of the general public as well as lawyers, clergy, physicians, coroners, funeral directors, and federal, provincial and municipal officials. The general public is interested in records for personal identification, lawyers are interested in records for legal requirements, the medical profession is interested in records for statistical purposes, and coroners and funeral directors require death certificates for burial."[224]

In 1987, the Government of Ontario announced that the ORG would be relocated from Toronto to Thunder Bay as part of the government's Northern Relocation Project. Art Daniels, the assistant deputy minister responsible for the ORG, saw this as an opportunity for innovation. In his words, "the relocation of ORG to Thunder Bay was viewed as a greenfield opportunity to build a model office that incorporates state of the art technology as a tool for new service-oriented team representatives, working in an organization that acknowledges and promotes learning and diversity."[225] As noted at the beginning of this book, the existing organization had many of the features of the bureaucratic model of organization. Several changes were made.

First, twelve functional "silos" were integrated into one multifunctional department. Two levels of management hierarchy and seven levels of clerical hierarchy were removed. Then the organization was formed into seven multifunctional teams headed by team managers responsible for leading a group of multiskilled team representatives. New technology was introduced to replace the antiquated paper-based production and records storage system; and workflow was redesigned to make it more efficient and people-friendly.

Once the re-location had been completed and the redesigned organization in Thunder Bay got over its start-up problems, productivity increased by fifty-five per cent from 1991 lows, and service times are now measured in minutes rather than days. Employees are trained cross-functionally, and the previous bureaucratic hierarchy has disappeared and been replaced by a "flat" organizational structure and a team-based production process, supported by state-of-the-art technology.

## Locally Shared Services

Imagine a large government building that houses several different departments and agencies. Each one has its own support services such as purchasing, mail and printing. This is not necessarily an efficient use of resources, and many government departments that are located in the same building complex or near each other are experimenting with the concept of "locally shared support services" (LSSS). An early example of LSSS occurred in Les Terrasses de la Chaudière, a Hull office complex across the Ottawa River from the Parliament Buildings, which contains 6,000 federal employees from a variety of federal departments and agencies. Looking for ways to reduce costs and improve service, representatives from Environment Canada, Indian and Northern Affairs Canada, Canadian Heritage, Revenue Canada, and three other agencies created an "administrative council" for the complex to pool resources and find economies through joint management of support services. For example, the council began its work by pooling and streamlining mail and courier services within the building. This resulted in savings of $300,000 per annum to the participating departments; this was followed by a further savings of close to $1,000,000 through the joint management of telephones and photocopying services. As of 1996, annual savings through the LSSS initiative were estimated at close to $3 million per annum.[226]

### Citizen-Centred Departmental Structures

The British Columbia Ministry for Families and Children, which was created in 1996, is an example of restructuring government in a more citizen-centred way. Prior to the creation of the ministry, services for families and children were delivered by five major government departments (Health; Education, Skills and Training; Women's Equality; Social Services; and the Office of the Attorney General), making one-window access to government programs virtually impossible for families with children: "The new minister, Penny Priddy, was directed to bring together services from five ministries to streamline child and family services and strengthen the province's child protection system."[227] The restructuring of these programs into one ministry resulted in an organization with 4,000 staff, a budget of $1.3 billion, and 400 offices around the province. The offices were structured into twenty regions, with a great deal of delivery autonomy, and with a focus on integrated service delivery.

According to the ministry's plan, integrated, client-centred service is based on four objectives: reduce the number of providers who serve a client; keep applicant processes to a minimum; ensure all providers involved in a case are in contact with each other and share information; and maintain links between services. The ministry established multidisciplinary teams to serve as the operational foundation for its concept of integrated, client-centred delivery. Another significant feature of the ministry's organizational restructuring is the reduction of five layers of bureaucracy, so that there are no more than four levels between the client and the deputy minister (similar to the ORG reforms discussed above). With all government programs for children now in one ministry, and with an integrated regional delivery structure, one-window delivery of provincial programs for families and children in British Columbia is now a reality.

As governments begin to examine organizational structures more from the citizen's perspective, we can expect to see many more departments and programs of government restructured around clusters of client needs. And as we move into the twenty-first century, government organizational structures will likely be less "silo-oriented" and more "horizontal" and citizen-centred.

## RE-ENGINEERING

We turn now to an examination of the trend in some innovative organizations to "re-engineer" delivery systems to achieve large breakthroughs in service improvement and cost reduction. The concept of re-engineering, explained at the beginning of this chapter, takes a "greenfield" approach to re-thinking current systems of delivery, resulting in the redesign of delivery systems from the ground up. We pointed out in Chapter 2 that many public-sector "re-engineering" projects do not meet the rigorous tests proposed by Michael Hammer and James Champy, the fathers of re-engineering.[228] These tests include the requirement to re-think delivery systems and processes from the ground up; to seek major breakthroughs in cycle times and productivity; and to avoid simply replacing existing manual processes with technological enhancements (commonly referred to as "paving over the cow paths").

Hammer and Champy also recommend a formal process of re-engineering within an organization that calls for the appointment of a re-engineering team led by a senior executive, with a strong mandate to "cause an organization to turn itself inside out and upside down to persuade people to accept the radical disruptions that reengineering brings."[229] The formal structure includes several key players. Ideally, the relationship among these players is as follows: "The leader appoints the process owner, who convenes a reengineering team to reengineer the process, with the assistance of the czar, and under the auspices of the steering committee."[230] In the public sector, few organizations have followed this very formal approach. Nonetheless, there are many examples of public organizations that have met the central test, that is, they have totally re-thought and redesigned the process of program delivery, in order to achieve quantum leaps in reducing costs and improving service. We have already seen how the Ontario Office of the Registrar General used the opportunity of its re-location to take a "greenfield" approach to the design of its organization and delivery systems. Some additional case examples are provided below.

### Re-engineering Supply Management of the Canadian Forces Base, Esquimalt

Prior to 1993, the base supply operations (the purchase and distribution of operational supplies) at Canadian Forces Base (CFB) Esquimalt in Victoria, B.C., were budget-funded. The base supply section had the budget for purchasing required goods like office supplies, which were then provided "free" to the operational units. It is not surprising that each fiscal year the entire budget was expended well before the year's end, and over-expenditures were common. In addition, the operational units – the "clients" of the base supply section – were dissatisfied with the service received, especially the long delays between ordering and receiving supplies, the quality of the goods purchased, and the difficulty of finding out the status of orders. In response to these problems, the Esquimalt base, in 1993, initiated a re-engineering project in cooperation with the staff of base supply section to try to re-think the supply operations system from the ground up. The staff were challenged to begin with the question: "What would we do, and how would we do it, if it were our own business?" The project led to major changes in the system of work, the system of management, and the system of delivery.

The first change (and one that Peter Drucker would applaud) was to distribute to each client organization an annual purchasing budget within which they had to manage. This created a new market relationship between the client organizations and the base supply section. Second, the client organizations were given the option of purchasing certain supplies from other sources, placing base supply in a revenue-dependent, competitive environment. Third, the existing assembly-line purchasing process was replaced by a system where each purchasing agent became responsible for ordering, obtaining and delivering specific goods to clients, so that clients could always hold someone accountable for their order. Fourth, hierarchical systems were replaced by a team-based approach, and new computer systems were developed to track purchasing operations. Fifth, goods were no longer placed in the warehouse but delivered directly to clients from private-sector suppliers – an important process re-engineering change. Sixth, clients were permitted to purchase by credit card – another useful process change. In addition to the process re-engineering that took place, there were changes to the management culture; for example, staff were empowered to find new ways of doing things. In the words of one staff member: "I wasn't required to think before – I would just do my job and leave."[231]

The results were impressive. To begin with, for the first time in eleven years, the procurement budget was not overspent. Second, the procurement process was cut down from 120 steps to seventeen steps, thereby reducing the time taken to get in-stock supplies from ten days to one. Third, clients can get feedback on where their order stands within an hour rather than within days. Fourth, administrative costs were reduced. Fifth, clients indicate a much higher level of satisfaction with the service provided and a greater sense of satisfaction with their own jobs. Thus, this re-engineering project seems to have succeeded on both the business side and the human-relations side of the organization.

### Human Resources Development Canada: Re-engineering the Record of Employment Project

In 1997, Human Resources Development Canada, the federal mega-department responsible for the Employment Insurance Program, won a coveted IPAC Award for Innovative Management for its Record of Employment (ROE) project. Businesses in Canada had long complained that the ROE, a document to report the insured earnings of employees who leave their jobs, was a major burden and an irritant in their dealings with the federal government. After an extensive consultation with the program's stakeholders, the new Employment Insurance Program adopted a much simpler and equitable structure for reporting workers' earnings. The employer guidebook has been reduced from thirty-five pages to four pages. The special rules for different types of pay periods – the major source of employer reporting errors – were eliminated through the re-engineering process: The department is "expecting a reduction by an estimated $100 million annually in employer administrative costs."[232]

### Canada Mortgage and Housing Corp. (CMHC): The "emili" System.

The Canada Mortgage and Housing Corp. (CMHC) is a large federal Crown corporation with responsibility for the government's mortgage insurance program. Through this program, the CMHC helps Canadians to buy houses with as little as five per cent down. In 1995, it had in place over $100 billion in mortgage insurance, which constituted over forty per cent of all residential mortgages in Canada. The CMHC works through 160 approved lenders in the banking and mortgage industry across the country. In the early 1990s, the financial services industry in Canada's private sector became much more competitive and mortgage lenders were using technology to speed up the mortgage approval process. Therefore, the financial services industry wanted much faster turnaround times from the

CMHC's approval process, as well as a link between the automated systems in the financial services industry and CMHC's systems. This led the CMHC to launch a re-engineering project in 1993. A new system known as "emili" was successfully introduced in 1996. It "automated the communications, analysis and decision making components associated with reviewing mortgage applications, which as a manual process took one to two days to complete, into a seamless electronic process that can render a decision within a few seconds."[233]

### The City of Vancouver's Neighbourhood Integrated Service Teams

This re-engineering project – the 1997 winner of IPAC's Gold Award for Innovative Management – provides an example of business process improvement, a key re-engineering concept. According to Hammer and Champy, "a business process is a collection of activities that takes one or more kinds of input and creates an output that is of value to the customer.[234] This Vancouver initiative grew out of a longstanding problem: "Residents of a local neighbourhood had been struggling for two years with a home on their block that was plagued with a seemingly never-ending string of noisy gatherings, brawls, and troublesome tenants. Although police, building inspectors and health board representatives paid many visits, the problem only escalated."[235] After neighbourhood residents stormed a city council meeting to vent their frustration with the continuing problem, the city set up an interdepartmental team that worked with residents and solved the problem: "The answer was not providing more staff in more departments, but rather cooperation, communication and teamwork between existing city staff and the public."[236]

Based on this successful experiment in re-engineering the process by which the city responded to neighbourhood problems, the approach was extended and formalized through the establishment of a Neighbourhood Integrated Service Team (NIST) for each of the 16 neighbourhoods in the city. Each NIST is composed of representatives of the major departments within the municipal government: police, fire, planning, parks, library, engineering, permits and licenses, health, and social planning, as well as some schools. Once a citizen identifies a problem that involves more than one city department, the NIST is put to work to resolve it in cooperation with the citizens affected. According to Nancy Cheung, the NIST coordinator, "[it's] an idea that's so innovative yet so simple ... [i]t includes the citizens and empowers the staff."[237] To make citizen access easy, Internet-capable computers have been placed in each library through which citizens can contact the NIST when they have a problem. The NIST experience has also prompted the city to re-engineer other operating systems. For example, city inspectors from different departments now do joint audits of problem hotels and restaurants, and citizens can now get "one-window" delivery of city licensing services from the licensing department. The Vancouver experience suggests that the benefits of re-engineering delivery systems can sometimes be achieved without a major formal re-engineering process. However, it is clear that the culture of the organization has to be one that promotes innovation and interdepartmental collaboration if new delivery systems that are more effective and responsive are to be implemented successfully.

## IMPLICATIONS AND IMPEDIMENTS

Perhaps the major learning point to be drawn from the *restructuring* initiatives discussed in this chapter is that new organizational models, if carefully chosen and effectively implemented, can help to improve dramatically the performance of public organizations, especially in terms of the values of productivity, responsiveness and service. *Re-engineering* projects that involve re-thinking and redesigning delivery processes while minimizing negative impacts on staff can yield similar improvements.

### Managerial and Organizational Considerations

Figure 5.2, which has been the anchor for much of this chapter, depicts the major trend in the 1990s towards greater autonomy and towards market and revenue dependency for public organizations. It is essential to keep in mind, however, that the organizations that have become SOAs, Crown corporations or private corporations have primarily been those organizations that generate large amounts of revenue from clients or from those they regulate. In Canada, we have made limited use of the British executive agency model for organizations that do not generate revenue from their services. (An exception is the proposed new revenue administration agency that will replace Revenue Canada; the agency will collect revenues, but not in exchange for services, as is the case with Parks Canada and the new Food Inspection Agency.) In both the federal and provincial spheres, we have seen a more pragmatic, more targeted approach. Examples include the introduction of SOAs for organizations that provide common services to government departments (e.g., Fleet Vehicles Agency in Manitoba); the use of SOAs (e.g., the Passport Office), service agencies (e.g., Parks Canada), and public–private partnership corporations (e.g., Ontario's Teranet) for programs that generate revenues from the sale of services; the contracting-out of services that can be provided more efficiently by the private sector (e.g., group homes in British Columbia);

Crown corporation status for commercial organizations that can compete in the private sector but that must also pursue a public interest (e.g., Canada Post); and privatization where the services are commercial with no public-interest component to the service (e.g., Canada Communications Group), or where the public-interest objective can be achieved by regulation (e.g., Air Canada).

The post-bureaucratic model suggests two considerations bearing on organizational structure. First, the public sector should use a wider range of organizational models than it has used in the past. Second, the model chosen should be aligned with the public purposes of the organization. This is easier said than done, however, because of the competing principles of organizational design (i.e., the criteria of purpose, place, process and persons). In keeping with Peter Drucker's view as to why public organizations do not perform well, experience to date suggests that holding public organizations accountable for results in exchange for less bureaucratic controls and processes leads to higher levels of organizational performance. Moreover, introducing appropriate market mechanisms to public-sector services can also improve performance.

What does the experience of Canadian governments teach us about re-engineering? Professor Arie Halachmi has asked, "Is re-engineering a real breakthrough in either management theory or practice or is it another concoction that management consultants are willing to dispense, for a fee, to those managers that are still seeking a cure-all for the ills of organizations?"[238] The answer is that if re-engineering is viewed as one more tool in the good manager's toolbox rather than as a management panacea, and if it is used in a pragmatic way to re-think service-delivery processes, then it can be a major force in reducing costs and improving service delivery.

As with other areas of public-sector reform, so with restructuring and re-engineering, what Kenneth Kernaghan has called the W5 question remains, that is, "What works well, where, and why?"[239] What structure is appropriate to particular types of public services, and what should the assessment criteria be? For example, a study by the Atmospheric Environment Service (the weather service that is part of Environment Canada) of how the weather service is organized in other countries showed that its structure varies from departmental division, to SOA, to executive agency, to public–private partnership, to Crown corporation. As we acquire more experience with new forms of organization, we must develop criteria to assist ministers and managers to choose the most appropriate form.

A related question is whether the use of more-autonomous organizational models (e.g., service agencies) necessarily leads to improved performance. Geert Bouckaert, who has studied organizational reform in OECD countries, including Canada, suggests that the enthusiasm for organizational reform may be greater than organizational theory or actual results may warrant: "As to the effects of decentralization on the performance of the unit, theories are not so unequivocally positive. This is in contrast with the 'euphoria' noticeable in many OECD countries. Therefore it should be useful to have a closer look at the empirical base for the presumed effect of decentralization on performance by evaluating these types of reforms more systematically and thoroughly."[240] The evidence provided in this chapter shows that organizational innovation in Canada had led to measurable improvements in such organizations as the Passport Office, the Ontario Office of the Registrar General, the Manitoba Fleet Vehicle Agency, and Canada Post. Thus, we can be confident in concluding that new organizational models, when properly chosen and implemented, can lead to improved performance.

A question that is more difficult to answer is whether similar results could have been achieved through better management within existing organizational forms. The Australian approach to public-sector reform during the 1980s and early 1990s concentrated much more on improving management systems than on changing organizational structures. The Australian experience (within the Administrative Services Department, for example) suggests that making existing organizations more accountable for results, subjecting them to more competition, and giving them more freedom from bureaucratic controls can also lead to improved performance. In this context, we should note that, by itself, making a monopoly service more autonomous in organizational structure may not automatically lead to better performance. The example of British Columbia Systems Corporation, when it became a Crown corporation in the late 1970s, suggests that structural change may have to be accompanied by improved management systems and the introduction of market forces to ensure significant improvement in performance.

Still another issue that has emerged from the creation of more autonomous delivery agencies is that of policy coordination: "Reforms such as 'Next Steps' in the United Kingdom, 'corporatization' in New Zealand, and similar reforms in other countries have divided large cabinet departments into a number of smaller specialized entities. ... As the 'ship of state' becomes a flotilla, producing effective coordination and cooperation becomes even more difficult than in the past."[241] It is also argued that there may be a loss of vertical coordination, between policy and operations, and that policy will suffer through the loss of feedback by operational managers in the policy development process. Figure 5.1 makes clear that decentralization into autonomous delivery units may make horizontally integrated (single-window) program delivery more difficult, although the Canadian Food Inspection Agency seems to have

119

overcome that problem by integrating several service delivery units into the new agency.

An important issue of human resource management arises from the implementation of re-engineering approaches in the public sector. Ole Ingstrup, former principal of the Canadian Centre for Management Development, has noted that re-engineering falls into one of the two main traditions of management thought – the scientific management school as opposed to the human relations school. He recommends an integrated approach to ensure that re-engineering does not occur at the expense of the people in the organization who may be displaced or discarded. In his view, "business process re-engineering will be successful to the degree it is implemented in the context of a balanced set of management approaches and tools. That is why the insights of the 'human relations' school of management ... must not be lost from view."[242]

## Political Considerations

While the issue of accountability is discussed in this section, it is so pervasive and important that it could easily be discussed under the headings of managerial/organizational and value/ethical considerations as well. It has been widely argued that new, decentralized organizational structures create new accountability issues.[243] For example, in reviewing the federal government's experience with SOAS, Alti Rodal identifies the accountability issue in this way: "How can the results-oriented accountability regime of SOAS, which encourages increased delegation of authority and flexibilities, be reconciled with the fact that deputy ministers and ministers remain fully accountable for the performance of the SOAS under their authority?"[244] This issue becomes even clearer when organizations move to separate agency status (e.g., the Canadian Food Inspection Agency) and when delivery organizations become engaged in delivery partnerships with other levels of government or with the private sector. Who is accountable when things go wrong? Is the minister accountable only for political issues, or is the minister also accountable to Parliament for delivery issues that have been delegated to an arm's-length agency? "In parliamentary systems the connection of operations through ministers to parliament is generally the crucial constitutional mechanism for accountability, and the separation of operations from direct ministerial control could weaken accountability."[245] In Britain, this issue arose with respect to the operations of the prison service (an executive agency) when the minister was held accountable in Parliament for the escape of prisoners, even though this was an operational issue delegated by formal agreement to the chief executive officer of the prison service.

In the Canadian context, what is the accountability regime for the Canadian Food Inspection Agency? If some food inspection is delegated to a provincial government to deliver, who is accountable when a public-health problem arises as a result of inadequate regulation – the head of the agency, the senior provincial official in charge of food inspection, the provincial minister or the federal minister? British experience suggests that the realities of political accountability can sometimes overtake an accountability regime that has been negotiated within and across governments. A good deal of thought needs to be given to this issue as new decentralized organizational forms come into potential conflict with the traditional Westminster form of ministerial accountability.

Another political issue arises when public organizations are transformed into entrepreneurial, revenue-dependent organizations that compete with the private sector. We saw this entrepreneurial spirit with the creation of the Fleet Vehicles Agency in Manitoba. The problem is that private-sector organizations may see such new, more entrepreneurial activity as a threat to their own aspirations to operate these services. If public organizations begin offering services in competition with the private sector, political pressure may be applied to rein in these activities. A possible solution to such problems may be to establish public–private partnerships such as Teranet, a partnership among the Ontario government, KPMG, and private-sector computer companies to provide land-registry services.

## Value and Ethical Considerations

As noted above, restructuring and re-engineering initiatives aim in part to promote such public-service values as efficiency, effectiveness, responsiveness and service. And we have just explained the pervasive importance of the value of accountability and the need to ensure that the search for values like efficiency and service does not undermine the accountability of either public-service managers or their ministers. It is often argued that when such values conflict they should be reconciled in the light of the public interest, which is widely viewed as both a democratic and an ethical value.

There is concern that in some instances innovative organizational forms may undermine the public interest. According to David Zussman, "these alternative service delivery agencies pose interesting and potentially worrisome issues. One of the most important is, what is the public interest?"[246] He notes that new decentralized organizational models increase service and efficiency but that there may be a consequent cost in terms of the public interest. For example, if Canada Post closes a rural post office, this may make sense in commercial terms but not in public interest – or political – terms: "[d]oes the public interest lie in a more efficient Post Office or in preserving rural communities? Or in some combination of the two? And who should get to make that decision?"[247] In the mid-1990s, the federal government asked Canada Post to freeze its closure of rural post offices, thereby exercising its power as shareholder to put the public interest ahead of a more narrow commercial interest.

Many regulatory agencies (e.g., the Food and Drug Directorate at Health Canada, the National Energy Board) are becoming more autonomous and, at the direction of government, more revenue dependent. The issue arising from these changes is that application by the agencies of the "user pay, user say" principle could be seen to tip the balance of regulation from the public interest towards the interest of those being regulated. Revenue-dependent regulatory agencies will have to ensure that the public interest is not jeopardized by the adoption of "the regulator pays for the regulation" approach.

## CONCLUSION

As part of the movement of public organizations towards the post-bureaucratic model, there is a huge amount of experimentation with new organizational forms. New structures and new processes are key elements of the drive to make the public sector more efficient, effective and service-oriented. These innovations raise new issues in governance and public management, so care must be taken to ensure that the organizational forms chosen are congruent with the range of roles that public organizations play in society and that the public interest is protected as reforms continue. Restructuring and re-engineering are two important tools for improving the performance of the public sector, but they are not a panacea; they must be used in harmony with other elements of the post-bureaucratic model if they are to achieve their full potential. Benchmarking of the performance of public organizations that are in the same business but that are using different organizational forms should be especially enlightening.

# 6

# Serving the Public

As explained in Chapter 1, the development of a much stronger focus on service to the public is a central characteristic of the post-bureaucratic model of public organization. Robert Denhardt, in *The Pursuit of Significance*, identifies serving the public as one of the five characteristics of the "revolution in public management." He states that the innovative public managers he interviewed in Canada, the United States, the United Kingdom and Australia each shared a strong commitment to improving service to the public:

The manager gives priority to service both to clients and citizens. That priority is supported by high standards of performance and accountability, and by a constant emphasis on quality. Most important, the manager recognizes that technical efforts alone will fail unless equal or greater attention is given to the human side, especially to building a sense of community within the organization, and a sense of cooperation outside.[248]

In Chapter 1, we noted that the traditional bureaucratic model of public organization tends to focus inwards to the organization's needs rather than outwards to the needs of clients and citizens. As Peter Drucker has noted, because public organizations tend to be monopolies and to be budget-funded rather than revenue-funded, there is much less incentive to provide excellent service to clients and customers than there is in the private sector.

This chapter examines the concept of client service in the public sector, with specific reference to the tools and strategies being used by public managers to improve service and to the lessons learned and issues encountered in implementing concepts of service excellence. We begin by examining the notions of citizen and customer in the public sector and comparing the role of service in the public and private sectors.

## MEANINGS AND FRAMEWORKS

To demonstrate his argument that service in the public sector is different from that in the private sector, management expert Tom Peters gave the following example. He said that when he wants approval to build an addition on his property, he wants fast service from city hall, but when his neighbour wants to build a similar garage on the neighbour's side of the fence, then Peters wants a slow consultative approval process to ensure that his interests are taken into account before his neighbour's proposal is adjudicated: "Suppose my neighbor wants to add almost the same addition? That's another matter. Now I want due process."[249] Clearly, public-sector service delivery takes place in an environment of competing interests that have to balance, and, in a democratic society, delivery processes must be fair to all concerned.

To understand service delivery in government, we need to be clear about the various governance roles that government plays in society. In the private sector, individuals and companies compete to sell goods and services to buyers who pay a market price. So there are several characteristics at play: there is *competition* among suppliers; *money is exchanged for the good or service; price is determined by market demand*; and when better service is provided, more customers are obtained or retained. But public-sector services seldom have these characteristics. As we saw in Chapter 1, the public sector is engaged in policy and legislation development, in regulation, and in the provision of tax-funded services. Most of the services it provides are not rendered in exchange for money; on the contrary, *many services are provided free*. In some cases people must qualify for the service in some way, and, in others, people actually receive money from the government rather than pay for a service.

Governments carry out a broad range of activities, including, for example, supplying park and recreation facilities; providing social assistance and pension payments; regulating the environment; and arresting, convicting and imprisoning people. These activities are summed up in Figure 6.1 as "the five Ps" – *parks, pensions, pollution, police and prisons* – and are portrayed on a continuum between the service role of government, where the client interest is dominant, and the control role of government, where the citizen interest is dominant. Governments must balance the interests of clients with the interests of citizens, and, sometimes, they must balance the interests of one set of citizens with that of another set. According to Denhardt, this balancing act is at the heart of public management: "When people act as customers [or clients] they tend to take one approach; when they act as citizens they take another. Basically, customers [and clients] focus on their own limited desires and wishes and how they can be expeditiously satisfied. Citizens, on the other hand, focus on the common

Figure 6.1. *The Client–Citizen Balance*

| | |
|---|---|
| *Client Interest Dominant* ........................................................................ | *Citizen Interest Dominant* |

parks .................. pensions .................. pollution ................ police ...................... prisons

| | |
|---|---|
| *Service Role* ............................................................................................. | *Control Role* |

good and on the long-term consequences to the community."[250] It is helpful to illustrate the need for balance by elaborating on the five Ps.

Even in organizations with a strong service dimension, like *parks* organizations, service to customers has to be balanced against the interests of the citizens as a whole. People who use the parks may want more services and more park development, while citizens in general may want strong conservation, along with limited development, of the park's resources for future generations.

In the case of *pensions*, protecting the interests of citizens (who are usually paying the bill) affects significantly the service role of pension managers. Under most pension programs, including the Canada Pension Plan and the Old Age Pension, clients have to meet a legislated qualification before they can receive benefits. Thus, managers have to ensure that only those who qualify get the benefits and that benefits are not paid, for example, to people who are dead! This control role changes the dynamic of the relationship between the client of the service and the providers. This relationship has some parallels in the private sector, where the insurance industry faces some of the same issues in providing good service to clients while controlling costs and preventing fraud.

In regard to activities like *pollution*, government has a regulatory function with little parallel in the private sector. The role of government is to protect the public interest. Thus, companies that are being inspected are not customers in the private-sector sense. In fact, one could argue that the customer (in this case, the beneficiary) is the citizen. On the other hand, shouldn't those being regulated by government be treated *like* customers in some ways, that is, be served courteously, promptly, professionally and equitably? In this sense, when you are stopped by a policeman for speeding or contacted by Revenue Canada for a tax audit, you want to be treated *like* a customer, even if you are not a customer in the pure sense of the word.

*Police* organizations enforce laws in the public interest, including arresting criminals to protect citizens. While those detained or arrested have rights to a certain degree of service, the main focus of police activity is serving the broader community through its control and law-enforcement role, and law-abiding citizens expect good service when they call their public law-enforcement agencies for help.

For a government activity like managing *prisons*, there is no obvious private-sector parallel. In this case, the interests of the citizens (which include keeping dangerous offenders behind bars) is the paramount consideration. Yet, it can be argued that even prisoners have certain rights to service (e.g., to have timely and fair parole hearings and to be secure from harm and abuse). The tragic incident in Kingston's Prison for Women in 1995, which resulted in the Arbour Commission Inquiry, demonstrated that in our society even prison inmates have certain basic "client" rights.

The preceding discussion demonstrates that service delivery is far more complex in the public than in the private sector. First, the tasks of government differ in fundamental ways from the simple market delivery of goods and services in the private sector. Second, government must balance the interests of citizens with the interests of program clients – a task that sometimes requires public managers to play a control rather than a service role. Such factors as public opinion and economic conditions can cause the balance to shift. For example, if the public believes that the welfare system is being abused by "cheaters" who do not legally qualify for benefits, the government may crack down on these cheaters. The balance will shift along the continuum in Figure 6.1 towards the interests of citizens and towards the control function. As a result, the agency's service performance, as perceived by claimants, may decline. But, to take a different example, if the government adopts a more lenient approach to university students who have trouble repaying their loans after graduation, the balance shifts towards the client and away from taxpaying citizens, who must bear the added cost.

A third major difference between service delivery in the public and private sectors is that the recipient of government programs is not a client or customer in the private-sector sense of someone who has a choice of suppliers and who pays directly for what he or she receives. The meaning of concepts like "client" and "customer" is more complex when applied to the public sector and must, therefore, be carefully defined. Figure 6.2, which draws on work by the federal Treasury Board of Canada and Professor Al Hyde of the Brookings Institution, shows that everyone is a *citizen*, who has both rights and responsibilities. But when a citizen comes into contact with government programs, he or she may also be a *customer* (someone who pays for a service, that may be available from other suppliers); a *client* (someone who receives a service from a professional on an ongoing basis); a *claimant* (a client who must qualify for a service); a *complier* (someone who is regulated by a public agency or someone required to pay a tax); or a *captive* (someone detained or incarcerated by a public agency). The determining factor is the type of program or service affecting the citizen.

Figure 6.2. *The Many Roles of the Citizen*

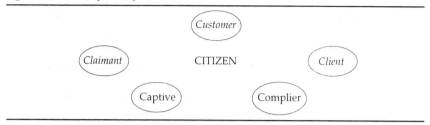

## WHY IMPROVE PUBLIC-SECTOR SERVICE DELIVERY?

### Overall Benefits

As explained below, the public believes that the service they receive from public organizations is generally inferior to that received from private-sector organizations. We shall see that this perception is not always supported by the facts. When in 1995 the federal Treasury Board launched its Quality Services Initiative it described the benefits of service improvement in terms of increased client satisfaction. However, it also identified significant benefits to clients, employees, managers and Canadians in general, as follows:

*Clients*: "When quality service becomes a priority, they see demonstrated value for tax dollars in the services they receive and find that those services are more accessible, responsive and affordable."

*Employees*: "They have opportunities to upgrade skills, diversify work, implement improvements and be part of a positive, constructive, client service-oriented culture."

*Managers and executives*: "By actively involving employees in setting organizational direction and celebrating successes, managers may reduce employee turnover, increase employee morale, and increase employee creativity and innovation."

*All Canadians*: "[B]oth stakeholders and taxpayers ... see value for money in affordable, accessible, responsive and relevant quality services. As well, they have greater confidence in the federal government, knowing that we are building more efficient and effective departments which, in turn, will make Canada a more competitive nation."[251]

What the Treasury Board did not explicitly say was that improving client satisfaction by providing better quality service might enhance the public's regard for the public sector and be a source of increased pride for public servants.

### Apples, Oranges and Public Perception of Service Performance

Surveys of public satisfaction with government services tend to deliver schizophrenic results. When asked about *government services as a whole*, citizens give government services low marks, compared to specific private-sector services such as banks and supermarkets. But, typically, when citizens are asked about *specific government services* they have experienced, client satisfaction levels are much higher and, indeed, are not dissimilar from ratings for private-sector services. For example, a 1987 Gallup survey reported that seventy-five per cent of clients of *specific* government services in Canada were either "very satisfied" or "quite satisfied."[252] In surveys at the local level in the United States, street repair services are given a sixty-per-cent satisfaction rating, while trash collection and fire services generally receive an eighty-per-cent rating.[253] In a 1993 survey by the British government, postal services received a ninety-two-per-cent ("well or very well") performance rating, compared to eighty-three per cent for refuse collection, seventy-eight per cent for customs, and seventy per cent for banks.[254] And a 1992 Ontario study showed that the ratings for individual elements of the service experience (e.g., courtesy and promptness) for specific government departments averaged about sixty-five per cent.[255]

Especially notable is a study by Georgia State University that compared citizen satisfaction with both public and private services and found that fire departments and private mail carriers ranked first at roughly eighty-per-cent satisfaction levels.[256] The lowest scores (about fifty-five per cent) were for two private-sector services: taxis and cable-TV providers. Moreover, the U.S. Post Office scored higher than doctors' offices and banks. Thus, the citizens of Georgia discriminated between good and poor service in both the public and private sectors and rated both sectors' individual services within similar ranges.

These studies provide an important backdrop to other surveys that compare apples with oranges, that is, they compare individual private-sector services (like a *bank*) with entire levels of government (like *provincial government*). Table 6.1 provides an example of this type of survey, undertaken for the Ontario government in 1992.[257] As noted above, however, the same study showed that citizens rated their actual service experience with provincial departments at much higher levels than the government as a whole: "The Public rate their satisfaction with each of the four generic services *higher* than they rate the quality of Ontario Government service in

Table 6.1. *Overall Quality of Service: Ontario Public, 1991*

| | |
|---|---|
| Your bank or trust company | 72 |
| A supermarket you go to | 71 |
| A department store you go to | 62 |
| Your municipal government | 55 |
| Canada Post | 49 |
| Ontario government | 45 |
| Federal government | 36 |

Rating scale: 0 = extremely poor; 100 = extremely good

Table 6.2. *Citizens' Satisfaction with Public- and Private-Sector Service Quality\**
*(Service satisfaction, on a scale of 0–100; N = 2900)*

| Service quality | | | |
|---|---|---|---|
| Fire departments | 86* | Health card | 62 |
| Libraries | 77 | Customs | 58 |
| Garbage disposal | 74 | Canada Post | 57 |
| Supermarkets | 74 | Taxis | 57 |
| Provincial parks | 71 | Revenue Canada, tax | 57 |
| Canada Pension/OAP | 68 | Insurance agencies | 55 |
| RCMP | 68 | Hospitals | 51 |
| Passport Office | 66 | Banks | 50 |
| Motor vehicle license | 66 | Road maintenance | 45 |
| Telephone companies | 63 | | |
| Electric utilities | 63 | | |
| Public-sector average | 62* | | |
| Private-sector average | 62** | | |

Note: *For public-sector services in the table, the ratings are for those services used by citizens in the past year.
**An average of seven services; for private-sector ratings in the study, citizens were not asked whether they had used the service in the past year.
Adapted from Erin Research, *Citizens First* (Ottawa: Canadian Centre for Management Development, 1998).

a global sense."[258] In fact, registration services and financial services programs were rated at the same level as department stores, at sixty-one per cent and sixty-two per cent, respectively. The Ontario government's explanation of this anomaly is probably correct: "Overall quality of service, when applied to an organization as large and diverse as the Ontario government is vague and unspecific, and may evoke a stereotyped image of "big government," while mention of a specific service may recall a personal experience."[259]

Table 6.2 shows the results of a more recent and sophisticated survey undertaken in 1998 by Erin Research for the federal government, Canada Post and three provincial governments.[260] This survey overturns the myth that private-sector service is superior to public-sector service. This survey, like the Georgia State and U.K. surveys, shows that citizens rate public- and private-sector services within the same general ranges and that many public-sector services out-perform private services in the minds of Canadians. In fact the highest-scoring services in this survey of 2900 Canadians were public-sector services. Even Revenue Canada, which has to ensure a balance between service and control, scores as well as or better than banks. There appears to be a considerable degree of mythology around the degree of citizen satisfaction with public-sector service. *In reality, poor service and excellent service exist in both sectors.* Nonetheless, no one would deny that citizens want public-sector agencies to improve their level of service and to provide faster, more convenient, less bureaucratic, and more responsive service. With this reality in mind, the Canadian Centre for Management Development undertook ground-breaking research in 1998 to determine public expectations of good service, especially with respect to service standards (a topic examined later in this chapter). Table 6.3 outlines the public expectations of selected types of government service. One of the most interesting findings from this research was that satisfaction ratings are largely driven by five important factors:

- timeliness
- staff competence
- courtesy
- fairness
- outcome

Over seventy per cent of the satisfaction ratings were driven by these five factors. Moreover, when all five factors were rated highly, the overall satisfaction rating of services averaged eighty-five out of one hundred – a very high score. The factor most likely to receive a low score was timeliness – thus suggesting an important priority for service improvement and an important area for establishing citizens' expectations for service standards.

What, then, are Canadians' expectations for service standards in the public sector? The *Citizens First* survey data showed that to satisfy the government's clients, telephones should be answered within thirty seconds, and the wait in line at a government office should take no longer than five minutes (Table 6.3). Knowing the expectations of clients is essential to achieving high levels of client satisfaction; if public managers don't know what clients expect, public managers are unlikely to try to attain service levels that will satisfy clients: the "service gap" will continue. The extent of the challenge to close the gap can be easily illustrated. The Oregon motor vehicle license office set a service standard for waiting in line of fifteen minutes. Based on the expectations of Canadians, meeting

Table 6.3. *Public Expectations of Service Standards in Canada*

| Service element | | Citizens' standard | Percentage of citizens that standard will satisfy |
|---|---|---|---|
| | | *Service standard/expectation* | |
| Telephones: | – Time before telephone answered | 30 secs. | 97 |
| | – Time to return a call | 4 hrs. | 76 |
| Office: | – Minutes in line | 5 | 68 |
| | – Number of people to deal with | 2 | 82 |
| Mail: | – Weeks to receive a reply | 2 | 87 |

Source: Erin Research, *Citizens First* (Ottawa: Canadian Centre for Management Development, 1998).

Table 6.4. *Assessment of Internal Services by Ontario Public Servants*

| Internal service | Importance (Rating scale = 0 to 100) | Service performance (Rating scale = 0 to 100) |
|---|---|---|
| Human resources | 70 | 48 |
| Information technology | 71 | 53 |
| Policy formulation | 65 | 47 |
| Communication | 63 | 52 |
| Finance | 59 | 50 |
| Purchasing | 56 | 49 |
| Legal services | 53 | 57 |
| Accommodation | 40 | 54 |

this exact standard one hundred per cent of the time would satisfy only sixteen per cent of the clients – the other eighty-four per cent of the driving public would go away disaffected with the government's service.

A final issue of service satisfaction levels that is important to examine is satisfaction with *internal services*, that is, the services provided *within* public organizations by staff functions such as personnel, legal, computer and building services. The Ontario government's 1992 survey provides one of the few reliable sources of information in this area. Line personnel generally have no option but to receive these services from within government, but, as explained in the previous chapter, the monopoly approach to internal services is gradually changing.

Table 6.4 shows both the importance and service performance ratings for eight internal services within Ontario government departments. (The respondents were public servants who rely on these services). The services most in need of improvement (the importance score minus the performance score) are human resources, information technology, and policy formulation, but the highest performance rating for any internal service is only fifty-seven, for legal services. These results suggest a substantial degree of client dissatisfaction with the whole range of internal services.

Some government departments are making major efforts to improve internal services. The federal Department of Justice, for example, provides legal service to all departments, and Department of Justice lawyers usually have offices within the headquarters of the operating departments. Following a study of expectations and satisfaction levels, the department signed formal *internal service agreements* with departments receiving its legal services. For example, the 1997 agreement with the deputy minister of health outlines Health Canada's legal priorities, the legal resources required from Justice Canada, and the process for establishing the *service standards* that Justice Canada will be responsible for meeting. Justice Canada undertakes annual satisfaction surveys to measure service performance on seventeen service elements within three dimensions – quality of legal services; timeliness of legal services; and courtesy of service. On a scale running from one (needs a lot of improvement) to five (excellent), the overall scores for 1996 averaged about 4.6 – an outstanding score for internal service and a substantial improvement over the 1995 scores. These results demonstrate how high client satisfaction levels can be achieved, even where the service is a monopoly, providing that commitment to client satisfaction and continuous improvement is followed up with the systematic application of service quality tools, including satisfaction surveys, service standards and a service improvement plan.

## HOW TO IMPROVE SERVICE: THREE MAJOR APPROACHES

During the 1980s, there was an explosion of private- and public-sector writings promoting service management and service improvement. This literature emerged in two streams: the total quality management (TQM) stream, which came out of the manufacturing sector and the U.S. military, and the service quality (SQ) stream, which came out of the service sector in Europe and North America. During the past decade, the public sector has adapted and experimented with concepts and tools from these two streams of thought and has made its own contributions to the TQM and SQ literature. Table 6.5 shows the genesis of these two approaches as well as the most important contributors, concepts and tools associated with them.

More recently, in the 1990s, the public-sector literature has added a third stream of its own, namely, alternative service delivery (ASD), which is examined later in this chapter.

### Total Quality Management: Concepts and Tools

Since TQM had its genesis in the manufacturing sector and developed out of the quality control movement, it is not surprising that its focus is on

Table 6.5. *The Total Quality Management and Service Quality Approach to Service Improvement*

| | Total quality management | | Service quality |
|---|---|---|---|
| *Genesis*: | Manufacturing sector | *Genesis*: | Service sector |
| *Gurus*: | Dr. Edwards Deming | *Gurus*: | Jan Carlzon |
| | Dr. Joseph Juran | | Ron Zemke |
| | Dr. Armand Feigenbaum | | Karl Albrecht |
| | Philip Crosby | | Leonard Berry |
| *Concepts*: | Continuous quality improvement | *Concepts*: | Customer satisfaction |
| | Employee involvement | | Customer expectations |
| | Zero defects | | The service gap |
| *Tools*: | Quality teams | *Tools*: | Customer surveys |
| | Statistical analysis of systems | | Service standards |
| | Plan, do, check, act | | Service skills training |
| | Flow charts | | Service improvement plans |
| | Benchmarking | | Service recognition |

improving product quality. While there are as many definitions of TQM as there are authors, the concept can be defined as "[i]nvolving everyone in an organization in controlling and continuously improving how work is done, in order to meet customer expectations of quality."[261] A study of the application of TQM in the public sector defines TQM more broadly:

Total quality management is a simple but revolutionary way of performing work. We define it as follows: *Total* implies the search for quality in every aspect of work, from identifying customer needs to aggressively evaluating whether a customer is satisfied. *Quality* means meeting and exceeding customer expectations. *Management* means developing and maintaining the organizational capacity to constantly improve quality."[262]

During World War II, Dr. Edwards Deming, of the U.S. Census Bureau and the Department of Agriculture, pioneered the concept of improving manufacturing processes using statistical process control techniques introduced by Dr. Walter Shewhart at Bell Laboratories in the 1920s. In 1947, Dr. Deming was invited to visit Japan to advise on a post-war census. While he was there, the Japanese Union of Scientists and Engineers asked Deming to lecture on the subject of quality improvement through statistical process control techniques. The rest is history. Dr. Deming's ideas (expanded by Dr. Joseph Juran when he went to lecture in Japan a few years later) were quickly implemented throughout Japanese industry, resulting in higher-quality Japanese products and reduced production costs. As a result, by the end of the 1970s, Japan was out-competing the United States and other western countries in many manufacturing sectors. It was at this time that Xerox, Ford and other major American companies

133

began to learn from Japan's experience and to adopt quality management techniques within American industry.

Many companies, including Xerox for example, credit their survival in the 1980s to the introduction of TQM methods within their companies.[263] In the public sector, the U.S. Navy adopted quality management techniques during the early 1980s in the area of aircraft and ship maintenance[264] and even claims to have coined the term total quality management to describe its approach to quality improvement. In 1988, the United States government created the Federal Quality Institute, under the aegis of the Office of Personnel Management, to introduce the TQM philosophy into government departments and agencies. Since 1990, the influence of TQM appears to have been waning in management circles. Nonetheless, some of the basic TQM concepts and tools have become an essential part of the innovative public manager's toolbox for improving service delivery. In Canada, the federal government (Department of National Defence) and the Government of Manitoba have used TQM techniques to improve their performance. And between 1985 and 1991, the U.S. Internal Revenue Service, using staff quality teams employing statistical techniques, claimed to have "saved $3,730,959, improved customer service and achieved intangible benefits. Other QM initiatives have saved $7,571,789. The total cost savings to the taxpayer? Over $11 million!"[265]

Table 6.6 outlines the basic toolbox used by practitioners of TQM. Based on the cycle of "plan, do, check, act," teams of employees analyse systems using tools such as flow charts and statistical analysis and find ways of reducing costs and improving system quality. A team in the B.C. Ministry of Finance obtained savings of $500,000 per year and achieved faster processing of property-tax payments by applying TQM techniques. Under a 1994 government–union agreement in British Columbia, training in quality tools has been provided for government employees with the purpose of enabling workplace teams to review work processes, identify opportunities for improvement, and make the improvements.

A final TQM tool is *benchmarking*. This involves a formal comparative analysis of the performance and systems of one organization with those of other organizations. The purpose of the analysis is to identify innovative ways of improving cost, quality and service performance so that these might be adapted to one's own organization.

## Service Quality: Concepts and Tools

The "service quality" (SQ) literature began with Thomas Peters and Robert Waterman's *In Search of Excellence*, which reported on the common characteristics of "excellent" manufacturing and service companies. The authors

Table 6.6. *The TQM Toolbox*

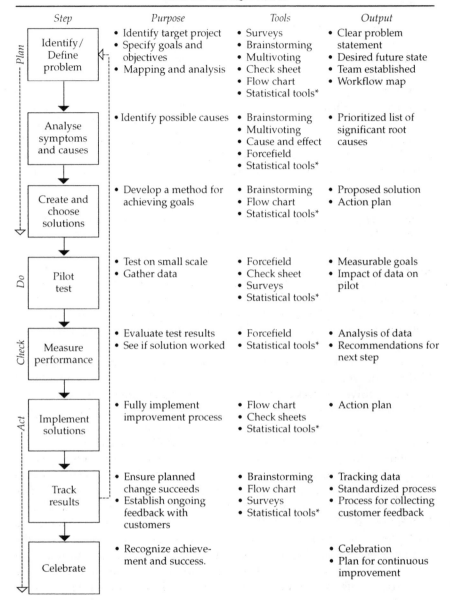

| Step | Purpose | Tools | Output |
|---|---|---|---|
| **Plan** — Identify/Define problem | • Identify target project<br>• Specify goals and objectives<br>• Mapping and analysis | • Surveys<br>• Brainstorming<br>• Multivoting<br>• Check sheet<br>• Flow chart<br>• Statistical tools* | • Clear problem statement<br>• Desired future state<br>• Team established<br>• Workflow map |
| Analyse symptoms and causes | • Identify possible causes | • Brainstorming<br>• Multivoting<br>• Cause and effect<br>• Forcefield<br>• Statistical tools* | • Prioritized list of significant root causes |
| Create and choose solutions | • Develop a method for achieving goals | • Brainstorming<br>• Flow chart<br>• Statistical tools* | • Proposed solution<br>• Action plan |
| **Do** — Pilot test | • Test on small scale<br>• Gather data | • Forcefield<br>• Check sheet<br>• Surveys<br>• Statistical tools* | • Measurable goals<br>• Impact of data on pilot |
| **Check** — Measure performance | • Evaluate test results<br>• See if solution worked | • Forcefield<br>• Statistical tools* | • Analysis of data<br>• Recommendations for next step |
| **Act** — Implement solutions | • Fully implement improvement process | • Flow chart<br>• Check sheets<br>• Statistical tools* | • Action plan |
| Track results | • Ensure planned change succeeds<br>• Establish ongoing feedback with customers | • Brainstorming<br>• Flow chart<br>• Surveys<br>• Statistical tools* | • Tracking data<br>• Standardized process<br>• Process for collecting customer feedback |
| Celebrate | • Recognize achievement and success. | | • Celebration<br>• Plan for continuous improvement |

*Statistical tools include Pareto, Run, Control, and Scatter Charts and Histograms.*

Source: Adapted from Denise Bragg, *Quality Management: An Introduction* (Victoria: Service Quality B.C. Secretariat, 1993), p. 33.

Figure 6.3. *The Service Quality Equation*

---

Customer satisfaction = Perceived service – Expectation

---

found that providing excellent service was one of the distinguishing features of these successful companies. A few years later, Karl Albrecht and Ron Zemke, in *Service America!* explained the service quality concepts used by such outstanding private-sector *service* companies as SAS airlines and the Disney Corporation to achieve customer satisfaction.[266] Subsequently, the book *Delivering Quality Service: Balancing Customer Perceptions and Expectations* by Valarie Zeithaml, A. Parasuraman and Leonard Berry finally provided an empirical foundation for understanding what customers of service organizations expect and how they evaluate service excellence.[267] In the mid- to late 1980s, innovative public-sector managers began to apply concepts and insights from these books to public-sector services.[268]

Since the service quality (sometimes called "quality service" or "total quality service") movement emerged from the *service* sector, it is not surprising that its underlying concepts and tools have found wide application in the public sector, which is largely in the service sector itself. Whereas TQM emerged from the manufacturing sector and had its roots in producing higher-quality *products*, SQ focuses on enhancing *service* and customer satisfaction. Since TQM emerged from the factory, its focus is on improving production systems; whereas SQ focuses more on customers, finding out what their expectations are and trying to exceed them. One of the most powerful concepts in the service management literature is the notion that customer satisfaction has a strong dimension of human psychology, which is reflected in the SQ concept that customer satisfaction equals perceived service delivery minus expectation (see Figure 6.3).

Assume, for example, that when you go to renew your driver's license you actually get served in about fifteen minutes. If you expected to wait twenty minutes you will be pleased, but if you expected to wait five minutes you will be displeased with exactly the same service experience. Moreover, you will measure the agency's performance by how long you *think* you were in line, not how long you *were* in line. That is why the Disney Corporation "snakes" its long lines and provides entertainment when lines get long – the wait seems shorter when you are moving and have something to look at. The importance of the equation in Figure 6.3 is that client satisfaction can be improved in two ways: 1) by improving perceived service, and 2) by reducing client expectations of the service. We are familiar with the reverse side of this equation in elections, where politicians over-promise to get elected, raise unrealistic expectations, then face an unhappy electorate when these expectations can't be met.

Several of the important management tools promoted by the service quality literature are as follows:

*Customer surveys*
These have three purposes:

1. to find out what customers want from the service (their expectations) and how important each element of the service is to them;

2. to find out how customers currently rate their satisfaction with the service (perceived current performance); and

3. to determine what elements of the service need to be improved in order to achieve enhanced customer satisfaction levels ("the service gap").

The British Columbia Pavilion Corporation, a public-sector agency that operates the Trade and Convention Centre on Vancouver Harbour, studied service quality with the Disney Corporation, then began surveying its customers. It found that the people who provided food services in the centre believed that a good coffee break was one that included hot, quality coffee on nicely skirted tables with flowers. When the customers were consulted, they said they wanted short lines so they could get two cups of coffee in fifteen minutes and be near a washroom and a telephone. Once the Pavilion Corporation knew what the customers' expectations were, they organized the coffee breaks much more differently and raised the level of customer satisfaction.

*The Service Improvement Matrix*
(sometimes called the "service quality window")
This is a powerful SQ tool that has been utilized by the Ontario and British Columbia governments in their service improvement programs. Table 6.7, which is adapted from the 1998 CCMD publication *Client Satisfaction Surveying: A Manager's Guide*, shows how the matrix can be used to identify those elements of service that clients rate as important and that are not being performed to their satisfaction.[269]

By asking clients (in this case, customers of a government purchasing agency) to identify the importance of each service element, as well as satisfaction levels, the service improvement priorities can be established by managers and progress plotted by re-doing the survey after some

Table 6.7. *The Service Improvement Matrix: B.C. Purchasing Commission Service*

| | Performance | |
| --- | --- | --- |
| *Importance* | *Low* | *High* |
| *High* | Priorities for improvement<br>– products arrive on time<br>– prompt handling of complaints | Service strengths<br>– courteous, helpful staff |
| *Low* | Low priority<br>– visits by customer service reps<br>– electronic billing | Possible redeployment<br>– electronic ordering<br>– electronic billing |

improvements have been put in place. In this example, staff courtesy is ranked high in terms of importance, and customers are relatively satisfied with it. On the other hand, the timeliness of service is not meeting customers' needs, and improving timeliness is the priority for service improvement. Notice that the items in the bottom right-hand column are not important to customers, and therefore the agency is using resources to expand its electronic ordering and billing services that might be better deployed on improving on-time service delivery. By using the service improvement matrix in this way, public managers can also identify those elements of the service that are candidates for service standards.

*Service Standards*

Since the 1990s, the governments of Canada, the United States, and the United Kingdom have all directed government departments to set service standards and communicate them to the public. Service standards are a "performance promise" to customers: "Setting customer-driven service standards and measuring how well the organization is doing are essential activities to providing customer-driven service. This is a continuous process. It means asking customers what service standards are reasonable."[270]

In the private sector, service standards take the form of "pizza delivered in twenty minutes or it's free" or "one-hour dry cleaning." In the public sector, a service standard can relate to such matters as the number of rings before a government telephone is answered; waiting times to cross the border; hours of service for government offices; processing times for passports; and the waiting time at an employment-insurance office. In the example depicted in Table 6.7, customers want service-delivery times improved at the B.C. Purchasing Commission. Management will have to survey their clients to find out what customers' expectations are for a reasonable waiting-time service standard. (Research indicates that a service standard of five minutes would meet or exceed the expectations of ninety per cent of clients of motor-vehicle licensing offices.) Once a service standard is established, it needs to be monitored to see if actual performance complies with the standard set.

Figure 6.4. *Five Dimensions of Service*

| | |
|---|---|
| *Reliability:* | The ability to perform the promised service dependably and accurately |
| *Tangibles:* | The appearance of physical facilities, equipment and personnel |
| *Responsiveness:* | The willingness to help customers and provide prompt service |
| *Assurance:* | The knowledge and courtesy of employees |
| *Empathy:* | The caring and individualized attention provided to customers |

### Training in Customer Service Skills

Many government agencies have taken a leaf out of the private-sector book by training their staff in skills for dealing with the customer. According to the empirical research of Zeithaml, Parasuraman and Berry, there are five dimensions to achieving client satisfaction with a service: reliability; tangibles; responsiveness; assurance; and empathy (Figure 6.4).[271] Notice how this list parallels the findings of the Citizens First research study with respect to the five drivers of service satisfaction. Clearly, responsiveness, assurance and empathy represent the human dimension of the service experience, and staff training in these factors can make a great difference to service and client satisfaction. Many government organizations such as Natural Resources Canada, British Columbia's Ministry of Finance, and the City of Calgary have provided customer-service skills training to staff who deal directly with clients.

### The Establishment of Customer-Friendly Policies and Procedures

A good example of this tool is the British Columbia government's review of the forms used for a seniors' rent-subsidy program and its discovery that the print was too small for many elderly clients to read. The program managers consulted the elderly and the Canadian National Institute for the Blind before producing a revised form with larger print and in a type-colour that was easy for the elderly to see. Likewise, many government departments have rewritten legislation and forms in "plain language" rather than in bureaucratese or legalese. In other cases, procedures have been simplified to make it easier for clients to access government services.

### The Use of Technology

As will be explained in Chapter 10, this is another important SQ tool. Technological initiatives can range from computerized information kiosks in shopping malls to the use of computerized on-line services like Access Montreal and BC Online. In the latter case, lawyers in British Columbia can now receive land-title information on-line in their offices instead of sending someone to the government office to do the title search. The new

Figure 6.5. *Continuous Improvement with Customer and Staff Involvement*

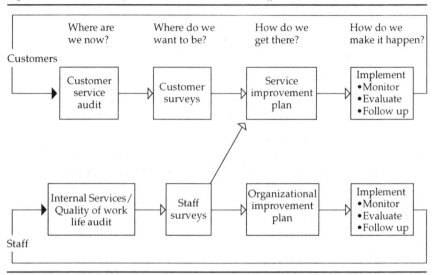

frontier of service quality in both the public and private sectors is the use of the Internet to provide direct service to citizens in their homes, communities and places of business.

*Service Quality Plans*

A Statistics Canada survey of service quality practices in the federal government found that the use of the Service Quality Plan was the most effective tool for service improvement: "The best indicator of the extent of use of these practices in an organizational unit is the presence of a written plan to improve or to maintain the quality of the service provided. ... In addition, the number of practices and the balance among the different types of practices used increased with the number of years this plan had been in place."[272] Typically these service quality plans (which include client surveys, satisfaction measurement, service standards, and the other tools noted above) plan, implement and monitor initiatives to improve service and client satisfaction. These plans sometimes include a parallel track for improving employee satisfaction. This two-track continuous improvement model has been used successfully by several public-sector agencies.[273] The model is outlined in Figure 6.5.

### Alternative Service Delivery: Concepts and Tools

In contrast to TQM and SQ, which originated in the private sector, the

Figure 6.6. *Types of Alternative Service Delivery*

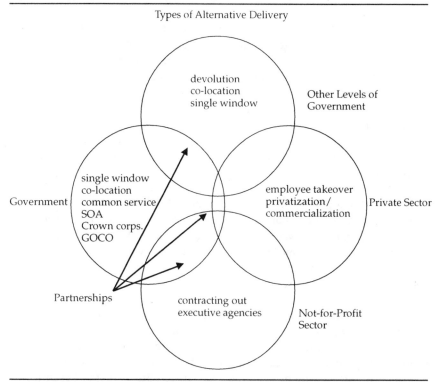

Source: Robin Ford and David Zussman, eds. *Alternative Service Delivery: Sharing Governance in Canada* (Toronto: KPMG and Institute of Public Administration of Canada, 1997), p. 6. Reprinted with permission.

alternative service-delivery approach (ASD) is specific to the public sector. It focuses on changing public-sector delivery structures to improve service to citizens. Alternative service delivery has been defined as "a creative and dynamic process of public sector restructuring that improves the delivery of services to clients by sharing governance functions with individuals, community groups and other government entities."[274]

Figure 6.6 depicts the various types of ASD that governments have implemented. Note the similarity between the content of this figure and that of Figure 5.2 in Chapter 5. While all of the structures described in Chapter 5 serve purposes other than service delivery, each can be considered a method of alternative service delivery. We will not describe these structures again; rather, we will focus on examples of additional ASD mechanisms that are new or that constitute innovative adaptation of more traditional mechanisms.

## The Single-Window Approach

The increasing use of the "single-window" mechanism can be exemplified by the British Columbia government agents system of one-stop delivery[275] and by Service New Brunswick.[276] These are examples of government offices where citizens can obtain a wide range of government services from a single office. The cooperation of many government departments is required to provide an integrated service at one site. Service New Brunswick (SNB) provides sixty government services, from vehicle registration to obtaining an electrical permit. These services can all be provided by the same clerk, who is cross-trained to deliver the services of many departments. In the words of one satisfied customer,

Well the first four months were very frustrating. I once waited over fifteen minutes. The staff were trained but not facile with all the programs and procedures. Frankly I thought that it was going to be a big bust. But the last two years have been spectacular, in that time I have never waited over two minutes. Oh, maybe at tax time it was five minutes. And the service was great. One stop, no matter what I need."[277]

Service New Brunswick was modelled after the sixty British Columbia government agents offices, each of which offer fifty programs on behalf of eighteen client ministries within the provincial government. The B.C. model was actually first developed in the 19th century, when the government agent was the government's representative in small communities and handled everything from marriages to taxes to death certificates. The agents offices gradually expanded across the province and provided an ever-wider range of government services. Twenty-eight of the sixty offices are "Access Centres" that co-locate the offices of several government departments with the agents office. In a 1994 survey, clients of individual agents offices gave their service an eighty-nine-per-cent to ninety-five-per-cent satisfaction rating (combining "very satisfied" and "completely satisfied" ratings), and a majority rated the service higher not only than other government services but higher than the private sector as well.[278]

The one-stop concept can also be extended to *service-delivery partnerships* among governments. The Canada Business Service Centres (CBSCS) are an example of federal and provincial governments (and, in some cases, municipal governments and the private sector) partnering to put all of their services to business under one roof, for the benefit of the client. The centres generally serve small-business clients, who previously had to contact several federal and provincial departments as well as local authorities to get the range of services needed to establish or expand a business. They can obtain everything from business-planning advice to financing to regulatory approvals and tax registration at one office. In 1992–93, the federal government launched pilot CBSCs in Edmonton and Halifax, and, by the end of 1994, they had been established in all ten provinces.

The Vancouver CBSC, for example, is the product of a formal agreement between the federal and B.C. governments. Located in a busy downtown storefront location, the centre is staffed by a combination of federal and provincial employees who work as a team under the direction of a manager drawn from one or the other level of government. Clients from the Vancouver business sector obtain seamless delivery of a range of federal and provincial government services to help them with their business ventures. New businesses can now file with several departments in one stop: "Automated work stations are simplifying registration for entrepreneurs in British Columbia. A job that used to mean filing several federal and provincial applications to several offices can now be done in one visit to a self-serve computer station. ... Through a single user-friendly program, it allows people to register a company as a partnership or sole proprietorship, apply for a Business Number, and register for GST or PST numbers and workers compensation coverage."[279]

Along with the federal and provincial partners, the CBSC in Edmonton includes the City of Edmonton as a partner, and the Montreal CBSC includes the Montreal Chamber of Commerce. In most CBSCs, there are about eighteen participating federal departments and a similar array of provincial departments. One reviewer of this initiative concluded that "[t]here seems little doubt that it has filled a need, that intergovernmental cooperation has played an important role, and that there is considerable potential for further expansion of this network of single window information centres."[280]

As with the CBSCs, so with *self-service kiosks* – another ASD initiative – the use of sophisticated *technology* is essential to service improvement. In 1993, Ontario launched a self-service kiosk project that used technology similar to automated banking machines (although they didn't dispense any money!). Initially, a project of the Ontario Ministry of Transport, the original eight ServiceOntario kiosks dispensed vehicle stickers and allowed clients to conduct record searches, record address changes, and pay fines. Later, the project was expanded to enable clients to order license plates and to access services of the Ministry of Consumer and Commercial Relations. Municipal governments are now able to arrange for fine payments to be made through these automated kiosks – another example of intergovernmental cooperation for service improvement.

Technology has also been important in the efforts of BC Online, a user-pay on-line information service of the B.C. government, to improve service. Established in 1989, BC Online offers a wide range of services to clients that formerly were only available from individual government departments across the counter. The clients of the services include lawyers, banks, real-estate companies and other business people who need to access government databases to conduct their business. For example, lawyers can access information from their office computer terminals to determine who legally owns title to residential or commercial properties they are conveying and what mortgages are registered against them. Lawyers and other registered clients of the system are billed automatically each time they access the service.

Alternative service-delivery innovations like those discussed above are now an integral part of efforts to improve service delivery and are an important complement to the use of TQM and SQ tools in the public sector.

## HOW TO IMPROVE SERVICE:
## CORPORATE AND ORGANIZATIONAL EXAMPLES

Service improvement initiatives can occur at both a government-wide level and at a department/agency level. We will begin at the government-wide level by drawing on experience in the United States and the United Kingdom and, in Canada, at the federal level and in the province of Ontario. We will then examine cases of individual public organizations that are considered leading-edge innovators in service improvement.

### Corporate Initiatives

From 1988 to 1992, the United States government, under President George Bush, used largely the TQM approach to service improvement. The government promoted TQM through the Federal Quality Institute attached to the Office of Personnel Management, with responsibility for educating departments about TQM and helping them mount service improvement programs utilizing TQM tools and techniques. Some departments, such as the Department of Defense, had been working with TQM techniques since the early 1980s and were early advocates of the approach. The Department of Defense and other departments were encouraged to apply for the President's Award for Quality, which was modelled after the Baldridge Award for quality developed for the private sector by the U.S. Department of Commerce. Agencies such as the Internal Revenue Service (mentioned earlier for its work with quality improvement teams) won several of these president's awards for service improvement and innovative approaches to employee involvement and cost reduction.

In 1993, President Clinton issued Executive Order 12862, which required all government departments to undertake client consultation and client surveys to establish service standards for each of their major services. He then established the National Performance Review (NPR), under the direction of Vice-President Al Gore. The NPR was greatly influenced by the Osborne/Gaebler book, *Reinventing Government*. As explained in Chapter 2, this best-selling book argued, among other things, for reducing costs and improving service by contracting-out, injecting competition into government services, focusing on the customer's needs, and holding government agencies accountable for results. Vice-President Gore's report on the NPR, entitled *Common Sense Government*, emphasizes three themes: getting results; putting customers first; and getting our money's worth. He noted that all departments and agencies were in the process of improving their services, and he supported the need for this by a quotation from a manager in the Social Security Administration: "We've always had our telephone lines open from 8.00 a.m. to 5.00 p.m., five days a week. Well, guess what? Everybody in this country works during those hours. It was ludicrous."[281] Gore noted also that the surveys ordered by the president's executive order had opened the eyes of many public managers, including those at Veterans' Affairs: "[The Department of Veterans' Affairs] assumed that vets didn't mind sitting around in waiting rooms at DVA hospitals because it gave them a chance to swap war stories. But when they finally talked to their customers, they found that vets dislike waiting as much as everyone else does. So the DVA set out to reduce waiting times."[282]

Another corporate approach to improving service delivery is provided by the British government, which has combined a Citizen's Charter approach with a restructuring approach involving the creation of executive agencies discussed in the previous chapter. Under the Citizen's Charter (Figure 6.7), proclaimed in 1991 by Prime Minister John Major, all government agencies are required to publish service standards and measure their performance. For example, at the Employment Service, clients are informed that the service standard for answering their calls is a maximum of thirty seconds, and letters are to be answered within five days.[283] The charter also requires that all agencies provide redress mechanisms so that "a swift and effective remedy" can be expected by the client "if things go wrong." Thus, for example, passengers on London's underground trains are guaranteed a refund if trains are delayed by more than fifteen minutes.

At the corporate level in Canada, efforts to improve service to the public have been under way for more than twenty years. As early as 1978, the federal Treasury Board established the task force on Service to the Public,

Figure 6.7. *The Provisions of the U.K. Citizen's Charter*

| Standards |
| --- |
| Setting, monitoring and publication of explicit standards for the services that individual users can reasonably expect. Publication of actual performance against these standards. |

| Information and Openness |
| --- |
| Full, accurate information readily available in plain language about how public services are run, what they cost, how well they perform and who is in charge. |

| Courtesy and Helpfulness |
| --- |
| Courteous and helpful service from public servants who will normally wear name badges. Services available equally to all who are entitled to them and run to suit their convenience. |

| Choice and Consultation |
| --- |
| The public sector should provide choice wherever practicable. There should be regular and systematic consultation with those who use services. Users' views about services, and their priorities for improving them, to be taken into account in final decisions on standards. |

| Putting Things Right |
| --- |
| If things go wrong, an apology, a full explanation and a swift and effective remedy. Well publicized and easy to use complaints procedures with independent review wherever possible. |

| Value for Money |
| --- |
| Efficient and economical delivery of public services within the resources the nation can afford. Independent validation of performance against standards. |

Source: London: Her Majesty's Stationery Office, 1991.

which appeared to have little long-term impact. A more influential project, known as Public Service 2000 (PS 2000), was initiated by Prime Minister Brian Mulroney's government in 1989. The PS 2000 report stated that "Deputy Ministers will establish clear standards of service and will be accountable for the reasonableness of those standards and for the quality of service provided to the public. They will ensure that information about client satisfaction and suggestions for improving service are regularly sought from both clients and employees.[284]

The 1990 report of the deputy ministers' task force on Service to the Public, established as part of PS 2000, recommended a variety of measures to improve service, but only modest progress was made over the next three years in implementing the recommendations. Then, as part of the February 1994 budget, a new government, headed by Prime Minister Jean Chrétien, announced a service improvement initiative that required the government-wide implementation of service standards: "Departments and agencies are to establish service standards through consultation, publish them, and make them available to clients at the points of service. Depart-

Figure 6.8. *Government of Canada: Declaration of Quality Services*

---

# QUALITY Services

**The Government of Canada is committed to delivering to Canadians quality services that:**

- are prompt, dependable and accurate;
- respect dignity, individual rights, privacy and safety;
- comply with the *Official Languages Act*;
- are good value for money, and consolidated for improved access and convenience;
- communicate applicable rules, decisions and regulations;
- are regularly reviewed and measured against published service standards;
- are improved wherever possible, based on client suggestions, concerns and expectations.

President of the Treasurry Board          Canadä

---

Source: Canada, Treasury Board Secretariat, "An Overview of Quality and Affordable Services for Canadians" [web site]. See <http://www.tbs-sct.gc.ca/pubs-pol>

ments and agencies are also required to publish measured performance against their service standards."[285]

By 1995, over two-thirds of departments had implemented service standards in at least some of their program areas.[286] At this point, the federal government expanded its service initiative by developing the Declaration of Quality Services (Figure 6.8) and by announcing an expanded Quality Services Initiative approved by cabinet in the summer of 1995.

Rather than relying exclusively on a service standards approach to service improvement, the Quality Services Initiative focused on improving *client satisfaction*. The strategy was to be phased in over three years and was to be based on four principles: "client involvement; leadership; employee involvement; and innovation."[287] Under the client involvement principle, departments are expected to do three things: consult clients, set and monitor service standards, and measure client satisfaction. By 1996, most progress had been made in the area of client consultation. Service standards were still not implemented in all departments, even though agencies like the Passport Office had installed service standards as early as 1993. By 1995, ninety-six per cent of over-the-counter passport applications were completed within the service standard of five days, and ninety-seven per cent of mailed applications were processed within the standard of ten days. Departments are required to report annually to Treasury Board and Parliament on their progress in improving service to Canadians. In 1998, the federal Treasury Board announced a new phase in federal service improvement, with the introduction of the concept of "citizen-centred service." The government stated that, under the new policy, additional emphasis would now be placed on horizontal (interdepartmental) and vertical (intergovernmental) service delivery in response to Canadians' desire to improved access to public-sector services and more seamless delivery.

The major government-wide service quality initiative mounted by Ontario in 1991 established the Customer Service Task Force under the leadership of Glenna Carr, the deputy minister of consumer and commercial relations. This task force of senior officials also included representation from the Ontario Public Service Employees Union. The task force's landmark study, *Best Value for Tax Dollars: Improving Service Quality in the Ontario Government* is perhaps the most sophisticated study ever done in Canada of public attitudes towards government service delivery.[288] On the basis of the task force's recommendations, each deputy minister was required to prepare a two-year plan for measuring client satisfaction and to involve employees in service improvement initiatives. Notwithstanding the implementation of Customer Service Week, service quality training, and an awards system for service improvement, the service quality initiative largely lost its corporate focus after Glenna Carr left the government in the summer of 1992. The major downsizing of the public service by premiers Bob Rae and Mike Harris also undermined corporate service improvement efforts. However, Ontario renewed its service quality improvement efforts under the Harris government by establishing government-wide service standards and by using electronic service delivery as a major tool for expanding integrated service delivery, including use of computerized service kiosks. Individual Ontario departments continue to be service leaders, and Ontario has become a North American pioneer in service quality innovation.

At the local level, municipalities across the country like Edmonton, Calgary, Oakville, Montreal and Halifax have implemented notable city-wide service quality initiatives. For example, the City of Montreal was the first winner of the IPAC Award for Innovative Management for its Accès Montreal centres, which provide citizens with one-stop shopping for a whole range of city services.

## Initiatives by Individual Public Organizations

By reputation, B.C. Parks is one of the best-managed parks services in North America. It attracts about the same number of visitors each year as Disney World – about twenty million people.[289] Since 1985, B.C. Parks has become one of the most sophisticated public organizations in Canada in managing service improvement. As we saw in Figure 6.5, leading-edge departments and agencies use a continuous improvement approach to service improvement and often parallel this with a continuous improvement approach to employee satisfaction. B.C. Parks has to concern itself, not only with *customers* who come to the parks, but with *citizens* who "own" the parks but who may not be park visitors. As explained earlier and depicted in Figure 6.1., B.C. Parks must balance these contending interests.

B.C. Parks is expert at finding out what customers and citizens want from the parks system. To determine the views of *citizens as a whole*, an annual householder survey has been undertaken for several years. In addition, when planning the future of the parks system, B.C. Parks undertakes extensive consultation with users and citizens. For example, in 1991–92, B.C. Parks managers met face-to-face with 11,000 British Columbians in meetings around the province to discuss long-term plans for the parks system.

To determine the views and satisfaction levels of *park users*, two major feedback instruments are used: comment cards and customer surveys. Comment cards are available at all park sites and offer customers the opportunity to make both their criticisms and kudos known to management on a continuous basis. The agency's annual survey of over 5,000 customers is one of the most sophisticated in the public sector, since it utilizes the service improvement matrix approach presented in Figure 6.7. Using this methodology, which asks customers to assess both the *importance and performance* of various service elements, B.C. Parks discovered that the most important component of service for its campground patrons

Table 6.8. *Service Improvement Matrix Data for B.C. Parks*

| Campground service element | Importance index | Customer satisfaction |
| --- | --- | --- |
| 1. Rest room cleanliness | 3.6 | 68% |
| 2. Campsite cleanliness | 1.4 | 84% |
| 3. Sense of security | 1.3 | 69% |
| 4. Condition of facilities | 1.3 | 76% |
| 5. Recreational things to do | 1.0 | 53% |
| 6. Control of noise | 0.7 | 65% |
| 7. Availability of firewood | 0.4 | 77% |
| 8. Value for fee | 0.3 | 60% |
| 9. Helpfulness of staff | 0.2 | 78% |

was not campsites or trails or things to do but, of all things, clean toilets. Customers rated clean toilets as ten times more important than helpful staff. This led one observer to comment that, for B.C. Parks, TQM did not mean total quality management but rather "toilet quality management"! This result demonstrates the effectiveness of using the importance-performance approach to client surveys, since the service elements that are the most important and that most need improvement in the eyes of customers are often not the ones that staff would select, or even think of.

The results of an early 1990s survey are shown in Table 6.8. For these same individual service elements, customer satisfaction levels ranged from fifty-three per cent ("excellent" and "above average"), for recreational things to do, to eighty-four per cent for cleanliness of campsites. In its comprehensive approach to service improvement, the agency sets satisfaction targets for each service element for each district manager as part of the operational plans for the next year, and actual performance is measured against these targets. This is the heart of the continuous improvement process outlined earlier in Figure 6.5.

Agencies such as B.C. Parks believe that excellent service and client satisfaction cannot be achieved without satisfied employees. Therefore, B.C. Parks also implements a continuous improvement approach to building employee satisfaction and a quality working environment. Some years ago, with staff participation, the agency established ten principles by which it would manage the organization and the people within it. Annual surveys of staff provide information on whether the organization is living up to its principles, and staff identify those principles that need particular attention in the following cycle. For example, in one annual survey, staff identified reduction of red tape, training and staff recognition as the priority areas for improvement in the next year.[290]

Another innovative public organization in the area of service quality is the Quebec Region of Human Resources Development Canada (HRDC),

Table 6.9. *Quebec Region of* HRDC, *Continuous Improvement Plan*

| Objectives | Measurement | Time-Frame |
|---|---|---|
| *Quality of service* | | |
| – overall client satisfaction | – 88% of clients satisfied | – 31 March 1997 |
| – timeliness of payments | – go from 78% to 85% of clients satisfied | – 31 March 1997 |
| – results of the process for the client | – go from 69% to 75% of clients satisfied | – 31 March 1997 |
| *Staff satisfaction* | | |
| – employee empowerment | – 70% of employees satisfied | – 31 March 1997 |
| – employee participation | – go from 65% to 75% employees satisfied | – 31 March 1997 |
| – problem-solving | – 75% of employees satisfied | – 31 March 1997 |
| – recognition | – go from 66% to 75% employees satisfied | – 31 March 1997 |

described in Chapter 2. As noted earlier in this chapter, the presence of a service improvement plan has been the biggest predictor of success in implementing service-quality concepts within federal departments and agencies.[291] The Quebec Region of HRDC developed an outstanding planning framework for improving both staff satisfaction and client satisfaction, based on the continuous improvement model described in Figure 6.5.

Three hallmarks of strong service-improvement plans are client surveys (*where are we now?*); improvement targets (*where do we want to be?*); and strategy (*how do we get there?*). Table 6.9 shows that the HRDC plan has all three elements. Moreover, the region developed a strategy to meet these targets, with time-targets along the way to ensure that milestones existed for each critical action in the plan, such as client surveys, staff surveys, implementation of service standards, training, and employee empowerment initiatives. This plan provides an excellent model for innovative public organizations to follow for continuously improving their levels of service and client satisfaction. The HRDC Quebec and B.C. Parks examples provide insights into innovative practices and lessons learned by innovative public organizations in improving service to the public.

## IMPLICATIONS AND IMPEDIMENTS

### Managerial and Organizational Considerations

The case examples in this chapter confirm the findings of a 1993 study of five public organizations (including B.C. Parks) that have made significant progress in improving service to the public.[292] The study identified ten common features that contributed to the organizations' success:

- leadership committed to service excellence;
- a mission statement committing the organization to satisfying its customers;
- formal measurement of customer expectations and satisfaction levels;
- training for staff in customer service skills and quality improvement tools;
- empowerment of staff to respond to customers' needs;
- setting customer-driven service standards and monitoring performance;
- reviewing policies, forms, procedures, hours of service and office locations for convenience and customer friendliness;
- utilizing technology to improve service;
- recognition and reward systems linked to the service strategy; and
- annual service improvement plans and organizational improvement plans.

This list shows clearly the relationship between the management of service delivery and various other management issues, including leadership, mission and value statements, technology, and employee empowerment and recognition, discussed elsewhere in this book. The list reinforces the need for public managers to consider the systemic relationships between the several components of the post-bureaucratic model.

Among the other learning points that can be drawn from this chapter are the need for public managers to build continuous service improvement approaches into the regular business-planning process; the need to think beyond the use of tools to the obtaining of results based on thorough understanding of client needs; the need to restructure service delivery from a client's point of view (ASD); and the importance of ensuring accountability by line managers for results. Total quality management approaches, because they focus on systems improvement, may lose sight of the clients' needs. Therefore, TQM-based improvement initiatives must be anchored in client surveys to ensure that the organization is working on those systems that are most important to the client. This consideration must be balanced, however, with the fact that the application of quality tools can often reduce delivery costs, which are of particular interest to the *citizens* who are taxed to pay for the services – and to the *politicians* who represent these citizens.

## Political Considerations

Over the past decade, in countries around the world, political leaders of diverse ideological and partisan stripes have supported public-sector reform in general and service improvement in particular. The reasons for their support can be found primarily in the political need to respond to the environmental forces discussed in Chapter 1 – globalization, technological advance, public demand for improved service and lower public expenditure, and the public's negative perception of government officials. However, given the strikingly different pressures on politicians compared to public servants, including the politicians' need for electoral success, it is not surprising that public servants' plans to enhance service delivery are often confounded by political considerations.

There is, for example, an understandable reluctance on the part of a newly elected government to associate itself with the public-sector reform programs of the previous government. British Columbia's New Democratic Party government abolished Service Quality B.C. and the Coordinators Council and set up its own service improvement program. Similarly, the federal Liberal government largely ignored the service improvement program launched by the previous government under the banner of PS 2000 and mounted a similar program of its own. While public servants can do much in the way of service improvement without strong political support, they can do a great deal more with it. It is not only the support of the government as a whole that is important but also the support of individual ministers for initiatives in their particular departments. Public managers are required to ensure that they have enough political support for their initiatives and to anticipate and ameliorate disruptions in service strategies when political – and public service – leaders change.

As noted earlier, there is a very close relationship between the use of alternative service-delivery mechanisms discussed above and the restructuring and re-engineering initiatives discussed in the previous chapter. As a result, much of the examination in that chapter of the accountability implications of reform applies to this chapter also. While politicians have good reason to support service improvement efforts, they have good reason also to be concerned about the political embarrassment of mistakes by innovative, risk-taking public servants. There are more than partisan political implications involved here. There are fundamental constitutional considerations as to the impact of service initiatives on relations between politicians and public servants, especially in the context of the constitutional convention of ministerial responsibility

## Value and Ethical Considerations

The primary emphasis in this chapter has been on the so-called "new" public-service value of service, which has much in common with the traditional values of responsiveness, efficiency and effectiveness. This focus on service, however, can clash with such other traditional values as accountability, equity and integrity. We have already discussed the tension between pursuing efficiency and ensuring accountability. Advocates of new service-delivery approaches must be sensitive to the implications of these approaches for accountability and to the need for innovative ways of ensuring it. For example, governments must find creative approaches to balancing accountability concerns with the benefits of citizen-centred ASD approaches, which involve intergovernmental cooperation in the form of joint administration.

The issue of accommodating various public-service values arises also from the need, discussed early on in this chapter, to balance the service and control dimensions in program and service delivery. The challenge is to strike a balance between client interests and citizen interests by reference to what the public interest requires. In practice, this can be a very difficult task because the determination of the public interest often involves an accommodation of conflicting values. For example, while the pursuit of improved service may call for greater emphasis on the professional value of efficiency, it is important to balance that emphasis with concern for the ethical value of equity in program delivery.

The enhanced focus on service has also given rise to new ethical problems in areas like conflict of interest. The kind of problem that can arise is illustrated by the case study entitled "Public Interest and Private Gain" (see box). Additional examples are provided in the discussion in other chapters of such matters as partnerships and employee empowerment.

---

Public Interest and Private Gain

The following conversation takes place between two senior officials in a department concerned with economic development.

SUZANNE: I guess I was wrong about conflict of interest.

RICK: What do you mean?

SUZANNE: Well, I've always argued that conflict of interest is the easiest ethical issue to manage; you just lay down the rules and enforce them vigorously. I'm beginning to think that there are subtleties and complexities in this area that a lot of us haven't recognized. And the importance of values other than integrity complicates things even further.

RICK: Something must have triggered this revelation.

---

SUZANNE: It's Gerry – and maybe some of the other economic development officers. We've encouraged them to focus on quality service to our clients and we've given them the discretionary authority to enable them to make decisions on individual cases. But I think Gerry in particular is getting too close to what he calls his customers. It's important to provide top-notch information and advice to our clients, but we need above all to keep in mind the public interest.

RICK: I'm not sure that I follow your argument.

SUZANNE: Maybe that's because I'm a little confused myself. My concern first arose when I heard a complaint from a businesswoman who is in competition with a firm that Gerry has been "advising." She thinks that Gerry has forgotten that he is a public servant. She even said: "Why doesn't he join the firm and get it over with?" And she asked why her tax money should be used to pay people who are giving an advantage to her competitors. She actually said: "Why should I provide the stick with which I am going to be beaten?"

RICK: Come to think of it, I heard a similar complaint about Dave Johnson. I'm not sure that Gerry and Dave understand the subtle transformation in their role that has occurred and how this impacts on considerations of equity and impartiality.

SUZANNE: My concern really bubbled over when I heard that Gerry was thinking about leaving the public service for the private sector. I hope that he is not joining one of his clients. I guess what bothers me most is the possibility that some of our people might give preferential treatment to clients in the hope that they might receive a job offer. I know that these issues are not new, but they seem to have been aggravated by the service-quality emphasis. I'm wondering also whether the current conflict of interest guidelines are sufficient to protect the public interest.

Source: Kenneth Kernaghan, "Cases on Public Service Values and Ethics," *Discussion Guide for A Strong Foundation: The Report of the Task Force on Public Service Values and Ethics* (Ottawa: Canadian Centre for Management Development, 1977), pp. 55–6.

## CONCLUSIONS

Notwithstanding the important challenges and impediments to public-sector service improvement, the evidence of the past decade, not only in Canada but in the United States and Britain as well, is that major improvements in service can be achieved within and across departments and governments. However, public managers need to be ever mindful that service improvement must always proceed in a "government-like" manner. Account must be taken of the complexities and special challenges of service delivery in the public sector that arise from the very nature of government's role in society, including the essential requirement to balance the needs of clients with the needs and rights of citizens.

# 7

# Empowering and Being Empowered

Many proponents of empowerment describe it as a major advance in human resource management. A study by the federal Office of the Auditor General on well-performing organizations noted that a common attribute of these organizations was that they empowered their employees. The report concluded that "[w]ell-performing organizations become and remain that way by developing and empowering their people. People are challenged, stretched and encouraged to grow by being given authority, responsibility and autonomy. They are given the power to act, to make decisions and to represent the organization based on their own best judgment."[293]

Some commentators laud the benefits of empowerment but emphasize the essential requirements that must be met for its successful implementation: "To feel empowered, people need formal authority and all the resources (like the budget, equipment, time, and training) necessary to do something with the new authority. They also need timely, accurate information to make good decisions. And they need a personal sense of accountability for the work."[294] Other commentators view empowerment as only the latest in a continuing series of passing fads in management reform. Still others argue that empowerment is especially difficult to implement in *public* organizations, compared to business organizations.

We shall see in this chapter that empowerment has become a central feature of management in many public organizations; we shall see also that its implementation has important political, value and ethical implications. Since conflicting views on the virtues of empowerment are based in part on misunderstanding of its meaning and purposes, it is important to explain the sense in which the term is used in this book.[295]

## MEANINGS AND FRAMEWORKS

### Empowerment Broadly Defined

The term empowerment is used with varying degrees of specificity. At its broadest level, it can be viewed as a growing international phenomenon involving demands by people all over the world to be recognized, consulted and valued. It is also used more narrowly to describe a wide range of efforts to enhance the power and the efficacy of individuals, groups and organizations in society. It has, for example, been used since the 1960s by social activists seeking to enhance the political power and personal efficacy of members of disadvantaged groups (e.g., the poor, visible minorities). In this chapter, empowerment is used in the still more narrow context of organization and management, with particular reference to the public sector.

### Empowerment Within and By Organizations

In the spheres of organization and management, empowerment has both external and internal dimensions. While this chapter focuses on internal empowerment, it is important to explain the nature of its external counterpart. External empowerment involves an organization's efforts to empower citizens and clients by involving them in its decision-making process. In the public sector, this involvement can be pursued through such means as partnership arrangements and various forms of community and client involvement. For example, in 1990, the Ontario Ministry of Natural Resources invited – and accepted – from local residents a strategy that turned a problematic waste-disposal site into a model site and saved public money. A side-effect was the creation by local citizens of a group to organize a recycling program. This external aspect of empowerment is very similar to higher-level forms of citizen participation in which citizens exercise real power rather than being manipulated or being involved in merely token participation. This point is further elaborated in the section of Chapter 9 on consultation.

Empowering individuals *within* organizations, especially those individuals closest to citizens, is likely to lead to a greater measure of external empowerment. Some organizations implement external and internal empowerment at the same time. For example, the Clinical Research and Treatment Institute (CRTI) of the Addiction Research Foundation of Ontario, encouraged by positive experience with participative practices, adopted "a continuous quality improvement approach that emphasizes staff, consumer and community participation and empowerment. Reorganizing into integrated treatment research units has resulted in a number of improvements in clinical services, most generated by front-line staff themselves. ... By suspending the hierarchical paradigm and empowering staff and stakeholders to participate in key change and planning processes, the CRTI is serving its clients and its community more effectively and responsively."[296]

The concept of empowerment, as it applies to managers and employees *inside* organizations, is a synthesis of several theories and practices in organizational behaviour and human resource management. It has been influenced by theories and techniques in such areas as participative management, quality circles, job enrichment, training, organizational design, and leadership, and it is especially closely related to the organizational development (OD) movement. There are obvious links between empowerment and such earlier innovations and emphases as management by objectives (MBO), theory Z management, the search for excellence, and strategic planning.[297]

Even in the specific context of organization and management, empowerment is interpreted in different ways. For many managers and management theorists, it is a relational concept meaning simply the delegation of power to subordinates. For others, empowerment is a more complicated concept that goes beyond delegation to the *enabling* of employees. Indeed, the term *enablement* is often used as a synonym for the overused term empowerment. To enable employees is to bring about conditions that will enhance their belief in their personal efficacy. Empowerment in this sense is "a process of enhancing feelings of self-efficacy among organizational members through the identification of conditions that foster powerlessness and through their removal by both formal organizational practices and informal techniques of providing efficacy information."[298]

## WHY EMPOWERMENT?

### Empowerment or Delegation?

The distinction between the related concepts of delegation and empowerment is captured well in the following statement:

In a command and control management culture, delegation is usually understood to involve handing over tasks to employees who follow guidelines, avoid taking risks and who carry out duties in traditional, sanctioned ways. Empowerment, by contrast, encourages managers, supervisors and employees to try new ways of achieving goals, motivating them to be creative and innovative in improving the service they deliver. Empowerment asks employees to assume responsibility for change and to be accountable for their actions within an environment which accepts a degree of risk-taking and acknowledges intent as well as results.[299]

Empowerment is not concerned with how managers can get employees to act as managers would like them to act; rather, it is concerned with what managers can do to foster individual and collective action by employees to the benefit of the organization, its managers and its employees. The objective is to make the best possible use of employees' knowledge and skills. The award-winning science fleet retroprofiling in the federal Department of Fisheries and Oceans involved a management strategy shift that "was made possible by the philosophy of empowered management. Managers acted as if they were the *owners*, actively examining alternative strategies, interested in the success of their organization, and determined to make existing resources work to their maximum potential. This new approach challenged managers to rethink the requirements for optimal service and program delivery, and to seek creative options for meeting these needs with available means."[300] On the basis of a study of seven business organizations committed to empowerment, Catharine Johnston and Carolyn Farquhar concluded that "[e]mpowerment is not just about giving power; it is about changing the conditions under which employees perform their jobs. It is about unleashing the potential of employees so that they feel and act from a true sense of ownership in the organization and so that their combined efforts meet the expectations of customers."[301]

### Empowerment and Participative Management

These two concepts are so closely related that empowerment is sometimes viewed as a mechanism for achieving participative management, and, on other occasions, participative management is viewed as a mechanism for achieving empowerment. Participative management is defined here as a philosophy requiring "that organizational decision making be made in such a way that *input* and *responsibility* are extended to the lowest level appropriate to the decision being made."[302] Its major components are involvement and empowerment. Involvement is a mechanism for ensuring that the employees' input is heard, and empowerment is a mechanism for conferring responsibility on employees, thereby enabling them to exercise more decision-making authority. A key element in the human resource strategy of B.C. Hydro's award-winning empowerment program was to "unleash the talent" of employees by changing the organization's culture to a more involving and empowering one.

The empowerment component of participative management has received much greater emphasis in recent years. Some organizations still view empowerment as consisting simply of such features as delegation of authority, employee involvement, improved communications, and openness. While these are important features of empowerment, organizations are increasingly supplementing them with commitment to such essential features as teamwork, risk-taking, employee "ownership" of jobs, employee recognition, performance feedback, and training. The Ontario Ministry of Community and Social Services' Southwestern Regional Centre, a home for severely developmentally handicapped persons, concluded that "merely having a 'participative management' oriented residence supervisor is not enough to develop the supportive environment created [here]. ... It is helpful ... but the maximum benefit is to be gained from the intensive type of team building and team development approach."[303]

### Empowerment and Service Quality

Empowerment is closely related also to the total quality management (TQM) movement, which in the public sector is often referred to as the service quality or service management movement. Total quality management has been defined as "involving everyone in an organization in controlling and continuously improving how work is done, in order to meet customer expectations of quality."[304] Among other things, TQM requires recognition of the employees' drive for achievement and their value to the organization, encouragement of risk-taking and tolerance of mistakes, cross-functional teamwork, a horizontal and decentralized organizational structure, and an emphasis on providing high-quality service through continuous improvement. There is considerable overlap in the features commonly attributed to empowerment and to TQM. However, a comparison of the main features of the two concepts suggests that *there can be empowerment without TQM, but there cannot be TQM without empowerment.*

Empowered managers and employees are essential to effective implementation of TQM. For example, the federal government's white paper on public-service renewal, which was based in part on TQM principles, called for a focus on service to clients; it also called for empowerment, which includes the belief that as many decisions as possible should be made by those employees closest to the clients.[305]

In the Ontario Region of Human Resources Development Canada, the motivation for their Quality Enhancement Initiative was to improve service quality. Their analysis showed "that the 'command and control' style of management was a serious impediment to empowered, flexible service delivery by local offices to their clients. Therefore, 'soft quality' Teambuilding was pursued first, so as to create a work environment where open communication, good ideas, innovation and some risk taking could flourish, so that 'hard quality' issues could then be addressed."[306]

## The Process of Empowerment

J.A. Conger and Rabindra Kanungo suggest a useful framework for analysis of empowerment in the form of a five-stage process.[307] The first stage involves an examination of conditions in the organization (e.g., the reward system) that lead to a psychological state of powerlessness among employees. In stage two, managers use various strategies and techniques (e.g., participative management) to eliminate some of the conditions that cause feelings of powerlessness, and, in stage three, managers provide employees with "self-efficacy information" (e.g., verbal persuasion, emotional arousal). This results in stage four in the empowerment of employees, which instils an enhanced belief in their self-efficacy. In the fifth and final stage, the behavioural effects of the empowerment process (e.g., persistence in the face of obstacles) begin to be noticed.

The empowerment process can also be depicted, in more concrete terms, as a multi-stage progression from very little to very substantial implementation of its main components. Near the beginning of the process, the organization has the following characteristics: most managers operate in a command-and-compliance mode, but at least some managers support employee involvement and teamwork; a small percentage of employees participate in team activities; there are only general, non-specific plans to expand employee involvement; the form and the number of employees' suggestions have been relatively stable over the past few years; and improvements to the organization's environment and human resource practices result from employee suggestions and complaints.[308] Subsequent stages of the process show gradual movement towards an empowered organization. Near the end of this empowerment process, a remarkable transformation has taken place; the organization now has these characteristics:

- Management uses innovative, effective approaches to increase employee involvement and teamwork; a high level of trust and respect exists between and among managers and employees.
- Cross-functional team cooperation occurs across the organization to meet customer/client needs more effectively.
- Trends towards team participation and other forms of employee participation include more employee suggestions being made and accepted.
- Employees have a strong feeling of empowerment; there is team owner-

ship of work processes, employees exhibit personal pride in the quality of work, and union and management cooperate to achieve quality improvement.

- Power, rewards, information and knowledge are moved to the lowest feasible levels; employee empowerment leads to a substantial flattening of the organization.
- Improvements resulting from employee participation are clearly evident in systems, processes, products and services.
- A regular formal survey process determines levels of employee satisfaction, follow-up actions are taken to improve human resource practices, and future plans address how to sustain momentum and enthusiasm.[309]

This framework of progressive empowerment provides a rudimentary checklist for assessing the degree to which an organization and its employees have been empowered. The characteristics of the final stage alert reformers to the extent of the change in organizational culture and structures required for full implementation of empowerment. This final stage exhibits also the employees' enhanced feelings of self-efficacy and their improved productivity. Over the past twenty years, various public organizations have begun to move along this continuum, but until recently few of them had approached its middle stages, much less its final stage. While it is clear that employees, as individuals, can be empowered, we explain later in this chapter that an emphasis on empowered *teams* is a common characteristic of empowered organizations.

A critical aspect of the theory of empowerment is that empowerment increases power in the organization by encouraging employees to share and work together:

It is an interactive process based on a synergistic, not a zero-sum, assumption about power; that is, the process of empowerment enlarges the power in the situation as opposed to merely redistributing it. ... Whereas most experts define power as A's ability to control or change B's behaviour, the concept of empowerment implies that A can influence or affect B so that A and B's interaction produces more power or influence for both of them.[310]

This means that in the initial stages of the empowerment process, managers increase employees' control over decisions, structures and resources with a view to expanding gradually the power of both managers and employees. It is argued that if managers vest operational decision-making power in others, they will have more time to think and plan in strategic terms.

The foregoing discussion suggests that the concept of empowerment can usefully be defined as "leadership and management practices and behaviours that empower employees by enabling them to exercise authority, with discretion and good judgment, over their areas of responsibility; placing authority as close as possible to the point of service delivery; removing obstacles and providing the framework and support needed for client-focused responsiveness and innovation."[311]

Among the most frequently cited benefits of empowerment in public organizations are reduced costs and improved service.[312] In 1993, the Township of Pittsburgh, Ontario, introduced a cost-management process, to reduce expenditures. The township adopted a "Just do it" approach that empowered employees "to implement cost savings, revenue enhancements or process improvements where the approval of the senior management or elected officials was not required."[313] After two years of considerable cost-savings, there was little room for further reductions, so the focus of the empowered workforce was shifted towards improving client service.

Another frequently cited benefit of empowerment is enhanced morale. For example, as a result of empowerment initiatives in B.C. Housing, there was "increased willingness to confront problems directly and seek constructive solutions."[314] Still other benefits claimed for empowerment are greater innovation and creativity, improved leadership, increased communication and teamwork, more group problem-solving, development of partnerships, removal of bureaucratic constraints on personal growth and flexibility, better career planning, more harmonious relations between management and unions, and a reduction in absenteeism and staff turnover.

## HOW TO EMPOWER

### Empowerment through Self-Directed Work Teams

As noted earlier, an empowered organization can be characterized not only by active employee participation, but also by *team* participation. Team-building initiatives can range from broad efforts to create a general commitment to teamwork, or working together, by such means as participative management, collegial decision-making and effective internal communications, to organizational restructuring based on the pervasive use of teams, including *empowered teams*.

It is important to set empowered teams in the broader context of teams in general. A team is "a small group of people with complementary skills who are committed to a common purpose, performance goals and approach for which they hold themselves mutually accountable."[315] The early literature on teams emphasized their contribution towards improving the quality of worklife and employee morale. Teams are now also viewed as an effective means of promoting high performance by both individuals and organizations; they are closely linked to such approaches as organizational learning and re-engineering. Teams can help to get things done faster (e.g., by making decisions without seeking authority from superiors); enhance the organization's capacity to solve complex issues; focus resources on serving clients; promote creativity and organizational learning (e.g., by bringing together people with complementary skills and experiences); and facilitate service integration (e.g., single-window service).[316]

The extent to which these objectives can be successfully pursued depends to a large extent on the type of team in question. While teams have been classified in a wide variety of ways, they can be grouped into three broad categories.[317] Problem-solving teams are established on an ad hoc basis to deal with particular problems or exploit particular opportunities. *Cross-functional* teams are widely used in both public and private organizations; they bring together employees performing different functions in the organization so as to promote such purposes as exchanging information, integrating services and providing a more complete picture of the organization as a whole.

The third category is *empowered*, or self-directed, work teams, which differ considerably in the extent to which they are empowered.[318] At one end of an empowerment continuum, teams enjoy only a modest measure of independent decision-making authority. At the other end, teams take responsibility for setting specific objectives within a framework of broad organizational objectives, for operational matters such as scheduling, and for group processes such as conflict management:

Self-Directed Teams are made up of natural work groups and are long term or permanent in nature. The team works on a specific product or service from start to finish with minimal support from others in the organization. This simplifies the production process, reduces errors, puts the right staff in the right place, and improves overall quality. Self-Directed team members become familiar with all the skills necessary to complete the task. The team has the authority to plan, implement and control all work processes, and may assume responsibilities for hiring, team performance reviews, and training needs.[319]

Empowered work teams are much less common in the public than in the private sector, but many public organizations have created such teams. B.C. Hydro's strategy for empowered work teams has been "to create a climate in which teams feel and use the freedom to act to achieve their goals in support of the corporate mission, objectives and climate goals."[320] Employees in empowered work teams are given decision-making authority and resources, and their manager alters his or her role from decision-maker/controller to facilitator/coach. In Industry Canada's Market Intelligence Service, employee empowerment "was not itself a goal, but a practical means to an end. We set out with the challenge of up-grading our out-dated [computer] technology. A participatory environment – which led to greater empowerment, and eventually the self-directed team – emerged as the most practical way to meet that challenge."[321] And, in Alberta's Department of Labour, "the team approach was seen as the best way of freeing people from the constraints of the hierarchy and empowering them to take ownership for customer relations, seeking new ways of doing business and giving them capability for reducing waste. ... [T]he senior management team opted for an organization-wide development of teams."[322]

In the Western Regional Office of Revenue Canada Taxation, regional offices were encouraged

to focus on client needs and leave most if not all the "how to's" to empowered employee teams. Instead of saying when individuals have to be at their jobs, we have an agreement on the essentials: being available for quality service to the client from this hour to that. How it is done – who works how long, when and where – is left to the team. This has had a tremendous effect – in offices that have tried it – on service quality and employee job satisfaction.[323]

And in Industry Canada's Market Intelligence Service:

Starting in June 1993, market research officers have met on a weekly basis to develop their own vision statement, and to define roles, operating procedures, and team performance measures. The performance measures – defined in terms of client satisfaction, operational output and overall team effectiveness – provide the key to effective self-management."[324]

The arguments for empowering teams are similar to those for empowering individuals, but team decision-making has the added benefit of tending to enhance the quality of decisions by utilizing the synergy created by people working together on a common problem. In the Market Intelligence Service, "the stress and frustration" of a major reorganization accompanied by continued resource reductions "has been more than offset by the renewed commitment, determination and enthusiasm gained through the experience of team building. ... Today we are a far more inspired, satisfied, efficient and effective team than ever before."[325]

## Empowerment through Leadership

Among the fundamental practices of exemplary leadership shown in Figure 3.1 (Chapter 3) the practices of "enabling others to act" and "encouraging the heart" are central to successful empowerment. To fulfil these practices, managers must be committed to strengthening employees "by giving power away, providing choice, developing competence, assigning critical tasks and offering visible support" and by recognizing "individual contributions to the success of every project" and "celebrating team accomplishments regularly."[326]

The kind of leadership skills required of public-service managers varies from one organizational level to another, and the skills developed at lower levels serve as building blocks for the skills needed at higher levels. For example, at the supervisor level an essential leadership skill is *motivating*, by seeking to achieve objectives "through the efforts of others," promoting teamwork, recognizing employees' contributions, and responding to their training and development needs. Four levels up the organization, at the level of assistant deputy minister, an essential leadership skill is *creating vision/values*, by instilling "a vision, a set of values and an organizational climate in which goals can be achieved"; being accessible and willing to become personally involved; fostering "innovation and adaptation to change"; and ensuring "that employees are trained and developed to meet the short- and long-term needs of the organization."[327] Thus, the processes of empowering and being empowered are important at all management levels.

A change of leadership (e.g., a new deputy minister, changes in the senior management team) is sometimes the key to bringing about an empowered organization. In B.C. Hydro, the new board chairman, who led that organization's renewal, has been described as "a charismatic, transformational leader" whose management bible was Tom Peters' *Thriving on Chaos*.[328]

## Empowerment through Reward and Recognition

The role of managers as coaches and facilitators includes providing employees with information and feedback that enhances their sense of personal efficacy. While an effective leader can accomplish this through various informal practices, there are many formal means of demonstrating that employees are valued, trusted and respected. Among these means are reward and recognition measures, including the encouragement and acceptance of employee suggestions, awarding bonuses for especially significant contributions, acknowledgement in newsletters of employees' achievements, and awards programs. (The federal Treasury Board Secretariat has developed a guide on recognition and rewards that provides definitions, advice and case examples.[329])

As part of its empowerment initiatives, the British Columbia Housing Management Commission developed an awards program to celebrate special successes. Outstanding performance awards are presented each year in five categories and an overall achievement award is made to the employee who best exemplifies the commission's "Can Do" spirit. In addition, all managers and supervisors are encouraged to recognize both achievement *and effort* with immediate rewards. Employee achievements are profiled in newsletters and on bulletin boards designated for "B.C. Housing Heroes."[330]

Also in British Columbia, in 1995, a government-wide Employee Recognition Program (ERP) replaced an earlier, award-winning Employee Suggestion Program, which is reported to have made net savings of $18.8 million between 1990 and 1995. The ERP "encourages employee initiative and creativity and provides recognition and cash awards for contributions to improvements in service, operations or the work environment; and provides funding of up to 30% of net cost savings to underwrite the improvement process and insulate it from budget cutbacks."[331] The ERP, among other improvements, provides more publicity for employee ideas and is more broadly based and team oriented.

### Empowerment through Training and Learning

Organizations that are genuinely committed to empowering their employees understand that training is an integral part of the empowerment process. For example, B.C. Hydro adopted a systematic training approach that included providing senior managers with a framework for understanding the concept and practice of empowered work teams; providing regional or functional management teams with a shared vision and action plans to develop, lead and support work teams; providing managers of potential work teams with a "prep session" to ensure that they understand the commitment required; and providing leaders and members of potential work teams with a workshop to expose them to the concepts involved in work teams and to enable them to make informed voluntary decisions. All this was followed, as appropriate, by more intensive skills development for the team and for individual team members in understanding and managing change, improving interpersonal communications, and enabling group problem-solving and decision-making and team-based performance management.[332]

An impresssive training program was mounted by the Staff Development Division of the Saskatchewan Public Service Commission. As part of a restructuring occasioned by a reduced workforce, the division created an Organizational Change Unit, with a mission of "empowering employees through learning." The division has helped to foster a corporate culture of empowerment in the public service, in part by providing specialized services in such areas as departmental mission statements and corporate culture and values and enhancing knowledge and skills in such fields as organizational development and change management. The division has been instrumental in the implementation of Coaching for Results – a process designed to enable employees to contribute effectively to their departmental mission and to provide high-quality service to the public and to other public servants. The name of the process reflects the changing role of the manager from director and controller to coach.[333]

The pay-off from training programs is notoriously difficult to measure. In 1989–90, the Ontario Region of the Canada Employment and Immigration Commission spent over $500,000 (sixteen per cent of its annual training budget) on team-building courses that included efforts to incorporate empowerment strategies and activities at each level of the region. A qualitative evaluation of the courses was "uniformly positive" in terms of improved teamwork. And a quantitative evaluation showed significant improvement in managerial attitudes towards teamwork and significant differences between managers who participated in the team-building courses and those who did not. However, continuing training and other team-building initatives were required to maintain the momentum. The most difficult problem was dealing with managers who wouldn't or couldn't adapt to the new environment: "A few may pay only lip service to the new approach and revert to autocratic styles when they return to their offices."[334]

## Empowerment through Structural Change

For many public organizations, a central feature of their empowerment initiatives has been structural change, which has taken the form primarily of the creation of teams, committees or task forces of varying degrees of sophistication and permanence. By mid-1991, B.C. Hydro, a leading public-sector organization in the use of empowered work teams, had about 2000 employees (half of its permanent workforce) functioning voluntarily in about 240 empowered work teams. In 1989–90, the Ontario

Regional Office of the federal Department of Employment and Immigration developed quality-oriented work units based on teamwork principles that crossed organizational boundaries and normal hierarchical structures; it also worked to turn the senior management group into a team.

In some organizations, empowerment initiatives facilitated, or were accompanied by, a flattening – or "de-layering" – of the organization: "Empowerment requires enabling organizational structures." The challenge is to find "an appropriate balance between flat structures that increase the individual's scope for decision-making and hierarchical structures that provide value-added leadership, direction and mentoring." Moreover, empowering organizations "use hierarchical structures in a flexible and adaptive way. They distribute authority so that each layer is both empowered and empowering – so that each brings to bear a progressively broader perspective on the organization."[335]

In 1989, the Finance and Administration Division of the Ontario Ministry of Community and Social Services announced a new organizational structure based on a project management approach under which hierarchical layers were reduced and structural barriers were eliminated. According to the division, this structural change was accompanied by a change in culture and values – "from territory, turf and fear to teamwork, trust and delegated responsibility."[336] In some instances, empowering employees by delegating decision-making power to them enables the organization to flatten the hierarchy by removing some middle managers; we shall see later that this prospect is a major reason for the reluctance of some middle managers to support empowerment initiatives.

## Empowerment through Cooperation with Unions

The desirability of cooperation between management and public-service unions is not an explicit element of the theory of empowerment. Nevertheless, both common sense and experience suggest that union support for empowerment initiatives is likely to facilitate their acceptance among unionized employees. As part of its cultural change process, the Nova Scotia Power Corporation, which has about half of its 2600 employees in unions, invited union leaders to participate in a leadership and values program that had been given to all managers and supervisors. According to management, the union leaders

were eager to participate but very leery, at the beginning at least, of the management propaganda or even brainwashing they were going to be subjected to. ... [They] emerged from the four days fully committed to helping change our corporate culture ... [and] offered to be ambassadors for the change process among their membership.[337]

Similarly, the management of B.C. Hydro and the International Brotherhood of Electrical Workers, which represents almost half of the unionized workforce, signed a statement of principles committing them to work jointly on the implementation of empowered work teams.

## A Case Example of Empowerment

Several of the steps towards effective empowerment discussed in this chapter can be demonstrated by reference to the response of Industry Canada's Industry Sector to the realization that its organizational structure – "branches operating as independent, vertically oriented 'silos' – was no longer a useful working model."[338] The sector adopted a flat, matrix-style organization based on self-directed teams.

The reform process began with the management team's adoption of a set of values (see Chapter 3), which included, among other values, commitment to client service, integrity, respect and trust for others and teamwork. A clear statement of objectives was flexible enough to permit experimentation to break through the traditional command-and-compliance approach. Training was made a priority; staff at all levels were involved in the process through such means as management retreats and branch focus sessions; a proactive communication plan was implemented; an anonymous "suggestion box" was used; and strong support was provided by the department's top public-service leadership. The team approach was introduced in all branches of the sector, but it became clear that this approach "did not suit all the tasks required of the various branches and that various types of teams were needed: self-managed teams, working groups and tasked individuals."[339] While it was realized that a significant culture shift within the sector would take time, short-term progress in quality outputs and new synergies were reported.

## IMPLICATIONS AND IMPEDIMENTS

### Managerial and Organizational Considerations

Several of the challenges involved in implementing empowerment successfully are implicit in the foregoing discussion of its major requirements. Organizations must transfer power and resources to their employees, turn their managers from controllers into coaches, promote teamwork, keep middle managers from backsliding, make structural changes, allocate more resources to training, provide increased recognition and rewards, and resolve the labour relations issues that develop. If organizations merely pay lip-service to these requirements, employee satisfaction and productivity are likely to be reduced rather than enhanced. Empowerment is not

a panacea for an organization's problems; rather, it is a lengthy and difficult process requiring sustained commitment from all levels of the organization and a signficant change in its culture. A fantasy version of an
empowered workforce is one composed of

energetic, dedicated workers who always seize the initiative (but only when
"appropriate"), who enjoy taking risks (but never *risky* ones), who volunteer their
ideas (but only brilliant ones), who solve problems on their own (but make no
mistakes), who aren't afraid to speak their minds (but never ruffle any feathers),
who always give their best to the company (but ask no unpleasant questions about
what the company is giving them back). How nice it would be ... to empower
workers without actually giving them any power.[340]

Much of the resistance to empowering employees comes from managers, especially middle managers. Some managers fear for their jobs, because successful empowerment can lead to a downsizing of the organization
through a flattening of the management ranks. Empowerment can take
place without downsizing, but for some organizations the desire to
downsize has provided an impetus for empowerment in the hope that the
decision-making responsibilities of managers who leave the organization
can be taken up by empowered employees at lower levels of the hierarchy.
In B.C. Hydro, the decision to empower employees *followed* substantial
downsizing of the organization, whereas, in the Oxford Regional Centre of
the Ontario Ministry of Community and Social Services, empowerment
initiatives *accompanied* downsizing in an effort to minimize the adverse
effects for employees.

Managers who have striven to acquire power and authority in the
organization are understandably reluctant to give it up; they may feel
disempowered as a result of their efforts to empower others. Some managers may be incapable of breaking out of the hierarchical mould to provide
the kind of leadership needed to empower employees. The Correctional
Service of Canada discovered during its process of organizational renewal
that some senior managers could not easily abandon the old ways of
doing things: "For all, the change came at a price. For a few, the shift was
just not possible. Consequently, some senior management changes were
made."[341] Managers who are used to playing the role of controller or
supervisor by making decisions and solving problems for their "subordinates" are now expected to play the role of coach by helping their "team
members" solve their own problems. In Revenue Canada, some of the
critics of empowerment "were managers who practice a traditional, controlling management style. Change is perceived as a threat to how they
were trained and are used to operating. One director went so far as to

resign since he felt his management style was at odds with departmental policy and the changes taking place in his local office."[342] And, in Human Resources Development Canada,

> while this is a gross over-generalization, the most significant obstacle has been resistance by middle managers, who have the most to lose (as they see it) by moving from a 'command and control' work environment to one which is participative, empowering and risk-taking. Senior managers know that empowerment is necessary and inevitable, working level staff are ready to work this way, but middle managers (consciously or unconsciously) resist the perceived loss of power which it brings.[343]

To the extent that empowerment has the synergistic effect of enlarging power and influence in an organization, the managers' concern about losing power will be ameliorated. Moreover, in certain organizations and in certain units and positions within organizations, the command-and-control mode must persist because empowerment is not warranted. In certain situations, innovative, risk-taking behaviour by air-traffic controllers or soldiers, for example, could have disastrous results. Clearly, managers require careful training in the skills needed to lead and manage the empowerment process.

Empowered work teams pose particularly difficult challenges for managers,[344] especially if the teams are given control over such supervisory/management tasks as setting work schedules, determining production goals, and handling performance problems.[345] In addition, when work teams operate with considerable autonomy, managers can be intimidated by a loss of control over, and lack of knowledge about, what is going on in the work teams. To empower employees successfully, managers must have a high level of trust – even faith – in employees. Managers must encourage innovation and creativity, and they must tolerate risk-taking and mistakes. Since team members are required to work closely and cooperatively with one another and to choose their own team leaders, managers must ensure that team members receive adequate training in such areas as group decision-making, interpersonal communications and leadership. In addition, compensation systems, which are usually based on individual merit pay, must be made compatible with the team approach to decision-making and operations. Finally, provision must be made for the placement of employees who are unable to cope with the requirements of an empowered organization. In Alberta's Department of Labour, managers "who were opposed to the team-based approach, or could not adapt, were able to negotiate severances from the department. About 15 percent actually left the department."[346]

The scale and complexity of government operations complicate the task of management and organizational reform. Efforts to implement empowerment face a more formidable set of obstacles in public- than in private-sector organizations – and successful empowerment is not easy in business organizations either.[347] The large size and the multipurpose nature of many government departments precludes or greatly complicates successful empowerment of the whole organization. Moreover, empowerment may be a tougher task in a government department than in a Crown corporation of equivalent size that enjoys a larger measure of autonomy in respect of human and financial resource management. Small administrative units usually enjoy more success in implementing participatory management, because face-to-face contacts are more common, relationships are more personal, decision-making responsibility is easier to pinpoint, and coordination is simpler.[348]

There are considerable differences among public organizations in the size of the unit or group that has been empowered. In most cases, an administrative unit within a government department is involved. In some instances, however, the whole department is the focus of empowerment (e.g., Quebec's Ministry of Agriculture, Fisheries and Food). But in the City of Burlington, Ontario, the animal shelter staff of 6.5 full- and part-time employees became a self-directed work team. In other instances, empowerment initiatives cut across departments. For example, the City of Toronto empowered a number of women employees by facilitating their movement into non-traditional occupations within the organization.[349] In the case of such organizations as Crown corporations, the whole organization can be involved (e.g., B.C. Hydro).

Another problem is that empowerment requires a considerable investment in staff training. The Correctional Service of Canada recognized that its belief that people have the potential to change must be backed up "with the tools and support to foster positive change" and that "authority could not be delegated without the appropriate training to allow for the effective exercising of new responsibilities."[350] While training that is related to empowerment is important for employees at all levels of the organization, it is especially important for middle managers; if they do not support and lead the empowerment process, it will not be effectively implemented. Compared to the private sector, governments have traditionally devoted limited resources to training, and in recent years the training budgets of many governments have been trimmed rather than expanded. Nevertheless, several public organizations have signficantly increased training that would help to advance their empowerment initiatives.

## Political Considerations

Critics of empowerment point to its potential conflict with accountability. As explained in Chapter 3, accountability is a centrally important value. The concept of accountability cuts across the political and value dimensions of public administration.

A significant obstacle to empowerment in public organizations is that they are subject to stricter accountability requirements than business organizations, especially through central agency rules that impede or discourage delegation of decision-making power; indeed, these rules tend to move decision-making to higher, rather than lower, levels of the public-service hierarchy. In addition, departmental managers are understandably anxious to avoid the risk of mistakes that result from pushing decision-making power down the hierarchy, especially when legislators, journalists and public interest groups can so quickly turn an apparently administrative issue into a political one. There is tension also between empowering lower-level employees and at the same time meeting the increased need in contemporary governments for better coordination of policies and programs, especially if empowerment is accompanied by the structural fragmentation of government.[351] An offsetting consideration is that if you empower employees to innovate by working with people in other organizations, the consequence is likely to be improved coordination. This is a central feaure of the holistic approach to innovation discussed in Chapter 4.

In most governments, central agencies are now putting relatively greater emphasis on accountability for results than for process and allowing more latitude for departmental empowerment initiatives by removing or simplifying rules and procedures. Moreover, governments are more aware that holding public servants accountable through a variety of formal controls is a necessary but insufficient means of ensuring responsible administrative conduct. Empowerment envisages increased emphasis on psychological or personal responsibility, in the sense of loyalty to, or identification with, organizational and program goals.

But is this emphasis on personal responsibility compatible with the constitutional convention of ministerial responsibility[352] and the related conventions of political neutrality and public-service anonymity? One reason why Canadian governments have made only modest progress in implementing participative forms of management in the past is concern that the bottom–up participative approach to decision-making is incompatible with the responsibility of ministers for the acts of departmental officials. This issue is even more important now because the concept and practice of empowerment go beyond the 1970s and 1980s notions of participatory management. Empowerment involves enabling employees to be innovative and, therefore, to take risks and to make mistakes that might come back to haunt their administrative and political superiors. Managers can easily envisage mistakes by creative, risk-taking employees that could embarrass the minister – or the government as a whole – and thereby injure their own career prospects.

It seems likely that empowerment will result in more administrative errors, but the danger should not be exaggerated. Despite significant empowerment initiatives over the past decade, there have been few reports of administrative errors or ministerial unhappiness resulting from them. While empowerment requires more tolerance of mistakes arising from creativity and innovation, it does not licence incompetence or bad judgement. Public servants will continue to be held accountable for their performance. The cultivation of personal responsibility is intended to reduce the need for accountability to hierarchical superiors, not to supplant it. In the words of one public servant, "Empowerment produces control because employees become more responsible."[353]

Under current applications of the convention of ministerial responsibility, ministers are unlikely to suffer resignation or demotion for the errors of departmental subordinates; they are, however, expected to answer to the legislature for these errors. Hence, ministers – and their senior advisers – have a major interest in ensuring that mistakes are not made or, if they are, that opposition legislators and the public will be more forgiving than they are now. Legislators – and government auditors – will need to view particular instances of maladministration within the larger context of a public service that is able to deliver efficiently a constantly expanding volume of services. The challenge is to change both the political culture and the public-service culture so that the intent, as well as the result, of administrative action will be taken into account.

Jocelyne Bourgon, Canada's former secretary to the cabinet, in her support for public-service innovation, has argued that "there can be no experimentation without *risk*. Ministers and senior officials must accept some of the uncertainty implicit in giving up a degree of control. Not every experiment will be a success. Some honest mistakes will be made. This needs to be understood and accepted. Our commitment should be to learn from these situations."[354] If this view is not shared and practised by public-service leaders across the government – if, for example, the reward system sends a different message – empowerment will be much less successful than it otherwise would be.

Empowerment requires a strengthening of ministerial responsibility in the sense that ministers must be willing to defend publicly those public servants who make mistakes while engaged in reasonable risk-taking. The related conventions of public-service anonymity and political neutrality will also be affected. Empowerment entails closer contacts between front-line public servants, who will have increased decision-making power, and their clients. Anonymity will necessarily decline, even at the senior levels of the public service. In addition, the more active involvement of public servants in partisan politics, if combined with significant delegation of decision-making power to lower levels of the hierarchy, may undermine the reality, and the perception, of a politically neutral public service.

## Value and Ethical Considerations

Empowerment is a means of achieving such "new" public-service values as innovation, service, quality and teamwork, but it must be reconciled with such traditional values as accountability, efficiency, effectiveness, fairness, equity, neutrality and integrity. A federal deputy minister has argued that employees must be empowered "without compromising such values as the wise use of public funds, consistency, and fairness in dealing with the public ... and probity in the conduct of government operations."[355] When the Air Carrier Operations of Transport Canada Aviation decided to empower its inspectors, it realized that it also had to provide "new levels of accountability, quality service to the client, and a workforce that is efficient, effective and motivated, while at the same time minimizing" the risk of loss or injury in aviation regulation.[356]

It is worth re-emphasizing that empowerment is not an invitation to public servants to do as they please. An empowering organization "provides a framework – a zone of comfort and safety – within which empowered individuals or groups can be innovative and, when appropriate, take reasonable risks."[357] This framework includes not only public-service values but also laws, regulations, policies and departmental missions: "[A]s we move to more empowerment to individual public servants and to public service agencies, clarity about authorities, obligations, performance measures and, above all, values becomes increasingly important."[358] Public servants must understand the components of the framework so that they can "answer such questions as: Will this proposal provide service value that is consistent with my organization's values and mission? Could this initiative be justified before a Parliamentary committee? Is this proposal consistent with what Canadians expect of their Public Service?"[359]

The need to impose reasonable limits on empowerment arises in the private sector also. Michele Darling, the cibc's executive vice-president for human resources, has asked: "How far should we go in removing the rules in an empowered organization? In an industry like ours, there are some very firm boundaries. The key lies in defining these boundaries, outside of which one may not tread, while at the same time allowing for tremendous flexibility within that framework. The president of our insurance company uses a term called the 'Empowerment Corral' to define the concept."[360]

Empowerment has significant implications for public-service ethics.[361] We have already mentioned the importance of accountability as an ethical as well as a democratic value. Another central ethical value is integrity. Successful empowerment requires that managers and employees have a high level of mutual trust in one another's integrity, especially if employees, or work teams, receive discretionary authority over financial and human resources. Concern about the ethical behaviour of public servants is also based on their power to affect the well-being of individuals and groups outside government. The delegation and decentralization of decision-making power will, for example, give more public servants opportunities to use their public office for financial – or even partisan – gain. It follows that more attention must be paid to providing employees with ethics guidelines and ethics education.

## CONCLUSIONS

Table 1.1 (Chapter 1) shows that empowerment is an important means by which public organizations can move towards the post-bureaucratic model of organization. Empowerment is not only an integral part of the movement from a rule-centred to a people-centred organization; it is also closely linked to such other characteristics of the post-bureaucratic model as quality service, shared values and participative decision-making, innovation and risk-taking, and accountability for results. Many public organizations have already made considerable progress towards empowerment. While in some instances entire departments have moved in that direction, it is notable that within departments, certain administrative units have been empowered, while other units have continued to operate largely in a command-and-control mode.

# 8

# Consulting and Partnering

"Effective *consultation* is about *partnership*. It implies a shared responsibility and ownership of the process and the outcome."[362] This assertion by a federal task force on service to the public recognizes that consultation and partnership are closely related concepts; certainly the process of partnering necessarily involves some measure of consultation. However, consultation can take place in isolation from partnership, and so-called "real" partnerships go beyond consultation to collaboration and include shared power, risks and benefits. Thus, while the close connections between consulting and partnering are noted in this chapter, these concepts are for the most part discussed separately.

Consulting and partnering are integral components of the move towards the new organizational forms and management approaches outlined in the post-bureaucratic model contained in Chapter 1 and elaborated in subsequent chapters. Chapters 3 and 4 explained that the espoused values and the actual innovations of a large number of public organizations are in tune with a shift towards more consultation and collaboration. And Chapters 6 and 7 showed that this shift is important for providing quality service to clients and for empowering employees.

## MEANINGS

A *consultation* is

an interactive and iterative process that seriously elicits and considers the ideas of citizens and encourages their involvement in decision-making in the tasks of vision-setting, policy development, issues resolution and in the design and delivery of government programs.[363]

While the term "citizen engagement" is now often used to describe this process,[364] the more conventional term consultation is used throughout this book.

*Partnering* is the process by which a partnership is created and maintained. A *partnership* is

a *relationship* that consists of shared and/or compatible objectives and an acknowledged distribution of specific roles and responsibilities among the participants which can be formal or informal, contractual or voluntary, between two or more parties. The implication here is that there is a cooperative investment of resources (time, funding, material) and therefore joint risk-taking, sharing of authority, and benefits for all partners.[365]

Thus, in contrast to consultation, partnership involves the pooling of resources such as money, information and labour to meet complementary or compatible objectives, *and* there is a sharing of decision-making power and of benefits and risks by the partners. We shall see, however, that many relationships routinely described as partnerships involve little in the way of power-sharing and that some mechanisms that are actually consultations are described as partnerships. Indeed, one major category of partnerships described later in this chapter is that of "consultative" partnerships. We turn now to an examination of consultation, followed by a more extensive treatment of partnership.

## CONSULTATION

Consultation, both *by* governments and *within* governments, was a central feature of governance in the late 1960s and early 1970s. The call for public participation, often described as participatory democracy, led to the adoption of a wide range of consultative mechanisms in all spheres of government. The greatly increased emphasis in Canada's political culture on *public participation* in government decision-making spawned a striking array of mechanisms for consultation between governments, on the one hand, and organizations, groups and individuals outside government, on the other. Moreover, technological advances in communications have made both broadly and narrowly targeted consultations much easier (see Chapter 10). We shall see that over time some of these consultative arrangements have evolved into partnerships.

Measures to enhance public participation in general, through such *indirect* means as the democratization of political parties, were complemented by measures to promote citizen participation in particular, through such *direct* means as advisory bodies that gave citizens the opportunity to

participate in government decision-making. Politicians and public servants were expected to seek out actively the views of those interests, especially citizen groups, that were affected by government decisions. It was
argued that the information that government obtained by consulting the
public would, among other things, make government more responsive to
public needs and more effective in fulfilling those needs.

Public participation, especially in the form of citizen involvement, had
an enduring impact on government. By the mid-1980s, government officials, particularly at the local level, were much more likely to seek public
input into government decisions than they were in the late 1960s. Still,
the practice of consultation, which is essential to successful public participation, had not become deeply ingrained in the public-service culture. Among the concerns about participation were that consultation can
be inefficient and ineffective because it is time consuming and decisions
are delayed. As a result, some public servants engaged in "phoney" and
manipulative consultation, rather than in genuine consultation, where
citizens' views were seriously taken into account and feedback was
provided; many members of the public were not fooled by the pretence
of consultation.

In the mid- to late 1980s, two factors led to renewed emphasis on
consultation. The first factor was the greatly increased emphasis in the
political culture on participation and, therefore, on consultation. The second factor was the onset of the service quality movement, which was
explained in Chapter 6. By the early 1990s, service had become a central
value in many public organizations – and consultation is often a precondition to satisfactory service.

Frances Abele et al. attribute the following features to genuine consultation (what they describe as citizen engagement):

1. It involves the participation of citizens as individuals.
2. It may be initiated by government, intermediary institutions or citizens
   themselves.
3. It includes the expression and exchange of views, group and individual
   deliberation, reflection and learning.
4. Sponsors have an obligation to provide adequate information in advance; participants have an obligation to inform themselves adequately.
5. The process is open, inclusive, fair and respectful and, most commonly,
   facilitated.
6. The process is sufficiently long to permit deliberation to a satisfactory
   end; it will rarely comprise a single isolated event.
7. The process is accountable: feedback about decisions and the reasons
   for decisions must be provided to the participants.[366]

## Why Consultation?

The overriding purpose of consultation is to improve the quality of decisions regarding the content and delivery of policies and programs. The discussion in Chapter 1 of forces driving public-service reform suggests some additional purposes: reducing costs, improving service delivery, and facilitating public participation. A survey of federal employees in the Department of Agriculture and the Treasury Board Secretariat identified still other reasons for consultation. The primary reason given was information-sharing, followed by developing solutions to a problem, obtaining stakeholders' views, building consensus, and creating dialogue.[367]

Consultation benefits both government officials and those with whom they consult. The benefits accruing to government include information and insights regarding the implications of actual and proposed decisions, the extent of support for these decisions, and better compliance with them. The benefits accruing to stakeholders include improvements in the quality of decisions affecting them and information on the government's future plans.

## Consultation with Whom?

The range of possible participants in the consultation process is as broad as that for the public policy process as a whole. Popular discussions of consultation tend to focus on government's interaction with individual citizens and groups of citizens, but consultation is an important element of relations between departments, between governments, and between governments, on the one hand, and a wide range of individuals, groups and organizations outside government, on the other. Environment Canada notes that the fact that it "shares its responsibility to protect the environment ... with other levels of government, business, interest groups and individual Canadians ... warrants their meaningful participation in the process of policy and program development and decision-making."[368]

While the number of participants varies from one policy field to another (e.g., from environmental policy to national security policy), decision-makers in virtually every policy field can benefit to some extent from consulting their stakeholders. Some consultation exercises are conducted at a very broad, or macro, level that involves large numbers of individual citizens and groups across the country (e.g., the Citizens' Forum on Canada's Future);[369] others are more narrowly focused but involve a large number of stakeholders (e.g., the Federal Pesticide Registration Review);[370] and still others involve a smaller number of stakeholders on a relatively narrow issue (e.g., numerous consultations on local environmental issues). The number and nature of stakeholders to be consulted is an important influence on the consultative mechanism that is adopted.

## How to Consult

By the end of the 1970s, a variety of new consultative mechanisms had been devised to supplement such traditional mechanisms as advisory bodies and public hearings. Subsequent advances in information and communications technology increased not only the rapidity and inclusiveness of the consultation process but also the innovative nature of the techniques employed. For example, the Citizen's Forum on Canada's Future used five major tools of consultation: an "Idea Line" for individual inputs; self-guided "group discussions" led by moderators and recorded by rapporteurs, with the content of the discussions entered into a database; unsolicited letters and briefs; a "Students' Forum" to seek ideas from elementary and secondary school students; and electronic town-hall meetings.[371]

Another notable example of an innovative approach to consultation is "SCAN NORTH," which was established in 1991 to assist the Ontario Ministry of Northern Development and Mines in its consultations with Northern Ontario residents on matters that affect them directly. The ministry develops a talent bank of representatives from such areas as business, labour, education and community development on whom the minister can call when advice is needed on particular issues. By 1992, six task teams had reported on such matters as value-added in the forest industry, recycling and waste management, and native economic development and the private sector.

The term "consultation" is interpreted in a variety of ways, "ranging from simple external communication with known clients ... to open comprehensive processes in which the public and private sector are partners working toward a consensus. It also includes a variety of methods, ranging from an informal chat to a royal commission."[372] Among the *formal* consultative mechanisms now available to governments are the following:

- advisory boards and councils
- committees and roundtables
- conferences and seminars
- expert panel hearings
- focus groups
- interviews
- networking
- open houses
- public hearings
- questionnaires
- requests for briefs
- royal commissions / task forces
- surveys
- toll-free telephone lines
- town-hall meetings
- workshops

Figure 8.1. *Scan North*

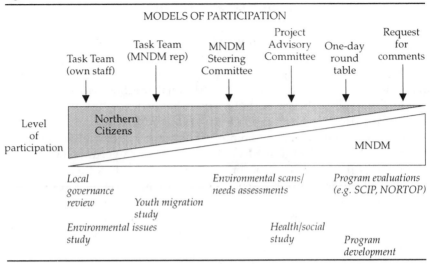

MODELS OF PARTICIPATION

Source: Ontario, Minisry of Northern Development and Mines, Policy and Program Development Branch, Strategic Consultation and Action Now (SCAN) NORTH. Submission to ipac Award for Innovative Management competition, 1992.

Such broad consultative mechanisms as advisory bodies, committees, roundtables, royal commissions and task forces often serve important purposes other than consultation, and, as shown above for the Citizens' Forum on Canada's Future (a royal commission), they often employ several other, more narrow mechanisms such as written briefs and town-hall meetings as part of their consultation process. Figure 8.1 illustrates six models utilized by SCAN NORTH; the model used depends on the desired level of citizen participation and ministry control.

The mechanism selected for a particular consultation will depend on such factors as the scope and nature of the issue to be discussed, the time available before a decision must be made, the number of people or groups to be consulted, and the kind of expertise and experience required.[373] For example, an expert panel is normally appointed for a period of time and is composed of persons with expertise on the issue under consideration (e.g., environmental protection), whereas a town-hall meeting is often a one-time event at which any member of the public with an interest in the issue can participate. SCAN NORTH specifically identifies such criteria as the sensitivity of the issue (degree of confidentiality required), degree of objectivity required, level of profile desired, and complexity of the issue.

Some of the mechanisms listed above are more in tune than others with the definition of consultation provided at the beginning of this chapter, where emphasis was put on the participants' genuine involvement in the decision-making process. Advisory bodies, for example, are more conducive to such involvement than are town-hall meetings or toll-free telephone lines.

While innovative approaches to consultation can bring substantial benefits, these approaches must be based on knowledge of the benefits and limitations of consultation and of the skills needed to plan and manage one. Some public organizations, on the basis of extensive and sometimes painful experience with consultation, have documented the lessons they learned and have developed principles for the assistance of others. The major lesson is that consultation can be a complicated process that should not be undertaken without careful consideration of the purposes to be served, the stakeholders to be consulted, the most appropriate consultative mechanisms to be employed, and the likely obstacles to success. Public organizations that adopt an unsophisticated or manipulative approach to consultation can badly damage their credibility with their stakeholders.

Appendix C provides a checklist of principles for public servants who wish to engage in consultation. This checklist is not a "how-to" manual; rather, it sets out the major general considerations to be kept in mind when planning and managing a consultation exercise. To strengthen both the ethic and the "how-to" of consultation, the Service to the Public Task Force mentioned earlier recommended that training programs be provided to develop skills in such areas as negotiations, communications and change management.[374] (A detailed road map for "what to do when" in the consultative process is provided in *Public Consultation Guide* by Peter Sterne and Sandra Zagon.[375])

### Impediments to Successful Consultation

The task force reported that the public service did not have a strong consultative culture; rather, public servants consulted "in the context of a culture which encourages a low-profile, risk-averse posture rather than a visible, open and accommodating stance vis-à-vis the public."[376] A weak consultative culture is clearly out of line with the post-bureaucratic model of public organization that was explained in Chapter 1. The client-centred, people-centred and results-oriented features of this model tend to promote consultation. Conversely, several features of the traditional bureaucratic model, which is organization-centred, rule-centred and process-oriented, tend to impede successful consultation: "Consultations with stakeholders are essential for transformation from a rules-oriented, control-dominated organization to a service-driven, quality-seeking organization."[377] Similarly, consultation is more compatible with some of the "new" public-service values, notably service, teamwork, empowerment and openness, than with some of the traditional ones, notably efficiency.

Many public organizations underestimate "the tensions between bureaucratic and consultative practice, as well as the extent of organizational changes required for meaningful consultation."[378] This was demonstrated by the efforts of the Correctional Service of Canada (csc) to increase public involvement in its activities. Initially, the csc tended to interpret public involvement as the management of information dissemination rather than as participative decision-making. The csc learned that consultation cannot be an add-on but must be integrated into its central decision-making structures and processes. The learning point for all public organizations is that "[a]n organization [that is] only reliant on bureaucratic practice will be unable to meet the challenge to be more consultative."[379]

Several roadblocks to effective consultation are implicit in the principles contained in Appendix C; a sure-fire route to unsuccessful consultation is to disregard the advice contained in these principles. The survey of employees in Agriculture Canada and the Treasury Board Secretariat noted earlier identified lack of time as the most important barrier to consultation; other significant barriers were lack of financial resources, lack of human resources, lack of authority/empowerment, lack of technological resources, and lack of skills/training.[380] We shall see in the next section that similar barriers exist on the road to partnerships.

## PARTNERSHIP

During the 1990s, partnerships became one of the most popular forms of public-sector innovation (see Chapter 4). This can be easily demonstrated by reference to their proliferation at all levels of government and across national borders and to the development of partnership networks within and between governmental and non-governmental organizations. Partnerships are not a new activity for public organizations. But the increased use of partnerships during the past decade and their innovative character are unprecedented. Whereas partnerships used to be adopted occasionally to deal with specific problems, they are now widely viewed as an effective alternative mechanism for program delivery and, to a lesser extent, policy development.

In 1992, more than 100 public organizations competed for the innovative management award of the Institute of Public Administration of Canada (IPAC) on the theme of partnership management; the submissions came from all orders of government and were of remarkable variety and creativity.[381] In the other years of the IPAC competition, when the themes have included service to the public, empowerment, doing better with less, re-shaping government, and managing diversity, a considerable number of submissions have also focused on partnerships. This is not surprising because partnerships provide a means of improving service, empowering stakeholders, reducing costs, and managing diversity – and they have certainly re-shaped government by providing an alternative mechanism for policy development and, especially, for program delivery.

But are partnerships just another passing fancy in the guise of a cure-all for economic, social and other ills facing governments? If partnerships served only to help public organizations reduce expenditures, it would be tempting to answer yes. However, as explained below, partnerships serve an impressive range of other purposes, not only for public organizations but for a broad range of non-governmental ones as well.[382] They are likely to be a permanent feature on the landscape of public organizations.

## Meaning and Typology of Partnerships

Near the beginning of this chapter, partnership was defined so as to distinguish it from consultation and devolution. An additional distinction should be made between *external* partnerships (between governments and partners outside government) and *internal* partnerships (between organizations within a single government). The basis for this distinction is the argument that, strictly speaking, a partnership must be between two or more *separate legal entities* (for example, between a government and a business firm). Since the various parts of government departments and the departments themselves are all part of a *single legal entity*, namely the Crown, it is argued that their collaborative interaction should be described as *networking* rather than as partnership. In practice, the term internal partnerships is more widely used than that of networking.

As will be explained later, there are important legal implications to the use of the partnership mechanism – and even of the term partnership. This term is used throughout this book, but in full recognition of the implications of using this term rather than such "safer" terms as strategic alliances and joint ventures.

Partnerships vary considerably in the extent to which decision-making power is shared. There are four major types of partnership that can be distinguished largely by the degree of power, in the form of control or influence, exercised by the partners.[383]

*Collaborative partnerships*, often referred to as real or power-sharing partnerships, are those in which each partner exercises power in the decision-making process. Partnerships of this type go beyond consultation to collaboration, that is, they involve the pooling of resources such as money, information and labour to meet shared or compatible objectives. Each partner gives up some autonomy. Ideally, decisions are made by building a consensus. Often, the prime impetus for consensus is that the partners face a problem that they cannot solve on their own; they are, therefore, mutually dependent. The purest variation of this type is a partnership in which the partners bring roughly equal resources to the decision-making table.

In the more typical collaborative partnership, a public organization surrenders some power to groups or organizations outside government. The public organization can either deliberately refrain from exercising control, thereby relying on influence, or it can delegate a measure of control to one or more partners. The first approach can be demonstrated by the British Columbia Financial Institutions Commission, which, in a partnership with the private sector, "has not used 'regulatory power' to obtain results, but rather active negotiation and appropriate compromise. It is important that all parties be vested with equal power and none be allowed to dominate others."[384] The second approach was adopted by Employment and Immigration Canada, which, in partnership with the country's six largest aboriginal organizations, established *co-managed* aboriginal/EIC boards at the local, regional and national levels to develop a trained aboriginal labour force.[385] Similarly, the Health Services Division of the B.C. Ministry of Social Services gave control over admission to a program for severely disabled children to a committee made up of parents, professionals and community representatives.[386]

Public organizations are often perceived as, or actually play the role of, "senior" partners because they are usually the source of any funding that may be required. The balance of power will be more equal in circumstances in which little or no funding is needed or in which the other partners can contribute money or equivalent resources. If public organizations take a dominant position at the decision-making table, little empowerment of the other participants will ensue and the partnership will be less successful. The Canadian Wildlife Service of Environment Canada attributes the success of its North American Waterfowl Management Plan in part to the realization that "individuals, organizations and governments must relinquish their 'control mentality' when trying to manage resources and they must form partnerships that recognize the importance and necessity of each Partner's role in the successful implementation of common goals."[387]

*Operational partnerships* are characterized by a sharing of work rather than of decision-making power. The emphasis is on working together at the operational level to achieve the same, or compatible, goals. Some partnerships of this type have a strong element of collaboration in that the partners share resources. For example, Ontario's Ministry of Natural Resources has made legal agreements with private-sector organizations to share the work and expense involved in conducting scientifically sound surveys of fish populations. And the Southwestern Regional Centre of the Ontario Ministry of Community and Social Services entered into partnership with school boards, teachers and students to share the costs and work involved in a cooperative program to encourage careers in the field of human services while promoting understanding and acceptance of handicapped people.[388]

In some operational partnerships, power, in the sense of control, is retained by one partner, almost invariably by the public organization involved, especially if it is providing the bulk of the resources. While this arrangement is less likely than a collaborative one to empower the participants, it can have other beneficial effects, such as more efficient or more responsive operations. Moreover, all partners can exercise influence over one another in a variety of informal ways.

Many federal–provincial partnerships are of the operational variety. At the heart of a large-scale, multipartner plan to clean up the St. Lawrence River are Environment Canada and two Quebec government departments. The federal and Quebec departments emphasized "harmonization of action rather than joint management" of their respective jurisdictions, and "the joint enforcement of acts and regulations established by both levels of government maximized the Plan's chances of success."[389]

It is notable that many collaborative and operational partnerships, especially intergovernmental ones like the St. Lawrence project, are characterized by a substantial measure of *coordination*. This is a process "in which two or more parties take one another into account for the purpose of bringing their decisions and/or activities into harmonious or reciprocal relation."[390] The Ontario Addiction Research Foundation achieved an impressive feat of coordination by establishing a registry to coordinate better the province's substance abuse treatment services. The registry's database, which is updated daily and includes more than 260 addiction treatment agencies, provides immediate information on available treatment beds.[391]

*Contributory partnerships* are those in which an organization, either public or private, agrees to provide sponsorship or support, usually in the form of funding, for an activity in which it will have little or no operational involvement. These are not generally considered true partnerships because they do not require active involvement in the decision-making process of all the players; a financial contribution alone is not considered

189

sufficient to make the contributor a real partner. There can be an element of collaboration in contributory partnerships in that the sponsoring organization can either propose or agree to the objectives of the partnership but play no decision-making role beyond that point. For example, Environment Canada, through its Environmental Partners Fund, contributed up to half of the cost of local, relatively small projects if private-sector organizations or local government authorities contributed the rest.

In so far as a sponsoring organization's contribution is essential to carrying out the activity, it retains ultimate control. In practice, however, the success of the partnership depends primarily on the performance of the partners receiving the support. A contributory partnership can empower persons outside the sponsoring organization by enabling them to carry out an activity and expressing faith in their ability to do so successfully.

*Consultative partnerships* are those in which a public organization solicits advice from individuals, groups and organizations outside government. As noted earlier, they have much in common with those forms of citizen participation that do little to empower the participants. Partnerships of this type are often distinguished from so-called true partnerships; they are certainly a sharp contrast to the power-sharing arrangements of collaborative partnerships. They usually take the form of advisory committees or councils whose main task is to advise government in relation to a particular policy field or policy issue. Environment Canada describes this type of partnership as a consultation. In its view, as noted earlier, a genuine consultation is "an interactive and iterative process that seriously elicits and considers the ideas of citizens and encourages their involvement in decision-making in the tasks of vision setting, policy development, issues resolution and in the design and delivery of government programs."[392]

Consultative partnerships serve useful purposes in the public policy process by providing government with information, ideas and insights for enhancing service quality. While control is retained by government, which ultimately decides the extent to which it will act upon the advice received, the other partners can often exercise considerable influence on government decisions. The degree of this influence depends on such factors as whether the partnership is formalized; whether its recommendations are made public; whether the policy issue is of broad public interest; and whether the non-governmental partners have credibility, both with the government and the public.

Consultative partnerships can gradually evolve towards collaborative relationships. For example, the Canadian Parks Service of Environment Canada consulted widely on a program to make accessible to persons with disabilities all of the 118 parks, sites and canals in its system. These consultations led to formal cooperative agreements with three national agencies representing disabled persons. Then, agencies representing these persons, joined by those representing seniors, "visited parks and sites with planners, met with parks staff and commented on (*and in a way gave their approval to*) draft plans."[393] These agencies now participate in such activities as staff training exercises, advising on the implementation of the access plans, and helping to market the parks and sites and their accessible programs and services. The initiative taken by the public servants involved led an official of the Canadian Paraplegic Association to say, "It's refreshing to be approached by a government official – usually we have to force ourselves on them."[394]

These four categories are not watertight compartments. Some partnerships evolve from one category to another (usually in the direction of increased collaboration), and some have elements of more than one category (e.g., a collaborative arrangement involving a few partners complemented by a consultative arrangement involving several others). Another possible category is "phoney" partnerships, that is, partnerships established, usually by a public organization, for the purpose of co-opting or otherwise manipulating various stakeholders; the likely result is disempowerment.

Partnerships vary significantly in the extent to which they are formalized by law (e.g., a legal agreement rather than a memorandum of understanding), by organizational structures (e.g., committees rather than informal interaction), and by procedures (e.g., regularly scheduled rather than ad hoc meetings). Formal arrangements tend to signal commitment and specify accountability. They also help to counter the inherent fragility of partnerships. Even partnerships based on strong mutual dependency require careful and continuous nurturing. Often, this task is performed by a "champion" from among the stakeholders – usually the same person who initiated the partnership. However, partnerships that depend largely on one individual for their success are especially fragile; formalization serves to keep the partnership alive when the champion moves on.

## Why Partnerships?

Partnerships serve several objectives. There is, however, considerable variety in the scope of these objectives. The Canadian Labour Force Development Board, a partnership involving government, business and labour, was created to "play a lead role in developing a commitment to training excellence in Canada" – a very broad objective.[395] In contrast, a partnership between the Newfoundland and Labrador Housing Corporation and community agencies was created to provide first-priority housing for victims of family violence.[396] Partnerships with relatively limited objectives are likely to require fewer partners and fewer resources; their results are likely to be more immediate, more visible, and more easily measurable; and they are more likely to be shorter-lived. Thus, they are easier to create and manage than are broadly focused partnerships seeking solutions to such large problems as unemployment and poverty and requiring several partners, extensive resources, and long-term commitment.

Chapter 1 described the major forces driving public-service reform, namely, globalization, technological advance, financial constraint, demands for quality service, a participative political culture, and changing demographics. We shall see below that these forces go a long way towards explaining the unprecedented emphasis on creating partnerships.

### Promoting Economic Productivity

Public-sector innovation can enhance Canada's competitiveness by such means as enhancing public-sector productivity, increasing service quality and lowering costs of production.[397] Innovative partnerships can help to achieve these objectives and thereby foster improved competitiveness.

To cope with the challenges of competing in the global marketplace, government, business and not-for-profit organizations have created a wide range of partnership arrangements for their mutual benefit. Consider, for example, the Quebec government's partnership for the purpose of establishing an "economic development strategy based on synergy, added-value, mobilization and improved competitiveness of companies."[398] Within this broad context, one partnership involved government collaboration with 138 business organizations and research centres to share the cost of producing a directory as a "tool for international promotion to develop technological alliances ... in this era of market globalization."[399]

### Empowering Clients, Stakeholders and the Disadvantaged

Partnership is closely related to empowerment – the process of enhancing feelings of personal efficacy by removing obstacles that create a sense of powerlessness. Governments can use partnerships to foster feelings of self-efficacy among their partners by permitting them to exercise genuine decision-making power: "The trust, sense of ownership and professional commitment that can be developed through partnership management can assist the partners in problem solving ... and have long-term benefits for the participants in their on-going relationships."[400]

Historically disadvantaged persons, such as the disabled and aboriginals, can be empowered through the use of partnerships. For example, the Registration Division in the Ontario Ministry of Consumer and Commercial Relations formed a partnership with a non-profit organization (Goodwill Industries) and a business firm (Andersen Consulting) to convert ten million government records from paper to electronic image.[401] To do the conversion work, the ministry hired eighty-six people who had difficulty getting a job because of cultural obstacles, disabilities, or a lack of Canadian work experience. And Environment Canada formed a partnership with technology companies and disabled persons organizations to establish the Adaptive Computer Technology Centre to improve job prospects in government for persons with mobility, sensory or visual disabilities and to enhance their productivity on the job.[402]

Governments have established a considerable number of partnerships with aboriginal organizations. For example, the Canadian Parks Service of Environment Canada formed several co-managed regimes with various aboriginal groups for the purpose of preserving the land and the cultural heritage of aboriginal peoples. And the Saskatchewan Department of Education worked with eleven partners to enhance the formal education and career prospects of northern residents, most of whom are aboriginals.[403]

*Adding Value*

All partners can receive "added value" from a partnership, because the pooling of resources will have a synergistic effect in that the combined impact will be greater than the sum of the efforts of each partner acting alone. Sharing power, work, support and information can stimulate creative problem-solving and permit a productive blending of resources (money, expertise, etc.) that otherwise would not be possible. Partnerships can also bring together stakeholders who, acting independently, might pursue conflicting goals or waste resources by duplicating the efforts of others.

The added value from partnerships can not only enhance the product or service resulting from the partnership; it can also enhance the partners themselves. "For example, in a partnership between a state-of-the-art software design company and a department, each party can reap benefits (in addition to the quality of the software developed) which *enhance* it (access to leading-edge expertise for the department, penetration of a large market for the company) without any increase in expenditures or use of additional internal resources."[404]

*Doing More or Better with Less*

The need to reduce the taxpayers' burden in a time of *financial constraint* while meeting their demands for *more and better service* is the dominant rationale for governments' use of partnerships. The benefit most often cited by the partnerships we studied was maintaining or expanding the current level of service with either the same or diminished resources. Partnerships can help to maintain service levels by preserving jobs; costs are cut by increasing efficiency rather than by reducing staff. The Registration Division of Ontario's Ministry of Consumer and Commercial Relations claims to have saved Ontario over $700,000 in social benefits by hiring disadvantaged persons as part of a partnership with Goodwill Industries. The Ontario Addiction Research Foundation, by establishing a registry to provide up-to-date information on available places for treating substance abuse, helped to reduce the number of applications for out-of-country treatment to less than ten per month from over 300 per month. And the Education Resources Unit of the Office for Seniors' Issues in the Ontario Ministry of Citizenship established partnerships with a variety of partners outside government so that its existing staff could respond to the increased needs of a rapidly expanding senior population.[405]

### Doing Good Rather than Doing Nothing

A related purpose of partnerships is to enable public organizations to carry out activities that otherwise would not be performed at all. Continuing fiscal pressures will oblige governments to conduct certain activities through partnerships or abandon the activities altogether. The British Columbia cabinet allocated $15 million to assist parents to keep severely disabled children at home, but all of this money had to go to the parents; no provision was made for the administrative costs of implementing the program. The Ministry of Health met this challenge successfully by creating a partnership that gave responsibility for program admission to parents, professionals and community representatives.[406]

### Avoiding Red Tape

Public–private partnerships enable private-sector organizations to carry out certain activities that, if performed by government, would be burdened by unavoidable rules, regulations, delays and other constraints. This is one of the reasons why Environment Canada approved the establishment of the Wastewater Technology Centre, a government-owned, contractor-operated facility. This partnership arrangement helped to avoid restrictive government regulations in such areas as conflict of interest that inhibited effective commercialization of technological innovations.[407]

### Coping with Demographic Change

Various demographic changes have stimulated increased use of partnerships. For example, one response to health-care concerns arising from Canada's aging population has been the creation of a large number of partnerships involving departments and agencies in the health-care field. Moreover, public–private partnerships involving the sharing of human resources may help to alleviate the anticipated shortage of skilled workers resulting from the aging workforce. And partnerships can help governments cope with the needs arising from the increasingly multicultural makeup of Canadian society, which leads, for example, to the concentration of certain ethnic groups in various urban areas. The City of Scarborough worked out a partnership with the Chinese community and a private-sector organization to develop the largest Chinese cultural centre in North America.[408]

## Utilizing Technology

There is a symbiotic relationship between partnerships and technology. Some partnerships enable public organizations to make use of sophisticated information and communications technology, and the availability of this technology makes other partnerships possible.

Consider the federal government's future-oriented plan for improving government services through the use of technology. The implementation of this "vision of affordable, accessible and responsive federal government services ... will require an effective and sustained partnership" not only among staff within departments but also with other departments, other levels of government and private-sector organizations: "Partnerships must be pursued and promoted aggressively to leverage common requirements, to take advantage of specific skills, to spread risks, and to share experience, innovation and investment."[409]

Then consider the extent to which the availability of technology in this information age facilitates partnerships to deal with policy and program issues that cross departmental boundaries and national borders. A notable example of a successful marriage of partnership and technology is the federal Department of Government Services' Open Bidding Service (OBS). This service "provides open access to $4 billion in federal procurement to all Canadians through the application of information technologies and private sector partnership."[410] Additional examples of skilful use of technology in partnering are provided in Chapter 11.

The remarkable capabilities of information technology suggest the possibility of looking beyond partnerships as we currently conceptualize them to consider the creation in the public sector of "virtual corporations." The concept of the virtual corporation (or the virtual *organization*) had its origins in the private sector[411] where it is used to refer to "a network of independent companies, which can include suppliers, customers and even competitors who can band together quickly to exploit brief windows of opportunity characteristic of fast-changing global markets. ... The alliance usually dissolves when the opportunity is exploited."[412] These arrangements give only the illusion of having an organizational structure. Robert Reich refers to such arrangements as enterprise webs.[413]

Figure 8.2. *Partnerships Between a Government Department and Other Organizations*

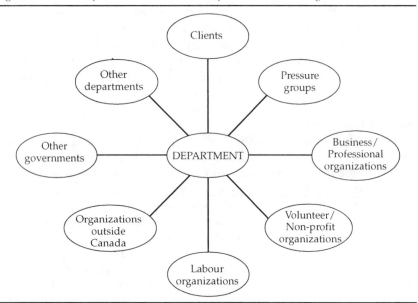

A virtual *public* organization would be one in which participants from different government departments, different governments and even non-governmental organizations share resources in a temporary alliance to "address immediate problems, carry out specific projects or exploit short-term opportunities."[414] Virtual public organizations would have features in common with conventional task forces and partnerships; they would, however, be distinguished by the flexibility and fluidity of their arrangements, facilitated by rapid communications through computer networks.

### Partners with Whom?

Much of the popular discussion of partnerships focuses on public–private partnerships – those between public organizations and business firms. Our discussion of the purposes of partnerships shows, however, that substantial benefits flow from the many partnerships between public organizations and a wide variety of other entities. Figure 8.2 illustrates the broad range of groups and organizations with which a single public organization can partner. Many partnerships have more than two partners. Figure 8.3 shows that a single partnership can involve many participants drawn from different segments of society.

A partnership should of course include all those stakeholders who can

Figure 8.3. *PARTNERSHIPS: Easing youth transition from school to work*

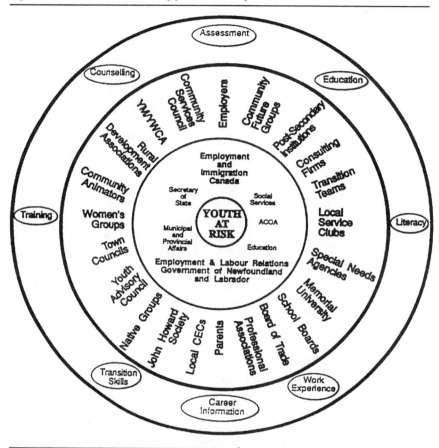

Source: Employment and Immigration Canada and Newfoundland Department of Employment and Labour Relations, 1992. (Submission to the IPAC Award for Innovative Management Competition.)

contribute significantly to attaining its objectives. Even groups and organizations with an adversarial relationship in the past or with clashing objectives (e.g., management and unions) can often find mutual benefits. However, those to whom only small benefits are likely to accrue should be excluded in the interests of expeditious decision-making and having partners contribute roughly equivalent resources.

Public organizations can partner with business, not-for-profit organizations, other government departments, other governments, labour unions, and entities in other countries. Each of these categories is discussed briefly in turn.

## With Business

The rapid expansion of partnerships (often called strategic alliances) among business organizations over the past decade has been complemented more recently by a dramatic increase in the number and diversity of partnerships between business and government. The use of partnerships fits well with the increasing realization that for many practical purposes the government and business sectors are complementary. Partnerships offer the possibility of choosing both government and business, rather than one or the other, for the conduct of certain activities.

The mutual benefits accruing from public–private partnerships have prompted many business organizations to seek, and even compete for, alliances with public organizations. Management consultants actively pursue partnership opportunities for their business clients, and public–private partnership networks have been developed.[415] Some of the benefits are the same for both parties – improving productivity, adding value, and reducing costs. Often, however, in the course of pursuing their corporate advantage, business firms can help governments achieve various public interest objectives.

## With Not-for-Profit Organizations

The development in recent years of a more participative political culture has helped to foster government involvement in partnerships with community and advocacy groups. A specific purpose of many of these partnerships has been to obtain client and stakeholder input as a means of improving policy development and service delivery, notably on environmental issues; such partnerships tend to be of the consultative variety.

Increasingly, partnerships involving not-for-profit organizations are established in association with business and government. For example, Forintek Canada Corporation involves the federal government, six provincial governments and 155 business firms in a not-for-profit corporation for the purpose of basic and applied research and development in wood products – an arrangement that "permits partners to draw benefits substantially in excess of their contributions. The partnership delivers 'private services' (such as market-oriented research) to industry members and 'public services' (such as public safety and environmental research) to government members."[416]

## With Other Organizations inside Government

As noted earlier, partnerships between organizations or between parts of organizations within a single government are described as internal partnerships or, more properly, as networking. Networking "implies not only the necessity of collaborating with one's immediate colleagues or those from other departments and agencies but also the necessity of compromising and consulting with one's colleagues/partners. Networking assumes that when preparing annual plans, setting organizational objectives, developing projects or approaching a client, the parties involved operate in a coherent and coordinated fashion."[417] A good example of networking across departmental boundaries is Ontario's Analytical Laboratories Council, which represents seven ministries and two agencies and which promotes partnerships within the analytical laboratory community by encouraging cooperation and circulating information of innovative practices in the delivery of scientific programs.

### With Other Governments
Intergovernmental partnerships are certainly not a new development but their use has greatly expanded in recent years. Federal–provincial partnerships in particular can not only save money but harmonize policy-making and program delivery. For example, the "innovative and creative aspects" of a partnership between Environment Canada and its Quebec counterpart is reported to have made possible the solution of two major problems that could have threatened the success of a plan to clean up the St. Lawrence River.[418]

Many intergovernmental partnerships not only involve all three orders of government but non-governmental organizations as well. The Lake Superior Programs Office in Thunder Bay, Ontario, is a coordinating agent for two provincial and two federal agencies with the common goal of restoring and protecting the Lake Superior ecosystem. The program is based on the realization that more can be achieved with fewer resources, if different agencies and governments with common goals are willing to share power. The office reports that by generating partnerships with municipalities, businesses and community groups it has produced synergy leading to reduced costs and increased public support. The governments' initial contribution of $3.3 million for restoration projects led to commitments from thirty-four community partners of $8.7 million: "The management style is participatory rather than hierarchical, largely because the organization is mission and project driven, rather than rule driven."[419]

### With Organizations in Other Countries
An increasing number of public organizations are involved in partnerships that cross national boundaries. At the 1992 Earth Summit in Rio de Janeiro, Canada proposed a model forest program to promote sustainable forest management. This idea emerged in the Canadian Forest Service of the federal Department of Natural Resources after extensive public con-

sultations forming part of a government-wide environmental action plan.[420] A Canadian network of ten model forest sites managed by a partnership of private, public and non-governmental organizations is part of an international network of sites in such countries as Mexico, Russia, Malaysia and the United States. International sites are twinned with Canadian sites to facilitate the transfer of Canadian knowledge, expertise and technology.

Another notable international partnership involves the Canadian Wildlife Service of Environment Canada and the United States Fish and Wildlife Service.[421] These two organizations jointly administer the North American Waterfowl Management Plan through joint ventures with provincial, territorial and state agencies as well as with private conservation organizations, business organizations, and individuals. And the City of Toronto participated in an international contributory partnership, with the support of several Canadian partners, to assist economic development in certain Latin American cities. In one project, fifty de-commissioned Toronto transit buses were shipped to Lima, Peru, where they were used to shuttle people between their homes in poor settlements and their workplace.[422]

*With Labour Unions*
Labour–management partnerships are relatively scarce in public organizations, but their number is gradually increasing and both management and the unions have attested to their success. The Canada Employment and Immigration Union agreed to "participate" and "cooperate" with management in the Quebec Region of the Department of Human Resources Development to improve quality. In the words of the union representatives, "Naturally, we have very different approaches: the employer's foremost aim is to provide higher quality service, while the union's chief aim is to improve the quality of working life. Nonetheless, both sides are convinced that these two goals are not mutually exclusive and can be pursued concurrently." Moreover, according to management, "the union's cooperation is essential since our common interests are at stake."[423] Another example involves B.C. Hydro, which developed several partnerships with the International Brotherhood of Electrical Workers, including a joint implementation team to introduce empowered work teams. One manager learned from this experience that "responsible partnerships are not formed overnight. They are built on a foundation of common values, shared vision and effective communications. They grow on the basis of taking increasing risks and deepening trust."[424]

## How to Partner

Partnering, like consulting, can be a complicated and risky enterprise.

Most partnerships of any consequence require rigorous examination of the purposes to be served, the partners to be included, the type of partnership to be created, and the possible impediments to success. The process of partnering can be conceptualized in distinct chronological stages beginning with planning and moving through development, implementation and evaluation to termination. Several public organizations have prepared a checklist of considerations to be taken into account at each stage of the partnering process. Heritage Canada, for example, prepared a partnership guide with several checkoff points for each of the following stages:

– deciding when to partner and identifying candidates
– developing an action plan
– assessing the candidates
– picking the winner(s)
– negotiating the terms
– issues and considerations
    – financial considerations
    – human resource issues
    – authorities and legal issues
    – communications/information
    – accountability and monitoring
– the agreement
    – terms and conditions
    – partnership instruments
– living with the agreement
    – monitor and evaluate
    – communicate
    – renegotiate
    – terminate
– learning from your experience[425]

Appendix D provides a checklist of general principles for public servants who are contemplating or involved in a partnership. While the checklist was designed for a specific department, the principles are generally applicable to all departments.

## Implications and Impediments

The principles in Appendix D suggest some of the barriers to successful partnerships faced by public organizations. Additional barriers will be identified in the following examination of the managerial, organizational, political, value and legal implications of partnering.

*Managerial and Organizational Considerations*

The use of partnerships is very much in tune with the emphasis of the post-bureaucratic model of public organization (Figure 1.2 in Chapter 1) on collaboration. Several other emphases of the post-bureaucratic model also tend to foster the use of partnerships. These include the emphases on alternative delivery mechanisms; quality service to clients and the general public; decentralization of authority and decision-making; empowering employees; accountability for results rather than process; and innovation, risk-taking and continuous improvement.

Partnerships provide an option to program delivery by operating departments, and, as noted above, their purpose is often to improve the quality of the service delivered. We have also noted that real (or collaborative) partnerships involve a sharing of power – a giving up of some decision-making authority to others, including non-governmental partners. There is a complementary emphasis in the post-bureaucratic model on going beyond delegation of authority to empowering public servants by pushing decision-making authority down the hierarchy and holding public servants accountable for the results they achieve rather than the way they do things. In this context, empowered public servants are more likely to be creative and innovative in the use of partnerships; they are more likely also to use partnerships to empower individuals and groups outside government (e.g., aboriginals, the poor) if they themselves are empowered.

While the post-bureaucratic model is more conducive to partnerships than the traditional model, we shall see that innovative partnerships, like other forms of public-sector innovation, can present significant risks for public managers – and for their political masters.

*Political Considerations*

Partnership is one of the few areas of public-service reform for which political leaders have publicly proclaimed their enthusiastic support. There are clear political benefits from partnerships that achieve such objectives as promoting economic productivity, reducing expenditures, and improving service to the public. The political payoff is especially evident in the use of public–private partnerships that enable governments to provide services that otherwise would not be provided at all.

Political benefits accrue also from the use of partnerships, especially of the collaborative type, that promote harmonious relations between governments. Notable examples include the intergovernmental partnerships described earlier in this chapter to clean up the St. Lawrence River and to restore the Lake Superior ecosystem. Partnerships can even be used to get around constitutional barriers to intergovernmental collaboration. Government departments in the federal, provincial and territorial spheres joined with the private sector to establish the Canadian Construction Materials Centre, a national program to evaluate the suitability of products, materials and systems for use in construction. One aspect of this partnership is that the National Research Council – a federal body – is permitted by a memorandum of understanding to take action in an area that is clearly within the constitutional competence of the provinces and territories.

Another political implication of partnerships is that their increased use can be seen as "a move away from support for interest advocacy and policy criticism to an emphasis on service delivery and implementation."[426] Using the rationale of budgetary constraints, governments have in recent years significantly reduced funding for various interest groups, including, for example, those advocating the interests of aboriginals and women. The influence of such groups, which use government funds partly to engage in public criticism of government policies, may consequently be reduced. Their influence may be further diminished by the increased emphasis on the need for governments to consult with "clients" rather than with the broader range of interests affected by government decisions. There is concern that advocacy groups, in seeking to maintain financial support and access to government, may allow themselves to be co-opted into partnerships – a position from which they cannot easily criticize government policy. On the other hand, if the partnerships are collaborative in that they allow for genuine power-sharing, the groups may still exercise influence on government decisions.

Collaborative partnerships involve sharing risk as well as power. Thus, both politicians and public servants need to keep in mind that they will be held accountable for the consequences of their involvement. This concern explains the difficulty faced by the Ontario Office of the Registrar General in "[o]btaining the necessary approvals to use the tripartite partnership model" and "to sole source" one of the partners for the award-winning conversion of records described earlier. The potentially adverse implications for ministerial responsibility and public-service accountability of empowerment that were discussed in Chapter 8 apply also to the use of partnerships. The policy of the Saskatchewan Department of Environment and Resource Management is that ministerial approval will not be given to partnerships involving a sharing of authority.[427] Further consideration of the accountability issue is contained in the next two sections on the value, ethical and legal ramifications of partnerships.

*Value and Ethical Considerations*
We explained in Chapter 3 that certain traditional values are now, and are

likely to remain, of central importance in the governance of public organizations. Foremost among these values are integrity, accountability and fairness/equity. However, new values have emerged that either complement or clash with traditional values. Among the most popular new values are service, quality, teamwork, innovation and openness. These new values are closely aligned with the characteristics of the post-bureaucratic model. They are also generally more compatible with the formation and maintenance of partnerships than are the traditional values. Indeed, partnerships are widely viewed as a means of fostering such values as service, quality and innovation.

However, partnerships are less compatible with certain other values, including accountability, a traditional value, and openness, a new one. There is a widespread and justifiable concern, for example, that emphasis on innovation in general and innovative partnerships in particular may clash with the need for democratic accountability explained above. As noted in the chapter on empowerment, innovation normally involves increased risk-taking that may lead to mistakes and to political embarrassment for cabinet ministers. Thus, governments need to ensure that public servants can be held adequately accountable for the creation and management of partnerships. Art Daniels, one of Canada's foremost champions of public-sector innovation, advises: "Encourage risk taking in the public service when the objective is one where significant benefits can be accrued both to the public service and outside the public service, and when the risk can be reasonably managed."[428]

A related issue is the emergence of openness as a central value in both our participative political culture and our public-service culture. Achieving an appropriate measure of openness among the participants in a partnership is difficult enough; a greater difficulty is deciding how much information the outside world needs to have about the partnership. This is not a problem with partnerships between business organizations. It can become a very significant problem for government–business partnerships, however, when the general public or the media demand to know, on the grounds of accountability for the expenditure of public funds, the details of the partnership agreement. For example, controversy arose when a business firm in partnership with the Ontario Ministry of Consumer and Commercial Relations used the Freedom of Information Act to keep secret certain information about the firm, including the names of its owners. While it is understandable that business firms may not wish to make public sensitive financial data, legislators have a legitimate interest in knowing how, and with what risk, their tax dollars are being spent. The auditor general of Canada has argued that "[d]elivering programs and services to the public through collaborative arrangements often requires more transparency than traditional delivery by a government department. Because partnerships are involved, it may be more difficult for citizens to know who is responsible. Consequently, the federal government needs to be as open as possible with information about agreements, decisions and results of these arrangements."[429]

Many of the value conflicts arising from use of the partnership mechanism are also *ethical* conflicts. Such values as accountability and openness have a substantial ethical content in that they relate to what is right or good. Consider, for example, the Drug and Alcohol Registry of Treatment developed by the Ontario Addiction Research Foundation, in partnership with government, researchers, service providers and consumers, to provide accurate, up-to-date and easily accessible information about the availability of alcohol and drug treatment. Among the questions raised in advance about the ethical implications of the registry were these: "Who may collect and release what information to whom and under what circumstances?" "Can the Registry collect client information? Can the Registry disclose client information to others?"[430]

A variety of other ethical issues can arise from the use of partnerships. Can a public organization simply enter into a partnership with any business firm that suits its purposes? Or do considerations of fairness and equity require that other firms have an opportunity to compete for involvement? Do the close relations between public servants and business people necessitated by partnerships create more opportunities for conflicts of interest? Do such partnerships, for example, increase the temptation for public servants to make personal use of confidential information or to grant preferential treatment in the hope of subsequent employment in the private sector? These and similar ethical issues have received very little attention in the partnership literature. However, one of the partnership principles of the Saskatchewan Department of Environment and Resource Management is that "[p]artnerships must be developed in an ethical manner, building on respect, trust, openness and common goals among partners."[431]

*Legal Considerations*

Significant *legal* issues arise from the involvement of public organizations in partnerships. The following were some legal questions that arose in connection with the substance abuse registry noted above: "What is the liability of professionals in the release of information to the Registry?" "What is the relation of the provincial freedom of information and protection of privacy legislation to a non-hospital based Registry?" "Is the health or social service professional or agency liable in any way in the event that a client death occurs and the provider has not consulted the Registry as part of the referral process?"[432]

Such questions indicate the importance of understanding the legal ramifications of creating partnerships – and the risk involved in using the word partnership to describe the arrangements. Ellen Fry warns that in technical legal terms a partnership refers to a "legal relationship whereby partners share profits and losses and the acts of each partner bind the others. ... [I]f the government were in partnership, it could be forced to pay debts incurred by the other parties to the relationship."[433] She provides the example of a court decision where the Canadian Mortgage and Housing Corp. (CMHC) was actually in a partnership relationship, not simply a lending relationship, with a builder and was, therefore, required to share the legal liability of the builder for deficient house construction.

Environment Canada's Legal Services has noted the risk of using the word partnership:

The risk of unintentional liability is significant in the use of the term partnership and, as such, it should be used only where it is understood that a liability is to be assumed. Terms such as alliance, cooperative agreement and collaborative activity should be used wherever appropriate to denote a joint activity or looser cooperative arrangement than a partnership.[434]

## CONCLUSION

There is ample evidence to demonstrate that public organizations can significantly improve policy formation and program delivery through the use of partnerships. We have shown also, however, that partnerships are not a panacea for economic and social problems and that careful account must be taken of their political, managerial, ethical and legal implications. Thus, public servants are well advised to learn the methods and implications of creating, implementing, evaluating and, when appropriate, terminating partnerships.

# 9

# Learning and Innovating Continuously

Public organizations can move towards the post-bureaucratic model by using individual and organizational learning to improve their performance and promote innovation: "The successful organizations appear increasingly to be those that have found a way to promote learning at both the individual level and at the level of the organization itself."[435] Table 1.1 in Chapter 1 shows that post-bureaucratic organizations embrace continuous improvement and innovation, whereas the traditional bureaucratic organization tends to be oriented more towards the status quo and avoiding risks and mistakes. In previous chapters we have seen that many public organizations have embraced innovation: not just a single innovation but continuous innovation and improvement through learning. In fact, many of the organizations that we have examined have developed, or are developing, a *corporate learning culture* – a culture "where learning is highly valued, where risks are encouraged and rewarded, and all have the responsibility for their own learning and the learning of others."[436]

This chapter begins by explaining the meaning of concepts related to organizational learning and by providing frameworks to promote understanding of its scope and its benefits. This is followed by a discussion of individual learning, organizational learning, and *strategic* organizational learning. The discussion of these three approaches contains advice on how to promote learning, and Appendix E contains a list of questions for managers to consider as a partial basis for creating a learning culture. The examination of organizational learning in the first part of the chapter is followed by a discussion of the closely related topic of innovation.

## THE LEARNING ORGANIZATION: MEANINGS AND FRAMEWORKS

The concept of "the learning organization" was popularized by Peter

Senge of MIT in his landmark book, *The Fifth Discipline: The Art and Practice of the Learning Organization.*[437] It is notable that a CCMD study differentiates between this concept and the concept of "organizational learning" and argues that "the term organizational learning puts the emphasis where it should be, on learning. And that is where it belongs."[438]

D.A. Schon, one of the earliest writers to analyse the links between organizational learning and organizational performance, suggested that an organization's long-term effectiveness is founded on its "continuing redesign in response to changing values and a changing context for action," including its ability to "design and redesign policies, structures and techniques in the face of constantly changing assumptions about self and environment."[439] Among other concepts, Schon invented the concept of "deutero learning," or "learning about learning," which refers to an organization's ability to examine critically its previous assumptions: "they discover what they did that eased or inhibited learning."[440]

Building on Schon's work, Senge argues that organizations must learn new skills in three important areas in order to be able to adapt successfully to continuously changing environments: building shared vision; surfacing and challenging mental models; and engaging in systems thinking. Senge identifies the new skills required in each of the three areas as follows:

1. *Building Shared Vision*
   - encourage sharing of personal vision
   - communicate and ask for support
   - recognize vision as an ongoing process
   - blend extrinsic and intrinsic visions
   - distinguish positive from negative visions
2. *Surfacing and Testing Mental Models*
   - see leaps of abstraction
   - balance inquiry and advocacy
   - distinguish "espoused theory" from "theory in use"
   - recognize and defuse defensive routines
3. *Systems Thinking*
   - see interrelationships and processes, not things and snapshots
   - move beyond blame
   - distinguish detail complexity from dynamic complexity
   - focus on areas of high leverage
   - avoid symptomatic solutions[441]

Senge argues that organizations must learn these new skill sets in order to become *learning* organizations.

Mike Pedlar and colleagues have developed an organizational learning

Figure 9.1. *Model—The Compleat Learning Organization*

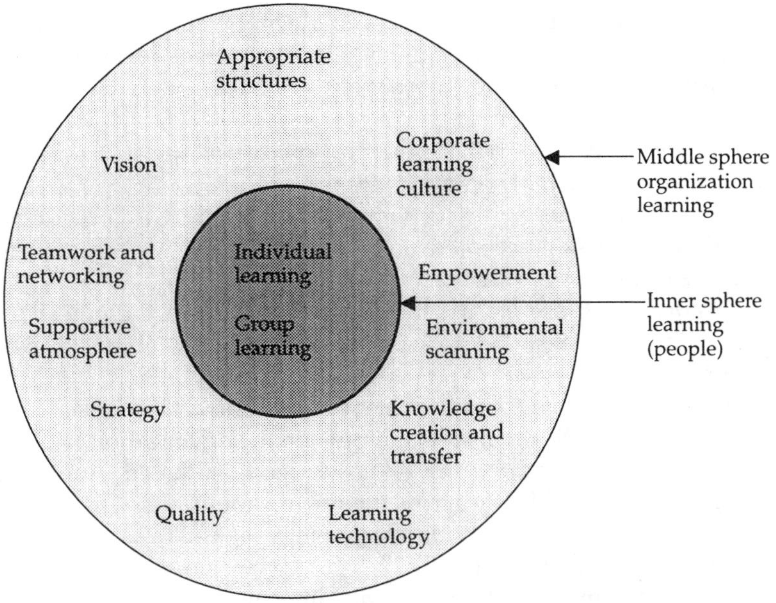

Source: Michael Marquardt and Angus Reynolds, *The Global Learning Organization* (New York: Irwin, 1993). Reprinted with permission.

model to describe how organizations with a strong learning culture promote learning at both the individual and organizational level.[442] According to this model, learning organizations promote learning in five ways: by *looking out* (external scanning and inter-organization learning), by *looking in* (internal exchange, rewarding flexibility), by *strategy* (learning approaches to strategy and consultative policy-making), by creating *learning opportunities* (learning climate and learning opportunities), and by *enabling structures*.

In their book *The Global Learning Organization*, Michael Marquardt and Angus Reynolds present a more holistic model of the learning organization, which is shown in a modified version as Figure 9.1. At the inner core of their "donut" model, they distinguish between individual and group learning. *Individual learning* is learning acquired by individual members of the organization through the organization's human resource development and training systems. *Group learning*, however, involves any learning by organizational units and teams, including through shared experiences. It is important to note that teams can be an especially powerful force for learning in that their members are more likely to share ideas and experiences, to develop leadership skills, and to be sources of creativity and innovation.

The second ring of the Marquardt and Reynolds model contains the eleven elements that they believe the organization needs to have in place to foster *organizational learning*. These are

1. *appropriate structures* – a flat organizational structure that promotes vertical and horizontal communication;
2. *corporate learning culture* – a corporate culture where learning is highly valued, where risk is accepted, and where everyone takes responsibility for learning;
3. *empowerment* – those closest to the client are given the power and responsibility to respond to client needs; learning occurs through responsibility;
4. *environmental scanning* – environmental scanning is undertaken regularly and systematically inside and outside the organization;
5. *knowledge creation and transfer* – knowledge is gathered, stored and communicated seamlessly across the organization;
6. *learning technology* – information technology is used to support learning and skill development;
7. *quality* – a commitment to continuous improvement and to personal mastery of essential skills by staff within the organization;
8. *strategy* – deliberate planning to make learning a key driver of the organization's success;
9. *supportive atmosphere* – employees are valued and nurtured;
10. *teamwork and networking* – the organization is committed to teamwork and team learning; and
11. *vision* – there is an organizational consensus on the future direction of the organization, as well as its mission, values and beliefs.[443]

The striking complementarity between these eleven elements and the characteristics of the post-bureaucratic model outlined in Chapter 1 indicates the importance of learning to the achievement of high levels of organizational performance. According to Mary Hale, public organizations lag private-sector organizations in adopting the learning organization model. She argues that the traditional bureaucratic model of public organization is an impediment to organizational learning: "The lag persists because public sector organizations remain embedded in bureaucratic structures that resist learning models."[444]

## INDIVIDUAL AND ORGANIZATIONAL LEARNING

Senge has pointed out that "[o]rganizations learn only through individuals who learn. Individual learning does not guarantee organizational learning, but without it no organizational learning occurs."[445] Similarly, a CCMD report asserts that individual and organizational learning are inextricably intertwined:

Individual and organizational learning are distinct but not separate. Each is the condition for the other. Individual learning is the condition for organizational learning since only individuals have minds that can learn. But organizations shape and mould the individuals in them: they help them to learn or prevent them from doing so. ... [O]rganizational learning has much to do with overcoming these negative patterns, and turning our places of work into the kinds of organizations that allow our better selves to emerge and flower.[446]

## Individual Learning: Formal and Informal

Writers in the field of learning distinguish between *formal learning*, which takes place in training courses and development programs, and *informal learning*, which takes place in the workplace and on the job. Recent research suggests that, while most organizations concentrate on formal individual learning programs to meet their learning objectives, the most effective learning is experiential and takes place on the job. For example, research at CCMD found that public-service managers identify various types of "on-the-job experience" as the most important source of their learning about leadership. Formal learning programs ranked fifth in terms of their importance as a source of learning for those senior managers who had risen to the executive category in the federal public service. These results will be discussed in more detail later in this section.

## Formal Learning

Public and private organizations that place a high value on learning commit substantial resources to formal training and development programs for staff at all levels. The amount committed tends to be substantially greater, however, in the private sector. For example, IBM Canada established a target of thirteen training days per year for each of its employees, while a major federal government department recently aimed to provide five days. In the mid-1990s, however, Statistics Canada set aside three per cent of its budget for training (up from one per cent).[447] In those public organizations strongly committed to learning, each person's learning needs may be assessed on an annual basis and an individual learning plan developed. Then the individual is enrolled in appropriate formal training courses that may be provided internally by the organization itself or by outside institutions such as universities, colleges and private training companies. This is the approach utilized at Indian Affairs and Northern Development, where employees are encouraged to develop one- to five-year training plans based on their individual personal development plans. The federal Public Service Commission maintains an assessment centre that identifies individual learning and development needs for candidates in "fast-track" development programs such as the Career Assignment Program (CAP) for middle managers.

In the private sector, and to an increasing degree in the public sector, individual formal learning programs have become more linked to the needs of the organization, both in the development of core competencies needed by the organization and in the inculcation of organizational values and strategies. In the private sector, many large corporations have founded "corporate universities" within their organizations and have in-sourced some of the generic training that used to be provided by universities and colleges. In this way, companies such as General Electric, Xerox, Motorola and the Bank of Montreal have begun to focus their skills training programs on the skills and knowledge needed within the organization, especially those skills needed for the future. In the federal public service, several large departments (e.g., Foreign Affairs and International Trade) have created internal training institutes to impart, in a more organized way, the individual skills and knowledge needed by their staff. Similarly, the Ontario government created the Centre for Leadership to impart required knowledge and skill sets to its managers, while the Government of Canada created the Canadian Centre for Management Development to provide focused management training for its senior managers and for participants in its accelerated development programs such as the Management Trainee Program.

Figure 9.2 depicts the hierarchy of formal training programs at the corporate level within the public service of Canada. There are three times in their careers when public managers receive formal government-wide training programs: at the supervisory level; at the middle-manager level; and when they move into the executive cadre. There are also special development programs within the management stream for those managers who are deemed to have high potential: the Management Trainee Program for recent university graduates; the Career Assignment Program for high-potential middle managers; and the Accelerated Executive Development Program at the executive level for those managers who have been identified as potential deputy ministers or assistant deputy ministers.

There are three important new trends in individual formal learning programs:

– the integration of "action learning" techniques into formal learning programs;

Figure 9.2. *Corporate Leadership Development Framework*

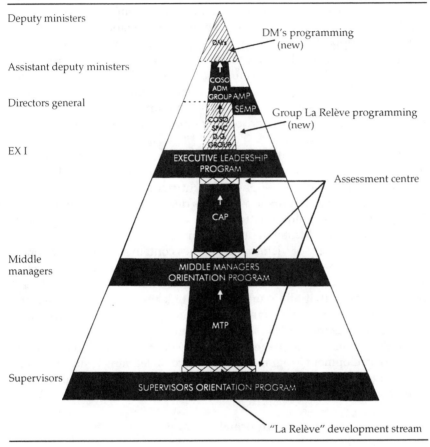

Deputy ministers

DM's programming
(new)

Assistant deputy ministers

Directors general

Group La Relève programming
(new)

EX I

EXECUTIVE LEADERSHIP
PROGRAM

Assessment centre

CAP

Middle
managers

MIDDLE MANAGERS
ORIENTATION PROGRAM

MTP

Supervisors

SUPERVISORS ORIENTATION PROGRAM

"La Relève" development stream

– the linkage of individual learning to organizational learning; and
– the linkage of formal learning to informal learning.[448]

Action learning refers to a learning process that is best described as a process of "learning, action, reflection." It refers to a system of learning where formal learning occurs in the classroom and is then applied in the workplace; later the participants return to the classroom to reflect on and analyse their experience with classmates and learning advisers.

The importance of the second trend – the formal linkage of individual learning to organizational learning – has already been noted. This is the process of ensuring that individual formal learning programs are linked to organizational strategy and to those organizational competencies required to implement the corporate strategy successfully. For example, in the mid-

213

1990s, the federal Department of Western Economic Diversification (WED) re-positioned itself from a supplier of financial resources to private companies to a value-added supplier of strategic information to private companies. To support this strategy, the department decided that it would work in future through partnerships with government, non-profit, and private organizations. This required the organization and its staff to acquire new competencies in the development and management of partnerships. A formal training program for WED employees was provided to support the new emphasis on partnerships as a way of delivering the organizations' programs.

The third trend is to link formal learning programs with informal learning. For example, an individual manager who wants to enhance his or her competency in policy development might traditionally take a course in policy development or pursue a master's degree in public administration. The trend now is to link this formal learning with practical experience (informal learning). Master in public administration programs, such as the one at the University of Victoria, sometimes contain a "co-op" component that allows the manager to gain experience in a policy development job in government. Departments such as Statistics Canada have formal rotational programs that allow managers to link their formal learning programs to developmental assignments in other areas of the organization, or in other organizations. The same holds true for programs such as the federal government's Management Trainee Program and Accelerated Executive Development Program, where classroom learning is supplemented with targeted rotational assignments that supplement formal learning with informal learning on the job.

### Informal Learning

While in the past organizations have focused much of their development efforts on *formal* learning programs, "the bulk of research to date seems to show that most individual learning in organizations occurs elsewhere, in the *informal* processes of everyday work."[449] This assertion confirms the findings of a study by the Centre for Creative Leadership in the United States, which concluded from a study of successful executives that development occurs largely through experiential learning on the job, including challenging new jobs, special assignments, and learning from bosses, good and bad.[450] A CCMD study based on interviews in 1997 and 1998 with over 600 federal executives found that formal learning programs, whether management development or university, ranked far behind informal on-the-job learning in terms of important sources of learning how to be an effective leader. "On-the-job experience" was identified as the number-one source of learning about leadership, closely followed by "observing bosses and other leaders"; in third place was "task forces and special assignments"; and in fourth place "informal mentors and coaches." It is significant that many participants indicated that they had also learned *how not to lead* by observing some of their bosses and the other leaders around them.

Organizations committed to individual and organizational learning, such as Statistics Canada, actively employ these methods of informal learning to "grow" their staff. By placing their managers in "stretch" jobs, and by offering rotational assignments both within and outside the organization, the powerful natural learning that takes place on the job is harnessed and maximized. In the same vein, the federal government and the provinces have for many years operated a program known as Executive Interchange whereby senior public-sector managers spend one or two years with another government or with a private-sector organization. Not only do participants return to the public service with greatly expanded experience, but these assignments also allow organizations to "import" ideas and innovations from other governments and organizations through the acquired knowledge of the manager who has been on the interchange assignment. The receiving organization benefits in a similar way. For example, CCMD regularly invites a "business fellow" from a leading private-sector company to spend two years on executive interchange at CCMD. During the 1990s, business fellows from IBM Canada, General Electric, and Nova Corporation spent two years each at CCMD. In the case of IBM and General Electric, the fellows passed on knowledge from their organizations to the federal public service in the areas of executive development, upward feedback, and WorkOut (GE's method of involving staff in finding ways of reducing work and "working smarter"). In the case of Nova Corporation, the business fellow was a vice-president who brought a knowledge of change management to the public service, just at the time when federal departments were managing through the post–Program Review downsizing process. The business fellow was able to provide advice to a number of different government departments in innovative practices in change management, based on her experience at Nova.

Special development assignments like these have been formalized by numerous public organizations, including Statistics Canada, the Canadian International Development Agency, and Natural Resources Canada. A notable example is the Corporate Assignments Program of Statistics Canada, "which, since 1983, has provided temporary lateral transfers on a voluntary basis and has contributed to second-language development, affirmative action, redeployment and relocation, as well as management development." Similarly, Natural Resources Canada "developed a Career

Enhancement Service that includes an Assignments Program, an Employee Voluntary Assistance Program, and a new Centre for Career Orientation."[451]

Some public organizations that are leading-edge in individual learning, reinforce on-the-job learning with periods of reflection and study about what is being learned through the work experience. This type of learning has been described as "Type 2" learning by management development expert Alan Mumford. "Type 1" learning is informal on-the-job experiential learning, while "Type 3" learning involves formal learning and development programs such as classroom learning. Type 2 learning fits in between the other two and involves the process of consciously integrating learning and managerial work.[452] Type 2 learning can be either prospective or retrospective. In *prospective* learning, managers identify their learning objectives for their assignment and consciously apply their on-the-job experience to these objectives. In *retrospective* learning, managers analyse and reflect on their learning during the most recent on-the-job experience. Sometimes these two forms of learning are integrated, as in the federal government's Accelerated Executive Development Program, initiated in 1997. In this program, rotational assignments are chosen for the candidate to fill in missing experience, such as in policy development, regional operations, or central agency work. Formal learning objectives may be developed with a participant by a personal mentor or coach prior to the rotational assignment, then candidates come together with the coach or with other participants to reflect on their on-the-job learning during the assignment period. This process can be strengthened through another learning device, the "learning log," which is a diary that the manager keeps during an assignment to record the learning or insights that he or she has each day or week.

Many innovative public organizations also help their staff to learn continuously through *self-development plans and processes*. Some of the approaches that are used include a personal-needs assessment, based on either 360-degree feedback instruments (feedback provided by peers, bosses and staff on the person's performance and development needs) or self-assessment questionnaires (technical competencies and interpersonal skills). Based on a variety of assessment tools, each person may develop a *personal learning plan*, which may include learning objectives for the next time-period, along with an identification of the formal learning programs, experience and personal learning that will achieve the learning objectives. Organizations employ a variety of supportive mechanisms to promote self-development programs. For example, Veterans Affairs Canada maintains a learning centre in its Charlottetown headquarters where all employees can use the computerized learning facilities, the book library or the video library to pursue their personal learning plan. Statistics Canada, the Department of Western Economic Diversification, and Natural Resources Canada also maintain self-directed learning centres for employees.

## ORGANIZATIONAL LEARNING

As noted above, individual learning, no matter how well organized and supported, is not the same as organizational learning: "The problem is that individual learning does not lead automatically or necessarily to learning by the organization to which the individual belongs. In many organizations it never does. Individual members of an organization may be learning things regularly about ways in which the organization could improve its performance. ... But unless the circumstances are propitious and the culture welcoming, this knowledge may remain forever private."[453] This gap between individual learning and organizational learning has been described by D.A. Schon and Chris Argyris as the difference between "single-loop learning" and "double-loop learning."[454] Single-loop learning refers to individual learning that is never transferred to the organization as a whole. Double-loop learning is learning that moves beyond the individual level to the whole organization. For example, if a government executive went to General Electric on an interchange assignment and learned GE's "WorkOut" techniques, this would be single-loop learning. If, after returning to government, he or she trained the whole organization in how to use "WorkOut" and the technique was used to improve the performance of the organization as a whole, this would be double-loop learning.

There are several specific means by which organizational learning occurs:

– systems thinking;
– anticipatory and loop learning;
– action learning;
– information systems;
– learning space; and
– benchmarking, and best practices.[455]

*Systems thinking* is the Senge concept referred to earlier – "a discipline for seeing wholes, a framework for seeing relationships rather than linear cause and effect chains, for seeing patterns of change rather than snapshots."[456] For example, a public organization that understands the changes in the public sector in terms of the forces producing change and the various elements of the emerging post-bureaucratic model is much better able to re-position itself to be successful in the future. *Anticipatory* and *loop learning* relate to our earlier description of single- and double-loop learning, except that anticipatory learning describes the organization's ability to think ahead to the various future "scenarios" that might affect it. Scenario planning, which was pioneered by Royal Dutch Shell, has been used extensively in some federal departments, including the Public Service Commission and Treasury Board Secretariat, to anticipate possible future environments and to consider how to prepare to meet them. The 1996 Deputy Minister's Task Force on the Future of the Public Service identified several "scenarios" that departments could use to think through, and plan for, their futures.[457]

*Action learning* is a method of organizational learning pioneered by England's Reginald Revans. In his book, *The ABC's of Action Learning*, he outlines an approach to organizational learning that involves establishing "learning sets" of individuals who "take real life problems as the raw material for learning, they alternate moments of reflection and analysis with periods of action, and they aim at learning not for its own sake alone but in order to produce concrete consequences from the learning achieved."[458] These action-learning groups may also be assisted by coaches or outside experts who serve as resources to the team. In some cases, the action-learning group may be drawn from a single work unit, while in other cases it may be drawn from across the organization or from several organizations. The cycle of discussion/action, discussion/action continues throughout the life of the action-learning set.

*Information systems*, in the writings of organizational learning expert Nancy Dixon, do not refer to computer systems but to the organizational learning process – the way in which an organization manages its information through five phases: acquisition; distribution; giving meaning; storage; and retrieval.[459] A learning organization successfully manages acquired information through all five steps. For example, in 1997, CCMD created five "knowledge centres" within the organization to manage knowledge the organization acquires in the areas of governance, leadership, organizational effectiveness, organizational culture, and learning.

The notion of *learning space* is also an essential element of organizational learning: "individuals need the physical, social and mental space to be creative and innovative; to listen; to slow things down, and to establish linkages; and to build on what's happening."[460] In the private sector, 3M is a company that has created learning space for its staff: "3M has undertaken many actions to create an innovative climate and encourage creativity in its organization. For example, 3M allows workers up to 15 percent of their paid work time to work on their own projects."[461]

Other tools used in organizational learning include the use of *benchmarking* and the organized gathering and analysis of *best practices*:

"Benchmarking is the process of understanding what is important to your organization's success (critical success factors), understanding your processes, finding and learning from others who do these processes better than yours, then adapting that learning to improve your performance."[462] Originally developed by the Xerox Corporation to improve its competitive performance, this technique is now routinely used by many world-class companies to learn from organizations that perform a particular function more efficiently than they do.

The process of formal benchmarking requires an organization to first measure its own "metrics" for a system (for example, the cost of producing a driver's license; or intercity delivery times in a national postal service) and then to visit another organization with better metrics to analyse how this organization manages to perform this function better. Once the benchmarking comparisons and analyses are complete, the final stage is to apply the learning to improve the organization's performance. Sometimes the benchmarking organization learns far more than how to improve the system under study. For example, a CCMD benchmarking team visited IBM Canada to study how that company produced so many student-days of learning per employee each year. The team learned that the company put all of its managers, company-wide, through a three-day training program when they gathered together each year and that the content was tied to the learning needs of the organization and IBM's strategic direction. Not only was this an efficient process for delivering executive education but it also contained a more strategic, high-impact philosophy of executive development than the approach CCMD was using at that time for federal departments. Many innovative public organizations now routinely use formal or informal benchmarking as a continuous learning tool. For example, payroll operations within the government of British Columbia have regularly benchmarked their performance against the best of the private and public sector in order to learn from those organizations operating large payroll systems more efficiently.

*Best practices* identification is a related tool used by public organizations that are committed to continuous learning and continuous improvement. Less rigorous than formal benchmarking, best-practices identification involves actively seeking out and applying innovations from other organizations, both public and private. For example, the Ontario government at the provincial level and Revenue Canada, the Treasury Board Secretariat and CCMD at the federal level maintain large computerized databases of best practices in public-sector management. Similarly, the Institute of Public Administration of Canada (IPAC) has a database of several hundred best practices flowing from its annual awards for innovative management, many of which have been cited in this book.

Organizations that use organizational learning to innovate continuously are constantly scanning the horizon for organizations that have discovered innovative ways of improving their performance. For example, Ontario is a best-practice site in the use of electronic kiosks to improve service delivery, while British Columbia has long been a best-practice site in the delivery of "single-window" government services through their Government Agents offices. Provinces such as Quebec and Nova Scotia have studied Ontario's kiosk system with a view to possibly adapting it to their jurisdiction. And in the early 1990s, after studying the British Columbia Government Agents system first-hand, New Brunswick established its Service New Brunswick offices to improve service delivery. Similarly, awards programs such as the one at IPAC are valuable to public-sector managers in making best-practice sites more widely known, but innovative sites also become known through such means as professional conferences and articles in professional journals. The difference between most public organizations and those that actively pursue organizational learning is that the latter actively and continuously seek out and learn from innovative organizations in both the public and private sectors.

So far we examined tools for individual learning and for organizational learning. We turn now to an examination of how public organizations are beginning to link the two together in order to build the desired corporate culture and to support the achievement of the organization's strategic goals.

## STRATEGIC ORGANIZATIONAL LEARNING

Faced with organizational pressures and the challenges of change, many top leaders are now using formal learning as a strategic tool within their organizations.[463] No longer providing just a "cafeteria" of learning through their training units, more and more organizations are placing formal learning programs under the direction of their top leadership. They are using their training and development programs to bring about more innovative, more people-centred and more client-centred cultures and to generate the competencies needed by the organization as it re-positions for the future. More broadly, the programs are being used to

- shape new cultures;
- communicate and implement new strategies;
- create new alignments and strategic unity;
- develop a shared vision and unity of purpose;
- build teamwork, networks and organizational "glue";
- establish a corporate identity;

- improve leadership;
- create a cadre of change agents;
- develop critical attitudes, knowledge and skills, especially the new skills the organization requires to meet its goals; and, through all this,
- to improve organizational productivity and performance.[464]

The Ontario government has adopted this new strategic approach to the use of formal learning programs through the creation of the Centre for Leadership, which reports through the Cabinet Office. In 1997, the secretary of cabinet endorsed a Human Resources Plan for the Ontario public service (OPS) executives that included the use of formal learning as a strategic tool to support the new directions for the Ontario public service: "At a time of major transformation in the role of government, the Ontario Public Service (OPS) must have a community of public service executives who can provide strategic leadership as well as excellence in public administration. This Human Resources Plan for the Senior Management Group of the OPS is designed to develop and foster current and future leaders who can manage the challenges of the changing environment."[465] The Ontario plan endorses the new strategic roles for management education, including many of those noted above: "Executive learning is key to renewal in the OPS. It will assist the organization to communicate and implement new strategic directions; develop the critical knowledge and skills needed to meet the government's business objectives; create a cadre of change agents; build networks, cross-ministry teams, and 'organizational glue'; and improve organizational and individual effectiveness and performance."[466]

The learning programs for senior Ontario managers are linked to core competencies identified for each executive level. For example, the most senior managers are expected to

- champion best models of delivery;
- manage medium-term risk;
- synchronize goals and resources to achieve both short-term and medium-term objectives;
- communicate strategically; and
- focus in, out, and across.

Based on these competencies, and on agency-specific knowledge and competencies, the learning program for Ontario senior managers is custom-designed to achieve these specific outcomes, as well as the development of a commitment to OPS values and the development of teamwork and corporate glue through shared learning experiences among managers. The Ontario model is mirrored at the federal level by the work of CCMD at the government-wide level and by internal training institutes within such departments as Foreign Affairs and International Trade and the Coast Guard.

According to emerging best practice, this more strategic approach to training and development includes the following factors: leadership from the top; internal provision and customization; new approaches to learning (experiential, active and action); new content; and new teachers.[467] Thus, organizational top leaders, not the human resources department, now manage the organizational learning function in order to link it to strategic direction. Moreover, instead of sending managers to generic executive development programs at universities and institutes, organizations are designing their own programs internally to customize leadership development to their specific needs and directions (although actual delivery may be contracted-out). And traditional classroom-based training programs are giving way to *experiential learning* (e.g., study tours to best-practice sites), *active learning* (e.g., preparing a report on an issue facing the organization), and *action learning* (e.g., studying and solving a work-based problem and taking action to apply the solution). At the federal level, all of these new learning techniques are now used in executive development programs for federal managers.

In terms of new content, leadership development programs are moving to include more "soft" people management skills as compared to the traditional "hard skills" like strategic planning. Moreover, there is a greater emphasis on *savoir faire* – actually knowing how to implement the learning. There are also "new teachers" in learning programs; there is much greater emphasis on using other managers rather than professional teachers to deliver the programs.

## INNOVATION IN PUBLIC ORGANIZATIONS

It is obvious that organizational learning plays an enormous part in organizational innovation. There has, therefore, been a strong interest in recent years in the question of how to build innovative public organizations. But organizational learning is not the only factor in organizational innovation. The public management literature suggests that innovative organizations differ from their non-innovative, bureaucratic counterparts in many ways, including culture, values and management systems.

As discussed in Chapter 4, Iain Gow has explained the important difference between invention, innovation and diffusion.[468] There appears to be a three-step process in innovation: from invention, to diffusion, to adop-

Table 9.1. *Steps in the Innovation-Adoption Process*

| Sequence | Description |
|----------|-------------|
| Step 1 | Knowledge |
| Step 2 | Persuasion |
| Step 3 | Decision |
| Step 4 | Adoption |
| Step 5 | Confirmation |

tion. A more complete model would involve the steps outlined in Table 9.1.

In his 1994 study of fifteen public-sector innovations, Gow concluded that emulation of other public organizations was a key driver of administrative innovations and that knowledge of innovations was communicated through a variety of channels, including professional associations and professional publications: "The great importance of emulation in the public sector provides the rationale for such new magazines as the Canadian Treasury Board's *Manager's Magazine* and IPAC's *Public Sector Management*. In sharing information about successful innovations, public sector managers have probably found the surest way to stimulate innovation in their community. This is why it is most encouraging that IPAC has created its Innovative Management Awards."[469]

A study in the United States found that two-thirds of *innovative* public managers attended meetings of professional associations, and more than a third belonged to two or more professional associations.[470] Linking this data with Figure 9.2 above suggests that *senior* public managers, who are the main source of many organizational innovations, may obtain many of their innovative ideas from professional meetings as well as from books and professional journals.

Building on this research, it is possible to create a model of organizational innovation, as a framework for analysing the degree to which a public organization exhibits a high degree of innovation. This framework is outlined in Table 9.2.

Clearly, an organization's "innovation index" reflects not only how actively the organization creates its own innovations internally and learns about the innovations employed in other organizations, but also how actively and successfully the organization communicates, assesses, adapts and implements the innovative ideas it has in its "innovations pool." Post-bureaucratic organizations actively seek out innovations to improve organizational performance. This may take the form of communicating with organizations that have received professional prizes for their innovations;

Table 9.2. *A Framework for Understanding Organizational Innovativeness*

| *Steps in the innovations process* | *Factors promoting innovative capacity* |
| --- | --- |
| 1. *Creation/documentation*<br>The pool of relevant innovations known to the organization is maximized:<br>– innovations gathered from outside the organization;<br>– innovations created inside the organization. | Professional memberships, professional conferences, benchmarking, and reading of journals and books are encouraged. Staff is encouraged to innovate through supportive corporate culture and management systems such as continuous improvement teams. |
| 2. *Communication/dissemination*<br>Knowledge of relevant innovations is widely communicated and disseminated within the organization. | The organization has internal communication instruments such as newsletters and innovation fairs that disseminate innovative ideas horizontally and vertically. |
| 3. *Assessment/evaluation*<br>Assessment of known innovations for potential application within the organization. | The organization has systematic ways of evaluating innovative ideas that the organization becomes aware of. |
| 4. *Adaptation*<br>The innovation is designed to meet the needs of the organization. | The organization has the capacity to be adaptive and to see how to custom-fit the innovation to the organization. |
| 5. *Adoption*<br>The decision is made to adopt an innovation. | The organization is open/decisive in adopting innovations that can improve performance. |
| 6. *Successful implementation*<br>Innovation is successfully put into operation. | The organization is adept at managing the implementation and change process associated with integrating innovations into the organization's operations. |

regularly seeking out innovations in organizations in other jurisdictions, including those in the same business lines; encouraging staff to visit other jurisdictions to seek out innovative ideas; or benchmarking with other organizations.

The Canadian Centre for Management Development serves as an "innovation pump" for itself and the federal public service in numerous ways: it maintains the International Governance Network of public management academics in a dozen countries to identify and assess public management innovations in industrialized countries and communicates these innovations to senior managers through seminars, presentations by visiting experts, and publications. It also maintains "good-practices databases" in key areas such as innovative service delivery, drawing on examples from the professional literature, from conferences, from action-learning programs, from action research, and from national and international awards programs. These innovative practices are communicated and disseminated through publications, presentations, innovations fairs, learning programs and the CCMD web site. The centre also critically assesses important management concepts such as total quality management, re-engineering and continuous learning and communicates these assessments to public managers through its publications.

Gow's study of public-sector innovation showed that the Province of Ontario has been an innovator for many years and that during the past two decades in particular has pioneered the introduction of many significant management innovations. As will be discussed later in Chapter 10, Ontario was the first jurisdiction in Canada to implement electronic kiosks for service delivery, and it was one of the first jurisdictions to implement a corporate learning centre tied to corporate strategy and corporate competencies. Ontario public organizations have also been frequent winners of the annual IPAC awards for innovative management. Not surprisingly, senior managers in the Ontario public service are actively involved in IPAC and have a reputation for seeking out innovations throughout Canada and the world and adapting these innovations to their own needs and circumstances. In 1998, officials in charge of Ontario's service quality improvement initiative helped to lead the process of identifying innovative ways of improving service delivery through the Citizen-Centred Service Delivery Network of senior officials created by CCMD. They also developed an inventory of innovative management practices within the Ontario public service for dissemination to government departments.

Similarly, in 1997 and 1998, officials from Quebec's innovative Ministry of Immigration and Citizen Relations studied service-delivery innovations in England, France, New Brunswick, Ontario and British Columbia as part of a strategy to improve service to the citizens of Quebec through technology and "single-window" storefront delivery of government services. In each case we observe public organizations that are constantly scanning innovations in other jurisdictions and continuously assessing and adapting the best ideas to improve the performance of their own organizations. Inevitably, these organizations find that some innovations do not succeed, but innovative organizations learn from their failures and work to minimize risk during the implementation of innovative ideas.

## IMPLICATIONS AND IMPEDIMENTS

### Managerial and Organizational Considerations

We have seen that public organizations wanting to become innovative, *learning* organizations need to make several changes in their management and organizational culture to achieve this result:

1. The organization must invest significant resources in both individual and organizational learning. Current good practice for formal learning is at least five days per annum for each employee.

2. Organizational learning should be actively managed by the executive team and consciously linked to organizational strategy.

3. The organization should harness both formal and informal learning techniques and use action and active-learning techniques to improve the impact of the learning experience.

4. The organization's culture and management systems should actively promote innovation and be outward-looking. They should continuously seek out innovations in other organizations that can be adapted to improve organizational performance.

The organization should also accept occasional failure as the inevitable cost of continuous improvement and learning initiatives, because there are substantial obstacles to success. Some of these obstacles are similar to those identified in earlier chapters. For example, such obstacles to organizational learning as resistance to increased funding for training and development, aversion to risk-taking, and low commitment to teamwork are also obstacles to organizational empowerment. Organizational learning is facilitated when "those closest to the client are given the power and responsibility to respond to client needs," "where risk is accepted" and "where the organization is committed to teamwork." These are elements of the post-bureaucratic model in general, and, where commitment to these elements does not exist, organizational learning is much less likely to occur.

### Political Considerations

Canada's adversarial political culture is supported by the efforts of such actors as the media and the auditor general in seeking out and publicizing mistakes and examples of waste in government. Active learning such as professional conferences, benchmarking and visits to other jurisdictions is viewed as "wasteful" spending by some elected politicians. Politicians who come from a small-business background are used to a system where skills are acquired via the person hired, since workers in small businesses tend to be mobile and investments in training cannot long be internalized in the firm. A provincial premier with a small-business background was heard to say, "If you need to send him for training, why did you hire him in the first place?" On the other hand, politicians with experience in large organizations know that training and development is an integral part of a large company's competitive strategy. While inadequate funding for formal training is a major impediment to organizational learning, it is difficult in a period of downsizing to protect and expand funds for learning activity.

Another barrier to organizational learning is risk aversion at the political level. Inevitably, politicians tend towards a risk-free approach to public management, where mistakes are avoided. Given the fish-bowl nature of public service and the many political actors waiting to pounce on mistakes, building an innovative culture in public organizations is an uphill battle. This makes it difficult for those public managers who try to develop a more innovative, risk-taking culture within their organizations. As one innovative public manager put it, "Either I try to play error-free ball, or I try to win the game; I can't do both at the same time."

### Value and Ethical Considerations

In Chapter 3, on sharing and managing values, we discussed the general importance of shared values to organizational success and the close links between an organization's vision, mission and values. With specific reference to organizational learning, Marquardt and Reynolds, as noted earlier, argue that in order to foster such learning, organizations need to have a vision: "Vision is organization-side consensus and support for the future directions. It includes the mission, values and beliefs of the organization. The common vision must be shared by and be challenging to everyone in the organization."[471]

All three types of public-service values discussed in Chapter 3 – professional, democratic and ethical values – are affected by efforts to promote organizational learning and innovation. For example, leadership is a professional value that is critical to organizational learning: "Learning-oriented leaders or 'learning champions' will create and nourish opportunities for learning. Leaders in the learning organization have the ability and drive to seek out new information and new ideas, to listen to criticism and dissenting views, and to help establish learning teams. They ensure that communication flows freely and that the momentum for change remains alive."[472] It is significant that several of the values identified by public-service executives and managers as being especially important in the future – namely, teamwork, collaboration and creativity – are professional values that are closely linked to the requirements for organizational learning.

Ethical values also come to the fore in organizational learning. Organizations that commit to continuous improvement through continuous learning and innovation must be sensitive to such ethical values as integrity, respect and caring. Many organizations commit themselves in their mission and values statement to the notion that "our employees are our most important resource." These organizations must "walk their talk" by striving to create an organizational climate where people are valued and are given a working environment where they can innovate, learn and contribute their best.

Honesty is another ethical value that is critical to successful organizational learning:

The essence of continuous and organizational learning is the pursuit and cultivation of truth in organizations. ... [O]rganizations that falter often do so because they ... have failed to develop the structures, habits, attitudes and values of learning and of honesty. They have allowed themselves to become insulated and distanced from these realities through ignorance, through oversight, and through the elaborate "organizational defences" that make it so difficult for ideas and perceptions to circulate freely, open and creatively. Organizational learning is about overcoming these defences and developing higher levels of perception, awareness, and honesty.[473]

## CONCLUSIONS

During the 1980s and 1990s, fiscal imperatives, public opinion, and changes in technology placed huge pressures on the public sector to find new ways of delivering public services within greatly reduced budgetary resources. The public sector, at all three levels of government, has responded by becoming much more innovative in reducing costs and improving service. This has required many public organizations to put much greater emphasis on organizational learning as a means of continuously finding ways to reduce costs and improve performance. Many of those organizations that have moved strongly towards the post-bureaucratic model have invested more resources in learning, have created a culture that values learning and innovation, and have put in place management systems that actively create and seek out innovative ways of improving performance.

# 10

# Enabling Change through Information Technology

## DEFINITION, FUNCTIONS AND EXAMPLES

The use of information technology was identified in Chapter 1 as one of the primary means of enabling public organizations to move towards the post-bureaucratic model. In that chapter we also discussed the technological revolution as one of the external forces stimulating the reform of public organizations in Canada. When information technology (IT) is introduced into the public sector, it can dramatically affect both internal operations and relations with the public. We would expect that any post-bureaucratic organization would be using up-to-date, and possibly leading edge, IT in ways compatible with its mission.

Information technology improves service quality by increasing accessibility (for example, by electronic access at any time of day instead of visits to government offices during business hours) and by making possible one-stop service. Information technology can facilitate participative leadership both within and outside public-sector organizations by making information widely available over the Internet and making it easier for citizens to express their views by sending e-mail or participating in discussion groups. It can facilitate decentralization by giving front-line workers the information necessary to make decisions themselves. And it can also help government become more revenue-driven by making it easier to measure and charge for the use of public services. For example, advances in information processing capacity have permitted a variety of public assets, such as clean water and air, landing rights at airports, or access to highways, to be bought and sold in markets.[474]

This chapter will show that IT is right at the core of post-bureaucratic public organizations in Canada. Seen in international perspective, Canadian governments are at the forefront in applying IT to the public sector. In part, this follows from a Canadian tradition of investing in state-of-the-art communications infrastructure to serve a population that is dispersed over a vast territory. In addition, as discussed in chapters 1 and 4, the fiscal crisis faced by Canadian governments has led them to look for the potential to reduce cost by substituting IT for labour. A simple way to see how extensive the information revolution is in Canadian government is to attend, or even to browse the program for, Technology in Government Week, a conference held annually since the early 1990s in Ottawa in mid-September. The program includes presentations by representatives of all levels of government on recent applications; presentations by industry representatives on the newest hardware, software and applications; discussions of the implications of IT for human resource management, training and privacy; and hundreds of exhibits by suppliers.

Chapters 5 to 9 have gone to some lengths to define relatively abstract concepts such as empowerment, consultation and partnership. In contrast, the concept of IT is quite concrete and easily defined. But because of the rapid advance of technological progress, it has numerous and often-changing realizations. Initially, we can define *information technology* as methods of compiling, storing, transferring and analysing information electronically. The notion of transferring makes clear the evolution and transformation of technology. For example, information can be transferred by dedicated wiring (ethernet), by telephone lines, or by wireless radio signals. In all three, the speed and quality of transmission have been improving markedly.

Canadian governments have been very active in introducing IT applications, some of which are listed below. This list makes no claim to being an exhaustive survey, and this classification of five types of technology is necessarily somewhat artificial. Given the rapidly evolving and readily transformable nature of IT, some of the technologies listed here may no longer be in use in a few years, or they may be re-combined in new ways.

First, the use of *electronic mail and the Internet* in government has taken off in the last three years. At this point, the federal government (www.gov.gc.ca), all the provinces (www.gov.on.ca, www.gov.ns.ca, etc.), and many municipalities have web sites and e-mail systems. The governmental e-mail systems are internally secure, in that internal communications are not accessible to outsiders, but links are provided for communication with the public through the Internet.[475] Among the items you will find if you browse through the different government web sites are the following: recent news releases, ministerial statements, statements of governmental priorities, commission reports, legislative information and debates, statistics, links to departmental web sites, areas where business can be transacted with government departments, business information directed at investors, electronic telephone directories of the public service, and opportunities for citizens to provide feedback.

In addition to these web sites that are providing mainly information about the public sector, governments have established other web sites containing information about various sectors of the economy and society and related electronic discussion groups. An example of this type of web site is "Strategis" (http://strategis.ic.gc.ca), Industry Canada's comprehensive business information source, incorporating a broad range of information about markets, industry sectors, and new technologies.[476] Another sectoral application is HealthNet. HealthNet has a web site and a discussion group that deals with health policy issues and government policy announcements, information about technological advances such as remote diagnosis, job postings, and requests for proposals.[477]

Another possibility is the use of the Internet for electronic democracy, that is, public discussion of political issues. Governments have only infrequently hosted such discussion groups; rather, individual citizens or interest groups have taken the initiative to launch such discussion groups themselves. A recent example is Citizens for Local Democracy, an Internet forum started by opponents of the Ontario government's proposals to amalgamate the municipalities of Metropolitan Toronto.[478] One would expect politicians to have some reluctance about going on-line and being exposed to the often vituperative reactions (flaming, in Netspeak) of the opponents of their policies.[479]

A second set of IT applications involves what we will call *remote electronic transactions*. At the federal level, two of the best-known examples are electronic tax filing and procurement. Electronic income-tax filing became available in 1993 and, by 1995, was being used by four million Canadians; due to security considerations, filing must be done by tax preparers using secure communications lines rather than by individuals using home computers.[480] Similarly, businesses are paying corporate income tax and personal income-tax deductions electronically, also through secure lines in financial institutions or payroll service bureaus. This program began in 1992 and by 1995 encompassed 40,000 companies making 500,000 payments annually for a value of $10.9 billion.[481]

The federal government's Open Bidding Service, now MERX, is a leading-edge application of IT to the procurement function. Information about most federal government contracts worth more than $50,000 – a total of $5 billion annually – is available on a web site (www.merx.cebra.com). The system is accessible around the clock in both official languages, with on-line support. Bidders can find out about past purchases as well as the other bidders who are ordering documents for a particular contract, so as to identify either competitors or potential bid partners. The system is

231

funded through user fees for electronic documents. The initiative stream-lined the bidding process, saves approximately $1.5 million per year in postage and labour, relative to the old paper-based system, and makes contract information available to a wider range of possible suppliers.[482]

At the provincial level, registry offices have been in the vanguard in developing the capability for remote electronic transactions. British Columbia and Ontario were the first to develop electronic systems of regis-tering and searching records of loans for the purchase of property other than real estate (personal property registries), and both applied to the Institute of Public Administration of Canada Award for Innovative Man-agement in 1993. British Columbia won first prize that year.[483] For clients, the benefits of electronic searching are substantial: the ability to work from their own offices instead of visiting a government office; faster and more accurate transactions; and longer hours of service. As a consequence, over eighty per cent of registrations and searches are now being performed electronically in both provinces.[484] The other provinces are now following British Columbia and Ontario's lead. The next area for electronic registra-tion is land titles.

A third example of IT is the *electronic kiosk*, in which the Ontario Ministry of Transportation has taken the lead. In conjunction with IBM, it has devel-oped electronic kiosks for the delivery of routine government products and services, such as vehicle registration renewals and change-of-address reporting. There is now in place a system of sixty ServiceOntario elec-tronic kiosks at government buildings and major urban shopping centres throughout the province, more conveniently located and open longer hours than government offices (www.gov.on.ca/MTO/English/kiosk/main.htm). This innovation was accomplished with no capital investment by the government and using a core staff of three people; IBM is being compensated on a commission basis.[485] The company has been running advertisements about the ServiceOntario kiosks in *Governing* magazine, directed at state and local governments in the United States.

Another Ontario government initiative is the Ministry of Consumer and Commercial Relations' Clearing the Path for Business Success project, which won the third prize in the 1996 IPAC Award for Innovative Manage-ment.[486] This project makes possible single-window service business registration, which incorporates name searches and registration, vendor registration, and registration for Retail Sales Tax, Employer Health Tax, and Workers' Compensation, all conducted electronically at one computer work-station.[487]

Human Resources Development Canada has established a system of 400 electronic kiosks throughout the country, most in locations where per-sonal assistance is also available, from which people can file applications for unemployment insurance, search for job vacancies in the National Job Bank, and obtain answers to questions about the labour market.[488]

A fourth example, and one in which Canada is in the lead internationally, is *electronic highway tolling*. The Province of Ontario wanted to build a major urban expressway to serve Toronto's northern suburbs; however, its fiscal situation precluded financing the road out of tax revenues or by incurring more debt. The solution was to use electronic technology to finance it from user fees. This is an example of G.B. Reschenthaler and Fred Thompson's point that computer technology has lowered the transactions costs of charging for the use of what were formerly viewed as public goods.[489] In the past, toll highways used toll booths, an expensive technology in terms of drivers' time, land cost (to widen the highway to accommodate toll plazas), and operating cost. As a consequence, urban expressways with numerous entrances and exits have not been able to use toll booths and thus have suffered from heavy traffic congestion. Ontario's Highway 407 has twenty-five interchanges in its sixty-nine kilometres but does not need to use toll booths. Drivers may acquire a transponder – a small electronic transmitter by which their cars can be identified and charged for use of the highway when they enter and exit. Drivers without transponders have a video-image taken of their license plates when entering and exiting. Both groups of drivers are charged per kilometre time-differentiated fees, with the highest fees during the morning and afternoon rush hours. Because video-imaging is more expensive than transponder technology, there is a $1 per trip surcharge for the former, designed to encourage frequent users to acquire transponders.[490] The technological advance was in the application of guided missile-tracking technology initially used in the Persian Gulf War; it distinguishes between cars with and without transponders and then directs cameras mounted on overhead gantries to video-image the rear license plates of cars without transponders.[491]

A fifth area into which Canadian governments are beginning to enter is the development of *debit cards or smart cards* to identify individuals and perform transactions.[492] The federal government has developed the Canpass, a credit-card-sized identification pass, which contains encoded fingerprints, used by frequent Canada–US. travellers to bypass customs queues.[493] A number of American states are delivering welfare and other benefits by debit or smart cards, and South Africa makes pension payments by means of smart cards with encoded fingerprints, a feature designed to deter cheating. The City of Toronto considered establishing such a system for welfare benefits but ultimately decided against it.[494] The Province of Ontario announced in its fall 1999 throne speech that it is considering the adoption of a smart card incorporating biometric identification for a wide range of transactions with citizens. Such a card could replace drivers' licenses, birth certificates, and health cards.[495]

## Local Heroes in Information Technology

Chapter 4 showed that in Canada, as in the United States, front-line public servants and middle managers play a very important role in initiating innovations. One very interesting finding from the United States data was that front-line workers or middle managers initiated seventy per cent of the information technology innovations, higher than the average of forty-eight per cent for all types of innovations and higher than for any other type of innovation. Looking at individual cases, the following picture of an information technology local hero emerges: a person who is close to and knowledgeable about a particular technology; who is aware of the evolution of that technology in other jurisdications and wants to match, if not exceed, its achievements elsewhere; who often has a long-term vision as to how the technology can grow to serve new purposes and markets; and, finally, who has leadership strengths by virtue of his or her ability to communicate this vision to others not familiar with the technology who control the resources needed to make the vision a reality.[496] Not your average techies! The success stories for IT innovations in Canada look similar. For example, the initiative for innovations such as the on-line registry systems in Ontario and British Columbia and the ServiceOntario electronic kiosks came from middle management, with assistant deputy ministers serving as high-level champions.

This portrait of the IT local hero has support from a recent survey of government officials in the United States and Canada about their perceptions of information technology reported by Jerry Mechling, a faculty member at the Kennedy School of Government. The survey found that, although over seventy-five per cent of respondents rated chief information officers in government and the technology community favourably in terms of the depth of their understanding of technology issues, the favourable ratings dropped to thirty-six per cent for budget and finance officers, twenty-eight per cent for government general managers, and eighteen per cent for legislators.[497] In the mid-1990s, at least, there was a critical knowledge-gap between the "techies" and the political and bureaucratic leadership, and successful innovators were the ones who, through their leadership and communication skills, had been able to transcend it. At the close of the decade, the political and bureaucratic leadership is more aware of the vast potential of IT, but the techies are still better informed about how it is evolving.

## Results Achieved

There are two ways of tracking the results of these IT initiatives. If the use of a new technology is voluntary and if users in large numbers are switching to it from an earlier technology, it is clear that the new technology is more convenient than the old. A second way to track the results is to measure cost reductions, decreases in waiting times, increases in convenience, and so on. Presumably, these two ways of measuring results should reinforce one another. Here are results that have been reported for the technologies discussed in the previous section:

- Electronic personal income-tax filing saved Revenue Canada $3.3 million in publishing and mailing costs in 1995; in addition, returns filed electronically are usually processed within two weeks, faster than for paper filing.[498]

- The Open Bidding Service (MERX) saves Supply and Services Canada $1.5 million annually on staff and document production and distribution.[499] While no attempt was made to measure reductions in procurement cost due to increased competition, a similar program in the State of Oregon is estimated to save ten per cent on the cost of goods purchased and to reduce the cost of operating the purchasing function by twenty per cent.[500]

- The British Columbia Personal Property Registry has reduced the turnaround time for transactions to two days. By its third year of operation, eighty per cent of registrations were done remotely, rather than in person, a convincing measure of customer acceptance. The staff was reduced from thirty-nine positions to twelve in four years. Finally, expenditures were reduced from $2.1 million in 1990 to $1.6 million in 1993.[501]

- The Ontario Personal Property Security Registry achieved similar results. In its third year of operation, eighty per cent of registrations and sixty-six per cent of inquiries were done electronically. Expenditures fell from $7 million to $4 million, and staffing was reduced from 100 positions to sixty over the same period. Finally, surveys indicated significant increases in customer satisfaction.[502]

- In its first two years of operation, Ontario's Clearing the Path project reduced the service time for business name searches from four weeks to five minutes and for business-name registration from six weeks to one.

In September 1996, instant on-line registrations were introduced. By 1996, fifty per cent of all registrations were being done electronically rather than in person.[503]

- The ServiceOntario kiosks have received a ninety-five-per-cent approval rating from consumers who were asked if the machines were easy to use, time-saving, and convenient, and if they would use the kiosks again. The kiosks now account for 700,000 transactions, approximately five to ten per cent of total transactions. The kiosks won second prize in the 1997 IPAC Award for Innovative Management (see www.gov.on.ca/english/news/ipac/htm).

- Because of some problems with the video-imaging technology, when Highway 407 opened in June 1997, fees were not charged. This free-use period had the benefit of introducing drivers – making 300,000 trips each weekday – to the highway. The technology problems were soon resolved, and pricing went into effect in October 1997. The highway now accommodates an average of more than 150,000 trips each weekday and brings in $6 million in revenue each month, both on target relative to plan. Two-thirds of trips are accounted for by drivers with transponders; a measure of the effectiveness of the technology is that over 99.5 per cent of transponder trips and ninety-five per cent of video trips are captured and billed.

  The Ontario government decided to privatize the highway, and in April 1999 it accepted a bid of $3.1 billion from a consortium comprising SNC-Lavallin Group, a Quebec engineering company; Caisse de dépôt et placement du Québec, the province's pension fund; the Bank of Montreal; and Grupo Ferrovial, Spain's second-largest construction company. The new owners are obligated to build another thirty-nine kilometres to complete the highway and are permitted to charge profit-maximizing tolls for the next ninety-nine years. The bid is substantially more than the government's original investment of approximately $1.5 billion.[504]

These IT innovations have achieved what was intended. They have improved service quality and have reduced costs, in some cases, such as the property registries, very substantially.

## IMPLICATIONS AND IMPEDIMENTS

### Managerial Considerations

To this point, this chapter has presented examples of successful public-sector IT projects. Going beyond cases, it is clear that IT has become increasingly essential to the public sector and a major factor in the production of public services. One measure of its importance is that, according to a 1994 estimate by the Treasury Board Secretariat, the Government of Canada was then spending over $3 billion annually on IT. This included the acquisition of new systems, as well as $1 billion in salaries for the 20,000 people who maintain and manage the technology.[505] Based on that report's estimate that IT staff expenditures were growing by six per cent per annum and other IT expenditures by nine per cent per annum, the federal government's annual IT expenditures now exceed $4 billion. Because the development of new software and enhancement in the capability of hardware are occurring rapidly and simultaneously, the useful life of existing systems is quite short; as a consequence, governments will continue to make major and frequent expenditures on new systems.

Managing IT is challenging, and there is a good deal of evidence that many managers have not been up to the challenge. A large percentage of IT projects, whether in the public or private sectors, suffer from one or more of the following three implementation failures: being over budget, being delivered late, or not meeting promised specifications. The Standish Group's frequently cited 1995 study of 8,400 IT projects in the public and private sectors in the United States found that thirty-one per cent were cancelled before completion; fifty-three per cent were completed, but over budget (by an average of 189 per cent) and with less than full functionality (providing on average only forty-two per cent of the proposed features and functions); and only sixteen per cent of the software projects were completed on time and within budget.[506]

Several large Canadian projects have also experienced similar problems: for example, SHL Systemhouse Inc. dropped a $10-million contract to modernize the computerized registry for Canada Savings Bonds; Public Works and Government Services Canada cancelled a $120-million contract with Andersen Consulting for a civil service compensation system, and Andersen Consulting sued the government in response; and Hughes Aircraft of Canada incurred significant cost overruns and major delays in its contract with Transport Canada to modernize the air-traffic control system.[507]

Given the seriousness of the problems with project management, there has now been substantial discussion about, as well as some progress in, doing it better.[508] The Treasury Board and auditor general have made a number of recommendations, such as ensuring that projects are aligned with departmental strategy and priorities, permitting more cooperation between government and the private sector during the bidding process so that bids can be more realistic, putting more emphasis on bidder capabilities than on promises of regional industrial benefits, replacing fixed price contracts with contracts incorporating both incentives and penalties, establishing clearer accountability for project management, training contract managers more effectively, monitoring the production period more diligently to make sure that contractors are meeting interim deadlines, and allowing for in-course changes in both the technology and the scope of the contract.

Managerial concerns about project management bring to the fore the private sector's role in the development of IT within government. The private sector inevitably will be playing a major role in providing hardware, software, and systems integration. For example, IBM pioneered electronic kiosk technology in California, then brought it to Ontario, and is now trying to market it elsewhere.[509]

From a private-sector point of view, the public sector is an ideal IT client. The public sector is providing services that could benefit from IT applications; in many areas, the public sector is technologically out-of-date; and, finally, the public sector is under pressure to produce savings. If the public sector is to enter into contracts with the private sector in the IT area, it needs people who are knowledgeable about IT and who are good negotiators, so that the deals that are struck benefit the public sector and, while ensuring that the private sector earns an appropriate risk-adjusted return on its investment, do not let the private-sector contractor earn excessive profits at public expense. Some governments have struck deals that align the incentives for the government and the private-sector contractor, for example, by paying the contractor on the basis of how much a technology is used if usage is voluntary, or by paying the contractor a share of the savings achieved.

However, the private sector's role in IT goes beyond that of contractor. We are now seeing technological convergence between the public and private sectors in the sense that both sectors are using the same technologies, such as electronic mail, the Internet, debit or smart cards, and electronic kiosks. For example, public-sector debit or smart cards for transfer payments use the banks' ATM systems, and private-sector debit cards can be used for payment at government kiosks. As was discussed in Chapter 6, user perceptions of the quality of technology-based public services will be influenced by their experience with technology-based private services. While one might argue that the public sector's IT applications should be somewhat less sophisticated than those of the private sector, because public-sector applications emphasize widespread accessibility of a service instead of targeting owners of the latest hardware or software, users may not permit the public sector to be far behind.

In addition to improving the management of big IT projects and handling relationships with the private sector, other managerial issues that governments are wrestling with include how to retain skilled IT staff, how to structure IT operations in line ministries, and the role and powers of the government's chief information officer.[510]

People with IT skills are in short supply everywhere, leading to a bid-up in IT salaries, particularly in the private sector. Governments have responded in a number of ways. They have tried to compete by emphasizing the intrinsic value of public-sector work and lifestyle advantages such as the amenities of the smaller cities in which many government departments are located. The federal government has recently responded to the market by increasing salaries of IT specialists by twenty per cent. Because many public-sector IT jobs are not purely technical but rather involve communicating between technicians and technology users (i.e., internal customers), they are increasingly going, not to computer science graduates, but to people who combine basic technical expertise with strong business and communication skills. Yet another alternative is out-sourcing some IT functions.

As IT becomes increasingly important, departments are establishing IT units headed by an assistant deputy minister, known as the department's chief information officer. His or her role is to ensure that systems are compatible within the department, to act as a champion for IT initiatives in the department, and to provide support for the department's IT infrastructure. The chief information officer is often a member of the department's senior management committee. Governments are also appointing government-wide chief information officers at the deputy-minister level. The chief information officer has a mandate as change agent and champion of new technology at the interdepartmental level. In some cases, particularly if they are part of, or closely allied with, a ministry of finance or treasury board, they have been able to exercise control over departmental IT budgets. They have often had a mandate to encourage common standards, for example ensuring that, as e-mail developed within the public sector, all departments would be able to communicate with one another. In addition, many technology applications, for example kiosks, can serve many departments, and it is the chief information officer's responsibility to ensure that departments cooperate in the development of these joint applications.

In addition to the considerations of organizational structure and staffing discussed above, IT also raises concerns regarding the management of service delivery. For example, if a new technology is more convenient for the customer and less expensive for the government than an old technology, the challenge for governments is to induce as many customers as possible to switch to the new technology. The experience of the British Columbia and Ontario personal-property security registry offices provides an excellent example of how this was done rapidly. Much of their business was accounted for by a small number of commercial customers, namely the major financial institutions.[511] The registries approached the institutions directly, made a business case for going on-line, and then provided good customer support. The Ontario registry provided an additional incentive to convert by adding a surcharge of $5 for manual transactions after the on-line system had been in operation for eighteen months.[512]

Despite such incentives, it is still likely that governments will be providing services by means of a number of different technologies simultaneously. For example, automobile registration may be done in person at government offices, in person at electronic kiosks, and, in the near future, remotely by Internet. In areas where the customers are individuals, rather than businesses, public opinion may resist surcharges levied on those who use old technologies, particularly if they tend to be those who are poor and/or old.

A second area involving the management of service delivery is the use of IT to facilitate single-window service delivery or one-stop shopping. Technically, it is easy to add functions to computer systems at government counters or to electronic kiosks. The more challenging issue is interdepartmental cooperation. How are costs of building the system to be shared, especially when the initial development cost is much greater than the cost of adding functions ? How is organizational or political credit to be allocated? One factor that might overcome resistance to change is fiscal pressure; departments facing severe budget cuts are often surprisingly innovative at finding ways of cooperating to reduce costs.

## Value and Ethical Considerations

*Equity and Accessibility*
There is substantial evidence that access to computers is unevenly distributed throughout Canadian society. A recent Statistics Canada study found that fifty-three per cent of households in the top fifth of the income distribution have a home computer, compared with only twelve per cent of those in the lowest fifth of the income distribution.[513] While computers have been hailed as a great equalizer by providing access to a vast and growing body of information through the Internet, they cannot play this role if they themselves are inequitably distributed. Given the importance of computers in education and in the workforce of the future, it is a particularly important policy objective to ensure access on the part of all young people. The main way that the federal and provincial governments have attempted to do this is by setting a goal of, and providing funding for, Internet access for all 23,000 schools and libraries by 1998.[514] Nevertheless, even if that goal is met, access will still be

limited, because, on average, schools have one computer for fifteen to twenty students.[515] Again, wealthier provinces and municipalities can be expected to do better than the national average. Wealthier families will provide computers for their children so that they can avoid the queues at school.

One federal government initiative to improve access is the Computers for Schools program (www.schoolnet.ca/cfs-ope/). The federal government has established forty-three workshops throughout the country to recycle its surplus computers (generally, 286, 386, and 486 models) for the schools. The repair and re-programming work in the National Capital Region is being done by paid technicians, many supported by HRDC's Youth Employment Program, and by volunteers. The work in the regions is being done by Telephone Pioneers, an association of current and retired telephone company employees.[516] Between the initiation of the program in 1993 and June 1998, over 55,000 computers have been donated; the program's goal is 250,000 donations by the end of the decade.

An example of an initiative explicitly targeted at the underprivileged is the Public Housing Commission of Lansing, Michigan's Computer Learning Centers, which won a Ford Foundation-Kennedy School of Government Innovation Award. These centres, located in public housing projects, use state-of-the-art (rather than recycled) technology and are available to students after school hours; impressive results have been achieved in terms of both the students' academic performance and a reduction of delinquency at the projects.[517]

Access to information technology is not just an education issue. For example, the Statistics Canada study of computer usage reported that eighty per cent of those between the ages of fifteen and twenty-four declared themselves to be computer literate, but fewer than ten per cent of those over the age of sixty-five made the same assessment. In part, the passing of time will solve this problem, but governments still might consider policies to increase computer literacy among seniors. Finally, there have been some programs to provide the assistance of information technology for the disadvantaged. For example, Seattle, Washington, with corporate support, established a program to provide voice mailboxes for homeless people; this program has been shown to be very effective at helping them find work and housing and has now been widely replicated in the U.S.[518] The United Way of Greater Toronto supports a similar program. While Canadian governments are under fiscal pressure, investments in increasing the availability of IT could pay high long-run returns in terms of better student performance in school and thereafter in the labour market. The challenge is to calculate these returns and, where justified, establish programs.

*Privacy and Anonymity*
The use of information technology for transactions with the public sector inevitably involves the creation, manipulation and potential sharing of databases that contain a great deal of personal information. This potential has led to many expressions of concern about invasions of privacy. Here are a few examples of concerns that have recently been expressed:

- Recently, the City of Victoria, British Columbia, put on the Internet its property-tax assessment roll, which had long been available in hard copy in the lobby of city hall. As a result of a story in the local newspaper, the assessment roll became a very popular web site, as people began searching to discover the value of their neighbour's properties, who owned a given property, and where any given individual owned properties. Within days, the city removed the assessment roll from the Internet, and the province's information and privacy commissioner began an investigation.[519]

- One of the reasons that the City of Toronto dropped its plan to produce a smart card for welfare recipients is that anti-poverty activists argued that finger-scanning welfare recipients would stigmatize them as criminals.[520]

- The Ontario government's recent throne speech proposal to introduce a multipurpose smart card met with an immediate expression of concern from the province's privacy commissioner, who announced that she expected the government to consult with her before introducing the cards and expressed her opposition to any use of the cards for tracking or surveillance.[521]

These stories suggest that a number of concerns are being expressed about IT. The reaction of anti-poverty activists to finger-scanning shows a view of social-safety net programs in which, in an uncertain world, it is considered better not to exclude someone who is entitled to benefits than to catch someone who is not entitled to benefits. However, in the government's view, putting in place a technology such as finger-scanning reduces uncertainty. In this view, it is an entirely appropriate response to fiscal constraint to employ finger-scanning to reduce fraud.[522]
The Victoria story shows how much more valuable a database becomes when it is readily accessible over the Internet. The British Columbia privacy commissioner's concern was primarily with the fact that people could use the linkage between property addresses and owners' names to find people who had legitimate reasons not to want to be found. Property

owners had lost their anonymity. The city was contemplating making the database available once more, but without names included.[523]

The federal government story also reflects a concern about the possibility of linking databases in inappropriate ways. The federal government, in its 1994 *Blueprint for Renewing Government Services Using Information Technology*, set forth as one of its guiding information principles that "information will be captured once, as close to the source as possible, then shared and re-used by authorized users."[524] The question that arises is who is an authorized user? For example, we appear to have accepted the principle that databases should be linked to permit the public sector to recover debts owed to it by individuals. Thus, student debts may be deducted from income-tax refunds, and provincial governments may calculate unpaid traffic- and parking-ticket liability and require people to pay it before they may renew their automobile registration or driver's license.[525] However, we are much less willing to allow government department A access to records gathered by department B to determine *whether* an individual violated statutes enforced by department A.

These three stories suggest that, as more uses are found for information technology and more databases are created, both legislation and case law will define principles to determine who in government (or elsewhere) should be authorized to use data gathered by another part of the government.

### Political Considerations

Because ever more of the public sector's work is being done through IT, the management of IT is becoming increasingly salient to Canada's politicians. Consider their interests in terms of issues of project management, equity and accessibility, public consultation, and privacy and anonymity.

If large IT projects – even ones completely internal to government – are managed poorly, resulting in cost overruns or contract cancellations, incumbent politicians will suffer, because it will create the image that they are poor public managers. In an era of deficits, budgetary restraint, and heavy and, in some cases, increasing taxes, this is not a desirable image. It is unlikely that the image of being poor public managers will defeat governments, but it certainly will not help re-elect them. Politicians have no expertise in managing complex projects, particularly in as rapidly changing an area as IT. Thus, it is unlikely that closer political supervision would improve project management. Indeed, there are some cases where political input into project management, for example choosing weaker contractors in order to deliver regional benefits, has exacerbated project management problems. Thus, politicians will have to rely on their central agencies such as treasury board secretariats or ministries of finance to develop and implement improved project management systems. Politicians should not be micro-managing these projects but should be holding their central agencies and line departments accountable for the results. Specifically, they should be asking public servants whether the projects were delivered on time, at cost, and with promised capabilities.

For politicians, the issues of equity and accessibility have a number of faces. First, programs to increase accessibility to computers and the Internet in the schools are politically popular, and all politicians, from prime ministers and presidents on down, want photo-ops delivering new computer systems to schools or watching as students surf the Internet on government-provided computers. In addition, donations of computers or software to schools are a way that private-sector firms can act as socially responsible citizens, and there is no shortage of private-sector partners. Not only is this true of programs helping the educational sector in general, but also of programs such as the Lansing Housing Corporation's Computer Learning Centers that provide computers and Internet access to the underprivileged. The demonstrated success of pilot programs in this area means that politicians, and their private-sector partners, are doing something – and can be seen to be doing something – about problems of youth poverty, unemployment and delinquency.[526] Thus, there is solid political support for such initiatives.

A second aspect of accessibility is the availability of older technologies for citizens who are not comfortable with the most up-to-date ones. It is likely that politicians will argue that it is necessary to continue to provide these technologies as long as there is any demand for their use. Very occasionally politicians have criticized new technologies, the most visible recent example being then-Toronto mayoral candidate Mel Lastman denouncing voice mail and promising that the new city would replace voice mail with human voices. That promise did not appear to have contributed much to his successful election campaign and, in the light of the new city's budget problems, it appears to have been forgotten. Thus, there appears to be little political mileage to be gained adopting Luddite tactics, especially if new technology delivers substantial cost-savings.

A third aspect of accessibility concerns user fees that have been implemented by means of IT, such as the tolls on Highway 407. The public has accepted that the tolls are being used to make users, rather than the general taxpayer, pay for the highway. Another reason for the public acceptance of Highway 407 is that no one is being forced to use it. There are alternative routes without tolls, including Highway 401, Highway 7, and Steeles Avenue. This case would suggest that the public will accept user fees implemented through IT if the fees are clearly explained and if there are alternatives to the premium service for which fees are charged.

While new technologies, such as Internet and e-mail, have the potential to be used for public consultation, politicians and citizens are still learning how to use them effectively. In addition to information on government web sites about government programs, there are ministerial profiles and copies of their speeches. Political parties have web sites that are being used to explain their positions on key issues, invite public reaction, communicate with party members, and sell memberships (see, for example, www.ontariopc.on.ca). The Internet is being used as a medium for citizens' groups that are organizing to oppose government policy. One interesting case is that in November 1997, messages circulated on the Internet to the effect that, should enough concerned citizens contact her office, Ontario's lieutenant-governor Hilary Weston would refuse to sign the Ontario government's controversial education bill. The lieutenant-governor's office took the unusual action of issuing on the Internet and elsewhere a press release stating that the messages were untrue and clarifying her constitutional role.[527] The Internet campaign did not stop the Harris government from passing the education bill, just as the Citizens for Local Democracy campaign on the Internet and other media did not stop the Harris government from creating the megacity. Nevertheless, the Internet does appear to be a medium that citizens' groups that oppose government policy can readily use, because it is inexpensive, uncensored, and reaches an ever-increasing percentage of the population.

Finally, politicians will have a keen interest in issues of privacy and anonymity raised by IT. We have seen that IT creates new possibilities for the sharing of information within the public sector, as well as enhanced accessibility by the public to information held by the government. In many instances these are "hot-button" issues. Inevitably, politicians will be deeply involved in public discussion about when information-sharing and enhanced accessibility are and are not appropriate, and the results of such discussions will ultimately be embodied in legislation. Public opinion about governmental priorities will play a major role in these decisions. For example, proposals to use IT to enforce child-support obligations will be argued as a choice between fathers' rights and cracking down on deadbeat dads. The political decisions that emerge are likely to differ throughout the country.

## CONCLUSIONS

This chapter has shown that IT is essential to the operation of the public sector in Canada and that post-bureaucratic organizations are deeply involved in the implementation and management of IT projects. Technology is advancing rapidly, opening up new possibilities we had scarcely imagined a few years ago. It is showing results in terms of faster and more convenient service – leading the public to reject old technologies in favour of new ones – as well as lower cost. However, IT is also controversial, and there are many issues to confront. These include managerial problems such as project management, relations with the private sector, and managing the IT function within the public service; there are also value considerations such as equity, accessibility and privacy. The managerial and value considerations inevitably raise political concerns. Information technology is one aspect of the post-bureaucratic organization where both the risks and rewards are great. Are Canada's public managers and politicians up to the challenge?

# 11

# Managing Policy

The process by which public policies are developed and implemented has an extremely important influence on policy outcomes. Thus, high-performance public organizations need to manage the policy process with a view to ensuring that they have sufficient policy capacity to develop sound policies and deliver them effectively: "Running a policy organization, whether engaged in applied research, program evaluation or general policy analysis, is a difficult and complex managerial task, quite different in some ways from program administration. But the managerial dimension of policy work has been relatively neglected."[528] This dimension has also been relatively neglected in previous chapters of this book. However, several matters discussed earlier, such as consultation and partnership, have significant implications for the development as well as the implementation of public policy.

## MEANINGS AND FRAMEWORKS

Policy management in government departments involves several interrelated functions, each of which is an important element of a government's overall policy capacity. The principal policy functions are

- theoretical research;
- statistics, applied research and modelling;
- environmental scanning, trends analysis and forecasting;
- policy analysis and advice;
- consultation and managing relations;
- communications; and
- program design, implementation, monitoring and evaluation.

Functional standards for each of these functions are contained in Appendix F.[529] In recognition of the importance of these functions, the federal Department of Human Resources Development, for example, sought to remedy systemic deficiencies in Canada's research capacity with respect to social and labour-market policy. This involved

building a statistical framework with Statistics Canada; creating networks with professional researchers, outside bodies, provinces and other departments; encouraging fact-based research; building structures and processes for the Minister to obtain advice; building expertise on horizontal design of programs and services and re-designing grants and contributions; and establishing missing local delivery structures.[530]

*Policy analysis* is widely viewed as the primary policy function in government. Ideally, in each government department,

[t]here is a proactive analytical and advisory function of high quality which bears heavily on actual decisions taken. Advice routinely incorporates both soft knowledge obtained from consultations and experience and hard knowledge obtained from data and research. There are regular exercises to identify major new strategic and horizontal issues and resources are dedicated to this function. Major objectives and planning priorities are frequently reviewed, are widely known within the department and have operational significance.[531]

The importance of the analytical function is reflected in the fact that the terms policy-making and policy analysis are often used interchangeably: "Policy making is central to what governments are about, and it is the policy development function of government that most distinguishes it from private sector organizations."[532] But policy capacity requires effective performance of all of the policy functions listed above, not just policy analysis and advice. The implementation function is especially important, because, if poorly done, it can offset the benefits of even high-quality policy analysis: "Policy development and decision making represent a comparatively small proportion of governmental activities. It is the implementation of policies that occupies the most governmental resources, and because it is highly visible, that ultimately forms the basis on which the effectiveness and the coherence of the government's action will be judged."[533] Thus, in the policy development process, careful account needs to be taken of implementation issues.

## The Decline and Rise of Policy Capacity

The current concern for improving policy capacity is a "renewed" emphasis rather than a new one. There is a considerable volume of literature and practice on policy coordination in the federal and provincial spheres dating from the late 1960s to the early 1980s. Among the notable coordinating mechanisms during this period were powerful cabinet committees, ministries of state for economic and for social development, and interdepartmental committees.[534] Thus, with respect to collaboration, there was considerable movement towards the post-bureaucratic model.

However, from the mid-1980s to the early 1990s the focus on improving governments' management capacity was accompanied by a relative lack of concern about the quality of their policy capacity. It is generally agreed that there was a decline in the capacity of governments to perform their policy functions effectively, especially their analytical and advisory roles.[535] Political executives actively downplayed the traditional policy advisory role of public servants and the importance of interdepartmental collaboration. Even some deputy ministers "denigrated the policy function and presided over the erosion of a good capacity they inherited."[536] At the same time, the policy role of political advisers and external consultants was elevated. Since the mid-1990s, there has been an effort to strengthen the policy capacity of the public service. Indeed, in 1995, improving policy capacity became one of the leading concerns of the federal public service.[537] The excellent reports of two deputy minister task forces – one on strengthening policy capacity and one on managing horizontal policy issues – contain sweeping proposals for reform of the federal government's policy-making process.[538]

In response to the need to improve its policy capacity, the federal government established in 1996 the Policy Research Initiative (PRI). The objective of the PRI is to "build a solid foundation of horizontal research upon which future public policy decisions can be based."[539] The PRI involves more than thirty departments and agencies and has established four interdepartmental research networks dealing with growth, human development, social cohesion, and global challenges and opportunities. A Policy Research Secretariat (PSR) has also been established to facilitate the integration cf the work of the research networks, to seek innovative ways of sharing policy research data, to develop knowledge partnerships with the broad policy research community in Canada, and to link up with policy researchers in international organizations and other countries.

This renewed emphasis on policy work has been partly a response to its previous neglect, but it has been primarily a response to the realization that high-quality policy work is essential to coping with the international and domestic forces examined in Chapter 1. These forces are similar to the "mega-trends" identified by the PRI; these mega-trends are globalization and North American integration, technological change and the information revolution, environmental pressures, changing demographics, fiscal

Table 11.1. *Paradigm Shift in Policy-Making*

| Element | From | To |
|---|---|---|
| Process | Closed | Open |
| Information and analysis | Hard | Soft and hard |
| Role of government | Rowing | Steering |
| Citizen participation | Selective | Rights |
| Policy analyst | Technical specialist | Generalist/team |
| Management | Vertical | Horizontal |

Printed with permission from Carl Taylor, formerly of the Canadian Centre for Management Development.

constraint, and multiple centres of power in the international environment.[540] The movement from the bureaucratic to the post-bureaucratic model that has been driven by such forces has implications for the policy capacity as well as the management capacity of public organizations. Both policy analysis and program delivery have been affected by the shift towards greater emphasis on such factors as service to clients and citizens; consultation and collaboration; decentralization of authority and control; cost recovery; and private-sector service delivery. In addition, as explained later, careful thought should be given to the implications of strengthening policy capacity for such public-service values as openness, loyalty and teamwork.

In Table 11.1, Carl Taylor conceptualizes recent and ongoing changes in policy-making as a "paradigm shift." This model complements the bureaucratic/post-bureaucratic framework that has been used throughout this book and that encompasses the movement towards a more open and participative culture, more use of "soft" knowledge obtained through consultation, and the increased emphasis on collaboration, horizontality and teamwork.

The rest of this chapter examines in turn the benefits of a strong policy capacity; the role of policy coordination in achieving these benefits; the obstacles that have to be overcome; and the political, managerial and value considerations involved. Although the primary focus is on the role of public organizations, reference is made to their links with organizations in other governments and with the policy research community outside government.

## WHY STRENGTHEN POLICY CAPACITY?

The overriding purpose of enhancing a government's policy capacity is to enable it to cope with the current and emerging challenges of a complex and rapidly changing policy environment. Consider the critical importance of effective and coordinated policy advice and program delivery in the many policy fields in which governments are involved, including, for example, foreign affairs, trade and the environment. We shall see below that one of the greatest anticipated benefits of a stronger policy capacity is improved management of horizontal policy issues. There is a pressing need to improve coordination among all policy actors through new and enhanced collaborative and consultative mechanisms such as partnerships and work teams. Increased collaboration and consultation can also lead to better policy by providing decision-makers with a clearer understanding of the substance and interdependence of policy issues (e.g., education and labour markets) and of the relationship of individual policy issues to the broader public interest.

Both the development and implementation of policy are significantly affected by the broad range of environmental forces discussed in Chapter 1: the international forces of globalization and the technological revolution; the domestic forces of financial constraint; increased public demand for services; a changing political culture; and demographic change. The phenomenon of globalization is used here to illustrate the potential benefits of a strong policy capacity. Globalization presents formidable challenges to policy-makers, in part because it requires that governments have the capacity to adapt quickly to changes in the global economy.

While the term globalization is interpreted in various ways, it usually refers to the emergence of a world-wide economy characterized by the increasing interdependence of national economies that results from the development of global markets for investment, production, distribution and consumption. Multinational enterprises, often described as global corporations, exercise enormous power in the global economy, and many of the rules for the conduct of economic activity are determined, not by national governments, but by such international institutions as the World Bank, the International Monetary Fund and the Organisation for Economic Co-operation and Development, and by such regional trading blocs as NAFTA and the European Union.

Not only have national governments given up substantial decision-making authority to such supra-national organizations, but in many states there has also been a devolution of decision-making from the central government to regional and local governments. It is widely argued that the first development threatens to undermine national autonomy and even national sovereignty and that the second development weakens the central government's capacity to negotiate on the international stage. Certainly, the policy options of national governments have become increasingly constrained, and the distinction between domestic issues and international issues has become blurred. Many decisions on "domestic" policy (e.g, on environmental regulation) have an impact in the international sphere, and many "international" decisions (e.g., on trade matters) have an impact on domestic policy.

In Canada, provincial and local governments have formal linkages with public- and private-sector organizations in other countries; similarly, since virtually every major policy issue has an international aspect, most federal departments and agencies have international "desks" to manage their relationships with other countries. As a result, "new international networks are developing between policy makers – who are linked as much by common policy interests as by national loyalties – while foreign ministries are progressively losing their monopoly in external relations. By blurring institutional and policy boundaries, globalisation is challenging governments' capacities to provide effective and coherent policy."[541] Given the importance of harmonizing the international activities of government departments, foreign affairs departments may have to play a more active "central agency" role in fostering interdepartmental policy coordination. Similarly, mechanisms are needed to coordinate the international activities of national and subnational governments.

These considerations demonstrate the critical importance of strong horizontal policy capacity for managing issues that cut across policy fields and across departmental, governmental and national boundaries. In the global economy, good policy capacity can bring substantial benefits to governments in such forms as better-quality policy decisions, ideas for policy innovation, and improved competitiveness in the global marketplace.

The management of horizontal policy issues is one of the weakest areas in the management of government's policy capacity. Our earlier examination of globalization showed the potential benefits of dealing effectively with policy issues that transcend departmental boundaries: "As policy makers, we should be concerned [about horizontal issues] because these do not fit 'in a box' – they don't respect turf, they don't fit within the jurisdiction of departments, they don't respect boundaries. They don't even fit within the constitutional definition of what level of government does what." Moreover, horizontal issues are "challenging because so many players control one tool, one 'key,' and all the keys need to be aligned at the same time to bring about a sustainable result."[542]

## IMPROVING POLICY COORDINATION

Policy coordination is the key to managing horizontal policy issues successfully. It requires that the decisions or actions of policy actors concerning the making and implementation of policy be brought into harmonious or reciprocal relation.[543] Collaboration, cooperation and consultation are

Figure 11.1. *Policy Coordination Scale*

---

9. Government strategy
8. Establishing central priorities
7. Setting limits on ministerial action
6. Arbitration of policy differences
5. Search for agreement among ministries
4. Avoiding divergences among ministries
3. Consultation with other ministries (feedback)
2. Communication with other ministries (information exchange)
1. Independent decision-making by ministries

---

Source: Les Metcalfe, "International policy coordination and public management reform," *International Review of Administrative Sciences* 60, no. 2 (June 1994), pp. 271–90.

the primary means of achieving policy coordination, both within government and between government and other policy actors. Policy coordination can help to ensure that public policies are mutually consistent, that duplication and overlap are avoided – or, at least, recognized – and that efficient, effective and responsive services are provided.

## The Policy Coordination Scale

Les Metcalfe has developed a nine-level policy coordination scale as a means of assessing and comparing, in qualitative terms, the coordination capacity of various governments (Figure 11.1). The nine components of the scale "are cumulative in the sense that higher-level co-ordination functions depend on the existence and reliability of the lower ones."[544] Although the scale was developed to assess the coordination capacity of national governments for the conduct of international relations, it can be applied to policy-making generally:

1. *Independent decision-making by ministries.* At this lowest level of the scale, each ministry retains independence of action within its own policy domain. It is at this level that attention is paid to the extent of coordination *within* ministries.

2. *Communication to other ministries (information exchange).* Ministries keep one another up to date on emerging issues and how they propose to deal with issues in their own areas. There must be reliable and accepted channels of regular communication.

3. *Consultation with other ministries (feedback).* This is a two-way process. Ministries not only inform other ministries as to what they are doing but also consult them in the process of developing their own policies.

253

4. *Avoiding divergences among ministries.* Ministries ensure that they do not take conflicting negotiating positions so that they can present at least the appearance of a united front (negative coordination).

5. *Interministerial search for agreement (seeking consensus).* Ministries work together voluntarily through such mechanisms as joint committees and project teams, because they recognize their interdependence and mutual interest in resolving policy differences.

6. *Arbitration of interministerial differences.* Where differences cannot be resolved by the horizontal processes at levels two to five, central machinery for third-party arbitration is needed.

7. *Setting parameters for ministries.* The centre of government plays a more active role, not by prescribing what ministries must do, but by defining what they must not do through such measures as budget constraints and limits on policy discretion.

8. *Establishing government priorities.* The centre plays a more positive role by laying down the main lines of policy and establishing priorities.

9. *Overall government strategy.* Strategic policy choices are made and handed down to ministries, and interministry coordination is taken for granted.

This scale demonstrates the many actors who can be involved in policy coordination at various levels of a single government. The following sections examine the coordination role of policy actors not only within a single government but in intergovernmental relations and with non-governmental actors as well.

### The Top and the Centre of Government

In Canada, the responsibility for overall government strategy and policy coordination belongs at the apex of government – with the prime minister (or provincial premier), the cabinet and cabinet committees. These political actors rely heavily for advice and support on the "centre of government," that is, on such central agencies as cabinet and management secretariats. In the federal sphere, for example, the Privy Council Office (PCO) provides policy advice and administrative support to cabinet committees responsible for coordinating social and economic policy. In the mid-1990s, the federal government strengthened the strategic role of cabinet by introducing an annual strategic planning cycle and integrating the budget-planning process into that cycle through a new expenditure management system. This development increased the need for long-term strategic policy advice by public servants. The strategic planning cycle is managed by the PCO and includes senior public servants as well as ministers. The intention is to extend the framework to all levels of the public service on the grounds that "[i]ncluding individual public servants in regular deliberations on the increasing number of horizontal issues can only serve to strengthen strategic, integrated and collaborative approaches to Public Service management."[545]

While most of the policy work in government must be done by the experts located in line departments, cabinet secretariats need to have a strong strategic capacity and play a vigorous coordinating role across line departments and policy fields. This role could include the functions of

- ensuring that there is an identification of strategic and major horizontal issues;
- setting system-wide priorities for developmental work on such issues;
- establishing mechanisms for interdepartmental collaborative work as and when needed;
- providing needed support to the functioning of such mechanisms; and
- encouraging the evolution of system-wide consensus, wherever possible, in problem definition and eventual assessment of options by providing mechanisms and fora for substantive interactions, exploration of competing views, timely resolution of dissension.[546]

Central agencies must play a major role in fostering and facilitating policy coordination between departments. The increased need for interdepartmental collaboration to deal with cross-cutting policy issues requires that departments go beyond the communication and consultation steps in the policy coordination scale to a search for consensus based on mutual benefits. This is in keeping with the emphasis in the post-bureaucratic model on collaboration, including increased use of interdepartmental committees, work teams and partnerships. As noted above, however, governments had extensive experience with interdepartmental collaborative arrangements from the mid-1960s to the early 1980s.

## Line Departments

Considerable responsibility for policy coordination remains with individual departments working through interdepartmental committees and subject to central agency regulations, directives and guidelines. In recent years, in both federal and provincial governments, an increase in the authority bestowed on departmental ministers has been accompanied by a decrease in the number of cabinet committees and in central agency controls over departments. Much of the onus for ensuring that policy proposals take adequate account of coordination considerations now rests with departments. In Ontario, for example, it is formally recognized that "[i]n today's increasingly complex policy environment, very few, if any, policy proposals affect only one ministry."[547] The ministry preparing the cabinet submission is required to undertake not only the necessary interministerial consultations but also to consult the minister's staff, the Cabinet Office and the Premier's Office, the Ministry of Finance and Management Board Secretariat, the public and stakeholders. When considering the impacts of different policy options, ministries are encouraged to consider the economic, regional and community, social, environmental, intergovernmental, trade agreement, legal and Charter, institutional and financial implications. In addition, ministries are required to outline a strategy that explains how the proposed policy will be implemented.

As a basis for seeking coordination with other policy actors, departments must ensure that they have adequate *internal* capacity for policy coordination. The Department of Indian Affairs and Northern Development, for example, has a "rigorous in-house policy process to promote quantity and quality control of products and a strategic approach to all policies." Policy proposals are channelled through a central policy branch that ensures coordination and quality standards before the proposals go to the senior policy committee. The responsibilities of this committee include "setting departmental priorities for the next year; making decisions on major policy issues to review and approving strategic plans of various program sectors; reviewing and approving the proposed Cabinet and legislative agenda for approval of new programs or major changes to programs; allocating funds for new proposals; and discussing and giving direction on high profile and major urgent issues."[548]

## Interdepartmental Committees

Successful policy coordination requires an effective system of interdepartmental committees. At the most senior level of the federal public service the weekly DM Breakfast brings together deputy ministers to exchange information, discuss urgent issues and decide how to deal with government-wide issues, and the coordinating committee of deputy ministers helps the clerk of the Privy Council with the overall coordination of both policy and management. In recognition of the need to strengthen the government's policy capacity, this committee has been split into separate policy and management components. One deputy described his first DM Breakfast as follows:

I put down each of the policy files that we were working on and beside that I put down the other departments that I needed as partners. There was not one issue that I could take forward – either to ministers, to the public interest groups that we were dealing with, or to my minister alone – without bringing along another department. I don't think there are very many of those issues left where you can say "I am sorry, it's none of your business! I've got this one."[549]

In addition, standing committees of senior managers have been established to promote interdepartmental policy coordination, but these committees have tended to focus on transactions rather than on policy planning and development. There are, however, some notable exceptions. The justice and legal affairs committee, chaired by the deputy minister of justice, is the primary mechanism for formulating and implementing long-term, multidisciplinary strategies in the sphere of social justice, and the committee on international affairs, chaired by the deputy minister of foreign affairs and international trade, is concerned with major cross-cutting issues of foreign policy. In 1995, four federal departments – Natural Resources, Fisheries and Oceans, Environment, and Agriculture and Agri-Food – signed a memorandum of understanding to encourage coordination and teamwork among departments in the use of science and technology for sustainable development. Partnerships have been created among the four departments and efforts are being made to collaborate with other departments.[550]

Some standing interdepartmental committees are supplemented by temporary interdepartmental task forces on such matters as policy planning and policy capacity. One of these task forces – Managing Horizontal Policy Issues – recommended that "mechanisms be developed to provide greater policy support to Cabinet committees, to streamline decision making systems so that more time is available for consideration of long term and strategic policy issues; and to encourage interdepartmental collaboration and cooperation among departments – on specific policy problems, as well as in particular policy areas."[551] The Privy Council Office has taken several initiatives to enhance interdepartmental policy work; these initiatives include having the current deputy ministers' committees pay more attention to policy matters, fostering more structured policy coordination among certain deputies, and having the PCO secretariats organize more policy discussions involving public servants from across the government.[552]

While policy coordination within and between departments is essential to coping with major changes in the policy-making environment, it is important also to improve coordination with other governments and with the research community outside government.

## Intergovernmental Relations

In Canada, all governments – and individual departments within these governments – need strong policy capacity to deal with other governments in the federation as well as governments in other countries. Despite the constitutional separation of powers between the federal and provincial governments, both orders of government have a shared interest in virtually every policy field. These governments have developed a large and complex infrastructure of intergovernmental bodies to seek policy coordination by promoting cooperation and collaboration and by reducing overlap and duplication. These bodies include departments or agencies responsible for the government-wide conduct of intergovernmental relations, administrative units within line departments, intergovernmental secretariats, and a host of intergovernmental committees. Nevertheless, Canada's formal structures for intergovernmental policy work are weak; indeed, these structures are weaker than those that Canada has developed with many international organizations, including, for example, the Organisation of Economic Co-operation and Development.[553] Part of the explanation lies in the fact that some provincial governments allocate relatively few resources to the conduct of intergovernmental affairs.

A study of sixteen cases in federal–provincial policy-making concluded that successful intergovernmental policy work depends in large part on three major factors: "building trust, which requires time, openness and careful attention to the interests of all the parties; working within existing mechanisms of cooperation, such as standing committees of officials ...; and a shared sense of the need to collaborate."[554] For example, the Federal–Provincial Working Group on Community Safety and Crime Prevention built trust between governments by emphasizing the open exchange of information; the Trucking Task Force used existing federal–provincial mechanisms (e.g., the Council of Transportation Ministers and its secretariat) to integrate the task force's recommendations and promote concrete results; and the Federal–Provincial Task Force on Regional Development Assistance recognized the need for collaboration to collect relevant data acceptable to both orders of government.[555]

In addition to the pursuit of their stated objectives, federal–provincial efforts in policy collaboration include such indirect objectives as

– improving the information base and the quality of analysis of information available;

- coordinating federal and provincial policies in areas of divided and concurrent jurisdiction;
- developing political support in federal and provincial governments for a new or established policy direction or program;
- achieving Canadian ("national") objectives in areas of provincial jurisdiction;
- moral suasion – raising the priority of an emerging issue;
- raising awareness and/or the quality of policy analysis on the subject within Canada;
- stimulating and shaping the policy debate; and
- improving service to provinces in areas where they are clients of federal services (e.g., justice statistics).[556]

There are also significant barriers to successful policy work. These include "the inconsistent quality of provincial participation, weak management of group dynamics [e.g., communications, scheduling] and a dysfunctional politicization of the issues."[557]

## Non-Governmental Players

Policy coordination between governments and the external policy research community, like that between the federal and provincial governments, is weak. Yet, "a healthy policy-research community outside government can play a vital role in enriching public understanding and debate of policy issues, and it serves as a natural complement to policy capacity within government."[558] The major components of this community are universities and policy institutes or "think-tanks." The latter component has been considerably weakened by the abolition of such federal advisory bodies as the Economic Council, the Science Council and the Law Reform Commission. The think-tanks that remain make a significant contribution to public policy debates, but they do not have sufficient resources to conduct the kind of basic research that governments need.

The universities are in a better position than either policy institutes or government departments to conduct not only basic research but – because of their autonomy and longer-term perspective – much valuable applied research as well. There is a complicated web of research relationships between governments and universities, and some government departments have developed strong and productive links with university scholars. Especially notable in this regard is the federal Department of Health, which has developed an impressive cadre of university experts who provide advice on health policy. Moreover, a few universities have health centres that are closely tied to provincial ministries of health. Similarly,

Statistics Canada has created several external advisory committees of academic experts. In June 1998, the federal government's PRI, described earlier, established a valuable web site (http://policy research.gc.ca) featuring hundreds of links to policy research organizations, including university research institutes, think-tanks and direct links to federal government policy research on the web. Governments can improve their research capacity in general and policy coordination in particular by exchanging and adopting best practices in the areas of "building external policy research capacity, commissioning applied research, and seeking policy analysis or advice."[559]

The task of policy coordination has been complicated over the past decade by the increasingly active role in the policy process of the general public, interest groups and the news media. As explained in Chapter 8, the emergence of a more participative political culture has obliged governments to consult more actively those citizens and groups affected by policy decisions. Moreover, the technological revolution has made it possible for policy actors to exchange large amounts of information more quickly and to use a variety of techniques to communicate their views. Policy coordination has become more difficult, because policy-makers must now take account of the divergent views of a larger number of players, including the news media, which can quickly mobilize and influence public opinion on policy issues.

## IMPLICATIONS AND IMPEDIMENTS

### Barriers to a Strong Policy Capacity

There are substantial obstacles to enhancing policy capacity. The experience of governments in Canada and elsewhere has shown that, while policy capacity has recently suffered a period of relative neglect, it has never enjoyed a golden age to which governments can now simply return. The Organisation for Economic Co-operation and Development (OECD) concluded from a study of its member countries that there is a gap between the need for policy coherence (defined as an overall state of mutual consistency among different policies) and the capacity of governments to achieve it: "The very notion of coherence needs to be adapted to the realities of a complex environment, and to the practical capacities of policy-making systems."[560]

An electronic discussion group organized by the Public Management Research Centre in Ottawa and composed of experts from within Canada and elsewhere identified the following barriers to strengthening the policy capacity of the federal government:

– the culture of secrecy pervading government that inhibits effective "outreach" and collaboration;
– the need to re-skill the policy capacity of government in view of the aging demographic profile of most policy analysts;
– the excessive focus on today's problems rather than on those of the next decade, that is, an emphasis on the urgent rather than the important;
– a weak policy capability in the federal government and little creativity by those working in the current environment;
– too little internal development of policy capabilities;
– the starving of policy capacity for budgetary reasons;
– poor links to external agencies like think-tanks and universities;
– the loss of confidence by many analysts in their own abilities and those of the state to find solutions to problems; and
– policy analysts who were unprepared for the new paradigms of alternative service delivery and public management.[561]

### Political Considerations

Political support, especially from the prime minister (or provincial premier) and cabinet, is extremely important for strengthening policy capacity and coordinating policy development. This support is much stronger in the early 2000s than it was a decade earlier, but there are certain political and constitutional realities that limit the extent to which political executives will support the rationalization of the policy process. Given the time-consuming political and other responsibilities of ministers, they are obliged to rely heavily on public servants for sound policy advice, which in turn requires strong policy capacity in the public service. Public servants must manage the policy process, with respect to both the substance and implementation of policy, within the constraints imposed by the political milieu in which they work. Canada's former top public servant has explained that "[a]s public servants, we owe decision makers not only our knowledge, our analysis of the options, but our best advice about how to make the desirable feasible, how to bring about enough consensus in Canadian society so that a policy option is in line with the values of Canadian society, so that it is feasible, implementable and sustainable."[562]

The search for policy coordination is complicated also by the requirements of the constitutional conventions of collective and individual ministerial responsibility. The collective responsibility of ministers requires that they recognize the interdependence of policy issues and seek to coordinate departmental interests so as to serve the broad public interest: "One of the principal challenges is to overcome the vertical stovepipes that divide government somewhat artificially into separate domains either of service delivery or of policy, and to knit them up again in a holistic fashion that reflects the real life of real people, and the connectedness of the real world."[563]

However, the requirements of individual ministerial responsibility work against this "whole-of-government" approach. Ministers have to answer to the legislature for their own actions and those of their departmental subordinates. Interdepartmental coordination often involves a diffusion of accountability, which tends to make both ministers and officials feel uncomfortable. Another consideration is that the reputation of ministers is enhanced much more by taking new policy initiatives in their own departments than by their contributions to the more nebulous collective and public interest. Ministers have few incentives to collaborate across departmental boundaries, especially if this means sharing the glory – or the blame – with other ministers. An incentive to collaborative innovation, however, is the consideration that shared glory is better than no glory.

These factors promote a culture of departmentalism where the emphasis is on vertical thinking and on interdepartmental competition rather than on collaboration: "There is a sense that the federal policy community is becoming less corporate, less collegial – with interdepartmental discussion focusing less on problem solving and more on departmental positioning and turf protection. Further, as departments have become larger, accountability is focused on the internal agenda; with few incentives to help 'tackle someone else's issues.'"[564] Yet, as explained earlier, there is a pressing need for governments to improve their capacity to manage cross-cutting policy issues.

## Managerial and Organizational Considerations

While cabinet and ministerial support for interdepartmental collaboration is important, the main responsibility in this area rests with public servants, both in central agencies and line departments. Public servants must help ministers appreciate the benefits of interdepartmental collaboration; they can, for example, encourage all those ministers with a departmental interest in a particular policy issue to work together at the beginning of the policy development process – as ministers did, for example, with respect to the reform of unemployment insurance policy.

Like ministers, public servants are affected by the requirements of collective and individual ministerial responsibility. While deputy ministers have a duty to serve the collective interest of the government of the day, their performance is measured primarily by how well they serve their ministers. In the past, the reward system has tended to encourage departmentalism and discourage collaboration across departments. More emphasis has been placed in recent years, however, on evaluating deputy ministers in terms of their contributions to interdepartmental collaboration. As explained earlier, if departments do not voluntarily seek policy coordination, central agencies must play a more active role. This has become a more difficult task in recent years because of the emphasis on reducing central agency controls over departmental operations and creating arm's-length agencies that enjoy considerable autonomy from both central agency and departmental control.

As explained earlier, there are several ways in which central agencies can encourage collaboration among departments. These agencies must, however, strike a delicate balance between fostering an appropriate measure of coordination and respecting the expertise and jurisdiction of individual departments. It will be important in future "to bring a greater degree of coherence to government policies while at the same time freeing government operations to the extent possible from centrally prescribed rules and regulations. This can only be accomplished if the centre develops a capacity 'to let go,' together with an ability to assess performance and to hold responsible actors accountable."[565]

## Value and Ethical Considerations

It is widely acknowledged that strengthening policy capacity requires a change in the culture of the public service. And, as explained in Chapter 3, values are widely viewed as the essence of organizational culture. It is essential, therefore, to consider the implications for public-service values of efforts to improve government's policy capacity, especially with respect to policy coordination: "True horizontality will require culture change – and a broad-based dialogue on the values that impede and those that would nurture a new approach. Horizontality will flourish in a public service that attaches high value to a 'whole of government approach,' an outlook that attaches adequate importance to the collective responsibility of ministers, oriented to the public interest."[566]

The values that are likely to nurture horizontality include democratic values such as openness and the public interest, ethical values such as loyalty and integrity, and new professional values such as teamwork and innovation. As noted earlier, a significant barrier to strengthening policy capacity is a "culture of secrecy," which pervades government and which impedes effective collaboration. The Metcalfe policy coordination scale (Figure 11.1) shows that what is required is a culture of *openness* and transparency to facilitate not simply an exchange of information but also a search for consensus. This will help to raise the sights of public servants from a focus on narrow departmental interests to a concern for the broader *public interest* manifested in part by a whole-of-government approach. Similarly, *loyalty* to one's minister must be tempered by loyalty to the government as a whole. *Integrity*, in the sense of congruence between one's values and actions, requires that senior public servants in particular "walk their talk" by taking the lead in promoting collaboration across departments and governments. We have already noted in earlier chapters the benefits accruing from *teamwork* and partnerships operating across departmental lines. It is expected that the knowledge and synergy gained from greater use of such mechanisms will stimulate *innovative* approaches to managing the policy process.

Certain key public-service values, if interpreted too narrowly, may impede rather than foster horizontality. For example, accountability, if interpreted in a strict hierarchical sense with emphasis on the way things are done rather on the results achieved, will tend to promote departmentalism. Similarly, respect for others, if it leads to undue sensitivity to the jurisdiction of other departments, will discourage interdepartmental collaboration.

## CONCLUSIONS

Successful management of the policy process depends heavily on the commitment of the public-service leadership to strengthen the policy capacity of individual departments and of the public service as a whole. The federal task force on horizontal policy issues concluded that "[t]he corporate values displayed by senior managers in practice are more powerful than any specific measures." Effective management of horizontal issues "requires a long term commitment and consistent actions supporting cooperation, collegiality, and collaboration within and across departments. If priority files are handled horizontally, there will be a shift in the Public Service culture towards horizontal approaches. If they are not, real and lasting change is unlikely"[567] As noted earlier, the federal government's PRI is designed to provide a foundation of horizontal research, in collaboration with other governments, non-governmental actors and the academic community.

The OECD, after reviewing the experience of its member states, developed a checklist of "tools of coherence." These are practical lessons to be considered by governments wishing to enhance policy capacity, especially for the effective management of horizontal policy issues:

– Commitment by the political leadership is a necessary precondition to coherence, and a tool to enhance it.

- Establishing a strategic policy framework helps ensure that individual policies are consistent with the government's goals and priorities.

- Decision-makers need advice based on a clear definition and good analysis of issues, with explicit indications of possible inconsistencies.

- The existence of a central overview and coordination capacity is essential to ensure horizontal consistency among policies.

- Mechanisms to anticipate, detect and resolve policy conflicts early in the process help identify inconsistencies and reduce incoherence.

- The decision-making process must be organized to achieve an effective reconciliation between policy priorities and budgetary imperatives.

- Implementation procedures and monitoring mechanisms must be designed to ensure that policies can be adjusted in the light of progress, new information, and changing circumstances.

- An administrative culture that promotes cross-sectoral cooperation and a systematic dialogue between different policy communities contributes to the strengthening of policy coherence.[568]

This checklist serves as a summary of many of the points about managing policy capacity that have been made in this chapter. It is notable, in conclusion, that this search for stronger policy capacity is in tune with several characteristics of the post-bureaucratic model, especially its emphasis on collaboration (Table 1.1 in Chapter 1). As already noted, however, there is tension *within* the model between the continuum leading to greater policy collaboration, on the one hand, and the continua leading to greater empowerment and decentralization, on the other. To ensure an appropriate balance between these contending emphases, public organizations will not be able to move as far along any one of these continua towards the post-bureaucratic model as they otherwise would.

# 12

# Sustaining the Momentum in the New Public Organization

We explained in Chapter 1 that the new public organization has two main features. First, it has moved along the continua between the bureaucratic and the post-bureaucratic model to the extent that is appropriate to the *type* of organization it is and the *functions* it performs. Second, it has learned to sustain the progress it has made and to improve continuously.

The bureaucratic/post-bureaucratic framework (Table 1.1 in Chapter 1) is shown in abbreviated form in Figure 12.1. While this framework has served an important analytical purpose throughout this book, we want to emphasize in this final chapter that the framework can also serve a *practical* purpose. It provides a tool for helping public managers to introduce reforms in their organizations and then to sustain those reforms and move

Figure 12.1. *From the Bureaucratic to the Post-Bureaucratic Organization*

| Bureaucratic organization | Post-bureaucratic organization |
|---|---|
| Organization-centred | Citizen-centred |
| Position power | Leadership |
| Rule-centred | People-centred |
| Independent action | Collaboration |
| Status-quo-oriented | Change-oriented |
| Process-oriented | Results-oriented |
| Centralization | Decentralized |
| Departmental form | Non-departmental forms |
| Budget-driven | Revenue-driven |
| Monopolistic | Competitive |

Figure 12.2. *Re-positioning the Organization*

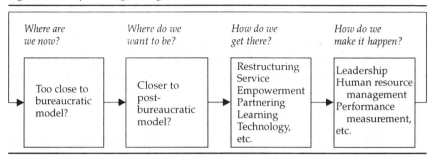

beyond them. The four questions shown in Figure 12.2 are crucial to using the framework for this purpose. Organizations need to answer these questions to determine to what extent they should move along the continua between the bureaucratic and post-bureaucratic models.

The primary focus of this final chapter is on the fourth question – how do we make it happen? We begin with a discussion of *leadership* – the dominant force for good governance in general and high-performance organizations in particular. This discussion includes an examination of the relationship between leadership, on the one hand, and human resource management and performance management, on the other. We then illustrate how the bureaucratic/post-bureaucratic framework can be used, in a practical way, to plan, implement and evaluate reforms. We conclude the chapter with an examination of the major learning points emerging from our analysis of the new public organization.

## POST-BUREAUCRATIC LEADERSHIP: PURPOSE, PEOPLE, PERFORMANCE AND POSITIONING

In Chapter 3, we noted the congruence between the characteristics of the post-bureaucratic model and the fundamental practices of exemplary leadership identified by James Kouzes and Barry Posner.[569] Adopting such practices as "challenging the process" through experimentation and risk-taking and "enabling others to act" by fostering collaboration and empowerment is "post-bureaucratic" leadership. So too are the practices of "inspiring a shared vision" by appealing to the values and interests of others and "modelling the way" by acting in accordance with shared values.

Not only are these leadership practices in accord with the post-bureaucratic model, but they are also very similar to the key themes of effective leadership identified by 279 public-service executives in a study by the

Canadian Centre for Management Development (CCMD).[570] The three major themes were

– *purpose*: The leader's role is to assess continuously the organization's changing external and internal environment to determine challenges, threats and opportunities, and to communicate them to staff. ... [T]he leader's role is to establish clear and relevant direction for the organization (vision, mission, strategy, values);

– *people*: The leader's role is to inspire and gain the commitment of staff to the goals and directions of the organization; and to serve as a role model for others; [and]

– *performance*: The leader's role is to create a culture and climate where staff can work together collaboratively to achieve high levels of performance and personal satisfaction.

Each of these themes is discussed below. While the primary focus is on leadership at the higher levels of the organization, we shall see that leadership must be recognized and nurtured at all levels.

## Purpose

The clearest expression of an organization's purpose is usually contained in its vision, mission and values statement, which is usually part of its strategic plan and which requires strategic leadership for its effective development and implementation. In Chapter 3, we noted the critical role of public-service leaders in articulating, diffusing and living the shared values of the organization. We also reported the results of a study that showed the dominant values contained in the vision, mission and value statements of public organizations across Canada.[571] Table 12.1 shows that these organizational values are very similar to the attributes (values, knowledge and competencies) that were most frequently associated with effective public-service *leaders* in the CCMD study mentioned above. The similarity is more striking if the leadership *values* are separated out from the list of overall attributes. These values, in order of priority, are honesty/integrity, respect/caring, team playing, commitment to service, recognition of staff, and professionalism.

As with the organizational values discussed in Chapter 3, so with leadership values, it is essential to consider the extent to which highly regarded values are actually practiced. Some evidence on this point can be gleaned from the CCMD study in which the major priorities for *improvement*

Table 12.1. *Organizational Values and Leadership Attributes*

| Organizational Values* | Leadership Attributes** |
|---|---|
| *Integrity* | *Honesty/integrity* |
| Accountability | *Communication skills* |
| *Respect* | *Respect*/caring |
| *Service* | *Team Player*/builder |
| Fairness/equity | Judgement/decision-making |
| Innovation | Visioning |
| *Teamwork* | Sets clear goals |
| Excellence | Inspires staff |
| *Honesty* | Knows the business |
| Commitment/dedication | Manages change well |
| Quality | Empowers staff |
| Openness | Strategic plan skills |
| *Communications* | Results-oriented |
| *Recognition* | *Committed to service* |
| *Responsiveness* | Evaluates org. environment |
| Trust | Gives staff job tools |
| Effectiveness | Manages stakeholders |
| *Professionalism* | Participative decisions |
| Leadership | *Recognizes staff* |
| Creativity | *Professional* |

*In rank order
**n = 279

in leadership values were found to be respect, communication, honesty and integrity.

In addition to leadership values, Table 12.1 shows the *knowledge* and *competencies* associated with effective leadership. Most of these attributes are important for leadership at any time, but several of them are especially important for leading an organization towards the post-bureaucratic model. Notable in this regard are the attributes of communication skills, visioning, managing change well, and empowering staff that are so central to fulfilling an organization's major purpose.

While these attributes are important for the top leaders of an organization, they are desirable attributes for employees below the top levels as well. It is now widely recognized that leaders at the middle and lower tiers of organizations play a major role in organizational success: "Leadership is now a strategic instrument, not a personal idiosyncrasy. It is also no longer confined to the top of an organization. Leadership is being found, and encouraged, at all levels."[572] A related point is that innovation "champions" can be found at all organizational levels and that a considerable percentage of innovations are in large part the result of their personal efforts. Evidence presented in Chapter 4 showed that the most frequent initiators of public management innovations are "local heroes," middle and front-line public servants who have visions and who are willing to take risks.

## People

The preceding analysis indicates the importance for building innovative, well-performing organizations of having highly motivated public servants at all organizational levels. Leaders at the top need to encourage the development and exercise of leadership throughout the organization: "The privilege and obligations of public service leadership are to be found throughout the public service, regardless of levels. ... Leaders [below the top] cannot simply wait for others more senior to act. ... We do not have to, and should not, wait for signals from others before undertaking the great tasks of public service leadership: exercising imagination, creativity and vigilance for the public good, and caring for the people entrusted to our charge."[573] Table 12.1 shows that effective leaders inspire, empower, involve and recognize employees. One innovative organization, in commenting on the most important things it learned from the innovation process, noted under the heading of "People" that

- senior executives involved were predisposed to entrepreneurship;
- most people involved were entrepreneurial, results-oriented, not process-oriented;
- good people were assigned, given responsibility and accountability and took ownership;
- [there was] willingness to take risks, be first, establish precedents;
- collaboration and loyalty to team and project characterized work relationships; [and]
- [there was] flexibility and willingness to change direction when necessary.[574]

These characteristics of post-bureaucratic leadership are reflected in the premises underpinning the federal government's La Relève initiative to revitalize the public service by improving its human resource management system. La Relève's first progress report noted that "[t]raditional hierarchical leadership ... is less effective than ever, and in many instances simply does not work. It is being replaced by *values-based leadership* which emphasizes trust, collaboration, inclusiveness and power sharing."[575] An earlier report, by the federal Consultative Review on Staffing, had envisioned a staffing system based not only on values (e.g., fairness, efficiency, integrity) but also "on a secure knowledge that decision makers understand and accept these values and that they are held accountable when they fail to support them."[576]

The La Relève report urged public-service leaders to understand that human resource management is just as important as the development and implementation of policies and programs. A conference organized by the federal Personnel Renewal Council to develop a human resource management framework for the year 2005 came to a similar conclusion. One of the vision statements in its report was that "managers are responsible and held accountable for the management of human resources. Managers are seen to place primary importance on the management of people in achieving their business objectives." Other notable vision statements were these:

- The mission of the [public-service] leadership is to enable each employee to achieve ... maximum potential. ... Work in the public service is team-based where each member is guided by shared values and feels personally accountable for results.
- People seek employment in the Public Service and love to work in it because it is rewarding, productive and creative.
- The public service is a model learning organization open to experimentation, creativity, and risk.
- Human resources are value-added, client-focused, efficient and effective, and continuously improving.[577]

These statements on the desirable future of human resource management are in harmony with the characteristics of the post-bureaucratic model. However, the current *reality* identified by the conference participants (in 1995) had many of the characteristics of the traditional bureaucratic model, including a command-and-control environment, an error-free approach to management, a one-size-fits-all mentality, and inadequate recognition and reward for good human resource management. As noted in Chapter 1, the legacy of earlier reforms in human management is a dismal one. In the federal sphere, for example, serious problems of morale and motivation remain, resulting in part from insufficient appreciation of public servants, both within and outside government. It is clear that effective human resource management is critical to the success of all public organizations, no matter where they are located in the bureaucratic/post-bureaucratic framework. Many of the organizations examined in this book would have benefited from paying more attention to the implications of their reform initiatives for their employees.

The issue of inadequate recognition and reward, not just for effective people management but for public service as a whole, has recently received unprecedented attention. The federal government, for example, has launched a long-term initiative led by senior public servants to enhance *pride* in the public service and *recognition* of its contributions. A federal deputy ministers' committee, Pride and Recognition, found that pride in the public service is tied to its ability to motivate and retain employees and to attract well-qualified new employees.[578] And a La Relève advisory committee, Workforce of the Future, concluded, after extensive consultations, that employees below the executive level "want to feel valued, respected and involved in their institution" and they "want managers to be accountable for creating conditions that can build employee morale." Some public servants think that a good beginning would be a survey that sets a benchmark of the extent to which they are currently feeling valued so that progress can be measured.[579]

Thus, it is argued that the overall performance of public-service leaders should be measured in part by their ability to model and enhance public-service pride and recognition. More generally, "public service leaders at all levels, but especially at senior levels, should be selected not just for effectiveness but also for the degree to which they exemplify ... the highest public service values. ... [I]n the process of evaluation, reward, and promotion, an assessment of the degree to which a leader exhibits public service values and models them for others should have an important role to play."[580] In this context, it is notable that the federal government created in June 1998 the Leadership Network, an agency with responsibility for promoting, developing and supporting networks of leaders at all levels of the public service and helping them in the ongoing challenge of implementing La Relève. The Leadership Network is a central participant in the program Rediscovering Public Service: Recognizing the Value of an Essential Institution, in partnership with the Institute of Public Administration of Canada, the Public Policy Forum, the Conference Board of Canada, and the Business Council on National Issues (http://lareleve.leadership.gc.ca). The primary purpose of this program is to foster understanding and appreciation of the challenges and achievements of public servants.

## Performance

Recent calls for increased accountability through performance management have not been directed to the top leadership alone. Indeed, the Workforce of the Future committee found that many public servants at other levels *want* to be held accountable for their performance, but they "want to be held accountable for the results they achieve, not the processes they use to achieve those results."[581] Public servants have become increasingly subject to a wide range of performance management techniques, including performance evaluation (employee appraisal), performance measurement, performance contracts, the setting of quality standards, and customer surveys. There is not space here to review the

Table 12.2. *The Balanced Scorecard Approach to Performance Measurement*

| Component | Sample indicator |
| --- | --- |
| financial | actual versus planned expenditures |
| client satisfaction | degree of service availability |
| internal business processes | setting/meeting targets |
| innovation and learning | staff motivation |

large body of literature and experience in the sphere of performance management, but it is important to note its relationship to the post-bureaucratic model.

The scope of the performance management function can be shown by reference to three broad *performance areas* that modern leaders need to manage and measure well:

1. The satisfaction of stakeholders (e.g., citizens, clients and politicians) with the current performance of the organization and of individual public servants.
2. The satisfaction of public servants with the organization's current culture and climate.
3. The satisfaction of both stakeholders and public servants with the organization's strategic direction and leadership of change.

Similarly, Robert Kaplan and David Norton recommend a "balanced scorecard" approach to measuring organizational performance.[582] This approach has four principal components, each with distinct performance indicators (see Table 12.2). The first three components of the scorecard relate primarily to the first performance area shown above. The innovation and learning component of the scorecard, which includes such indicators as employee suggestions for program and service innovations, levels of staff involvement in decision-making and degree of staff recognition, is in line with the second performance area. The third performance area, which has been comparatively neglected, draws attention to the importance of *strategic leadership of change,* a subject to which we return in the next section.

Current efforts to enhance performance management are focused primarily on the first performance area – satisfying stakeholders about organizational and individual performance. Many governments are now engaged in what is commonly described as results-based management, involving the development of performance indicators and measures related to an organization's business objectives, measuring the outputs and outcomes of programs and services, and using these data to evaluate the performance of the organization and its employees.

In the Ontario government, for example, performance measurement is an integral part of its formal accountability framework. Performance expectations set out the measures by which performance will be assessed, including the performance standards or service levels being sought. Performance is reported on and monitored against these measures, and there are consequences for the organization and for individuals of meeting, or failing to meet, the performance expectations. Performance measurement is an integral part of each ministry's business plan. In the Ministry of Consumer and Commercial Relations, for example, one of the core businesses is Vital Statistics; the outcome desired is improved service levels and productivity standards; and the proposed performance measures are average service times for issuance of birth and marriage certificates, for processing change of name applications, and for delayed birth registration. In the Ontario system, performance is measured at all levels of the organization: thus, there are core business (macro-level) measures; program and activity (micro-level) measures; and individual performance measures. These data are made available to the legislature and the general public.

This emphasis on using performance measurement to promote accountability, efficiency, effectiveness and service is in keeping with the results orientation of the post-bureaucratic model as well as with the movement towards such goals as greater cost recovery and improved service delivery. Performance measures can help organizations to assess where they are located on the various continua. We have shown in previous chapters that a considerable variety of performance measures is being used – ranging from sophisticated cost-benefit measures through the results of citizen surveys to benchmarking studies.

There are significant analytical, financial and cultural difficulties in implementing performance measurement systems.[583] Developing effective performance measurement systems can be costly and time consuming, and integrating performance measurement into the decision-making process requires a substantial cultural change in most public organizations. Moreover, although more sophisticated measurement techniques have gradually been developed, it is still difficult to measure accurately the actual outcomes, as opposed to the outputs, of government activity.[584] It is, however, important to measure outputs, even if you can't link them easily to outcomes. There are *political* difficulties as well, including the risk that the media and the public will use certain performance reports to embarrass politicians. Despite such concerns, it is clear that performance measures are an important tool for assessing where organizations stand in relation to the bureaucratic and post-bureaucratic models. They are also a potentially important means of holding public servants accountable for their performance.

In the federal government, the Independent Review Panel on Modernization of Comptrollership recommended in 1997 that the function of performance measurement be set within the broader context of an emerging emphasis on "modernized comptrollership." The four main elements of this concept are 1) performance information – financial and non-financial, historical and prospective; 2) risk management; 3) control systems; 4) ethics, ethical practices and values (beyond a focus on legal compliance).[585] The panel's hope is that senior officials in departments and central agencies will play the lead role in imbedding these elements in every management activity.

## Positioning and Re-Positioning

All three dimensions of leadership – purpose, people and performance – are important for achieving high-performance organizations. In this time of rapid and extensive change the criterion of *purpose* as defined through *strategic* leadership is especially important. As explained above, strategic leaders assess "continuously the organization's changing external and internal environment to determine challenges, threats and opportunities, and to communicate them to staff. ... The leader's role is to establish clear and relevant direction for the organization."[586] Note the emphasis on *continuous* assessment. The organization's top leaders need to position the organization strategically to perform at its highest possible level and then to *re-position* it by anticipating and responding to environmental changes. Strategic leadership of change is particularly important in rapidly changing times. An organization may perform well in the current environment but may be unable to sustain its position when its external environment (e.g., political, fiscal, social, technological) or its internal environment (e.g., staff morale, staff diversity) changes. Increasingly, public organizations that perform poorly or that no longer perform an important function are being disbanded, transferred to the private sector, or restructured beyond recognition.

A major reason for the decline and even the disappearance of some successful private-sector firms has been their failure to re-position themselves at the strategic level: "In a learning-based organization it is everyone's business to question and challenge the paradigms that are shaping their work. The leaders, though, are ultimately responsible for creating an environment where innovation and change are possible, valued and encouraged"[587] – and where local heroes can flourish.

The bureaucratic/post-bureaucratic framework provides a tool to help public managers re-position their organizations. Senior managers can build this tool into their organization's strategic and business planning. On a regular and formalized basis, they can ask where they are on each of the continua of the framework, where they want to be, how to get there, and how to make it happen (Figure 12.2). In this book we have provided a basis for answering each of these questions. We have explained the differences between the bureaucratic model and the post-bureaucratic model (towards which many organizations would benefit from moving). We have also explained how organizations can get there – by using such means as citizen-centred service delivery, partnering and technology to move along the various continua of the framework. We have described, especially in Chapter 2, the substantial transformation of certain organizations that have used these means to move a long way towards the post-bureaucratic model. We have noted also the benefits accruing to organizations that have moved only a short distance along several continua or a considerable distance along only a few continua. We are not, however, recommending change for the sake of change. As explained in Chapter 1, there are sound reasons for organizations, or parts of organizations, to adhere closely to certain features of the traditional bureaucratic organization.

Figure 12.2 indicates how managers can utilize the framework in their strategic and business planning by asking as many as possible of the right questions. Consider, by way of illustration, movement along the continuum from the traditional organization-centred approach, where emphasis is on the needs of the organization, to the citizen-centred approach, where emphasis is on providing the best possible service to citizens. Among the major questions to be asked at each stage are the following:

1. *Where are we now?*
   Who are our customers and stakeholders?
   What are their expectations and current levels of satisfaction?
   What is the current level of satisfaction within the organization?

2. *Where do we want to be?*
   What level of customer, stakeholder and staff satisfaction do we want to achieve?
   What should our targets be for each time-period?

3. *How do we get there?*
   At a broad level:
   Which of the following approaches to public-service reform will enhance citizen-centred service?
   – creating a citizen-centred organizational culture
   – encouraging innovation
   – restructuring and/or re-engineering

- improving service delivery
- empowering employees
- improving consultative mechanisms
- establishing partnerships
- promoting individual and organizational learning
- using information technology
- improving policy capacity

At a more specific level (using improved service delivery by way of example):

What are customers', stakeholders' and staffs' priorities for improvement?

What actions will we need to take to improve our performance in these areas (e.g., training, new systems, policies, procedures, delegation, service standards)?

How do we build these actions into our annual business improvement plan?

4. *How do we make it happen?*

Who will be made responsible and accountable for achieving the improvements?

How will we regularly monitor the implementation of the business improvement plan?

When will we re-measure customer, stakeholder and staff satisfaction to measure our progress and to update our continuous improvement plan?

While managers can use the bureaucratic/post-bureaucratic framework to assess the need for reform and while continuous assessment of this need is desirable, they must avoid the saturation psychosis discussed in Chapter 2. Organizations do not have unlimited capacity for change. After identifying reforms that are likely to improve the organization, managers must prioritize them in the light of available resources and the prospects of saturation psychosis.

## LESSONS LEARNED

In earlier chapters we discussed the learning points emerging from our discussion of the various means of moving towards the post-bureaucratic model. Under the heading of "Implications and Impediments," we examined the managerial, organizational, political, value and ethical ramifications of using such instruments as restructuring, continuous learning and technology. In this final chapter, we draw out lessons that cut across the chapters of the book and that include important learning points for students and practitioners of public-service reform.

### Remember that the Public Sector Really is Different

Public organizations face significant obstacles to reform that are not present in, or are less important in, the private sector. This point is reinforced in several of the learning points noted below, including those relating to the uniqueness of public-service values, the importance of accountability, and the issue of risk-taking. In 1997, the conclusion was drawn on the basis of roundtable discussions involving Canadian business leaders that "change is much easier to implement in the business world. ... [These leaders] were cognizant of the fundamental differences based on accountability and governance, which restrict the public sector from simply adapting or adopting private sector, business-like solutions."[588]

The political context of public-service reform has an especially strong influence on its success: "Ensure you have deputy minister and ministerial support" is the first item on the list of important things learned from the innovation experience of the Registration Division of Ontario's Ministry of Consumer and Commercial Relations.[589] Reformers need to keep in mind that leading public-service reform does not rank highly in the reward system for politicians and that reform programs can be used for partisan political purposes. A change of government can undermine reform initiatives launched under the auspices of a previous government or even of a previous minister. Yet, in the Correctional Service of Canada, a reform plan developed jointly in 1988 by the minister and the commissioner was supported by several subsequent ministers.

While many reforms can be carried out within the existing authority of public servants, even these reforms are likely to be more successful with firm political support – and major reform initiatives are very difficult without it. While lack of political support can weaken reform efforts, active political opposition will almost certainly kill them. Despite problems in implementing the Thunder Bay reforms in Ontario's Office of the Registrar General and the consequent political criticism, the minister (and the deputy minister) stuck by the reforms' champion and shared in the subsequent glory of this celebrated innovation. And the highly regarded literacy initiative in New Brunswick received strong support from Premier Frank McKenna who was the most vigorous advocate of the initiative "both on a public policy basis and on a personal basis."[590] He used fundraising letters to seek financial assistance from the private sector; he donated to the initiative all his honoraria from such activities as giving speeches; and he participated in all of the main literacy celebrations.

## Get the Values Right

Getting government right requires that the public service get its values right. Moreover, these values must be firmly imbedded in both individual and organizational decisions. We have shown in this book the pervasive influence of values in public administration generally and in public-service reform in particular. We have shown also that movement towards the post-bureaucratic model involves an emphasis on so-called "new" values like innovation, service and teamwork. As noted earlier in this chapter, these new values are among those required for successful leadership in the new public organization.

Attention to new values cannot, however, be to the neglect of fundamental traditional values like democratic accountability and integrity. Some advocates of the new public management approach to reform pay little or no explicit attention to public-service values, and many of those who do discuss values focus on the new values, most of which are *professional* ones (e.g., service, quality, entrepreneurship). The new public organization recognizes the need to balance professional values with democratic and ethical ones – and thereby to ask more of the relevant values questions. Thus, in assessing a potential reform, officials should ask not only whether improved service will result but what the implications will be for values like accountability, openness, integrity and respect.

Experience in other countries suggests that governments need to ensure that they have the values right *before* embarking on major public-service reforms. In the United Kingdom and New Zealand, for example, too much of the concern about the value and ethical consequences of reforms came *after* the reforms had been substantially implemented; this concern was manifested largely in the drafting of statements on public-service values and ethics. The more pragmatic, incremental approach to reform taken by governments in Canada has permitted both public servants and politicians to ask many of the important value questions while the reform is being contemplated. The federal government, for example, took a cautious and limited approach to the creation of service agencies (e.g., the Canadian Food Inspection Agency, Parks Canada) rather than following the British or New Zealand "big-bang" approach.

Few governments in Canada have developed a statement of service-wide values that can be used as a partial basis for assessing actual and proposed reforms. However, the Government of Ontario has developed a "Statement of Values" in the form of a list that includes most of the values ranked highly by public organizations across the country. Moreover, many individual organizations at all levels of government have adopted value statements. The 1996 report of the federal Deputy Ministers' Task Force on

Public Service Values and Ethics stimulated considerable emphasis on public-service values. Discourse on values and ethics has become much more pervasive in the federal public service in recent years and has been especially evident in the work of La Relève, the initiative to revitalize human resource management, and of the Leadership Network, with its commitment to values-based leadership.

A major political and public-service concern about service agencies – and indeed about many other proposed reforms – is their implications for accountability. A persuasive argument can be made that accountability is the dominant public-service value – at least in the realm of public-service reform. Accountability is both an ethical value and a democratic one, that is, people must be held accountable for the power they exercise over others in society generally, and, in the specific context of Canada's parliamentary democracy, officials must account for their use of the coercive power of the state. Accountability has been a central theme in our discussion of the political and value implications of various approaches to reform. We have noted, for example, the obstacle that the need for political and public service accountability poses for such measures as employee empowerment, the creation of service agencies, and interdepartmental policy collaboration. We have also examined ways in which such measures can be adopted without undue damage to accountability.

It is clear that accountability must be reconciled with other values, both traditional and new ones – hence the importance of getting the values right by identifying those values, along with accountability, that are most central to public service. These values have been aptly described as "the great principles of public service";[591] they provide a firm foundation on which the new public organization can be built. They define the essence of public service and help to distinguish it from the private sector.

### Take Reasonable Risks

Some element of risk-taking is a feature of virtually all innovations. The nature and extent of the risk range all the way from the unforeseen consequences of modest innovations (e.g., demands for *more* service resulting from *improved* service) to "high-wire" risks (e.g., investing substantial public resources in a public–private partnership). Risk-taking, by definition, admits the possibility of making mistakes. In this respect, innovators in the Township of Pittsburgh argue that "[l]earning by doing is not an admission of failure" and quote management guru Henry Mintzberg as saying that "[t]he really great success stories are ones where people made all kinds of mistakes, not the ones where they had glorious plans."[592] The Saskatchewan Department of Environment and Resource Management notes that "[w]e are all on a learning curve and will make mistakes which we must learn from."[593]

Many local heroes have become heroes largely because of their willingness to take risks. Reformers must, however, assess carefully the extent of the risk and of the need for formal approval. Experience with the kiosk innovation in Ontario's Ministry of Transportation suggested that "[i]f it makes sense act on your innovation. It is much easier to ask forgiveness than to seek permission."[594] For some innovations in some organizations, following this advice could be unduly hazardous to public servants' career prospects. A more generally applicable piece of advice based on the experience of Ontario's Office of the Registrar General is that risk-taking should be encouraged "when the objective is one where significant benefits can be accrued both to the public service and outside the public service, and *when the risk can be reasonably managed.*" In this particular case, the risk was reported to have worked "because it was:

– a technically correct solution;
– skilled resources were brought to bear;
– the partners were united in objective and commitment; [and]
– we became a team with a mission."[595]

Our earlier discussion of the political context of public-service reform – and of the importance of accountability – suggests that public servants, compared to their private-sector counterparts, must be acutely sensitive to the political risks of innovation. It is no simple matter to square the risk-taking emphasis of the post-bureaucratic model with the adversarial nature of politics in the federal and provincial spheres of government, where opposition parties and the media embarrass government by publicizing its mistakes. Given the political consequences of mistakes, it is not surprising that some ministers equate *public-service* risk-taking to *political* risk-taking. A more hopeful attitude, expressed by a former-deputy-minister-turned-politician, is that "it is crucial that public servants continue looking for new and innovative ways of managing performance within government. ... Leaders within government need to create a culture where it is safer to try and then fail, than not to try at all."[596]

### Involve the Key Stakeholders

This learning point was mentioned frequently by respondents to our questionnaire on public-sector innovation. The advice of the B.C. Ministry of Finance and Corporate Relations, for example, was to "ensure that all parties who will be affected by a change are included in making and developing the change."[597] And the B.C. Ministry of Transportation and Highways recommended the involvement of "as many stakeholders as logistically possible in the decision making process, planning and implementation of the initiative."[598] The distinction between involving "all parties who will be affected" and "as many stakeholders as logistically possible" is an important one. There are often practical limitations on the number of affected parties that can be involved, especially if the consultative process "seriously elicits and considers the ideas" of these parties and "encourages their involvement in decision-making in the tasks of vision-setting, policy development, issues resolution and in the design and delivery of government programs."[599]

As explained in Chapter 8, the practice of consultation has become more deeply ingrained in the public-service culture since the mid-1980s, largely because of greater emphasis on public participation in the political culture and of the movement in most governments towards citizen-centred service delivery. Public servants are now required to have much more sophisticated skills in consultation – or in what is often described as "citizen engagement." These skills are especially important in the initiation and implementation of public-service reform. Consultation is a key instrument for moving organizations towards the post-bureaucratic model, not only by improving service delivery but also by facilitating participative decision-making, continuous learning, and policy coordination.

The use of consultation for these purposes is in tune with several of the new public-service values, especially professional values like service and teamwork. But successful consultation also requires commitment, by all the participants, to traditional ethical values like honesty and democratic values like participation. The federal government's consultation guidelines note that "[t]o be effective, consultation must be based on values of openness, honesty, trust, and transparency of purpose and process" (Appendix C). Public servants are left with the difficult task of balancing these values, but the democratic value of participation will weigh more heavily in the balance than it did in the past.

### Heed the Learning Paradox

The *learning paradox* refers to "a Catch-22 type scenario whereby our future will increasingly depend on our ability to learn and change. Yet what we fear most is the sense of discomfort we feel when learning and changing."[600] This whole book has been about learning and changing, both now and in the future. Change has become a constant in the public sector, so we have stressed the importance of continous learning, not only for individuals throughout the organization but also for the organization as a whole under the guidance of a strategic leader attuned to the importance of re-positioning the organization.

A recurring theme in case studies of public-sector innovation is resistance to change – *from all levels of the organization*. It has been middle managers, however, who have been most severely criticized for impeding change. It is argued that they have less incentive than the senior or lower levels of the organization to promote and support change, especially in the form of major restructuring or downsizing, which may substantially alter, or even eliminate, their jobs. Experience has shown that their fear about losing their jobs is well founded. Middle managers are perfectly situated in the hierarchy to impede – or to foster – change initiatives flowing down from the top or bubbling up from the bottom. We explained in Chapter 8, for example, that in many organizations, middle managers have provided the stiffest resistance to employee empowerment. The fear of job change or job loss is compounded by the need to give up some power and authority to others, especially if empowerment takes the form of empowered work teams.

Empowerment is only one of several approaches to change, all of which must cope with the constraints of traditional bureaucratic systems. For each of the major approaches examined in this book we have discussed organizational, managerial and political obstacles to change and ways of overcoming these obstacles. Dealing with the paradox of change is of course much easier in organizational cultures that value continuous improvement, organizations that ask "what can we improve next?" rather than "why change?" Bringing about genuine cultural change in an organization can take as much as a decade of concerted effort. However, one way of fostering shared commitment to continuous improvement is, as suggested earlier, to institutionalize the process of asking where the organization stands in relation to each of the characteristics of the post-bureaucratic model.

### Invest in the Reform Process

Continuous improvement requires continuous change and, therefore, continuous learning. We saw in Chapter 9, however, that individual and organizational learning require a considerable investment of human and financial resources. Both in an absolute sense and in comparison to their private-sector counterparts, most public organizations commit too few resources to the education, training and development of their employees. Yet, the scope and pace of change have made such learning opportunities much more important than in the past. Consider, for example, the individual learning required to meet the increasing need for sophisticated technological and leadership skills throughout the organization. It is notable that some public organizations, like Statistics Canada, have committed increased resources to learning, despite tight financial constraints.

The resources required for *organizational* learning are considerably greater than for individual learning. As explained in Chapter 9, Michael Marquardt and Angus Reynolds argue that to foster organizational learning an organization needs to have in place, among other things, empowerment, commitment to continuous improvement, strategic planning, appropriate (flatter) structures, teamwork and vision. In other words, organizational learning will be enhanced by moving along many of the continua towards the post-bureaucratic model. The reforms required to do this can impose heavy costs in time and money (e.g., consultation, training costs).

An offsetting consideration is that certain reforms can reduce costs, either in the short or the long run, or both. Shifts from budget-driven to revenue-driven methods of financing programs and from a government monopoly to competition with the private sector for service-delivery are designed to save money while maintaining or improving service. But market-driven reforms are only part of the total reform package represented by the post-bureaucratic model. Some initiatives to improve citizen-centred service delivery, for example, increase costs, especially in the short term, which may not be offset by long-term savings. A single-window service delivery initiative like Ontario Business Connects requires initial expenditures on information technology that may never be offset by improved efficiencies. But Ontario's investment in technology for the Property Registry reform and for the Used Vehicle Information Program was offset by savings. The effectiveness of such service-window initiatives as Edmonton Business Link and the Aboriginal Single Window Initiative in Winnipeg suffered from insufficient investment in human and financial resources. However, the effectiveness of such service-window operations as Service New Brunswick and the Edmonton Business Link has been improved by investing time and money in training.[601]

Before they embark on reforms, public organizations need to assess carefully whether adequate resources will be available and, in particular, what the balance will be between increased costs and increased benefits.

## Balance Words and Actions

The concept of balance is important to understanding the field of public administration – a field that is permeated by tensions, contradictions, paradoxes and inconsistencies. The discussion throughout this book of the need to reconcile old and new values as well as democratic, professional and ethical values shows the inherent nature of tension and conflict in public-service reform. We have examined ways of reducing tensions arising from reform initiatives. We addressed, for example, the issue of balancing employee empowerment and accountability by stressing the importance of setting empowerment within an appropriate accountability framework. We discussed the importance of reconciling political and public-service interests. David Wright, a management consultant in the federal public service, goes so far as to argue that "the success of the entire process of structural and managerial innovation will depend upon the extent to which a community of interest and a climate of trust exists between the government and the public service."[602]

One of the most critical balances to be struck is between words and actions. The seemingly trite advice to "walk the talk" has such staying power because it expresses so succinctly a concern about values like integrity and promise-keeping. Matching words and actions is by no means a new issue in the public service, but it has taken on new importance in the context of reform where innovation and reasonable risk-taking are so central to success. Public servants are subjected to mixed messages, from both political and public-service leaders, as to whether reform initiatives will be rewarded – or even accepted. They receive strong encouragement to be innovative but often from risk-averse leaders; they are encouraged to take risks while their jobs are being threatened by downsizing; and reforms that they have been urged to adopt become the target of budget cuts.

Most of the public- and private-sector executives consulted by the federal Independent Review Panel on Modernization of Comptrollership felt that "risk taking is important to modern government and an essential element of achieving the government's policy goals in a world of constrained resources."[603] And the general perception of a substantial number of present and former federal public-service executives "was that the current structure and culture of the federal government are not conducive to taking risks. ... [F]or those who seek to take risks there must be some formal recognition that the organization will support them. ... There [is] a great deal of talk regarding a new emphasis in the federal government to encourage more risk-taking among its employees. However, the reality is that when mistakes are made, the individual is 'hoisted up the flagpole'."[604] Yet, fear of being hoisted has not prevented the introduction of impressive innovations at all levels of government, including the federal level. Developing a culture that *is* more conducive to risk-taking will undoubtedly stimulate more innovation and, thereby, foster high performance. The fact remains that public servants must keep in mind "the tension between innovation and risk taking (tolerate honest mistakes, not recklessness) and how to bridge the technical (hazard management) and political dimensions (outrage management)."[605]

The new public organization is a high-performance one that continues to move, to the extent appropriate to its form and function, along the continua between the bureaucratic and post-bureaucratic models. While many public organizations have taken measures to foster high performance, many others still have a considerable distance to go. A major purpose of this book has been to help them make the journey by explaining the opportunities and obstacles on the road to becoming a new public organization. Another major purpose has been to provide a foundation for further research that will help to illuminate the opportunities and eliminate the obstacles.

# Appendices

Appendix A-1

**Canada, Department of Energy, Mines and Resources**
[1992]
[now the Department of Natural Resources]

[in the context of a mission statement that contains several points of elaboration on each of the values shown below]

## OUR VALUES

*EMR's Statement of Values*
Trust, honesty, equity, fairness and integrity are the basis of our relationships with the people we serve, and with each other. We believe that:

- quality service to our clients is our standard
- the Canadian public interest is paramount
- people are our principal strength
- every job is important
- effective communication is a shared responsibility
- managerial excellence is essential.

*Values are Important*
Values form the core of our identity, both as individuals and as an organization. They reflect our fundamental beliefs, guide our behaviour and influence our decision-making. As one person expressed, "Values take their form in actions, not in words; they are expressed not by what we say, but by what we do."

Values can be used to harness the human energy of an organization and to create an atmosphere of vitality, loyalty and pride. With this in mind, EMR has adopted a Statement of Values that reflects the importance of people rather than processes, of results rather than regulations. In doing so, it has joined a Public-Service wide movement away from administrative controls and toward trust and empowerment of employees.

Over the past several months, EMR employees have played the central role in defining the values which will guide this department. Based on their input, the Statement of Values sets up a clear standard of behaviour for each of us. These values are our ideals and we can take pride in them while recognizing the challenge they represent.

*Building for the Future*
EMR is now looking to its future and the opportunities and challenges that a new century will bring. Through our values, we are challenging ourselves to achieve excellent quality service to the public, recognize our employees as a critical resource, and to strive for excellence in management.

By aligning our actions to these values, in everything we do, we will reaffirm, through our behaviour, a continuing commitment to them.

## Appendix A-2

### Saskatchewan Department of Economic Development
[1992]
[in the context of a strategic plan]

### CORE VALUES

The way we do business

In dealing with our colleagues and stakeholders we value and demonstrate:

– Effective Communication
– Respect for Others
– Personal and Professional Development
– Quality Service
– Honesty and Integrity
– Innovation and Improvement
– Leadership and Initiative
– Teamwork and Partnership

## Appendix A-3

### City of Vancouver
[1992]

[in the context of a statement of mission, objectives and values]

### VALUES

*Integrity*
- To be open and honest
- To honour our commitments

*Excellence*
- To strive for the best result

*Responsiveness*
- To listen to all the people we work with and serve
- To act in a timely and sensitive way

*Learning*
- To increase knowledge and understanding in the workplace and in the community
- To grow through our successes and our mistakes

*Fairness*
- To apply unbiased judgement and sensitivity

*Leadership*
- To set examples that others will choose to follow.

## Appendix B

### Questionnaire on Public-Sector Innovation in Canada

1. Please provide a brief description of your program or policy initiative. This description should touch upon the program's purposes, goals, or objectives; its principal clients and activities; and the resources at the core of the program or policy initiative.
2. What makes your program or policy initiative innovative? Compare it with other programs currently operating in your region, province, or

nationally that address the same problem. How does your approach differ?

3. Please describe the target population served by your program or policy initiative.

4. How many clients *per year* does your program or policy initiative currently serve?

5. What percentage of the potential clientele does this represent?

6. How does the program or policy initiative identify and select its clients?

7. What is your program's current operating budget? What are its funding sources (e.g., federal, provincial, local, user fees, non-profit or private sector grants or in-kind contributions)? What percentage of annual income is derived from each?

8. Does your program have a capital budget? If so, what is its capital budget this year? What are its funding sources for the capital budget (e.g., federal, provincial, local, user fees, non-profit or private sector grants or in-kind contributions)? What percentage of the capital budget is derived from each?

9. Briefly describe the composition, role, and reporting relationships of any government departments, boards or committees involved in the policy-setting or administration of your program or policy initiative. Include any subcontractual relationships with outside organizations or individuals. It may be useful to attach an organizational chart to show the current number, responsibilities, and reporting relationships of key program employees or staff.

10. When and how was the program or policy initiative originally conceived in your jurisdiction? Please describe any specific incidents or circumstances that led to the initiative. (If your program or policy initiative is an adaptation or replication of another innovation, please identify the original program or policy initiative. In what ways has your program or policy initiative adapted or improved on the original?)

11. What individuals or groups are considered the primary initiators of the program or policy initiative? Please specify their position or organizational affiliation at the time they initiated the program or policy initiative.

12. Please identify the key milestones in program or policy development and implementation when they occurred (e.g., cabinet authorizes a pilot program in June 1991; pilot program accepted first clients, August 1991; expanded program approved by cabinet in October 1992).

13. How has the implementation strategy of your program or policy

initiative evolved over time? How has it evolved since you made your application to the IPAC Award for Innovative Management?

14. In recent years, some students of public management have argued that innovation is often characterized by a process referred to in the literature as "groping along," whereby innovators began with loosely defined goals and, over time and as a result of trial and error, moved towards those goals. Others have argued that innovations result from clear and comprehensive plans, for the organization as a whole and/ or for the innovation itself. Please explain whether your innovation is more accurately described by the "groping along" model or the "comprehensive planning" model?

15. Please describe the most significant obstacle(s) encountered thus far by your program or policy initiative. How did you deal with each of the obstacles? Which implementation obstacles or difficulties remain?

16. Besides the originators of the program or policy initiative, what other individuals or organizations have played the most significant roles in a) program development, and b) ongoing implementation and operations? What roles have they played?

17. What individuals or organizations are the strongest supporters of the program or policy initiative and why?

18. What individuals or organizations are the strongest critics of the program or policy initiative and why? What is the nature of their criticism?

19. What are the *three most important measures* you use to evaluate your program or policy initiative? In qualitative or quantitative terms for each measure, please provide the outcomes of the last full year of program operation and at least one prior year.

20. What would you describe as the program's or policy initiative's single-most important achievement to date?

21. What are the program's most significant remaining shortcomings?

22. Has your program or policy initiative been *formally evaluated or audited by an independent organization or group*? If it has, please indicate who did the evaluation or audit and please summarize the principal findings of the independent evaluator(s) and/or auditor(s).

23. How do you believe the principal problem(s) addressed by your program or policy initiative will evolve over the next five years and how are you going to respond?

24. To what extent do you believe your program or policy initiative is potentially replicable within other jurisdictions and why? To your knowledge, have any other jurisdictions or organizations established programs or implemented policies modelled specifically on your own?

25. Has the program or policy initiative received any awards or other

honours? If yes, please list and describe the awards and the sponsoring organizations.

26. Has the program or policy initiative received any press or other media coverage to date? If yes, please list the sources and briefly describe relevant coverage.

27. What are the most important things you have learned from initiating and/or implementing this innovation? Is there any advice you would give to a would-be innovator?

## Appendix C

### Principles for Consultation

1. Consultation between government and the public is intrinsic to effective public policy development and service to the public. It should be a first thought, not an after-thought.

2. Mutual respect for the legitimacy and point of view of all participants is basic to successful consultation.

3. Whenever possible, consultation should involve all parties who can contribute to or are affected by the outcome of consultation.

4. Some participants may not have the resources or expertise required to participate, and financial assistance or other support may be needed for their representation to be assured.

5. The initiative to consult may come from inside government or outside – it should be up to the other to respond.

6. The agenda and process of consultation should be negotiable. The issues, objectives and constraints should be established at the outset.

7. The outcome of consultation should not be predetermined. Consultation should not be used to communicate decisions already taken.

8. A clear, mutual understanding of the purpose and expectations of all parties to the consultation is necessary from the outset.

9. The skills required for effective consultation are listening, communicating, negotiating and consensus building. Participants should be trained in these skills.

10. To be effective, consultation must be based on values of openness, honesty, trust, and transparency of purpose and process.

11. Participants in a consultation should have clear mandates. Participants should have influence over the outcome and a stake in implementing.

12. All participants must have reasonable access to relevant information and commit themselves to sharing information.

13. Participants should have a realistic idea of how much time a consultation is likely to take and plan for this in designing the process.

14. Effective consultation is about partnership. It implies a shared responsibility and ownership of the process and the outcome.

15. Effective consultation will not always lead to agreement; however, it should lead to better understanding of each other's positions.

16. Where consultation does lead to agreement, whenever possible, participants should hold themselves accountable for implementing the resulting recommendations.

Source: Canada, Public Service 2000, *Service to the Public Task Force Report* (Ottawa: Privy Council Office, 1990), p. 47.

## Appendix D

### Heritage Canada
### The Partnership Guide
### Guiding Principles
### [1995]

*Introduction*
The following guiding principles are based on working collaboratively with the private and not-for-profit sectors. These principles provide the context for Canadian Heritage to enter into agreements with these sectors for the purposes of revenue generation, message/mandate communication, program/facility cost sharing, event sponsorship and the like.

*Guiding Principles*
– Partnerships are not a panacea but rather one of many tools to be used in the quest for increased efficiency, effectiveness and economy;

- All partnership activities must directly or indirectly contribute to the achievement of the Government, Departmental, and Sector vision, goals and objectives;
- All partnership arrangements must act in the public interest and not be seen as giving preferential or special treatment to special interest groups;
- All partnership arrangements must have a value added which enhances each partner as an entity;
- All inherent risks must be identified and mitigated/managed so as to minimize any potential negative impact;
- Partnership agreements may not be undertaken with organizations whose products or services are not in keeping with the image of the Government and/or the Department;
- It is a valid and acceptable objective that all partners gain a direct or indirect benefit from their partnering activity;
- Partners may be either active or passive participants in the partnership arrangement;
- Partnership arrangements should not lead to an increase in the "machinery of government";
- Government regulations, policies, delegations and authorities must be respected throughout the life of the partnership agreement.

Source: Canada, Department of Canadian Heritage, *The Partnership Guide* (Ottawa: Department, 1995).

## Appendix E

### Questions to ask as basis for creating a learning culture

- Has the organization articulated an overall purpose? Do its members understand it? Are they committed to it? Is there provision to re-examine the purpose periodically in light of changing circumstances?

- Does the organization have a framework of values and operating principles that must be observed, but within which members are encouraged to learn and to find innovative ways of improving performance?

- Do all members of the organization feel that their work is valued and that they contribute to the creation of the organization's products, satisfy customers' needs and add to the well-being of society?

- Does the organization see change as an opportunity to be welcomed instead of as a threat to be resisted?

– Is the organization aware that mental models are often acquired and held unconsciously yet govern the organization's strategies and actions?

– Does the organization regularly examine and challenge its mental models of reality to ensure that they fit with reality itself?

– Are people at all levels of the organization encouraged to learn, to acquire new skills, to experiment, participate in pilot projects, and make suggestions for innovation?

– Are the results of individual learning being distributed throughout the organization? Are they being embedded in the practices and processes of the organization as a whole?

– Does the organization use both success and failure as sources of learning that will lead to future improvement?

– Is the organization receptive to a diversity of views and new ideas from both within and outside the organization?

– Does the organization seek to discover and deal with the causes of problems rather than simply addressing their symptoms? Is it aware that problems may be caused by several interrelated factors?

– Is the organization periodically reassessing who its customers are and how it can sustain a productive learning partnership with them?

– Does the organization understand that organizational learning is a continuous process rather than a one-time transformation?

## Appendix F

### Possible Functional Standards for use in a Review of Departmental Policy Capacity

*Theoretical research*: There is a good understanding of and consensus on the relevant theoretical issues underlying the policy area.

*Statistics, applied research and modelling*: There is a clear view of the statistical or data requirements for policy work, including what is needed to follow trends and analyse the critical factors affecting outcomes. Where applicable, it will include proactive measures to develop the necessary statistical frameworks or data; and systematic monitoring of relevant Canadian and foreign applied research in the policy area. This knowledge is actually used in policy-making. Priority gaps in applied research are identified and addressed. The department has a good working relationship with the external policy research community. It routinely provides quantitative estimates of the impact of possible policy options, and these estimates are based on sound methods of modelling and analysis.

*Environmental scanning, trend analysis and forecasting*: There is systematic identification of factors most likely to influence policy in the middle to longer-term, including budgets, demographic change, shifts in public opinion and technology. The department uses a variety of techniques, such as scenarios and contingency plans, in developing its longer-range frameworks.

*Policy analysis and advice*: There is a proactive analytical and advisory function of high quality that bears heavily on actual decisions taken. Advice routinely incorporates both soft knowledge obtained from consultations and experience and the hard knowledge obtained from data and research. There are regular exercises to identify major new strategic and horizontal issues, and resources are dedicated to this function. Major objectives and planning priorities are frequently reviewed, are widely known within the department and have operational significance.

*Consultations and managing relations*: There is a regular and systematic review of the evaluation of its performance by interested parties: minister, deputy, departmental colleagues, central agencies, main stakeholders and the policy staff itself. Consultations on policy are well conceived, based on experience and norms. The consultations reflect a clear sense of the roles of the key players, including the possible contributions of those outside government, so as to minimize wasteful duplication and fill gaps.

*Strategic communications:* The strategic communications function operates closely with the other policy functions, especially policy analysis and advice.

*Program design, monitoring and evaluation*: The evaluation function is closely linked to policy, is based on best practices of evaluation, and is used in program redesign and policy reviews. Programs are designed in such a manner that the expected outcomes are specified in an explicit manner capable of subsequent evaluation.

*Personnel management*: Senior management places a high priority on and is directly involved in all personnel management activities including human resources planning, recruitment, training and development, staff rotation, and reviewing management performance. A competency profile has been developed to evaluate skill mix and determine training and development needs.

*Organization and internal processes*: The department has reviewed its mandate and organized policy functions to maximize coverage and integration and make best use of available resources. The mandate of any policy branch is clear and the workload is manageable. A systematic review of organizational linkages across policy functions has been conducted, and appropriate mechanisms to ensure participation and coordination have been developed.

# Notes

1 See n.a. [IPAC], "Re-shaping government: a case study of the Office of Registrar General, Thunder Bay, Ontario," *Public Sector Management* 5, no. 1 (Spring 1994), pp. 4–7, at p. 6. Ontario, Ministry of Consumer and Commercial Relations, Registration Division, "Maximizing Opportunity, Office of the Registrar General: A Case of Re-shaping Government." Submission to the IPAC Award for Innovative Management competition, 1994.

2 Peter Aucoin, "The design of public organizations for the 21$^{st}$ century: why bureaucracy will survive in public management," CANADIAN PUBLIC ADMINISTRATION 40, no 2 (Summer 1997), pp. 290–306, at p. 292.

3 This framework is a slightly revised version of the one first presented by Kenneth Kernaghan, "Beyond Bureaucracy: Towards a Framework for Analysis of Public Sector Reform." Paper presented at the annual conference of the Canadian Political Science Association, Brock University, 4 June 1996. The term post-bureaucratic *paradigm* was, to our knowledge, first used by Michael Barzelay and Babak J. Armajani, "Managing state government operations: changing visions of staff agencies," *Journal of Policy Analysis and Management* 9, no. 3 (Summer 1990), pp. 307–38.

4 James Iain Gow, *Learning from Others: Administrative Innovations Among Canadian Governments*. Monographs on Canadian Public Administration – No. 16 (Toronto: Institute of Public Administration of Canada, 1994), p. 121.

5 Sam Overman and Kathy Boyd, "Best practices research and postbureaucratic reform," *Journal of Public Administration Research and Theory* 4, no. 1 (January 1994), pp. 67–83.

6 James O. Finckenauer, *Scared Straight! and the Panacea Phenomenon* (Englewood Cliffs, N.J.: Prentice-Hall, 1982).

7 Nancy J. Adler, *Globalization, Government and Competitiveness. The John L. Manion Lecture of the Canadian Centre for Management Development* (Ottawa: Supply and Services Canada, 1994), p. 1.

8 Sandford Borins, "Public Sector Innovation: Its Contribution to Canadian Competitiveness." Discussion Paper Series, Government and Competitiveness, School of Policy Studies, Queen's University, 1994, p. 66.

9 Steven A. Rosell, *Governing in an Information Society* (Halifax: Institute for Research on Public Policy, 1992), p. 30.

10 H. Brinton Milward, "Implications of Contracting Out: New Roles for the Hollow State," in Patricia W. Ingraham, Barbara S. Romsek and Assocs. ed., *New Paradigms for Government* (San Francisco: Jossey-Bass, 1994), pp. 42ff.

11 John Manion, "Career public service in Canada: reflections and predictions," *International Review of Administrative Sciences* 57, no. 3 (September 1991), pp. 361–72, p. 367.

12 H.L. Laframboise, "Administrative reform in the federal public service: signs of a saturation psychosis," CANADIAN PUBLIC ADMINISTRATION 14, no. 3 (Fall 1971), pp. 303–25.

13 David Zussman and Jak Jabes, *The Vertical Solitude: Managing in the Public Service* (Halifax: Institute for Research on Public Policy, 1989), p. 196.

14 Manion, "Career public service in Canada," *International Review of Administrative Sciences*, p. 364.

15 Zussman and Jabes, *The Vertical Solitude*, pp. 207–17.

16 Manion, "Career public service in Canada," *International Review of Administrative Sciences*, p. 364.

17 Ibid.

18 Linda Duxbury, Lorraine Dyke and Natalie Lam, *Career Development in the Federal Public Service: Building a World-Class Workforce* (Ottawa: Treasury Board Secretariat, 1999), p. 119.

19 Robert R. Fowler, "Base delegation or authority and accountability trial management through innovation," *Public Sector Management* 4, no. 3 (Autumn 1993), pp. 14–16.

20 Joan Barton and Brian Marson, *Service Quality: An Introduction* (Victoria: Service Quality B.C. Secretariat, 1991), p. 13.

21 Ibid., pp. 8–9.

22 Peter Drucker, *Management: Tasks, Responsibilities, Practices* (New York: Harper & Row, 1974), p. 137.

23 Ibid. Note that Drucker uses the term "public-service institution" to refer not only to government agencies, the armed services, schools and universities, research laboratories, and hospitals but also to such entities as labour unions, professional practices such as large law firms and trade associations.

24 Ibid., p. 146.

25 Ibid., p. 157.

26 Ibid., pp. 158–9. Drucker presents similar arguments in a widely quoted article. See Peter Drucker, "Really reinventing government," *The Atlantic Monthly* (February 1995), pp. 49–61.

27 Ole Ingstrup, *Public Service Renewal: From Means to Ends* (Ottawa: Canadian Centre for Management Development, 1995), p. 5.

28 Thomas J. Peters and Robert H. Waterman, *In Search of Excellence: Lessons from America's Best-Run Companies* (New York: Harper & Row, 1982).

29 Gow, *Learning from Others*, p. 52.

30 Kenneth Kernaghan, "The emerging public service culture: values, ethics and reforms," CANADIAN PUBLIC ADMINISTRATION 37, no. 4 (Winter 1994), pp. 614–30, at p. 620.

31 David Osborne and Ted Gaebler, *Reinventing Government: How the Entrepreneurial Spirit is Transforming the Public Sector From Schoolhouse to State House, City Hall to Pentagon* (Reading, Mass.: Addison-Wesley, 1992).

32 Al Gore, *Creating a Government that Works Better and Costs Less* (New York: Penguin, 1993).

33 Osborne and Gaebler, *Reinventing Government*, p. xxii; 19–20.

34 David Osborne and Peter Plastrik, *Banishing Bureaucracy: The Five Strategies for Reinventing Government* (Reading, Mass.: Addison-Wesley, 1997).

35 Ibid., pp. 39ff.

36 Michael Barzelay, with the collaboration of Babak J. Armajani, *Breaking Through Bureaucracy: A New Vision for Managing in Government* (Berkeley and Los Angeles: University of California Press, 1992).

37 Ibid., p. 118.

38 Sandford Borins, "Summary: Government in Transition – a new paradigm in public administration," in Commonwealth Association for Public Administration and Management, *Government in Transition* (Toronto: CAPAM, 1995), p. 4 (emphasis in the original).

39 Robert B. Denhardt, *The Pursuit of Significance: Strategies for Managerial Success in Public Organizations* (Belmont, Calif.: Wadsworth Publishing, 1993).

40 Ibid., p. 283.

41 Ibid., pp. 17–18.

42 Canada, Office of the Auditor General, *Annual Report* (Ottawa: Supply and Services Canada, 1988), Chapter 4.

43 Ibid., Section 4.64.

44 Canada, Office of the Auditor General, *Annual Report* (Ottawa: Supply and Services Canada, 1990), Chapter 7.

45 Ole Ingstrup and Paul Crookall, *The Three Pillars of Public Management* (Montreal and Kingston: McGill-Queen's University Press, 1998).

46 Michael Hammer and James Champy, *Reengineering the Corporation: A Manifesto for Business Revolution* (New York: HarperCollins, 1993).

47 Ibid., p. 32.

48 Ibid., p. 3.

49 James Champy, *Reengineering Management: The Mandate for New Leadership* (New York: HarperCollins, 1995).

50 Ibid., p. 75.

51 Christopher Hood, "A public management for all seasons?" *Public Administration* 69, no. 1 (Spring 1991), pp. 3–19, at p. 5.

52 William Niskanen, *Bureaucracy and Representative Government* (Chicago: Aldine Atherton, 1971).

53 Peter Aucoin, "Administrative reform in public management: paradigms, principles, paradoxes and pendulums," *Governance* 3, no. 2 (April 1990), pp. 115–37, at p. 116.

54 Ibid., p. 118.

55 Michael E. Milakovich, "Total quality management in the public sector," *National Productivity Review* 15, no. 2 (Spring 1991), pp. 195–213; Albert C. Hyde, "The proverbs of total quality management: recharting the path to

quality improvement in the public sector," *Public Productivity and Management Review* 16, no. 1 (Fall, 1992), pp. 25–38; James Swiss, "Adapting total quality management (TQM) to government," *Public Administration Review* 52, no. 4 (July/August 1992), pp. 356–62.

56 Canada, Public Service 2000, *The Renewal of the Public Service of Canada* (Ottawa: Supply and Services Canada, 1990).

57 Alasdair Roberts, "Worrying about misconduct: the control lobby and the PS 2000 reforms," CANADIAN PUBLIC ADMINISTRATION 39, no. 4 (Winter 1996), pp. 489–523.

58 Donald J. Savoie, *Thatcher, Reagan, Mulroney: In Search of a New Bureaucracy* (Toronto: University of Toronto Press, 1994); Peter Aucoin, *The New Public Management: Canada in Comparative Perspective* (Montreal: Institute for Research on Public Policy, 1995).

59 Canada, Office of the Auditor General, *Annual Report* (Ottawa: Supply and Services Canada, 1993), p. 178.

60 Aucoin, "Design of public organizations for the 21st Century," CANADIAN PUBLIC ADMINISTRATION, p. 15.

61 Manitoba, Fleet Vehicles Agency, *1997–98 Annual Report* (Winnipeg: Queen's Printer, 1997), p. 8.

62 Ibid.

63 Ibid., p. 4.

64 André Gladu, "Human Resources Development Canada, Quebec Region" [unpublished paper, 1996], p. 2.

65 Ibid., p. 3.

66 Ibid.

67 Marie Blythe and Brian Marson, *Good Practices in Citizen-Centred Service* (Ottawa: Canadian Centre for Management Development, 1998), p. 25.

68 Ibid., p. 30.

69 Carolyn Farquhar, *Business and Organizational Planning Case Study Series. Case # 4: Ontario Ministry of Consumer and Commercial Relations* (Toronto: Cabinet Office, Centre for Leadership, 1996).

70 Judith Wolfson, "The MCCR Story: A New Approach to Governance." Notes for a speech at the University of Toronto, 16 February 1995.

71 Ontario, Ministry of Consumer and Commercial Relations, Registration Division, Personal Property Security Registration Branch, "Direct Access: Maximizing People with Technology." Completed questionnaire on public-sector innovation in Canada, 1996; Ontario, Ministry of Consumer and Commercial Relations, "Maximizing Opportunity." Completed questionnaire on public-sector innovation in Canada, 1996; n.a. [Institute of Public Administration of Canada], "Ontario Ministry of Consumer and Commercial Relations: Clearing the Path for Business Success," *Public Sector Management* 7, no. 2 (Summer 1996), pp. 12–14.

72 Arthur Daniels, "Taking Strategic Alliances to the World: Ontario's Teranet," in Robin Ford and David Zussman, eds., *Alternative Service Delivery: Sharing Governance in Canada* (Toronto: Institute of Public Administration of Canada and KPMG Centre for Government Foundation, 1997), pp. 235–45.

73 Ontario, Ministry of Consumer and Commercial Relations, Registration Division and Business Practices Division, "Reshaping Government: The 'Used Vehicle Information Program.'" Completed questionnaire on public-sector innovation in Canada, 1995.

74 Ontario, Ministry of Consumer and Commercial Relations, "Maximizing Opportunity." Questionnaire.

75 Ontario, Ministry of Consumer and Commercial Relations, "The Companies Branch Night Shift Project." Completed questionnaire on public-sector innovation in Canada, 1996; Ontario, Ministry of Consumer and Commercial Relations, Registration Division, "Partners in Goodwill." Completed questionnaire on public-sector innovation in Canada, 1996.

76 Ontario, Ministry of Consumer and Commercial Relations, "The Triple Handshake: Ontario's Industry Self-Management Paradigm." Submission to the IPAC Award for Innovative Management competition, 1998.

77 Mohga Badran and Sandford Borins, "Innovation and Transformation in a Canadian Public Sector Organization." Paper presented to the annual conference of the International Institute of Schools and Institutes of Administration, Quebec City, 1997.

78 Standards Council of Canada, "What is ISO Registration/Certification" [web site, 2000]. See http://www.scc.ca/iso9000/ques9000.html.

79 Richard Parisotto, chief administrative officer, Town of Ajax. Interview, August 1998.

80 Canada Post, "Angus Reid Group Public Opinion Survey of Canadians Concerning Canada Post and Postal Issues," *Canada Post Press Release*, 11 March 1996 (Ottawa: Canada Post, 1996), p. 1.

81 Canadian Centre for Management Development, *Public Service Culture: Results of the SYMLOG Survey* (Ottawa: CCMD, 1997).

82 Canada, Passport Office, *Annual Report 1995–96* (Ottawa: Public Works and Government Services Canada, 1996), p. 12.

83 G. Bruce Doern, *The Road to Better Public Services: Progress and Constraints in Five Canadian Federal Agencies* (Montreal: Institute for Research on Public Policy, 1994), p. 40.

84 Canada, Passport Office, *Annual Report 1995–96*, p. 15.

85 Ibid., p. 22.

86 Kernaghan, "The emerging public service culture," CANADIAN PUBLIC ADMINISTRATION.

87 Denhardt, *Pursuit of Significance*, p. 23.

88 Jim Clemmer, *Pathways to Performance* (Toronto: Macmillan, 1995), p. 93.

89 This is taken from the federal Department of Energy, Mines and Resources (now the Department of Natural Resources) [1992], "Our Values," which is reproduced in Appendix A-1.

90 A few sections of this chapter are drawn from Kernaghan, "Emerging public service culture," CANADIAN PUBLIC ADMINISTRATION.

91 Milton Rokeach, *The Nature of Human Values* (New York: Free Press, 1973), p. 5.

92 Canada, Office of the Auditor General, *Annual Report* [1990], p. 176.

93 Kenneth Kernaghan, "Shaking the Foundation: New versus Traditional Public-Service Values," in Mohamed Charih and Arthur Daniels, eds., *New Public Management and Public Administration in Canada*. Monographs on Canadian Public Administration – No. 20 (Toronto: Institute of Public Administration of Canada, 1997), pp. 47–65, at pp. 48–9.

94 Some authors use the term "managerial values" rather than "organizational values." The latter term, in the sense of the values associated with the organization, permits the inclusion not only of managerial values but also of values that would not generally be considered specifically managerial.

95 Kenneth Kernaghan, "Changing concepts of power and responsibility in the Canadian public service," CANADIAN PUBLIC ADMINISTRATION 21, no. 3 (Fall 1978), pp. 389–406.

96 Several of these values (effectiveness, representativeness, fairness and equity) have become much more important since the early 1960s. While fairness and equity do not mean precisely the same thing, they are frequently used interchangeably.

97 A study of the dominant values appearing in the mandates of five commissions or study groups reporting between 1962 and 1990 and of the mandate of the Canadian Centre for Management Development support the centrality of these traditional values. See James Iain Gow, *Innovation in the Public Service* (Ottawa: Canadian Centre for Management Development, 1991), p. 4.

98 Canada, Committee on Governing Values, *Governing Values* (Ottawa: Supply and Services, 1987), p. 7.

99 For an examination of the distinction between "espoused values" and "values in use," see Chris Argyris, "Double loop learning in organizations," *Harvard Business Review* 55, no. 5 (September/October 1977), pp. 115–25.

100 Nancy Hughes Anthony [former deputy minister, Department of Veterans Affairs, Government of Canada], "Speaking Notes for a Meeting of the Prince Edward Island Regional Group of the Institute of Public Administration of Canada," 21 September 1993.

101 Zussman and Jabes, *The Vertical Solitude*, p. 86.

102 Barbara Wake Carroll and David Siegel, "Two Solitudes or One Big Happy Family: Head Office–Field Office Relations in Government Organizations." Paper presented to the annual meeting of the Canadian Political Science Association, Montreal, 6 June 1995, p. 15.

103 Ibid., p. 18.

104 Jim Vantour, ed., *Our Story: Organizational Renewal in Federal Corrections* (Ottawa: Canadian Centre for Management Development, 1991), p. 35.

105 Denhardt, *Pursuit of Significance*, p. 22.

106 Canada, Public Service 2000, Task Force on the Management Category, *Report* (Ottawa: Privy Council Office, 1990), p. iv.

107 Canada, Deputy Minister's Task Force on Public Service Values and Ethics, *A Strong Foundation. Report* (Ottawa: Privy Council Office, 1996), p. 77.

108 I.D. Clark, "Getting the Incentives Right: Towards a Productivity-Oriented Management Framework for the Public Service." Background paper for an

armchair discussion at the Canadian Centre for Management Development, 1993, p. 4.

109 Canada, Deputy Ministers' Task Force on Service Delivery Models, *Report. Part II* (Ottawa: Privy Council Office, 1996), p. 12.

110 Kernaghan, "The emerging public service culture," CANADIAN PUBLIC ADMINISTRATION.

111 Canada, Deputy Minister's Task Force on Public Service Values and Ethics, *A Strong Foundation. Report*, pp. 2–3.

112 Canadian Centre for Management Development, *Public Service Culture: Results of the SYMLOG Survey*.

113 Canada, Treasury Board Secretariat and Public Service Commission, *Profile of Public Service Leaders and Managers* (Ottawa: TBS and PSC, 1990), p. 7.

114 James M. Kouzes and Barry Z. Posner, *The Leadership Challenge* (San Francisco: Jossey-Bass, 1995), p. 18.

115 Phillip Selznick, *Leadership in Administration: A Sociological Interpretation* (New York: Harper & Row, 1957), p. 28.

116 Denhardt, *Pursuit of Significance*, p. 36.

117 We are grateful to Victor Rocine for this framework. A well-documented study of the development and the early stages of implementation of a value statement as part of a strategic plan is found in Vantour, *Our Story*.

118 John L. Manion [former federal deputy minister and first principal of the Canadian Centre for Management Development], *A Management Model* (Ottawa: Canadian Centre for Management Development, 1989), p. 95.

119 For brief case studies of the formulation and implementation of value statements, see also the corporate philosophy approach used by Tandem Computers, described in Diane Filipowski, "The Tao of Tandem," *Personnel Journal* (October 1991), pp. 72–8.

120 Alberta, Department of Labour, Department of Business and Organizational Planning, *Case Study Series: # 1* (Toronto: Ontario Centre for Leadership and Ottawa: Conference Board of Canada, 1995), p. 4.

121 Zussman and Jabes, *The Vertical Solitude*, pp. 96ff.

122 Letter dated 9 June 1993 (emphasis added).

123 Tandem Computers, *Tandem Value System* (Tandem Computers, 1990), p. 1.

124 Canada, Public Service 2000, Task Force on Workforce Adaptiveness, *Managing Change in the Public Service – A Guide for the Perplexed* (Ottawa: Supply and Services Canada, 1991), p. 15; Clemmer, *Pathways to Performance*, pp. 98–103.

125 There are four sequential elements to the values audit in strategic planning: the values audit itself; the examination of the organization's operating philosophy; an analysis of the organization's culture; and a stakeholder analysis. See J. William Pfeiffer, Leonard D. Goodstein and Timothy Nolan, *Shaping Strategic Planning* (Glenview, Ill.: Scott, Foresman, 1989), p. 96.

126 Zussman and Jabes, *The Vertical Solitude*, p. 96.

127 Canada, Public Service 2000, Service to the Public Task Force, *Report* (Ottawa: Privy Council Office, 1990), p. 25 (emphasis in the original).

128 Clemmer, *Pathways to Performance*, p. 96.

129 Canada, Committee on Governing Values, *Governing Values*, p. 11.

130 The committee's report asks on p. 18: "Is RESPECT a common value – does it cover the spectrum from respect for the law through to self-respect; does it include our relationships with our political masters, with our clients, with our employees, and with each other? Is RESPONSIBILITY another common value – does it include the people to whom we have obligations and the things for which we are accountable? Is RESPONSIVENESS a third value – does it provide for meeting the changing needs of Government, and for dealing with the public when that is applicable?"

131 Clemmer, *Pathways to Performance*, p. 95.

132 Filipowski, "Tao of Tandem," *Personnel Journal*, p. 75.

133 Canada, Deputy Minister's Task Force on Public Service Values and Ethics, *A Strong Foundation. Report*, pp. 77, 78.

134 Kenneth Gold, *A Comparative Analysis of Successful Organizations* (Washington, D.C.: U.S. Office of Personnel Management, Workforce Effectiveness and Development Group, 1981), cited in Michael L. Vasu et al., *Organization Behavior and Public Management*, 2nd edition (New York: Marcel Dekker, 1990), p. 227.

135 Peters and Waterman, *In Search of Excellence*.

136 Barry Z. Posner, James M. Kouzes and Warren H. Schmidt, "Shared values make a difference: an empirical test of culture," *Human Resource Management* 24, no. 3 (Fall 1985), pp. 293–309.

137 Kernaghan, "The emerging public service culture," CANADIAN PUBLIC ADMINISTRATION, p. 620.

138 Denhardt, *Pursuit of Significance*, p. 22.

139 Paul G. Thomas, "Coping with Change: How Public and Private Organizations Read and Respond to Turbulent External Environments," in F. Leslie Seidle, ed., *Rethinking Government: Reform or Reinvention?* (Montreal: Institute for Research on Public Policy, 1993), pp. 31–62, at p. 57. See also Alan L. Wilkins and William G. Ouchi, "Efficient cultures: exploring the relationship between culture and organizational performance," *Administrative Science Quarterly* 28, no. 4 (December 1983), pp. 468–81. For a more positive view see Posner, Kouzes and Schmidt, "Shared values make a difference," *Human Resource Management*.

140 Francine Séguin, "Service to the public: a major strategic change," CANADIAN PUBLIC ADMINISTRATION 34, no. 3 (Fall 1991), pp. 465–73, p. 471.

141 Frank Swift, *Strategic Management in the Public Service: The Changing Role of the Deputy Minister* (Ottawa: Supply and Services Canada for the Canadian Centre for Management Development, 1993), p. 18.

142 Séguin, "Service to the public: a major strategic change," CANADIAN PUBLIC ADMINISTRATION, p. 471.

143 Thomas, "Coping with Change," in Seidle, *Rethinking Government*, p. 57. In support of these assertions, he cites John P. Kotter and James L. Heskett, *Corporate Cultures and Performance* (Boston: Harvard Business School Press,

1992); Danny Miller, *The Icarus Paradox: How Exceptional Companies Bring About their Own Downfall* (New York: HarperCollins, 1990).

144 Zussman and Jabes, *The Vertical Solitude*, pp. 111, 112.

145 Vijay Sathe, "Implications of corporate culture: a manager's guide to action," *Organizational Dynamics* (Autumn 1983), pp. 5–23.

146 Posner, Kouzes and Schmidt, "Shared values make a difference," *Human Resource Management*, p. 303.

147 Letter dated 15 June 1993.

148 Gow, *Learning from Others*, p. 3.

149 Sandford Borins, *Innovating with Integrity: How Local Heroes are Transforming American Government* (Washington, D.C.: Georgetown University Press, 1998).

150 Ibid., pp. 12–18.

151 Aucoin, *New Public Management*; Leslie Seidle, *Rethinking the Delivery of Public Services to Citizens* (Montreal: Institute for Research on Public Policy, 1995).

152 To measure the similarity of Canadian and U.S. distributions, we have calculated correlation coefficients. A correlation coefficient is a statistical measure of association between two variables, varying between $-1$ and $+1$. A coefficient of $+1$ indicates a strong positive relationship, $-1$ a strong negative relationship, and zero no relationship. It is necessary to test whether the coefficient calculated is significantly different from zero. This is done by calculating a t-statistic; the larger the t-statistic, the more the correlation coefficient is significantly different from 0. A t-statistic that is significant at the .01 level means that we would expect the correlation coefficient to be different from 0 ninety-nine out of 100 times. Generally, statisticians do significance tests at the .05 level. (See Morris Hamburg, *Statistical Analysis for Decision Making* [New York: Harcourt, Brace, 1970], pp. 486–98.) Correlation coefficients and significance tests are reported in the tables.

153 Environment Canada, Atmospheric Environment Service, "Development of the Ozone Watch and UV Index Programs." Completed questionnaire on public-sector innovation in Canada, 1995.

154 It might be argued that the applicants' frequent citing of holism to describe their innovations is at variance with our discussion in Chapter 5 about the creation of relatively autonomous special operating agencies. In response, we would say that the optimal context for a special operating agency is a function that is independent of the rest of the public sector. Holistic innovations can occur when existing organizations, while retaining their identity, cooperate in delivering a particular program; in this case, the program is being delivered by a "virtual organization." In some instances, cooperation in service delivery could lead to the creation of a new organization, generally referred to as a service agency. Service agencies are also discussed in Chapter 5.

155 Ontario, Ministry of Consumer and Commercial Relations, Registration Division and Business Practices Division, "Re-shaping Government: The Used Vehicle Information Program." Questionnaire.

156 Rosabeth Kanter, "When a thousand flowers bloom: structural, collective, and social conditions for innovation in organizations," in Barry M. Staw and L.L. Cummings, eds., *Research in Organizational Behaviour*. Vol. 10 (Greenwich, Conn.: JAI Press, 1988), pp. 169–211, at p. 171.

157 Alberta, Department of Labour, "The Third Option: Alberta Labour's Approach to Public Sector Reform." Completed questionnaire on public-sector innovation in Canada, 1995; Ontario, Ministry of Natural Resources, "Partnerships in Resource Management." Completed questionnaire on public-sector innovation in Canada, 1995; Saskatchewan, Environment and Resource Management, "Partnership Program." Completed questionnaire on public-sector innovation in Canada, 1995.

158 Alberta, Department of Transportation and Utilities, "Alberta Transportation and Utilities' Transition Project." Completed questionnaire on public-sector innovation in Canada, 1995; British Columbia, Ministry of Transportation and Highways, "Privatization of Road and Bridge Maintenance." Completed questionnaire on public-sector innovation in Canada, 1995; Ontario, Ministry of Transportation, Safety and Regulation, "ServiceOntario Self-Service Kiosks." Completed questionnaire on public-sector innovation in Canada, 1996

159 Ontario, Soil and Crop Improvement Association, "Land Stewardship Program." Completed questionnaire on public-sector innovation in Canada, 1995.

160 Alberta Workers' Compensation Board, Rehabilitation Centre, "Work Hardening." Completed questionnaire on public-sector innovation in Canada, 1996.

161 Township of Pittsburgh [Ontario], Municipal Office [Sheilagh Dunn], "Cost management in Action: How to be lean and keen while having fun." Completed questionnaire on public-sector innovation in Canada, 1995.

162 Human Resources Development Canada, "Teambuilding: Changing Managerial Attitudes and Behaviour." Completed questionnaire on public-sector innovation in Canada, 1995.

163 Barzelay, with Armajani, *Breaking Through Bureaucracy*; Donald Savoie, What's wrong with the new public management?" CANADIAN PUBLIC ADMINISTRATION 38, no. 1 (Spring 1995), pp. 112–21.

164 Gow, *Learning from Others*, p. 47.

165 Environment Canada, Canadian Parks Service, "Parks Canada Accessibility Program for Seniors and People with Disabilities." Completed questionnaire on public-sector innovation in Canada, 1995.

166 Alan Altshuler and Marc Zegans, "Innovation and creativity: comparisons between public management and private enterprise," *Cities* 1, no. 1 (February 1990), pp. 16–24.

167 Sandford Borins, "Public management innovation awards in the US and Canada," in Hermann Hill and Helmut Klages, eds., *Trends in Public Service Renewal* (Frankfurt: Peter Lang, 1995), pp. 213–40. The IPAC questionnaire is much shorter than the Ford-KSG questionnaire and had only a few questions that were comparable.

168 Township of Pittsburgh [Ontario], Municipal Office [Sheilagh Dunn], "Cost management in action: How to be lean and keen while having fun." Questionnaire.

169 The category "stakeholder dissatisfaction" was rejected by Borins in later research because it was insufficiently specific.

170 Alberta, Department of Transportation and Utilities, "Alberta Transportation and Utilities' Transition Project." Questionnaire; Alberta, Department of Labour, Department of Business and Organizational Planning, *Case Study Series # 1*; British Columbia, Ministry of Transportation and Highways, "Privatization of Road and Bridge Maintenance." Questionnaire.

171 British Columbia, Ministry of Finance and Corporate Relations, "Personal Property Registry System." Completed questionnaire on public-sector innovation in Canada, 1996; Ontario, Ministry of Consumer and Commercial Relations, Registration Division, Personal Property Security Registration Branch, "Direct Access: Maximizing People with Technology." Questionnaire.

172 Ontario, Ministry of Consumer and Commercial Relations, Registration Division, "Maximizing Opportunity." Questionnaire.

173 Martin Levin and Mary Bryna Sanger, *Making Government Work: How Entrepreneurial Executives Turn Bright Ideas into Real Results* (San Francisco: Jossey-Bass, 1994); James Q. Wilson, "Innovation in Organization: Notes toward a Theory," in J.D. Thompson, ed., *Approaches in Organization Design* (Pittsburgh: University of Pittsburgh Press, 1966), pp. 194–218.

174 Nigel King, "Innovation at Work: the Research Literature," in M.A. West and J.L. Farr, eds., *Innovation and Creativity at Work* (New York: Wiley, 1990), pp. 15–59.

175 This correlation used the frequency of political initiatives in the larger Canadian sample rather than the small Canadian sample. The other frequencies were from the small Canadian sample.

176 Robert Behn, "Management by groping along," *Journal of Policy Analysis and Management 7*, no. 4 (Fall 1988), pp. 643–63; Olivia Golden, "Innovation in public sector human services programs: the implications of innovation by 'groping along,'" *Journal of Policy Analysis and Management 9*, no. 2 (Spring 1990), pp. 219–48; Martin Levin and Mary Bryna Sanger, "Using old stuff in new ways: innovation as a case of evolutionary tinkering," *Journal of Policy Analysis and Management 11*, no. 1 (Winter 1992), pp. 88–115; Levin and Sanger, *Making Government Work*.

177 In both Canada and the U.S. fewer than ten per cent of the innovations were derived from a strategic planning for the entire organization. This finding is consistent with Henry Mintzberg's work on strategic planning in the private sector, which finds that few organizations had overall strategic plans. See Henry Mintzberg, *The Rise and Fall of Strategic Planning: Reconceiving Roles for Planning, Plans, and Planners* (New York: Free Press, 1994).

178 In an extended case study of the implementation of public school choice in Minnesota, Nancy Roberts and Paula King found evidence of both planning and groping. See Nancy Roberts and Paula King, *Transforming Public Policy:*

*Dynamics of Policy Entrepreneurship and Innovation* (San Francisco: Jossey-Bass, 1996).

179 Township of Pittsburgh [Ontario], Municipal Office [Sheilagh Dunn], "Cost management in action: How to be lean and keen while having fun." Questionnaire, p. 11.

180 Environment Canada, Atmospheric Environment Service, "Development of the Ozone Watch and UV Index Programs." Questionnaire.

181 Ontario, Ministry of Consumer and Commercial Relations, Registration Division, "Maximizing Opportunity." Questionnaire, p. 16.

182 Ontario, Ministry of Consumer and Commercial Relations, Registration Division, Personal Property Security Registration Branch,"Direct Access: Maximizing People with Technology." Questionnaire, p. 19 and p. 20, respectively.

183 Saskatchewan, Economic and Cooperative Development, "Partnership for Renewal – An Economic Strategy for Saskatchewan." Completed questionnaire on public-sector innovation in Canada, 1995.

184 Environment Canada, Canadian Parks Service, "Parks Canada Accessibility Program for Seniors and People with Disabilities." Questionnaire.

185 Ontario, Ministry of Consumer and Commercial Relations, Registration Division and Business Practices Division, "Reshaping Government: The Used Vehicle Information Program." Questionnaire.

186 Borins, *Innovating with Integrity*, p. 67.

187 New Brunswick, Department of Advanced Education and Labour, Department of Advocacy Services, "New Brunswick's Literacy Initiative." Completed questionnaire on public-sector innovation in Canada, 1995.

188 Ontario, Ministry of Transportation, Safety and Regulation, "ServiceOntario Self-Service Kiosks." Questionnaire.

189 Township of Pittsburgh [Ontario], Municipal Office [Sheilagh Dunn], "Cost management in action: How to be lean and keen while having fun." Questionnaire, p. 11.

190 Ontario, Ministry of Consumer and Commercial Relations, "The Companies Branch Night Shift Project." Questionnaire.

191 Respectively, Township of Pittsburgh [Ontario], Muncipal Office [Sheilagh Dunn], "Cost management in action: How to be lean and keen while having fun." Questionnaire; British Columbia, Ministry of Finance and Corporate Relations, Personal Property Registry System." Questionnaire; Environment Canada, Canadian Parks Service, "Parks Canada Accessibility Program for Seniors and People with Disabilities." Questionnaire; Ontario, Ministry of Consumer and Commercial Relations, Registration Division and Business Practices Division, "Reshaping Government: The Used Vehicle Information Program." Questionnaire; New Brunswick, Department of Advanced Education and Labour, Department of Advocacy Services, "New Brunswick's Literacy Initiative." Questionnaire; Ontario, Ministry of Consumer and Commercial Relations, "Maximizing Opportunity." Questionnaire; Environment Canada, Atmospheric Environment Services, "Development of the Ozone Watch and UV Index Programs." Questionnaire; Township of Pittsburgh

[Ontario], Municipal Office [Sheilagh Dunn], "Cost management in Action: How to be lean and keen while having fun." Questionnaire; British Columbia, Ministry of Finance and Corporate Relations, "Personal Property Registry System." Questionnaire; Ontario, Ministry of Consumer and Commercial Relations, "The Companies Branch Night Shift Project." Questionnaire.

192 Township of Pittsburgh [Ontario], Municipal Office [Sheilagh Dunn], "Cost management in action: How to be lean and keen while having fun." Questionnaire.

193 British Columbia, Ministry of Health, "Pregnancy Outreach Program." Completed questionnaire on public-sector innovation in Canada, 1995.

194 British Columbia, Ministry of Finance and Corporate Relations, "Personal Property Registry System." Questionnaire; Ontario, Ministry of Consumer and Commercial Relations, Registration Division, Personal Property Security Registration Branch, "Direct Access: Maximizing People with Technology." Questionnaire.

195 Ontario, Soil and Crop Improvement Association, "Land Stewardship Program." Questionnaire.

196 n.a. [Institute of Public Administration of Canada], "Alberta Workers' Compensation Board Rehabilitation Centre," *Public Sector Management* 4, no. 1 (Spring 1993), p. 8; Alberta Workers' Compensation Board, Rehabilitation Centre, "Work Hardening." Questionnaire.

197 Revenue Canada, "Harnessing the Power within the Corporation." Completed questionnaire on public-sector innovation in Canada, 1996.

198 Manitoba, Government Services, Fleet Vehicles Agency, "Fleet Vehicles Special Operating Agency." Completed questionnaire on public-sector innovation in Canada, 1995.

199 An expression of interest was coded when it was not clear that actual replication had occurred. However, even though interest would naturally precede replication in any given case, we did not code both when there was actual replication.

200 Ontario, Ministry of Citizenship, Office for Seniors' Issues, Education Resources Unit, "Seniors' Issues Group." Completed questionnaire on public-sector innovation in Canada, 1995; Environment Canada, Atmospheric Environment Services, "Development of the Ozone Watch and UV Index Programs." Questionnaire; Environment Canada, Canadian Parks Service, "Parks Canada Accessibility Program for Seniors and People with Disabilities." Questionnaire.

201 Hammer and Champy *Reengineering the Corporation*, p. 32.

202 Brian Marson, "1998–99 deputy ministers' issues survey," *Public Sector Management* 10, no. 1 (Spring 1999), pp. 5–10.

203 Brian Marson, "Leading strategic change in the public sector," *The Public Manager* 26, no. 4 (Winter 1997–8), pp. 26–30, at p. 27.

204 John Edwards and Nick Mulder, "Round table on alternative organizational forms," *Optimum* 23, no. 1 (1992), pp. 3–5, at p. 3.

205 Canada, Treasury Board Secretariat, *Framework for Alternative Program Delivery* (Ottawa: Treasury Board Secretariat, 1995), p. 1.

206 David Wright, *Special Operating Agencies–Autonomy, Accountability and Performance Measurement* (Ottawa: Canadian Centre for Management Development, 1995), p. vii.

207 Kenneth Kernaghan and David Siegel, *Public Administration in Canada: A Text*, 4th edition (Toronto: Nelson, 1999), p. 265.

208 Canada, Canadian Tourism Commission, *Annual Report, 1996* (Ottawa: Commission, 1997).

209 Dennis Ducharme, "Manitoba Fleet Vehicles – Testing the SOA Concept," *Public Sector Management* 6, no. 1 (Winter 1995), pp. 22–3.

210 Eric Huffy, " The creation of autonomous service units – a change more fundamental than it appears" [English translation of French article], *Public Sector Management* 7, no. 4 (Winter 1997), pp. 19, 31, at p. 31.

211 Alti Rodal, *Special Operating Agencies: Issues for Parent Departments and Central Agencies* (Ottawa: Canadian Centre for Management Development, 1996), p. 5.

212 Canada, Department of Finance, *Budget Plan* (Ottawa: Finance Canada, 1996), p. 46.

213 Ronald Doering, "Alternative Service Delivery: the Case of the Canadian Food Inspection Agency" [unpublished paper] (Ottawa: Canadian Food Inspection Agency, 1997), p. 1.

214 Ibid., p. 3.

215 Ibid, p. 2.

216 Barry Stemshorn, "The Canadian Food Inspection Agency – A Work in Progress." Paper presented to the B.C. Federal Regional Council ASD Workshop, 1998, p. 11.

217 Tom Beaver, "Accountability of Alternative Service Delivery Organizations: the Case of the Canadian Food Inspection Agency" [unpublished paper] (Ottawa: Canadian Food Inspection Agency, 1997), p. 13.

218 Canada, Deputy Ministers' Task Force on Service Delivery Models, *Report. Part II*, p. 36.

219 Ibid., p. 37.

220 Ibid., p. 41.

221 Murray Skinner, "Building on heritage: CCG and St. Joseph Corporation," *The Focus Report* 6, no. 4 (August 1997), pp. 10–15, p. 12.

222 Ibid., p. 17.

223 James McDavid and D. Brian Marson, eds., *The Well Performing Government Organization* (Toronto: Institute of Public Administration of Canada, 1993), p. 61.

224 n.a. [Institute of Public Administration of Canada], "Re-shaping government – a case study of the Office of the Registrar General, Thunder Bay, Ontario," *Public Sector Management* 5, no. 1 (Spring 1994), pp. 4–7, at p. 4.

225 Ibid., p. 6.

226 Jean Bilodeau, "Locally shared support services: a success story," *Optimum* 66, no. 3 (Winter 1996), pp. 35–8, at p. 37.

227 British Columbia, Ministry for Children and Families, *Building the Ministry for Children and Families* (Victoria: Ministry, 1997), p. 4.

228 Hammer and Champy, *Reengineering the Corporation*.

229 Ibid., p. 103.

230 Ibid.

231 Canada, Department of National Defence, "A Re-engineering Success Story" [video] (Ottawa: DGPA-National Defence Headquarters, 1995).

232 n.a. [Institute of Public Administration of Canada], "Human Resources Development Canada: a collaborative approach to change management: re-engineering the Record of Employment (ROE)," *Public Sector Management* 8, no. 2 (Summer 1997), pp. 11, 16, at p. 16.

233 Gérard LaFrance, "Managing reengineering projects for results," *Optimum* 27, no. 3 (Winter 1997), pp. 8–13.

234 Hammer and Champy, *Reengineering the Corporation*, p. 35.

235 n.a. [Institute of Public Administration of Canada], "City of Vancouver: Neighbourhood Integrated Service Teams," *Public Sector Management* 8, no. 2 (Summer 1997), p. 8.

236 Ibid.

237 Ibid.

238 Arie Halachmi, "Business process reengineering in the public sector: trying to get another frog to fly?" *National Productivity Review* 15, no. 3 (Summer 1996), pp. 9–18.

239 Kenneth Kernaghan and Mohamed Charih, "The challenges of change: emerging issues in contemporary public administration," CANADIAN PUBLIC ADMINISTRATION 40, no. 2 (Summer 1997), pp. 218–33, at p. 223.

240 Geert Bouckaert and K. Verhoest, "A Comparative Perspective on Perform-ance Management in the Public Sector." Round Table of the International Institute of Administrative Sciences, 14–17 July 1997, Quebec City, p. 21.

241 Guy Peters, *Managing Horizontal Government: The Politics of Coordination* (Ottawa: Canadian Centre for Management Development, 1998), p. 12.

242 Ole Ingstrup, *Reengineering in the Public Service: Promise or Peril?* (Ottawa: Canadian Centre for Management Development, 1995), p. 17.

243 Brian Marson, "Report on the IPAC 1996–97 Deputy Ministers' Issues Sur-vey – Public Service Renewal Agenda," *Public Sector Management* 7, no. 4 (Winter 1997), pp. 11–17; Rodal, *Special Operating Agencies*.

244 Rodal, *Special Operating Agencies*, p. 31.

245 Guy Peters, *Policy and Operations* (Ottawa: Canadian Centre for Management Development, 1997), p. 5.

246 David Zussman, "Government's new style," *Public Sector Management* 8, no. 2 (Summer 1997), pp. 21–3, p. 22.

247 Ibid.

248 Denhardt, *Pursuit of Significance*, p. 17.

249 Thomas Peters, "Excellence in government? I'm all for it! Maybe," *The Bureaucrat* 20, no. 1 (Spring 1991), pp. 3–8, p. 6.

250 Denhardt, *Pursuit of Significance*, p. 8.

251 Canada, Treasury Board Secretariat, *Who is the Client – A Discussion Paper* (Ottawa: Supply and Services Canada, 1996), p. 3.

252 Seidle, *Rethinking the Delivery of Public Services to Citizens*, p. 76.

253 Thomas Miller, *Citizen Surveys* (Washington, D.C.: International City/ County Management Association, 1991), p. 115.

254 ICM Research, *Citizen's Charter Customer Survey: Research Report* (London: Citizen's Charter Unit, 1993).

255 Ontario, Management Board of Cabinet, *Best Value for Tax Dollars: Improving Service Quality in the Ontario Government* (Toronto: Management Board, 1992), p. 39.

256 Theodore Poister and Gary Henry, "Citizen ratings of public and private service quality: a comparative perspective," *Public Administration Review* 54, no. 2 (March/April 1994), pp. 155–60, at p. 157.

257 Ontario, Management Board of Cabinet, *Best Value for Tax Dollars*, p. 69.

258 Ibid., p. 78.

259 Ibid.

260 Erin Research, *Citizens First* (Ottawa: Canadian Centre for Management Development, 1998).

261 David Carr and Ian Littman, *Excellence in Government: Total Quality Management in the 1990s* (Arlington, Va.: Coopers & Lybrand, 1990), p. 3.

262 Steven Cohen and Ronald Brand, *Total Quality Management in Government: A Practical Guide for the Real World* (San Francisco: Jossey-Bass, 1993), p. xi.

263 Richard Palermo and Gregory Watson, *A World of Quality: the Timeless Passport* (Milwaukee: ASQC Press, 1993), p. 11.

264 Carr and Littman, *Excellence in Government*, p. 8.

265 Denise Bragg, *Quality Management: An Introduction* (Victoria: Service Quality B.C. Secretariat, 1993), p. 4.

266 Karl Albrecht and Ron Zemke, *Service America!* (Homewood, Ill.: Dow-Jones Irwin, 1985).

267 Valarie Zeithaml, A. Parasuraman and Leonard Berry, *Delivering Quality Service: Balancing Customer Perceptions and Expectations* (New York: Free Press, 1990).

268 Brian Marson, "Building customer focused public organizations," *Public Administration Quarterly* 17, no. 1 (Spring 1993), pp. 30–41.

269 Faye Schmidt and Teresa Strickland, *Client Satisfaction Surveying: A Manager's Guide* (Ottawa: Canadian Centre for Management Development, 1998), p. 14.

270 Barton and Marson, *Service Quality*, p. 29.

271 Zeithaml et al., *Delivering Quality Service*; Leonard Berry, *On Great Service* (New York: The Free Press, 1995).

272 Paul Johanis, *Serving Canadians: A Survey of Practices in Support of Quality Services in the Federal Public Service of Canada* (Ottawa: Statistics Canada, 1995), p. 2.

273 Marson, "Building customer focused public organizations," *Public Administration Quarterly*.

274 Robin Ford and David Zussman, "Alternative Service Delivery: Transcending Boundaries," in Ford and Zussman, *Alternative Service Delivery*, pp. 1–14, at p. 7.

275 McDavid and Marson, *The Well Performing Government Organization*, p. 68.

276 Canada, Deputy Ministers' Task Force on Service Delivery Models, *Report. Part II*, p. 101.

277 Seidle, *Rethinking the Delivery of Public Services to Citizens*, p. 101.

278 Ibid., p. 120.

279 Canada, Business Service Centres Secretariat, "One more one-stop service," *InterConnexion* 1, no. 3 (January 1997) [newsletter], p. 2.

280 Seidle, *Rethinking the Delivery of Public Services to Citizens*, p. 129.

281 Al Gore, *Common Sense Government* (New York: Random House, 1995), p. 79.

282 Ibid., p. 83.

283 Seidle, *Rethinking the Delivery of Public Services to Citizens*, p. 34.

284 Canada, Public Service 2000, *The Renewal of the Public Service of Canada*, p. 55.

285 Commonwealth Secretariat, *Current Good Practices and New Developments in Public Service Management – A Profile of the Public Service of Canada* (London: Commonwealth Secretariat, 1994), p. 104.

286 Seidle, *Rethinking the Delivery of Public Services to Citizens*, p. 89.

287 Canada, Deputy Ministers' Task Force on Service Delivery Models, *Report*, p. ii.

288 Ontario, Management Board of Cabinet, *Best Value for Tax Dollars*.

289 Barton and Marson, *Service Quality*, p. 10.

290 Marson, "Building customer focused public organizations," *Public Administration Quarterly*, p. 38.

291 Johanis, *Serving Canadians*.

292 Marson, "Building customer focused public organizations," *Public Administration Quarterly*.

293 Canada, Office of the Auditor General, *Annual Report* [1988], Chapter 4, Section 4.74.

294 Kimball Fisher, *Leading Self-Directed Work Teams* (New York: McGraw-Hill, 1993), p. 13.

295 This chapter is based in part on Kenneth Kernaghan, "Empowerment and public administration: revolutionary advance or passing fancy," CANADIAN PUBLIC ADMINISTRATION 35, no. 2 (Summer 1992), pp. 194–214.

296 n.a. [Institute of Public Administration of Canada], "Clinical Research and Treatment Institute: Addiction Research Foundation of Ontario," *Public Sector Management* 5, no. 1 (Spring 1994), pp. 14–15.

297 Kernaghan and Siegel, *Public Administration in Canada*, chapters 4 and 22.

298 J.A. Conger and Rabindra N. Kanungo, "The empowerment process: integrating theory and practice," *Academy of Management Review* 13, no. 3 (1988), pp. 471–82, at p. 474.

299 Canada, Public Service 2000, *Highlights of the White Paper on Public Service 2000. The Renewal of the Public Service of Canada* (Ottawa: Privy Council Office, 1990), pp. 51–2.

300 Art Silverman quoted in n.a. [Institute of Public Administration of Canada], "Fisheries and Oceans Canada: management strategy shift produces increased efficiency and effectiveness of DFO's science fleet," *Public Sector Management* 4, no. 1 (Spring 1993), pp. 10–12, at p. 12.

301 Catharine G. Johnston and Carolyn Farquhar, *Empowered People Satisfy Customers* (Ottawa: Conference Board of Canada, 1992), p. 15.

302 Lorne C. Plunkett and Robert Fournier, *Participative Management: Implementing Empowerment* (New York: John Wiley, 1991), p. 5.

303 Ontario, Ministry of Community and Social Services, Southwestern Regional Centre, "Social Demonstration Project." Submission to the IPAC Award for Innovative Management competition, 1991, p. 3.

304 Victor Rocine, "Total quality management: excellence by design," *Public Sector Management* 2, no. 1 (Spring 1991), pp. 18–21, at p. 18.

305 Canada, Public Service 2000, Service to the Public Task Force, *Report*, p. 46.

306 Human Resources Development Canada, "Teambuilding: Changing Managerial Attitudes and Behaviour." Questionnaire, p. 7.

307 Conger and Kanungo, "Empowerment process," *Academy of Management Review*, pp. 474–6.

308 Federal Quality Institute, *Criteria and Scoring Guidelines for the President's Award for Quality and Productivity Improvement*. Federal Total Quality Management Handbook (Ottawa: Institute, 1990), pp. 26–7.

309 Ibid., p. 24.

310 Judith Vogt and Kenneth Murrell, *Empowerment in Organizations* (San Diego, Calif.: University Associates, 1990), pp. 8–9.

311 Canada, Human Resources Development Council, *Strategies for People: An Integrated Approach to Changing Public Service Culture* (Ottawa: Treasury Board Secretariat, 1992), p. 33.

312 This is based in part on submissions to the IPAC Award for Innovative Management, completed questionnaires on public-sector innovation, interviews, and a CCMD report of visits to federal organizations involved with empowered work teams.

313 Township of Pittsburgh [Ontario], Municipal Office [Sheilagh Dunn], "Cost management in action: How to be lean and keen while having fun." Questionnaire, p. 4.

314 British Columbia Housing Management Commission. Submission to IPAC Award for Innovative Management competition, 1991.

315 Jon R. Katzenbach and Douglas K. Smith, *The Wisdom of Teams: Creating the High-Performance Organization* (Boston: Harvard Business School Press, 1993), p. 45.

316 Ibid., pp. 15–19; Glenn M. Parker, *Cross-Functional Teams: Working with Allies, Enemies, and Other Strangers* (San Francisco: Jossey Bass, 1994), pp. 6ff.

317 John H. Zenger, Ed Musselwhite, Kathleen Hurson and Craig Perrin, *Leading Teams: Mastering the New Role* (New York: Irwin, 1994), pp. 12–13; Parker, *Cross-Functional Teams*, pp. 34–7.

318 Fisher, *Leading Self-Directed Work Teams*.

319 Canada, Treasury Board Secretariat, *Innovations: Best Practices Notes. Note #15. Teamwork: Combined Effort* (Ottawa: TBS, 1994). Also available at http://www.tbs-sct.gc.ca.

320 Bruce Young, manager, Team Effectiveness, B.C. Hydro. Interview, 27 August 1991.

321 Anne Clapperton, "Reshaping government – technology as a catalyst for management change," *Public Sector Management* 5, no. 2 (Summer 1994), pp. 23–5, at p. 25.

322 Alberta, Department of Labour, Department of Business and Organizational Planning, *Case Study Series # 1*, p. 10.

323 Canada, Human Resources Development Council, *Empowerment* (Ottawa: Treasury Board Secretariat, 1992), p. 21.

324 Clapperton, "Reshaping government," *Public Sector Management*, p. 24.

325 Ibid.

326 Kouzes and Posner, *The Leadership Challenge*, p. 18.

327 Canada, Treasury Board Secretariat and Public Service Commission, *Profile of Public Service Leaders and Managers*, p. 7.

328 Young, B.C. Hydro, interview.

329 Canada, Treasury Board Secretariat, *Guides to Quality Service. Quality Services Guide V – Recognition* (Ottawa: TBS, 1996). Also available at http://www.tbs-sct.gc.ca.

330 British Columbia Housing Management Commission. Awards submission.

331 British Columbia, Public Service Employee Relations Commission. Employee Recognition Program, "Public Service Through Employee Involvement and Recognition." Submission to IPAC Award for Innovative Management competition, 1996, p.2.

332 British Columbia Hydro, Labour Relations Department. Submission to the IPAC Award for Innovative Management competition, 1992.

333 Saskatchewan, Public Service Commission, Staff Development Division. Submission to the IPAC Award for Innovative Management competition, 1991.

334 David Morley, "Team building: changing managerial attitudes and behaviour in a quality environment," *Optimum* 22, no. 3 (1991–92), pp. 17–24, at p. 23.

335 Canada, Human Resources Development Council, *Empowerment*, p. 15.

336 Ontario, Ministry of Community and Social Services, Southwestern Regional Centre," Social Demonstration Project." Awards submission, p. 4.

337 Nova Scotia Power Corporation. Submission to the IPAC Award for Innovative Management competition, 1991, pp. 6–7.

338 Industry Canada, Industry Sector, "Managing Change in the Industry Sector." Submission to the IPAC Award for Innovative Management competition, 1996, p. 1.

339 Ibid., Appendix 6.

340 Peter Kizilos, "Crazy about empowerment?" *Training* 27 (December 1990), pp. 47–56, at p. 56.

341 Vantour, *Our Story*, p. 64.

342 Revenue Canada [Bruce Lawrence]. Completed questionnaire on public-sector innovation in Canada, 1996, p. 7.

343 Human Resources Development Canada, "Teambuilding: Changing Managerial Attitudes and Behaviour." Questionnaire, p. 8.

344 Fisher, *Leading Self-Directed Work Teams*, pp. 211–44; Katzenbach and Smith, *The Wisdom of Teams*, pp. 149ff; Parker, *Cross-Functional Teams*, pp. 43ff.

345 Michael Verespej, "When you put the team in charge," *Industry Week* no. 239 (3 December 1990), pp. 30–2.

346 Alberta, Department of Labour, Department of Business and Organizational Planning, *Case Study Series* # 1, p. 12.

347 Michele Darling, "Empowerment: myth or reality?" *Executive Speeches* 10, no. 6 (June/July 1996), pp. 23–8; Margaret Houston and John Talbott, "Worker empowerment works – sometimes," *CMA Magazine* 70, no. 4 (July/August 1996), pp. 16–18.

348 Bengt Abrahamsson, *Bureaucracy or Participation: The Logic of Organization* (Beverly Hills, Calif.: Sage Publications, 1977); Ray Loveridge, "What is participation? A review of the literature and some methodological problems," *British Journal of Industrial Relations* 18, no. 3 (November 1980), pp. 297–317.

349 City of Burlington, City Clerk's Department, "Burlington Animal Control Self-Directed Work Team." Submission to IPAC Award for Innovative Management Competition, 1996; City of Toronto, "Bridges Program." Submission to the IPAC Award for Innovative Management competition, 1991.

350 Vantour, *Our Story*, p. 61.

351 Guy Peters and Donald J. Savoie, *Governance in a Changing Environment* (Montreal and Kingston: McGill-Queen's University Press, 1995).

352 S.A. Sutherland, "The Al-Mashat affair: administrative accountability in parliamentary institutions," CANADIAN PUBLIC ADMINISTRATION 34, no. 4 (Winter 1991), pp. 573–603, at p. 583.

353 Canada, Office of the Auditor General, "The Learning Organization," *Annual Report* (Ottawa: Supply and Services Canada, 1992), p. 133.

354 Canada, Clerk of the Privy Council [Jocelyne Bourgon], *Fourth Annual Report to the Prime Minister on the Public Service of Canada* (Ottawa: Privy Council Office, 1997), Chapter 4.

355 Bruce Rawson, "Public Service 2000 Service to the Public Task Force: findings and implications," CANADIAN PUBLIC ADMINISTRATION 34, no. 3 (Fall 1991), pp. 490–500, at p. 495.

356 Transport Canada, Air Carrier Operations, Ontario Region, "Aviation District Office Project." Submission to the IPAC Award for Innovative Management competition, 1996, p. 2.

357 Canada, Human Resources Development Council, *Empowerment*, p. 27.

358 Canada, Deputy Minister's Task Force on Public Service Values and Ethics, *A Strong Foundation. Report*, p. 72.

359 Ibid., pp. 27–8.

360 Darling, "Empowerment," *Executive Speeches*, p. 93.

361 For an examination of the ethical dimension of empowerment based on a study of business organizations, see Jeffrey Gandz and Federick G. Bird, "The ethics of empowerment," *Journal of Business Ethics* 15, no. 2 (April 1996), pp. 383–92.

362 Canada, Public Service 2000, Service to the Public Task Force, *Report*, p. 47 (emphasis added).

363 Canada, Department of the Environment, Transition Team Steering Committee on Consultation and Partnerships, *Consultations and Partnerships: Working
Together with Canadians* (Ottawa: Environment Canada, 1992), p. i.

364 Frances Abele, Katherine Graham, Alex Ker, Antonia Maioni, Susan Phillips,
*Talking with Canadians: Citizen Engagement and the Social Union* (Ottawa:
Canadian Council on Social Development, 1998), pp. 8–10.

365 Canada, Department of the Environment, Transition Team Steering Committee on Consultation and Partnerships, *Consultations and Partnerships*, p. i.

366 Abele et al., *Talking with Canadians*, p. 1.

367 Sharon Varette, "Consultation in the public service: a question of skills,"
*Optimum* 24, no 4 (Spring 1993), pp. 28–39, at p. 31.

368 Canada, Department of the Environment, Transition Team Steering Committee on Consultation and Partnerships, *Consultations and Partnerships*, Annex
11–1.

369 Robert P. Shepherd, "The citizens' forum: a case study in public consultation," *Optimum* 23, no. 4 (Spring 1993), pp. 18–27.

370 Hajo Versteeg, *A Case Study in Multi-Stakeholder Consultation: The Corporate
History of the Federal Pesticide Registration Review or How We Got From There to
Here. Volume 1 – General Principles for Decision Makers. Volume 2 – Practical
Considerations for Process Managers and Participants* (Ottawa: Canadian Centre
for Management Development, 1992).

371 Patricia Lane, "Ontario's Fair Tax Commission: an innovative approach to
public consultation," *Optimum* 23, no. 4 (Spring 1993), pp. 7–17; Shepherd,
"The citizens' forum," *Optimum*, pp. 20–2.

372 Canada, Public Service 2000, Service to the Public Task Force, *Report*, p. 41.

373 For a detailed examination of the meaning and effectiveness of consultative
mechanisms, see Peter Sterne and Sandra Zagon, *Public Consultation Guide*.
Canadian Centre for Management Development, Management Practices # 19
(Ottawa: Supply and Services Canada, 1997), pp. 69–84.

374 For an examination of consultation and training, seeVarette, "Consultation
in the public service," *Optimum*.

375 Sterne and Zagon, *Public Consultation Guide*, pp. 25–65.

376 Canada, Public Service 2000, Service to the Public Task Force, *Report*, p. 45.

377 Ibid., p. 37.

378 Debora L. VanNijnatten and Sheila Wray Gregoire, "Bureaucracy and consultation: the Correctional Service of Canada and the requirements of being
democratic," CANADIAN PUBLIC ADMINISTRATION 38, no. 2 (Summer
1995), pp. 204–21, p. 205.

379 Ibid., p. 220.

380 Varette, "Consultation in the public service," *Optimum*, p. 28.

381 For an examination of the types, objectives and benefits of partnerships
involving public organizations, see James L. Armstrong, "Innovation in
public management: toward partnerships," *Optimum* 23, no. 1 (1992–93), pp.
17–26; Kenneth Kernaghan, "Partnership and public administration: conceptual and practical considerations," CANADIAN PUBLIC ADMINISTRA-

TION 36, no. 1 (Spring 1993), pp. 57–76; Alti Rodal and Nick Mulder, "Partnerships, devolution and power-sharing: issues and implications for management," *Optimum* 23, no. 1 (1992–93), pp. 27–45, at p. 29.

382 Alan Gratias and Melanie Boyd, "Beyond government: can the public sector meet the challenges of public–private partnering?" *Optimum* 26, no. 1 (Summer 1995), pp. 3–14.

383 Relations between organizations, including those involved in partnerships, are usually characterized by the exercise of power in the sense of influence that takes such forms as persuasion, suggestion and the exchange of information with a view to reaching a compromise or consensus. For elaboration on power conceptualized as control and influence in intra-organizational and inter-organizational relations, see Kenneth Kernaghan and Olivia Kuper, *Coordination in Canadian Governments: A Case Study of Aging Policy.* Monographs on Canadian Public Administration – No. 8 (Toronto: Institute of Public Administration of Canada, 1983), pp. 6–12.

384 British Columbia, Financial Institutions Commission (FICOM) and Ministry of Finance and Corporate Relations. Submission to the IPAC Award for Innovative Management competition, 1992, p. 5.

385 Employment and Immigration Canada, Canadian Labour Force Development Board (CLFDB). Submission to IPAC Award for Innovative Management competition, 1992.

386 British Columbia, Ministry of Social Services, Health Services Division, "At Home Program." Submission to IPAC Award for Innovative Management competition, 1992.

387 Environment Canada, Canadian Wildlife Service, "The North American Waterfowl Management Plan." Submission to the IPAC Award for Innovative Management competition, 1992, p. 9.

388 Ontario, Ministry of Natural Resources, "Partnerships in Resource Management." Questionnaire; Ontario, Ministry of Community and Social Services, Southwestern Regional Centre, "Social Demonstration Project." Awards submission.

389 Environment Canada, Environmental Conservation and Protection, "The St. Lawrence Action Plan." Submission to the IPAC Award for Innovative Management competition, 1992, p. 6.

390 Kernaghan and Kuper, *Coordination in Canadian Governments*, p. 13.

391 Addiction Research Foundation, "Drug and Alcohol Registry of Treatment (DART)." Submission to the IPAC Award for Innovative Management competition, 1992. Appended document entitled "Some Legal and Ethical Issues Related to the Ontario Substance Abuse Treatment Registry."

392 Environment Canada, Canadian Wildlife Service, "The North American Waterfowl Management Plan." Awards submission, Preface.

393 Environment Canada, Canadian Parks Service, National Parks, "Visitor Activities." Submission to the IPAC Award for Innovative Management competition, 1992, p. 2 (emphasis added).

394 Ibid., p. 4.

395 Employment and Immigration Canada, Canadian Labour Force Development Board (CLFDB). Awards submission, p. 2.
396 Newfoundland and Labrador, Housing Corporation, "Housing Initiatives 92
– Partnerships for Better Housing." Submission to the IPAC Award for
Innovative Management competition, 1992.
397 Borins, "Public Sector Innovation." Discussion Paper, p. 66.
398 Quebec, Ministry of Industry, Trade, Science and Technology, "'Quebec: A
Technological Partner' Index." Submission to the IPAC Award for Innovative
Management competition, 1995, p. 5. The general objectives of the partnership were to facilitate access to Quebec businesses and research centres that
have significant technological assets in international networks and business
linkages; to promote Quebec's comparative advantages likely to attract
technological investments; and to support promotional activities of Quebec
offices in Canada, all economic agents in Quebec agencies located abroad,
and Canadian embassies and consulates by providing them with a promotional tool for technological alliances.
399 Ibid., p. 9. For another example, note Investment Canada's partnership
program, which focuses on attracting investment to Canada in strategic
technology sectors by helping small- and medium-sized businesses "to find
the capital, technology, joint ventures or other forms of strategic alliances
they are seeking." See Investment Canada. Submission to the IPAC Award
for Innovative Management competition, 1993.
400 New Brunswick, Department of Health and Community Services, "'Single
entry point' model. Submission to the IPAC Award for Innovative Management competition, 1992.
401 Ontario, Ministry of Consumer and Commercial Relations, Registration
Division, "Partners in Goodwill." Questionnaire.
402 Environment Canada, Finance and Administration [Adaptive Computer
Technology Centre]. Submission to the IPAC Award for Innovative Management competition, 1992.
403 Environment Canada, Canadian Parks Service, "Cooperative Arrangements
with First Nations for the Management of National Parks." Submission to
the IPAC Award for Innovative Management competition, 1992; Saskatchewan, Department of Education, Northern Education Services Branch,
"Multi-Party Training Plan." Submission to the IPAC Award for Innovative
Management competition, 1996.
404 Canada, Interdepartmental Committee of Heads of Training, *Partnerships: An
Introductory Guide* (Ottawa: Supply and Services Canada, 1994), p. 49 (emphasis in the original).
405 Ontario, Ministry of Consumer and Commercial Relations, Registration
Division, "Partners in Goodwill." Questionnaire; Addiction Research Foundation, "Drug and Alcohol Registry of Treatment (DART)," Appended
document. Awards submission; Ontario, Ministry of Citizenship, Office for
Seniors' Issues, Education Resources Unit, "Seniors' Issues Group." Questionnaire.

406 British Columbia, Ministry of Health, "Street Nurse Outreach Program." Submission to the IPAC Award for Innovative Management Competition, 1991.

407 Environment Canada, Environmental Conservation and Protection, "Wastewater Technology Centre." Submission to the IPAC Award for Innovative Management competition, 1992.

408 City of Scarborough, "Image Committee." Submission to the IPAC Award for Innovative Management competition, 1992.

409 Canada, Treasury Board Secretariat, *An Overview of Quality and Affordable Service for Canadians* (Ottawa: Supply and Services Canada), pp. i, 8.

410 Government Services Canada, "Open Bidding Service (OBS)." Submission to IPAC Award for Innovative Management competition, 1993. See also the article by the same title in *Public Sector Management* 4, no. 1 (Spring 1993), p. 13.

411 William H. Davidow and Michael S. Malone, *The Virtual Corporation* (New York: Harper Business, 1992).

412 Rodal and Mulder, "Partnerships, devolution and power-sharing," *Optimum*, p. 40.

413 Robert Reich, *The Work of Nations* (New York: Vintage Books, 1992), p. 99.

414 Rodal and Mulder, "Partnerships, devolution and power-sharing," *Optimum*, p. 40.

415 These include the Canadian Council for Public–Private Partnerships and the Ontario Public Service Partnerships Network. See also the large volume of information at the Public–Private Partnering web site: http://www.ppp. beyondgov.ca.

416 Canada, Clerk of the Privy Council [Jocelyne Bourgon], *Fourth Annual Report*, Chapter 2, p. 6.

417 Canada, Interdepartmental Committee of Heads of Training, *Partnerships*, p. 46.

418 Environment Canada, Environmental Conservation and Protection, "The St. Lawrence Action Plan." Awards submission, p. 7.

419 Federal/Provincial Environmental Programs on Lake Superior, Lake Superior Programs Office, "Lake Superior Programs Office." Submission to the IPAC Award for Innovative Management competition, 1994, p. 4.

420 Natural Resources Canada, Canadian Forest Service, "The Model Forest Program." Submission to the IPAC Award for Innovative Management competition, 1996.

421 Environment Canada, Canadian Wildlife Service, "The North American Waterfowl Management Plan." Awards submission.

422 City of Toronto, Management Services Department, Municipal Professional Exchange Program, "Toronto–Lima Bus Project." Submission to the IPAC Award for Innovative Management competition, 1992.

423 Canada, Department of Human Resources Development, "The Union's Vision of Quality," *Service Quality: Strategy 1994–1997* (Ottawa: Department, 1994).

424 British Columbia Hydro, Labour Relations Department. Awards submission, p. 1.

425 Canada, Department of Canadian Heritage, *The Partnership Guide* (Ottawa: Heritage Canada, 1995).

426 Susan D. Phillips, "How Ottawa Blends: Shifting Government Relationships with Interest Groups," in Frances Abele, ed., *How Ottawa Spends. 1991–92: The Politics of Fragmentation*. Carleton Public Policy Series #13 (Ottawa: Carleton University Press, 1991), pp. 183–227, at p. 211.

427 Ontario, Ministry of Consumer and Commercial Relations, "Partners in Goodwill." Questionnaire; Saskatchewan, Department of Environment and Resource Management, "Partnership Program." Questionnaire, p. 14.

428 Ontario, Ministry of Consumer and Commercial Relations, "Partners in Goodwill." Questionnaire, p. 21.

429 Canada, Office of the Auditor General, "Collaborative Arrangements: Issues for the Federal Government," *Annual Report* (Ottawa: Supply and Services Canada, 1999), Chapter 5.

430 Addiction Research Foundation, "Drug and Alcohol Registry of Treatment (DART)." Appended document. Awards submission, Appendix.

431 Saskatchewan, Department of Environment and Resource Management, "Partnership Program." Questionnaire, p. 4.

432 Addiction Research Foundation, "Drug and Alcohol Registry of Treatment (DART)." Appended document. Awards submission.

433 Ellen Fry, "The perils of partnership," *Justice Echo* no. 15 (July 1992), p. 4.

434 Canada, Department of the Environment, Transition Team Steering Committee on Consultation and Partnerships, *Consultations and Partnerships*, Preface.

435 Canadian Centre for Management Development, *Continuous Learning. A CCMD Report* (Ottawa: CCMD, 1994), p. 1.

436 Michael Marquardt and Angus Reynolds, *The Global Learning Organization* (New York: Irwin, 1993), p. 31.

437 Peter Senge, *The Fifth Discipline: The Art and Practice of the Learning Organization* (New York: Doubleday/Currency, 1990).

438 Canadian Centre for Management Development, *Continuous Learning*, p. 23.

439 D.A. Schon, "Deutero-learning in organizations: learning for increased effectiveness," *Organizational Dynamics* 4, no. 1 (Summer 1995), pp. 2–16, at p. 10.

440 Marquardt and Reynolds, *The Global Learning Organization*, p. 40.

441 Senge, *Fifth Discipline*, p. 143.

442 Mike Pedlar, *Action Learning in Theory and Practice* (Aldershot, U.K.: Gower Publishing, 1991), p. 31.

443 Marquardt and Reynolds, *The Global Learning Organization*, p. 52.

444 Mary M. Hale, "Learning organizations and mentoring," *Public Productivity Review* 9, no. 4 (June 1996), pp. 422–33, at p. 424.

445 Senge, *The Fifth Discipline*, p. 236.

446 Canadian Centre for Management Development, *Continuous Learning*, p. 5.

447 Ibid., p. 6.

448 Ibid., pp. 8–9.

449 Ibid., p. 10.
450 Morgan McCall, *Developing Executives through Work Experience* (Greensboro, N.C.: Centre for Creative Leadership, 1988).
451 Canadian Centre for Management Development, *Continuous Learning*, p. 12.
452 Alan Mumford, *Management Development: Strategies for Action* (London: Institute of Personnel Management, 1989).
453 Canadian Centre for Management Development, *Continuous Learning*, p. 24.
454 Schon, "Deutero-learning in organizations," *Organizational Dynamics*; Chris Argyris, *Knowledge for Action: A Guide to Overcoming Barriers to Organizational Change* (San Francisco: Jossey-Bass, 1993).
455 Senge, *The Fifth Discipline*; Marquardt and Reynolds, *The Global Learning Organization*; Canadian Centre for Management Development, *Continuous Learning*.
456 Senge, *The Fifth Discipline*, p. 68.
457 Canada, Deputy Ministers' Task Force on the Future of the Public Service, *Report* (Ottawa: Privy Council Office, 1996).
458 R.W. Revans, *Action Learning* (London: Blond and Briggs, 1980); Canadian Centre for Management Development, *Continuous Learning*, p. 48.
459 Nancy M. Dixon, *Organizational Learning* (Ottawa: Conference Board of Canada, 1993).
460 Marquardt and Reynolds, *The Global Learning Organization*, p. 42.
461 Ibid., p. 55.
462 Rocine, "Total quality management," *Public Sector Management*, p. 27.
463 Ole Ingstrup, *The Strategic Revolution in Executive Development* (Ottawa: Canadian Centre for Management Development, 1995).
464 Ibid., p. 5.
465 Ontario, Executive Development Committee, *Human Resources Plan for the Senior Management Group* (Toronto: The Cabinet Office, 1997).
466 Ibid., p. 25.
467 Ingstrup, *The Strategic Revolution in Executive Development*.
468 Gow, *Learning from Others*, p. 3.
469 Ibid., p. 127.
470 Dennis O'Grady and Keon Chi, "The Origins of Innovation in State Government." Paper presented at the conference of the American Society of Public Administration, Washington, D.C., March 1991. Cited in Ibid, p. 14.
471 Marquardt and Reynolds, *The Global Learning Organization*, p. 74.
472 Canada, Office of the Auditor General, "The Learning Organization," *Annual Report* [1992], Chapter 5, p. 151.
473 Canadian Centre for Management Development, *Continuous Learning*, p. 57.
474 G.B. Reschenthaler and Fred Thompson, "The information revolution and the new public management," *Journal of Public Administration and Theory* 6, no. 1 (January 1996), pp. 125–43.
475 Canada, n.a., "Relevant and Reliable E-Mail System Connects Federal Government Departments," *Blueprint in Action No. 17* [flyer] (Ottawa: Supply and Services Canada, n.d.).
476 Richard Simpson, "Making government a 'model user' of the Information

Highway – Canada's progress to date," *Public Administration and Development* 17, no. 1 (February 1997), pp. 103–7.

477 Richard Simpson, "The Information Highway: An Update on Canada." Paper presented to the second biennial conference of the Commonwealth Association for Public Administration and Management, San Gorg, Malta, April 1996.

478 Mary Gooderham, "Participatory democracy thriving on the Internet," *The Globe and Mail* (Toronto) 4 March 1997, p. A10.

479 The oldest discussion group established by a government is the Public Electronic Network in Santa Monica, California, which has been of value in policy discussions but which has also exposed local councillors to vigorous flaming. See Christopher Conte, "Teledemocracy for better or worse," *Governing* 8, no. 6 (June 1995), pp. 33–41. See also Monica Gattinger, "Local Governments On-Line: How are They Doing it and What Does it Mean?" in Katherine A. Graham and Susan D. Phillips, eds., *Citizen Engagement: Lessons in Participation from Local Government*. Monographs on Canadian Public Administration – No. 22 (Toronto: Institute of Public Administration of Canada, 1998), pp. 200–22, who argues that governments will attract more participation in their on-line forums if they exercise as little control as possible.

480 Canada, n.a., "Electronic Tax Filing Speeds up Process," *Blueprint in Action No. 14* [flyer] (Ottawa: Supply and Services Canada, n.d.).

481 Canada, n.a., "Paying Taxes Electronically Catches on in Business Community," *Blueprint in Action No. 16* [flyer] (Ottawa: Supply and Services Canada, n.d.).

482 Shirley Won, "How to sew up government work," *The Globe and Mail* (Toronto) 4 September 1995, p. B5.

483 n.a. [Institute of Public Administration of Canada], "Personal Property Registration," *Public Sector Management* 4, no. 1 (Spring 1993), pp. 4, 6.

484 British Columbia, Ministry of Finance and Corporate Relations, "Personal Property Registry System." Questionnaire; Ontario, Ministry of Consumer and Commercial Relations, Registration Division, Personal Property Security Registration Branch, "Direct Access: Maximizing People with Technology." Questionnaire.

485 Ontario, Ministry of Transportation, Safety and Regulation, "ServiceOntario Self-Service Kiosks." Questionnaire.

486 n.a. [Institute of Public Administration of Canada], "Ontario Ministry of Consumer and Commercial Relations: Clearing the Path for Business Success," *Public Sector Management* 7, no. 2 (Summer 1996), pp. 12–14.

487 Seidle, *Rethinking the Delivery of Public Services to Citizens*, pp. 125–7.

488 Ibid., pp. 129–31.

489 Reschenthaler and Thompson, "The information revolution and the new public management," *Journal of Public Administration and Theory*.

490 Ontario, Transportation Capital Corporation, "Highway 407 Info Brochure II" (Toronto: Corporation, 1995).

491 Phillip Sellers, "New Information Highway almost ready as finishing touches put on the 407," *Computing Canada* (6 January 1997), pp. 1, 4.

492 Smart cards are plastic cards that contain a microchip and memory capacity that allow their contents to be read and altered by a computer. A simple example in increasingly common use in North America is the telephone card. While smart cards look like the cards variously referred to as bank cards, debit cards, or credit cards, the difference is that the latter cards contain much less information and cannot be altered by a computer; they are used primarily for on-line access to bank accounts or records stored in mainframe computers, and it is these records that are altered.

493 Barrie McKenna, "Your life on a chip," *The Globe and Mail* (Toronto) 23 November 1995, p. B7.

494 Margaret Philp, "Toronto planning welfare ID card," *The Globe and Mail* (Toronto) 26 March 1996, pp. A1–A2; Margaret Philp, "Metro to debate welfare ID technology," *The Globe and Mail* (Toronto) 30 April 1996, p. A6; Lila Sarick and Gay Abbate, "Fingerprint plan approved for Metro welfare recipients," *The Globe and Mail* (Toronto) 20 June 1996, p. A7.

495 R. Mackie, "Ontario's ID plan spurs privacy fears," *The Globe and Mail* (Toronto) 22 October 1999, pp. A1, A4.

496 Borins, *Innovating with Integrity*.

497 Jerry Mechling, "Leadership and the knowledge gap," *Governing* 9, no. 12 (December 1995), p. 68.

498 Canada, n.a., "Electronic Tax Filing Speeds up Process," *Blueprint in Action No. 14*.

499 n.a. [Institute of Public Administration of Canada], "Government Services Canada: Open Bidding Service (OBS)," *Public Sector Management* 4, no. 1 (Spring 1993), p. 13.

500 Oregon, Department of General Services, "Vendor Information Program." Semi-finalist submission to the Innovations in American Government Awards program, 1993.

501 British Columbia, Ministry of Finance and Corporate Relations, "Personal Property Registry System." Questionnaire; n.a. [Institute of Public Administration of Canada], "B.C. Ministry of Finance and Corporate Relations: Personal Property Registration," *Public Sector Management* 4, no. 1 (Spring 1993), pp. 4, 6.

502 Ontario, Ministry of Consumer and Commercial Relations, Registration Division, Personal Property Security Registration Branch, "Direct Access: Maximizing People with Technology." Questionnaire.

503 n.a. [Institute of Public Administration of Canada], "Ontario Ministry of Consumer and Commercial Relations: Clearing the Path for Business Success," *Public Sector Management* 7, no. 2 (Summer 1996), pp. 12, 14.

504 E. Reguly, "Quebec-led group wins bidding war for Highway 407," *The Globe and Mail* (Toronto) 10 April 1999, pp. B1, B4.

505 Canada, Office of the Auditor General, "Information Technology: Reaping the Benefits and Managing the Risks," *Annual Report* (Ottawa: Supply and Services Canada, 1994), Chapter 8.

506 Standish Group International, *Chaos (Application Project and Failure)*. Available at www.standishgroup.com.

507 Barrie McKenna, "A deal way off course," *The Globe and Mail* (Toronto) 13 May 1995, pp. B1, B5; Barrie McKenna, "Cancelled contracts cost Ottawa millions," *The Globe and Mail* (Toronto) 4 September 1996, pp. B1, B23.

508 Canada, Office of the Auditor General, "Systems under Development: Managing the Risks," *Annual Report* (Ottawa: Supply and Services Canada, 1995), Chapter 12; Canada, Office of the Auditor General, "Systems under Development: Getting Results," *Annual Report* (Ottawa: Supply and Services Canada, 1996), Chapter 24; Canada, Treasury Board Secretariat, *Guides to Quality Service*.

509 California, Health and Welfare Agency Data Center, "Info/California." Semi-finalist application to the Innovations in American Government Awards program, 1993.

510 Sandford Borins and David Wolf, *Realizing the Potential of Information Technology in the Public Sector: An Organizational Challenge* (Toronto: KPMG Centre for Government Foundation, 1999).

511 This is yet another illustration of Pareto's Law (also known as the "80–20 rule"), namely that twenty per cent of the customers account for eighty per cent of the business.

512 Ontario, Ministry of Consumer and Commercial Relations, Registration Division, Personal Property Security Registration Branch, "Direct Access: Maximizing People with Technology." Questionnaire.

513 Jennifer Lewington, "Computer gap hurts poor, report says: skills and access are concentrated in the hands of rich Canadians, Statscan study finds," *The Globe and Mail* (Toronto) 1 November 1996, p. A5; Bruce Little, "Poor left behind in computer revolution: richest Canadians more than four times as likely to own a PC than lower-income households," *The Globe and Mail* (Toronto) 15 January 1996, p. B11.

514 David Roberts, "Ottawa adds $55 million to venture," *The Globe and Mail* (Toronto) 9 June 1998, p. A5.

515 Lewington, "Computer gap hurts poor, report says," *Globe and Mail*.

516 Hugh Winsor, "Salvaged computers teach valuable lessons, *The Globe and Mail* (Toronto) 24 December 1997, p. A4.

517 Lansing, Michigan Housing Commission. "Computer Learning Centers." Semi-finalist application to Innovations in American Government Awards program, 1993.

518 Seattle Workers' Center, "Community Voice Mail." Semi-finalist submission to Innovations in American Government Awards program, 1993.

519 Craig McInnes, "Victoria data site pulled off Internet," *The Globe and Mail* (Toronto) 27 September 1996, p. A6.

520 Philp, "Toronto planning welfare ID card," *The Globe and Mail*.

521 Mackie, "Cancelled contracts cost Ottawa millions," *Globe and Mail*.

522 Sarick and Abbate, "Fingerprint plan approved for Metro welfare recipients," *The Globe and Mail*.

523 McInnes, "Victoria data site pulled off Internet," *Globe and Mail*.

524 Canada, Treasury Board Secretariat, *Blueprint for Renewing Government Services Using Information Technology: Executive Summary (Discussion Draft)* (Ottawa: Treasury Board Secretariat, 1994), p. 28.

525 The State of Massachusetts has taken this principle one step further. It has established an automated child-support enforcement program that involves computer scanning of all the state's financial databases to find income or assets that can be seized to enforce child-support obligations. See Massachusetts, Department of Revenue, "Automated Child Support Enforcement System." Semi-finalist application to the Innovations in American Government Awards program, 1993.

526 Two very successful British projects involving partnerships between government and the computer firm ICL are Merseyside Education On Line (www.icl.com) and the South Bristol Learning Network (www.sbln.org.uk). See Sandford Borins, *The Shifting Boundaries of Government : A United Kingdom International Conference: A Report* (Toronto: CAPAM, 1998).

527 Ontario, Office of the Lieutenant Governor, "The Honourable Hilary M. Weston, Lieutenant Governor of Ontario, Concerned about Erroneous Message on Bill 160," *Press Release*, 17 November 1997 (Toronto: Queen's Printer, 1997).

528 George Anderson, "The new focus on the policy capacity of the federal government," CANADIAN PUBLIC ADMINISTRATION 39, no. 4 (Winter 1996), pp. 469–88, at p. 484.

529 For elaboration on each of these functions, see Canada, Deputy Ministers' Task Force on Strengthening Policy Capacity, *Report*, pp. 4–7.

530 Canada, Department of Human Resources Development, "Teambuilding: Changing Managerial Attitudes and Behaviour." Questionnaire, Annex 8.

531 Canada, Deputy Minister's Task Force on Strengthening Policy Capacity, *Report*, Annex 3.

532 Canada, Deputy Minister's Task Force on Managing Horizontal Policy Issues, *Report* (Ottawa: Privy Council Office, 1996), p. 2.

533 Organisation for Economic Co-operation and Development, *Building Policy Coherence: Tools and Tensions* (Paris: OECD, 1996), p. 25.

534 G. Bruce Doern and Peter Aucoin, eds., *Public Policy in Canada* (Toronto: Macmillan, 1979); Audrey Doerr, *The Machinery of Government in Canada* (Toronto: Methuen, 1981); Kernaghan and Kuper, *Coordination in Canadian Governments*.

535 Savoie, *Thatcher, Reagan, Mulroney*, pp. 173–4; 340–5.

536 Anderson, "New focus on the policy capacity of the federal government," CANADIAN PUBLIC ADMINISTRATION, p. 478.

537 Canada, Clerk of the Privy Council [Jocelyne Bourgon], *Third Annual Report to the Prime Minister on the Public Service of Canada* (Ottawa: Privy Council Office, 1995), p. 43.

538 Canada, Deputy Minister's Task Force on Strengthening Policy Capacity, *Report*; Canada, Deputy Minister's Task Force on Managing Horizontal Policy Issues, *Report*.

539 Canada, Policy Research Initiative, 1999, available at http://
policyresearch.schoolnet.ca.

540 Ibid.

541 Organisation for Economic Co-operation and Development,
*Globalisation:What Challenges and Opportunities for Governments?* (Paris:
OECD, 1996), p. 4.

542 Jocelyne Bourgon, "Plenary Report – Strengthening Our Policy Capacity," in
Canadian Centre for Management Development, *Strengthening Policy Capacity: Conference Proceedings* (Ottawa: CCMD, 1996), p. 28.

543 Kernaghan and Kuper, *Coordination in Canadian Governments*, p. 13.

544 Les Metcalfe, "International policy coordination and public management
reform," *International Review of Administrative Sciences* 60, no. 2 (June 1994),
pp. 271–90, at p. 281.

545 Canada, Clerk of the Privy Council [Jocelyne Bourgon], *Fourth Annual
Report*, Chapter 5.

546 Canada, Deputy Minister's Task Force on Strengthening Policy Capacity,
*Report*, p. 15.

547 Ontario, Cabinet Office, *The Ontario Cabinet Decision-Making System: Procedures Guide* (Toronto: Queen's Printer, 1997), Chapter 2, p. 5.

548 Canada, Deputy Minister's Task Force on Strengthening Policy Capacity,
*Report*, Annex 2.

549 Mel Cappe, "False Dichotomies," in John C. Tait and Mel Cappe, *Rethinking
Policy: Perspectives on Public Policy* (Ottawa: Canadian Centre for Management Development, 1995), p. 34.

550 Canada, *On the Memorandum of Understanding among the Four Natural Resource Departments on Science and Technology for Sustainable Development.
Annual Report: 1996–1997* (Ottawa: Public Works and Government Services,
1997).

551 Canada, Deputy Minister's Task Force on Managing Horizontal Policy
Issues, *Report*, p. 22.

552 Anderson, "New focus on the policy capacity of the federal government,"
CANADIAN PUBLIC ADMINISTRATION, p. 482.

553 Canada, Deputy Minister's Task Force on Strengthening Policy Capacity,
*Report*, p. 32.

554 Allen Sutherland and John Knubley, *Case Studies in Federal–Provincial Analysis and Policy Making: Lessons and Conclusions* (Ottawa: Intergovernmental
Affairs Secretariat, Privy Council Office, 1995), pp. 3–4.

555 Ibid., pp. 4–7.

556 Ibid., pp. 3–4.

557 Canada, Deputy Minister's Task Force on Strengthening Policy Capacity,
*Report*, p. 33.

558 Anderson, "New focus on the policy capacity of the federal government,"
CANADIAN PUBLIC ADMINISTRATION, p. 486.

559 Canada, Deputy Minister's Task Force on Strengthening Policy Capacity,
*Report*, p. 31.

560 Organisation for Economic Co-operation and Development, *Building Policy Coherence*, p. 8.

561 David Zussman, "Developing Policy Capacity for Government: The Canadian Experience." Paper presented to the third international conference of the International Institute of Administrative Sciences, Beijing, October 1996, p. 10.

562 Bourgon, "Strengthening Our Policy Capacity," *Conference Proceedings*, p. 25.

563 Canada, Deputy Ministers' Task Force on Public Service Values and Ethics, *A Strong Foundation. Report*, p. 42.

564 Canada, Deputy Minister's Task Force on Managing Horizontal Policy Issues, *Report*, p. 25.

565 Donald J. Savoie, "Central Agencies: A Government of Canada Perspective," in J.M. Bourgault, M. Demers and C. Williams, eds., *Public Administration and Public Management: Experiences in Canada* (Quebec City: Les Publications du Québec, 1997), pp. 59–69, at p. 68.

566 Canada, Deputy Ministers' Task Force on Public Service Values and Ethics, *A Strong Foundation. Report*, p. 43.

567 Canada, Deputy Minister's Task Force on Managing Horizontal Policy Issues, *Report*, p. 29.

568 Organisation for Economic Co-operation and Development, *Building Policy Coherence*, pp. 10; 41–2.

569 Kouzes and Posner, *The Leadership Challenge*, p. 18.

570 D. Brian Marson and Geoff Dinsdale, *Effective Public Service Leadership: Results of EL Participants Survey of Senior Managers* (Ottawa: Canadian Centre for Management Development, 1999), p. 8.

571 Kernaghan, "The emerging public service culture," CANADIAN PUBLIC ADMINISTRATION.

572 Ingstrup and Crookall, *The Three Pillars of Public Management*, p. 53.

573 Canada, Deputy Ministers' Task Force on Public Service Values and Ethics, *A Strong Foundation. Report*, p. 59.

574 Ontario, Ministry of Consumer and Commercial Relations, Registration Division, "Partners in Goodwill." Questionnaire, p. 26.

575 Canada, La Relève, *First Report on La Relève: A Commitment to Action. Overview* (Ottawa: Canada Communications Group, 1998), p. 11 (emphasis added).

576 Canada, Public Service Commission, Consultative Review of Staffing, *A New Framework for Resourcing the Workforce: Report* (Ottawa: Public Service Commission, 1996), p. 24.

577 Canada, Personnel Renewal Council, "Human Resource Management in the Public Service: Framework for the Future." Report from the roundtable conference organized by the Personnel Renewal Council, Hull, Quebec, 8–10 November 1995, pp. 5–7.

578 Canada, La Relève, COSO Sub-Committee on Pride and Recognition, *Pride and Recognition: Keys to an Outstanding Public Service. An Interim Report* (Ottawa: La Relève, 1997).

579 Canada, La Relève, Advisory Committee on the Workforce of the Future, *Valuing Our People. Report* (Ottawa: La Relève, 1997), pp. 2–4.

580 Canada, Deputy Minister's Task Force on Public Service Values and Ethics, *A Strong Foundation. Report*, p. 66.

581 Canada, La Relève, Advisory Committee on the Workforce of the Future, *Valuing Our People. Report*, p. 3.

582 Robert S. Kaplan and David P. Norton, *The Balanced Scorecard: Translating Strategy into Action* (Boston: Harvard Business School Press, 1996).

583 Arie Halachmi and Geert Bouckaert, eds., *Organizational Performance and Measurement in the Public Sector: Toward Service, Effort and Accomplishment Reporting* (Westport, Conn.: Quorum Books, 1996); John Mayne and Eduardo Zapico-Goni, *Monitoring Performance in the Public Sector: Future Directions from International Experience* (New Brunswick, N.J.: Transaction Publishers, 1997); Aucoin, "Design of public organizations for the 21st Century," CANADIAN PUBLIC ADMINISTRATION.

584 Paul Thomas, "The politics of performance measurement," *Public Sector Management* 8, no. 2 (Summer 1997), pp. 17–19.

585 Canada, Independent Review Panel on Modernization of Comptrollership in the Government of Canada, *Report* (Ottawa: Treasury Board Secretariat, 1997), p. 4. Also available at http://www.tbs-sct.gc.ca.

586 Marson and Dinsdale, *Effective Public Service Leadership*, p. 8.

587 Jim Harris, *The Learning Paradox: Gaining Success and Security in a World of Change* (Toronto: Macmillan, 1998), p. 45.

588 Public Management Research Centre, *Federal Executive Compensation and Retention: Perspectives from the Private Sector* (Ottawa: Public Management Research Centre, 1997), p. 3.

589 Ontario, Ministry of Consumer and Commercial Relations, Registration Division, "Partners in Goodwill." Questionnaire, p. 25.

590 New Brunswick, Department of Advanced Education and Labour, Department of Advocacy Services, "New Brunswick's Literacy Initiative." Questionnaire, p. 14.

591 Canada, Deputy Minister's Task Force on Public Service Values and Ethics, *A Strong Foundation. Report*, p. 78.

592 Mintzberg, *The Rise and Fall of Strategic Planning*, p. 18.

593 Saskatchewan, Department of Environment and Resource Management, "Partnership Program." Questionnaire, p. 21.

594 Ontario, Ministry of Transportation, Safety and Regulation, "ServiceOntario Self-Service Kiosks." Questionnaire, p. 11.

595 Ontario, Ministry of Consumer and Commercial Relations, Registration Division and Business Practices Division, "Reshaping Government: The Used Vehicle Information Program." Questionnaire, p. 21 (emphasis added).

596 Ronald Duhamel, "Performance management: What is it? Why does it matter?" *Insights* 3 (February/March 1998), pp. 1–2, at p. 2.

597 British Columbia, Ministry of Finance and Corporate Relations, "Personal Property Registry System." Questionnaire, p. 22.

598 British Columbia, Ministry of Transportation and Highways, "Privatization of Road and Bridge Maintenance." Questionnaire, p. 21.

599 Canada, Department of the Environment, Transition Team Steering Committee on Consultation and Partnerships, *Consultations and Partnerships*, p. i.

600 Harris, *The Learning Paradox*, p. 6.

601 Stephen Bent, Kenneth Kernaghan and Brian Marson, *Innovations and Good Practices in Single-Window Service* (Ottawa: Canadian Centre for Management Development, 1999).

602 David Wright, "Structural innovation in government organizations," *Optimum* 23, no. 1 (1992–93), pp. 27–36, p. 36.

603 Canada, Independent Review Panel on Modernization of Comptrollership in the Government of Canada, *Report*, pp. 39–40.

604 Public Management Research Centre, *Final Report: Executive Consultations on Issues Related to Organizational Retention and Compensation* (Ottawa: Public Management Research Centre, 1997), pp. 19–20.

605 Canada, Treasury Board Secretariat, *Risk Management in the Federal Public Service: Action Plan to Develop Integrated TBS Policy Guidance* (Ottawa: Treasury Board Secretariat, 1999). Also available at http://www.tbs-sct.gc.ca.

# Bibliography

SUBMISSIONS TO INNOVATIONS IN AMERICAN GOVERNMENT AWARDS
[FORMERLY STATE AND LOCAL GOVERNMENT INNOVATIONS AWARDS]

California, Health and Welfare Agency Data Center, "Info/California." Semi-finalist, 1993.

Lansing, Michigan Housing Commission, "Computer Learning Centers." Semi-finalist, 1993.

Massachusetts, Department of Revenue, "Automated Child Support Enforcement System." Semi-finalist, 1993.

Oregon, Department of General Services, "Vendor Information Program." Semi-finalist, 1993.

Seattle Workers' Center, "Community Voice Mail." Semi-finalist, 1993.

SUBMISSIONS TO IPAC'S AWARD FOR INNOVATIVE MANAGEMENT COMPETITION

*1991*

British Columbia Housing Management Commission [finalist]. See also "British Columbia Housing Management Commission people power," *Public Sector Management* 2, no. 2 (Summer 1991), p. 12.

British Columbia, Ministry of Health, "Street Nurse Outreach Program."

Nova Scotia Power Corporation.

Ontario, Ministry of Community and Social Services, Southwestern Regional Centre, "Social Demonstration Project."

Saskatchewan, Public Service Commission, Staff Development Division.

City of Toronto, "Bridges Program" [finalist]. See also "City of Toronto Bridges Program," *Public Sector Management* 2, no. 2 (Summer 1991), p. 12.

*1992*

Addiction Research Foundation, "Drug and Alcohol Registry of Treatment (DART)." Appended document entitled "Some Legal and Ethical Issues Related to the Ontario Substance Abuse Treatment Registry" [finalist]. See also "Drug Alcohol Registry of Treatment (DART) Addiction Research Foundation (Ontario)," *Public Sector Management* 3, no. 3 (Fall 1992), p. 14.

British Columbia, Financial Institutions Commission (FICOM) and Ministry of Finance and Corporate Relations.

British Columbia Hydro, Labour Relations Department.

British Columbia, Ministry of Health, "Pregnancy Outreach Program."

British Columbia, Ministry of Social Services, Health Services Division, "At Home Program" [finalist]. See also "At Home Program," *Public Sector Management* 3, no. 3 (Fall 1992), p. 15.

Employment and Immigration Canada, Canadian Labour Force Development Board (CLFDB).

Environment Canada, Canadian Parks Service, "Cooperative Arrangements with First Nations for the Management of National Parks."

Environment Canada, Canadian Parks Service, National Parks, "Visitor Activities."

Environment Canada, Canadian Wildlife Service, "The North American Waterfowl Management Plan."

Environment Canada, Environmental Conservation and Protection, "The St. Lawrence Action Plan."

Environment Canada, Environmental Conservation and Protection, "Wastewater Technology Centre."

Environment Canada, Finance and Administration [Adaptive Computer Technology Centre].

New Brunswick, Department of Health and Community Services, "'Single entry point' model."

Newfoundland and Labrador, Housing Corporation, "Housing Initiatives 92 – Partnerships for Better Housing."

Ontario, Ministry of Citizenship, Office for Seniors' Issues, Education Resources Unit, "Seniors' Issues Group" [silver award winner]. See article "Education Resources Unit, Office for Senior's Issues, Ontario Ministry of Citizenship, Enhancing the quality of life of seniors," *Public Sector Management* 3, no. 3 (Fall 1992), pp. 8, 10.

Ontario, Ministry of Consumer and Commercial Relations, Registration Division, "Partners in Goodwill" [finalist]. See also "Partners in Goodwill, Registration Division, Ontario Ministry of Consumer and Commercial Relations," *Public Sector Management* 3, no. 3 (Fall 1992), p. 14.

Ontario, Ministry of Natural Resources, "Strategic Initiatives" [gold award winner]. See also "Ontario, Ministry of Natural Resources, Partnerships in Resource Management," *Public Sector Management* 3, no. 3 (Fall 1992), pp. 4, 6.

Ontario, Ministry of Northern Development and Mines, Policy and Program Development Branch, "Strategic Consultation and Action Now (SCAN) NORTH."

City of Scarborough, "Image Committee."

City of Toronto, Management Services Department, Municipal Professional Exchange Program, "Toronto–Lima Bus Project."

*1993*

Alberta, Workers' Compensation Board, Rehabilitation Centre, "Work Hardening" [silver award winner]. See also "Innovative management and the Rehabilitation Centre," *Public Sector Management* 4, no. 1 (Spring 1996), p. 8.

British Columbia, Ministry of Finance and Corporate Relations, "Personal Property Registry System" [gold award winner]. See also "Personal Property
Registration," *Public Sector Management* 4, no. 1 (Spring 1996), pp. 4, 6.

Canada, Fisheries and Oceans, Corporate Management, "Science Fleet" [bronze
award winner]. See also "Management strategy shift produces increased
efficiency and effectiveness of DFO's science fleet," *Public Sector Management* 4,
no. 1 (Spring 1993), pp. 10, 12.

Government Services Canada, "Open Bidding Service (OBS)" [finalist]. See also
"Open Bidding Service (OBS)," *Public Sector Management* 4, no. 1 (Spring 1993),
p. 13.

Investment Canada.

Ontario, Ministry of Consumer and Commercial Relations, Registration Division,
Personal Property Security Registration Branch."

*1994*

Environment Canada, Atmospheric Environment Services, "Development of the
Ozone Watch and UV Index Programs."

Federal/Provincial Environmental Programs on Lake Superior, Lake Superior
Programs Office, "Lake Superior Programs Office" [finalist]. See also "Lake
Superior Programs Office, *Public Sector Management* 5, no. 1 (Spring 1994), p. 16.

Manitoba, Government Services, Fleet Vehicles Agency, "Fleet Vehicles Special
Operating Agency."

Ontario, Ministry of Consumer and Commercial Relations, Registration Division,
"Maximizing Opportunity, Office of the Registrar General: A Case Study in Re-
shaping Government" [gold award winner]. See also "Re-shaping government:
a case study of the Office of Registrar General, Thunder Bay, Ontario," *Public
Sector Management* 5, no. 1 (Spring 1994), pp. 4, 6–7.

Ontario, Ministry of Consumer and Commercial Relations, Registration Division
and Business Practices Division, "Reshaping Government: The Used Vehicle
Information Program."

Ontario, Ministry of Transportation, Safety and Regulation, "ServiceOntario, A
Self-Service Kiosk Pilot Project."

Township of Pittsburgh [Ontario], Municipal Office [Sheilagh Dunn] [finalist],
"Cost management in action: How to be lean and keen while having fun." See
also "Township of Pittsburgh," *Public Sector Management* 5, no. 1 (Spring 1994),
p. 17.

Saskatchewan, Economic and Cooperative Development, "Partnership for
Renewal – A Strategy for the Saskatchewan Economy."

*1995*

New Brunswick, Department of Advanced Education and Labour, Department of
Advocacy Services, "Community Academic Services Program" [bronze award

winner]. See also "Making diversity work for everyone – re-engineering literacy training: New Brunswick's Community Academic Services Program," *Public Sector Management* 6, no. 2 (Summer 1995), pp. 11, 13.

Quebec, Ministry of Industry, Trade, Science and Technology, "'Quebec: A Technological Partner' Index."

*1996*

Alberta, Department of Labour, "The Third Option: Alberta Labour's Approach."

British Columbia, Public Service Employee Relations Commission, Employee Recognition Program, "Public Service Renewal Through Employee Involvement and Recognition."

City of Burlington, City Clerk's Department, "Burlington Animal Control Self-Directed Work Team."

Industry Canada, Industry Sector, "Managing Change in the Industry Sector."

Natural Resources Canada, Canadian Forest Service, "The Model Forest Program."

Ontario, Ministry of Consumer and Commercial Relations, Business Division, "Clearing the Path for Business Success" [bronze award winner]. See "Ontario Ministry of Consumer and Commercial Relations: Clearing the path for business success," *Public Sector Management* 7, no. 2 (Summer 1996), pp. 12, 14.

Saskatchewan, Department of Education, Northern Education Services Branch, "Multi-Party Training Plan."

Transport Canada, Air Carrier Operations, Ontario Region, "Aviation District Office Project."

*1997*

Human Resources Development Canada, Insurance Program Services, "Re-engineering the Record of Employment" [bronze award winner]. See also "1997 IPAC Award for Innovative Management – Breakthroughs: connecting citizen and government," and "Human Resources Development Canada – a collaborative approach to change management: re-engineering the Record of Employment (ROE)," *Public Sector Management* 8, no. 2 (Summer 1997), pp. 4, 6 and 11, 16, respectively.

*1998*

Ontario, Ministry of Consumer and Commercial Relations, "The Triple Handshake: Ontario's Industry Self-Management Paradigm."

QUESTIONNAIRES ON PUBLIC-SECTOR INNOVATION IN CANADA

Alberta, Department of Labour, "The Third Option: Alberta Labour's Approach to Public Sector Reform," 1995. (Submission to IPAC's Award for Innovative Management competition made in 1993.)

Alberta, Department of Transportation and Utilities, "Alberta Transportation and Utilities' Transition Project," 1995. (Submission to IPAC's Award for Innovative Management competition made in 1994.)

Alberta Workers' Compensation Board, Rehabilitation Centre, "Work Hardening," 1996. (Silver award winner in IPAC's Award for Innovative Management
competition in 1993.) See also "Innovative Management and the Rehabilitation
Centre," *Public Sector Management* 4, no. 1 (Spring 1996), p. 8.
British Columbia, Ministry of Finance and Corporate Relations, "Personal Prop-
erty Registry System," 1996. (Gold award winner in IPAC's Award for Innova-
tive Management competition in 1993.) See also the article in *Public Sector
Management* 4, no. 1 (Spring 1993), pp. 4, 6.
British Columbia, Ministry of Health, "Pregnancy Outreach Program," 1995.
(Submission to IPAC's Award for Innovative Management competition made
in 1992.)
British Columbia, Ministry of Transportation and Highways, "Privatization of
Road and Bridge Maintenance," 1995. (Submission to IPAC's Award for Inno-
vative Management competition made in 1990.)
Environment Canada, Atmospheric Environment Services, "Development of the
Ozone Watch and UV Index Programs," 1995. (Submission to IPAC's Award
for Innovative Management competition made in 1994.)
Environment Canada, Canadian Parks Service, "Parks Canada Accessibility
Program for Seniors and People with Disabilities," 1995. (Submission to IPAC's
Award for Innovative Management competition made in 1992.)
Human Resources Development Canada, "Teambuilding: Changing Managerial
Attitudes and Behaviour," 1995. (Submission to IPAC's Award for Innovative
Management competition made in 1991.)
Manitoba, Government Services, Fleet Vehicles Agency, "Fleet Vehicles Special
Operating Agency," 1995. (Submission to IPAC's Award for Innovative Man-
agement competition made in 1994.)
New Brunswick, Department of Advanced Education and Labour, Department
of Advocacy Services, "New Brunswick's Literacy Initiative," 1995. (Sub-
mission to IPAC's Award for Innovative Management competition made in
1993.)
Ontario, Ministry of Agriculture and Food, Resources Management Branch, Soil
and Crop Improvement Association, "Land Stewardship Program," 1995.
(Submission to IPAC's Award for Innovation Management competition made
in 1992.)
Ontario, Ministry of Citizenship, Office for Seniors' Issues, Education Resources
Unit, "Seniors' Issues Group," 1995. (Silver award winner in IPAC's Innovative
Management competition in 1992.) See article "Enhancing the quality of life of
seniors," *Public Sector Management* 3, no. 2 (Summer 1992), pp. 8, 10.
Ontario, Ministry of Consumer and Commercial Relations, Registration Division
and Business Practices Division, "Reshaping Government: The Used Vehicle
Information Program," 1995. (Submission to IPAC's Award for Innovative
Management competition made in 1994.)
Ontario, Ministry of Consumer and Commercial Relations, "The Companies
Branch Night Shift Project," 1996. (Submission to IPAC's Award for Innovative
Management competition made in 1990.)
Ontario, Ministry of Consumer and Commercial Relations, Registration Division,

337

Personal Property Security Registration Branch, "Direct Access: Maximizing People with Technology," 1996. (Submission to IPAC's Award for Innovative Management competition made in 1993.)

Ontario, Ministry of Consumer and Commercial Relations, "Maximizing Opportunity," 1996. (Submission to IPAC's Award for Innovative Management competition made in 1994.)

Ontario, Ministry of Consumer and Commercial Relations, Registration Division, "Partners in Goodwill," 1996. (Finalist in IPAC's Award for Innovative Management competition made in 1992.) See also article in *Public Sector Management* 3, no. 3 (Fall 1992), p. 14.

Ontario, Ministry of Natural Resources, "Partnerships in Resource Management," 1995. (Gold award winner in IPAC's Innovative Management competition in 1992.) See also article in *Public Sector Management* 3, no. 3 (Fall 1992), pp. 4, 6.

Ontario, Ministry of Transportation, Safety and Regulation, "ServiceOntario, Self-Service Kiosks," 1996. (Submissions to IPAC's Award for Innovative Management competition made in 1994 and 1996.)

Township of Pittsburgh [Ontario], Municipal Office [Sheilagh Dunn] [finalist], "Cost management in action: How to be lean and keen while having fun," 1995. (Submission to IPAC's Award for Innovative Management competition made in 1994.)

Revenue Canada, "Harnessing the Power within the Corporation," 1996. (Submission to IPAC's Award for Innovative Management competition made in 1991.)

Saskatchewan, Economic and Cooperative Development, "Partnership for Renewal – A Strategy for the Saskatchewan Economy," 1995. (Submission to IPAC's Award for Innovative Management competition made in 1994.)

Saskatchewan, Environment and Resource Management, "Partnership Program," 1995. (Submission to IPAC's Award for Innovative Management competition made in 1992.)

### BOOK, ARTICLES AND GOVERNMENT DOCUMENTS

Abele, Frances, ed. *How Ottawa Spends. 1991–92: The Politics of Fragmentation.* Carleton Public Policy Series # 13. Ottawa: Carleton University Press, 1991.

—, Katherine Graham, Alex Ker, Antonia Maioni and Susan Phillips. *Talking with Canadians: Citizen Engagement and the Social Union.* Ottawa: Canadian Council on Social Development, 1998.

Abrahamsson, Bengt. *Bureaucracy or Participation: The Logic of Organization.* Beverly Hills, Calif.: Sage Publications, 1977.

Adler, Nancy J. *Globalization, Government and Competitiveness. The John L. Manion Lecture of the Canadian Centre for Management Development* (Ottawa: Supply and Services Canada, 1994).

Alberta. Department of Labour. Department of Business and Organizational Planning. *Case Study Series:* # 1. Toronto: Ontario Centre for Leadership and Ottawa: Conference Board of Canada, 1995.

Albrecht, Karl, and Ron Zemke. *Service America!* Homewood, Ill.: Dow-Jones Irwin, 1985.

Altshuler, Alan, and Marc Zegans. "Innovation and creativity: comparisons between public management and private enterprise," *Cities* 1, no. 1 (February 1990): 16–24.

Anderson, George. "The new focus on the policy capacity of the federal government." CANADIAN PUBLIC ADMINISTRATION 39: 4 (Winter 1996): 469–88.

Argyris, Chris. "Double loop learning in organizations." *Harvard Business Review* 55: 5 (September/October 1977): 115–25.

—. *Knowledge for Action: A Guide to Overcoming Barriers to Organizational Change.* San Francisco: Jossey-Bass, 1993.

Armstrong, James L. "Innovation in public management: toward partnerships." *Optimum* 23:1 (1992–93): 17–26.

Aucoin, Peter. "Administrative reform in public management: paradigms, principles, paradoxes and pendulums." *Governance* 3:2 (April 1990): 115–37.

—. "The design of public organizations for the 21st century: why bureaucracy will survive in public management." CANADIAN PUBLIC ADMINISTRATION 40:2 (Summer 1997): 290–306.

—. *The New Public Management: Canada in Comparative Perspective.* Montreal: Institute for Research on Public Policy, 1995.

Badran, Mohga, and Sandford Borins. "Innovation and Transformation in a Canadian Public Sector Organization." Paper presented to the annual conference of the International Institute of Schools and Institutes of Administration, Quebec City, 1997.

Barton, Joan A., and D. Brian Marson. *Service Quality: An Introduction.* Victoria: Service Quality B.C. Secretariat, 1991.

Barzelay, Michael, and Babak J. Armajani. "Managing state government operations: changing visions of staff agencies." *Journal of Policy Analysis and Management* 9, no. 3 (Summer 1990): 307–38.

—, with the collaboration of Babak J. Armajani. *Breaking Through Bureaucracy: A New Vision for Managing in Government.* Berkeley and Los Angeles: University of California Press, 1992.

Beaver, Tom. "Accountability of Alternative Service Delivery Organizations: the Case of the Canadian Food Inspection Agency." Ottawa: Canadian Food Inspection Agency, 1997.

Behn, Robert. "Management by groping along." *Journal of Policy Analysis and Management* 7, no. 4 (Fall 1988): 643–63.

Bent, Stephen, Kenneth Kernaghan and Brian Marson. *Innovations and Good Practices in Single-Window Service.* Ottawa: Canadian Centre for Management Development, 1999.

Berry, Leonard. *On Great Service.* New York: The Free Press, 1995.

Bilodeau, Jean. "Locally shared support services: a success story." *Optimum* 66:3 (Winter 1996): 35–8.

Blythe, Marie, and Brian Marson. *Good Practices in Citizen-Centred Service.* Ottawa: Canadian Centre for Management Development, 1998.

Borins, Sandford. *Innovating with Integrity: How Local Heroes are Transforming American Government*. Washington, D.C.: Georgetown University Press, 1998.

—. "Public management innovation awards in the US and Canada." In Hermann Hill and Helmut Klages, eds. *Trends in Public Service Renewal*. Frankfurt: Peter Lang, 1995.

—. "Public Sector Innovation: Its Contribution to Canadian Competitiveness." Discussion Paper Series, Government and Competitiveness, School of Policy Studies, Queen's University, 1994.

—. *The Shifting Boundaries of Government: A United Kingdom International Conference: A Report*. Toronto: CAPAM, 1998.

—. "Summary: Government in Transition – a new paradigm in public administration." In Commonwealth Association for Public Administration and Management. *Government in Transition*. Toronto: CAPAM, 1995.

—, and David Wolf. *Realizing the Potential of Information Technology in the Public Sector: An Organizational Challenge*. Toronto: KPMG Centre for Government Foundation, 1999.

Bouckaert, Geert, and K. Verhoest. "A Comparative Perspective on Performance Management in the Public Sector." Round Table of the International Institute of Administrative Sciences, 14–17 July 1997, Quebec City.

Bourgon, Jocelyne. "Plenary Report – Strengthening Our Policy Capacity." In Canadian Centre for Management Development. *Strengthening Policy Capacity: Conference Proceedings*. Ottawa: CCMD, 1996.

Bragg, Denise. *Quality Management: An Introduction*. Victoria: Service Quality B.C. Secretariat, 1993.

British Columbia. Ministry for Children and Families. *Building the Ministry for Children and Families*. Victoria: Ministry, 1997.

Canada. Business Service Centres Secretariat. "One more one-stop service." *InterConnexion* 1:3 (January 1997) [newsletter]: 2.

—. Clerk of the Privy Council [Jocelyne Bourgon]. *Third Annual Report to the Prime Minister on the Public Service of Canada*. Ottawa: Privy Council Office, 1995.

—. —. *Fourth Annual Report to the Prime Minister on the Public Service of Canada*. Ottawa: Privy Council Office, 1997.

—. Committee on Governing Values. *Governing Values*. Ottawa: Supply and Services, 1987.

—. Department of Canadian Heritage. *The Partnership Guide*. Ottawa: Heritage Canada, 1995.

—. Department of Energy, Mines and Resources (now the Department of Natural Resources). "Our Values" [1992].

—. Department of the Environment. Transition Team Steering Committee on Consultation and Partnerships. *Consultations and Partnerships: Working Together with Canadians*. Ottawa: Environment Canada, 1992.

—. Department of Finance. *Budget Plan*. Ottawa: Finance Canada, 1996.

—. Department of Human Resources Development. "The Union's Vision of Quality." *Service Quality: Strategy 1994–1997*. Ottawa: Human Resources Development Canada, 1994.

—. Department of National Defence. *A Re-engineering Success Story* [video]. Ottawa: DGPA-National Defence Headquarters, 1995.

—. Deputy Minister's Task Force on the Future of the Public Service (Ottawa: Privy Council Office, 1996).

—. Deputy Minister's Task Force on Managing Horizontal Policy Issues. *Report.* Ottawa: Privy Council Office, 1996.

—. Deputy Minister's Task Force on Public Service Values and Ethics. *A Strong Foundation. Report.* Ottawa: Privy Council Office, 1996.

—. Deputy Ministers' Task Force on Service Delivery Models. *Report. PartII.* Ottawa: Privy Council Office, 1996.

—. Deputy Minister's Task Force on Strengthening Policy Capacity. *Report.* Ottawa: Privy Council Office, 1995.

—. Human Resources Development Council. *Empowerment.* Ottawa: Treasury Board Secretariat, 1992.

—. —. *Strategies for People: An Integrated Approach to Changing Public Service Culture.* Ottawa: Treasury Board Secretariat, 1992.

—. Independent Review Panel on Modernization of Comptrollership in the Government of Canada. *Report.* Ottawa: Treasury Board Secretariat, 1997.

—. Interdepartmental Committee of Heads of Training. *Partnerships: An Introductory Guide.* Ottawa: Supply and Services Canada, 1994.

—. La Relève. COSO Sub-Committee on Pride and Recognition. *Pride and Recognition: Keys to an Outstanding Public Service. An Interim Report.* Ottawa: La Relève, 1997.

—. —. Advisory Committee on the Workforce of the Future. *Valuing Our People. Report.* Ottawa: La Relève, 1997.

—. —. *First Report on La Relève: A Commitment to Action. Overview.* Ottawa: Canada Communications Group, 1998.

—. n.a. "Electronic Tax Filing Speeds up Process." *Blueprint in Action No. 14* [flyer]. Ottawa: Supply and Services Canada, n.d.

—. —. "Paying Taxes Electronically Catches on in Business Community." *Blueprint in Action No. 16* [flyer].Ottawa: Supply and Services Canada, n.d.

—. —. "Relevant and Reliable E-Mail System Connects Federal Government Departments." *Blueprint in Action No. 17* [flyer]. Ottawa: Supply and Services Canada, n.d.

—. —. *On the Memorandum of Understanding among the Four Natural Resource Departments on Science and Technology for Sustainable Development. Annual Report: 1996–1997.* Ottawa: Public Works and Government Services, 1997.

—. Office of the Auditor General. *Annual Report.* Ottawa: Supply and Services Canada, 1988.

—. —. *Annual Report.* Ottawa: Supply and Services Canada, 1990.

—. —. *Annual Report.* Ottawa: Supply and Services Canada, 1992.

—. —. *Annual Report.* Ottawa: Supply and Services Canada, 1993.

—. —. *Annual Report.* Ottawa: Supply and Services Canada, 1994.

—. —. *Annual Report.* Ottawa: Supply and Services Canada, 1995.

—. —. *Annual Report.* Ottawa: Supply and Services Canada, 1996.

—. —. *Annual Report.* Ottawa: Supply and Services Canada, 1999.

—. Passport Office. *Annual Report 1995–96.* Ottawa: Public Works and Government Services Canada, 1996.

—. Personnel Renewal Council. "Human Resource Management in the Public Service: Framework for the Future." Report from the roundtable conference organized by the Personnel Renewal Council. Hull, Quebec, 8–10 November 1995.

—. Public Service Commission. Consultative Review of Staffing. *A New Framework for Resourcing the Workforce: Report.* Ottawa: PSC, 1996.

—. Public Service 2000. *Highlights of the White Paper on Public Service 2000. The Renewal of the Public Service of Canada.* Ottawa: Privy Council Office, 1990.

—. —. *The Renewal of the Public Service of Canada.* Ottawa: Supply and Services Canada, 1990.

—. —. Service to the Public Task Force. *Report.* Ottawa: Privy Council Office, 1990.

—. —. Task Force on the Management Category. *Report.* Ottawa: Privy Council Office, 1990.

—. —. Task Force on Workforce Adaptiveness. *Managing Change in the Public Service – A Guide for the Perplexed.* Ottawa: Supply and Services Canada, 1991.

—. Treasury Board Secretariat. *An Overview of Quality and Affordable Service for Canadians.* Ottawa: Supply and Services Canada, 1994.

—. —. *Blueprint for Renewing Government Services Using Information Technology: Executive Summary (Discussion Draft).* Ottawa: TBS, 1994.

—. —. *Framework for Alternative Program Delivery.* Ottawa: TBS, 1995.

—. —. *Guides to Quality Service. Quality Services Guide V – Recognition.* Ottawa: TBS, 1996.

—. —. *Innovations: Best Practices Notes. Note # 15. Teamwork: Combined Effort.* Ottawa: Supply and Services Canada, 1994.

—. —. *Quality Services: An Overview.* Ottawa: Supply and Services Canada, 1995.

—. —. *Risk Management in the Federal Public Service: Action Plan to Develop Integrated TBS Policy Guidance.* Ottawa: TBS, 1999.

—. —. *Who is the Client – A Discussion Paper.* Ottawa: Supply and Services Canada, 1996.

—. —, and Public Service Commission. *Profile of Public Service Leaders and Managers.* Ottawa: TBS and PSC, 1990.

Canada Post. "Angus Reid Group Public Opinion Survey of Canadians Concerning Canada Post and Postal Issues." *Canada Post Press Release,* 11 March 1996. Ottawa: Canada Post, 1996.

Canadian Centre for Management Development. *Continuous Learning. A CCMD Report.* Ottawa: CCMD, 1994.

—. *Public Service Culture: Results of the SYMLOG Survey.* Ottawa: CCMD, 1997.

Canadian Tourism Commission. *Annual Report, 1996.* Ottawa: Commission, 1997.

Cappe, Mel. "False Dichotomies." In John C. Tait and Mel Cappe. *Rethinking Policy: Perspectives on Public Policy.* Ottawa: Canadian Centre for Management Development, 1995.

Carr, David, and Ian Littman. *Excellence in Government: Total Quality Management in the 1990s.* Arlington, Va.: Coopers & Lybrand, 1990.

Carroll, Barbara Wake, and David Siegel. "Two Solitudes or One Big Happy Family: Head Office–Field Office Relations in Government Organizations." Paper presented to the annual meeting of the Canadian Political Science Association, Montreal, 6 June 1995.

Champy, James. *Reengineering Management: The Mandate for New Leadership.* New York: HarperCollins, 1995.

Clapperton, Anne. "Reshaping government – technology as a catalyst for management change." *Public Sector Management* 5:2 (Summer 1994): 23–5.

Clark, I.D. "Getting the Incentives Right: Towards a Productivity-Oriented Management Framework for the Public Service." Background paper for an armchair discussion at the Canadian Centre for Management Development, 1993

Clemmer, Jim. *Pathways to Performance.* Toronto: Macmillan, 1995.

Cohen, Steven, and Ronald Brand. *Total Quality Management in Government: A Practical Guide for the Real World.* San Francisco: Jossey-Bass, 1993.

Commonwealth Secretariat. *Current Good Practices and New Developments in Public Service Management – A Profile of the Public Service of Canada.* London: Commonwealth Secretariat, 1994.

Conger, J.A., and Rabindra N. Kanungo. "The empowerment process: Integrating theory and practice." *Academy of Management Review* 13:3 (1988): 471–82.

Conte, Christopher. "Teledemocracy for better or worse." *Governing* 8:6 (June 1995): 33–41.

Daniels, Arthur. "Taking Strategic Alliances to the World: Ontario's Teranet." In Robin Ford and David Zussman, eds. *Alternative Service Delivery: Sharing Governance in Canada.* Toronto: Institute of Public Administration of Canada and KPMG Centre for Government Foundation, 1997.

Darling, Michele. "Empowerment: myth or reality?" *Executive Speeches* 10: 6 (June/July 1996): 23–8.

Davidow, William H., and Michael S. Malone. *The Virtual Corporation.* New York: Harper Business, 1992.

Denhardt, Robert B. *The Pursuit of Significance: Strategies for Managerial Success in Public Organizations.* Belmont, Calif.: Wadsworth Publishing, 1993.

Dixon, Nancy. M. *Organizational Learning.* Ottawa: Conference Board of Canada, 1993.

Doering, Ronald. "Alternative Service Delivery: the Case of the Canadian Food Inspection Agency" [unpublished paper]. Ottawa: Canadian Food Inspection Agency, 1997.

Doern, G. Bruce. *The Road to Better Public Services: Progress and Constraints in Five Canadian Federal Agencies.* Montreal: Institute for Research on Public Policy, 1994.

—, and Peter Aucoin, eds. *Public Policy in Canada.* Toronto: Macmillan, 1979.

Doerr, Audrey. *The Machinery of Government in Canada.* Toronto: Methuen, 1981.

Drucker, Peter. *Management: Tasks, Responsibilities, Practices.* New York: Harper & Row, 1974.

—. "Really reinventing government." *The Atlantic Monthly* (February 1995): 49–61.

Ducharme, Dennis. "Manitoba Fleet Vehicles – Testing the SOA Concept." *Public Sector Management* 6:1 (Winter 1995): 22–3.

Duhamel, Ronald. "Performance management: What is it? Why does it matter?" *Insights* 3 (February/March 1998): 1–2.

Duxbury, Linda, Lorraine Dyke and Natalie Lam. *Career Development in the Federal Public Service: Building a World-Class Workforce.* Ottawa: Treasury Board Secretariat, 1999.

Edwards, John, and Nick Mulder. "Round table on alternative organizational forms." *Optimum* 23:1 (1992): 3–5.

Erin Research. *Citizens First.* Ottawa: Canadian Centre for Management Development, 1998.

Farquhar, Carolyn. *Business and Organizational Planning Case Study Series. Case # 4: Ontario Ministry of Consumer and Commercial Relations.* Toronto: Cabinet Office, Centre for Leadership, 1996.

Federal Quality Institute. *Criteria and Scoring Guidelines for the President's Award for Quality and Productivity Improvement.* Federal Total Quality Management Handbook. Ottawa: Institute, 1990.

Filipowski, Diane. "The Tao of Tandem." *Personnel Journal* (October 1991): 72–8.

Finckenauer, James O. *Scared Straight! And the Panacea Phenomenon.* Englewood Cliffs, N.J.: Prentice-Hall, 1982.

Fisher, Kimball. *Leading Self-Directed Work Teams.* New York: McGraw-Hill, 1993.

Ford, Robin, and David Zussman. "Alternative Service Delivery: Transcending Boundaries." In Robin Ford and David Zussman, eds. *Alternative Service Delivery: Sharing Governance in Canada.* Toronto: IPAC and KPMG Centre for Government Foundation, 1997.

Fowler, Robert R. "Base delegation or authority and accountability trial management through innovation." *Public Sector Management* 4:3 (Autumn 1993): 14–16.

Fry, Ellen. "The perils of partnership." *Justice Echo* no. 15 (July 1992): 4.

Gandz, Jeffrey, and Federick G. Bird. "The ethics of empowerment." *Journal of Business Ethics* 15:2 (April 1996): 383–92.

Gattinger, Monica. "Local Governments On-Line: How are They Doing it and What Does it Mean?" In Katherine A. Graham and Susan D. Phillips, eds. *Citizen Engagement: Lessons in Participation from Local Government.* Monographs on Canadian Public Administration – No. 22. Toronto: Institute of Public Administration of Canada, 1998.

Gladu, André. "Human Resources Development Canada, Quebec Region" [unpublished paper, 1996].

Gold, Kenneth. *A Comparative Analysis of Successful Organizations.* Washington, D.C.: U.S. Office of Personnel Management, Workforce Effectiveness and Development Group, 1981. Cited in Michael L. Vasu et al. *Organization Behavior and Public Management*, 2nd edition. New York: Marcel Dekker, 1990.

Golden, Olivia. "Innovation in public sector human services programs: The implications of innovation by 'groping along.'" *Journal of Policy Analysis and Management* 9:2 (Spring 1990): 219–48.

Gooderham, Mary. "Participatory democracy thriving on the Internet." *The Globe and Mail* (Toronto) 4 March 1997, p. A10.

Gore, Al. *Creating a Government that Works Better and Costs Less.* New York: Penguin, 1993.

—. *Common Sense Government.* New York: Random House, 1995.

Gow, James Iain. *Innovations in the Public Service.* Ottawa: Canadian Centre for Management Development, 1991.

—. *Learning from Others: Administrative Innovations Among Canadian Governments.* Monographs on Canadian Public Administration – No. 16. Toronto: Institute of Public Administration of Canada, 1994.

Gratias, Alan, and Melanie Boyd. "Beyond government: can the public sector meet the challenges of public – private partnering?" *Optimum* 26:1 (Summer 1995): 3–14.

Halachmi, Arie. "Business process reengineering in the public sector: trying to get another frog to fly?" *National Productivity Review* 15:3 (Summer 1996): 9–18.

Halachmi, Arie, and Geert Bouchaert, eds. *Organizational Performance and Measurement in the Public Sector: Toward Service, Effort and Accomplishment Reporting.* Westport, Conn.: Quorum Books, 1996.

Hale, Mary M. "Learning organizations and mentoring." *Public Productivity Review* 9:4 (June 1996): 422–33.

Hamburg, Morris. *Statistical Analysis for Decision Making.* New York: Harcourt, Brace, 1970.

Hammer, Michael, and James Champy. *Reengineering the Corporation: A Manifesto for Business Revolution.* New York: HarperCollins, 1993.

Harris, Jim. *The Learning Paradox: Gaining Success and Security in a World of Change.* Toronto: Macmillan, 1998.

Hood, Christopher. "A public management for all seasons?" *Public Administration* 69:1 (Spring 1991): 3–19.

Houston, Margaret, and John Talbott. "Worker empowerment works – sometimes." *CMA Magazine* 70 (July/August 1996): 16–18.

Huffy, Eric. "The creation of autonomous service units – a change more fundamental than it appears" [English translation of French article]. *Public Sector Management* 7:4 (Winter 1997): 19, 31.

Hughes Anthony, Nancy [former deputy minister, Department of Veterans Affairs, Government of Canada]. "Speaking Notes for a Meeting of the Prince Edward Island Regional Group of the Institute of Public Administration of Canada," 21 September 1993.

Hyde, Albert C. "The proverbs of total quality management: recharting the path to quality improvement in the public sector." *Public Productivity and Management Review* 16:1 (Fall 1992): 25–38.

ICM Research. *Citizen's Charter Customer Survey: Research Report.* London: Citizen's Charter Unit, 1993.

Ingstrup, Ole. *Public Service Renewal: From Means to Ends.* Ottawa: Canadian Centre for Management Development, 1995.

—. *Reengineering in the Public Service – Promise or Peril.* Ottawa: Canadian Centre for Management Development, 1995.

—. *The Strategic Revolution in Executive Development*. Ottawa: Canadian Centre for Management Development, 1995.

—, and Paul Crookall. *The Three Pillars of Public Management*. Montreal and Kingston: McGill-Queen's University Press, 1998.

Johanis, Paul. *Serving Canadians: A Survey of Practices in Support of Quality Services in the Federal Public Service of Canada*. Ottawa: Statistics Canada, 1995.

Johnston, Catharine G., and Carolyn Farquhar. *Empowered People Satisfy Customers*. Ottawa: Conference Board of Canada, 1992.

Kanter, Rosabeth. "When a thousand flowers bloom: structural, collective, and social conditions for innovation in organizations." In Barry M. Staw and L.L. Cummings, eds. *Research in Organizational Behaviour*. Vol. 10. Greenwich, Conn.: JAI Press, 1988.

Kaplan, Robert S., and David P. Norton. *The Balanced Scorecard: Translating Strategy into Action*. Boston: Harvard Business School Press, 1996.

Katzenbach, Jon R., and Douglas K. Smith. *The Wisdom of Teams: Creating the High-Performance Organization*. Boston: Harvard Business School Press, 1993.

Kernaghan, Kenneth. "Beyond Bureaucracy: Towards a Framework for Analysis of Public Sector Reform." Paper presented at the annual conference of the Canadian Political Science Association, Brock University, 4 June 1996.

—. "Changing concepts of power and responsibility in the Canadian public service." CANADIAN PUBLIC ADMINISTRATION 21:3 (Fall 1978): 389–406.

—. "The emerging public service culture: values, ethics and reforms." CANADIAN PUBLIC ADMINISTRATION 37:4 (Winter 1994): 614–30.

—. "Empowerment and public administration: revolutionary advance or passing fancy." CANADIAN PUBLIC ADMINISTRATION 35:2 (Summer 1992): 194–214.

—. "Partnership and public administration: conceptual and practical considerations." CANADIAN PUBLIC ADMINISTRATION 36:1 (Spring 1993): 57–76.

—. "Shaking the Foundation: New versus Traditional Public-Service Values." In Mohamed Charih and Arthur Daniels, eds. *New Public Management and Public Administration in Canada*. Monographs on Canadian Public Administration – No. 20. Toronto: Institute of Public Administration of Canada, 1997.

—, and Mohamed Charih. "The challenges of change: emerging issues in contemporary public administration." CANADIAN PUBLIC ADMINISTRATION 40:2 (Summer 1997): 218–33.

—, and Olivia Kuper. *Coordination in Canadian Governments: A Case Study of Aging Policy*. Toronto: Institute of Public Administration of Canada, 1983.

—, and David Siegel. *Public Administration in Canada: A Text*, 4th edition. Toronto: Nelson, 1999.

King, Nigel. "Innovation at Work: the Research Literature." In M.A. West and J.L. Farr, eds. *Innovation and Creativity at Work*. New York: Wiley, 1990.

Kizilos, Peter. "Crazy about empowerment?" *Training* 27 (December 1990): 47–56.

Kotter, John P., and James L. Heskett. *Corporate Cultures and Performance*. Boston: Harvard Business School Press, 1992.

Kouzes, James M., and Barry Z. Posner. *The Leadership Challenge*. San Francisco: Jossey-Bass, 1995.

Laframboise, H.L. "Administrative reform in the federal public service: signs of a saturation psychosis." CANADIAN PUBLIC ADMINISTRATION 14:3 (Fall 1971): 303–25.

LaFrance, Gérard. "Managing reengineering projects for results." *Optimum* 27:3 (Winter 1997): 8–13.

Lane, Patricia. "Ontario's Fair Tax Commission: an innovative approach to public consultation." *Optimum* 23:4 (Spring 1993): 7–17.

Levin, Martin, and Mary Bryna Sanger. *Making Government Work: How Entrepreneurial Executives Turn Bright Ideas into Real Results.* San Francisco: Jossey-Bass, 1994.

—. "Using old stuff in new ways: innovation as a case of evolutionary tinkering." *Journal of Policy Analysis and Management* 11:1 (Winter 1992): 88–115.

Lewington, Jennifer. "Computer gap hurts poor, report says: skills and access are concentrated in the hands of rich Canadians, Statscan study finds." *The Globe and Mail* (Toronto) 1 November 1996, p. A5.

Little, Bruce. "Poor left behind in computer revolution: richest Canadians more than four times as likely to own a PC than lower-income households." *The Globe and Mail* (Toronto) 15 January 1996, p. B11.

Loveridge, Ray. "What is participation? A review of the literature and some methodological problems." *British Journal of Industrial Relations* 18:3 (November 1980): 297–317.

Mackie, R. "Ontario's ID plan spurs privacy fears." *The Globe and Mail* (Toronto) 22 October 1999, pp. A1, A4.

Manion, John. "Career public service in Canada: reflections and predictions." *International Review of Administrative Sciences* 57:3 (September 1991): 361–72.

—. *A Management Model.* Ottawa: Canadian Centre for Management Development, 1989.

Manitoba, Fleet Vehicles Agency. *1997–98 Annual Report.* Winnipeg: Queen's Printer, 1997.

Mayne, John, and Eduardo Zapico-Goni. *Monitoring Performance in the Public Sector: Future Directions from International Experience.* New Brunswick, N.J.: Transaction Publishers, 1997.

Marquardt, Michael, and Angus Reynolds. *The Global Learning Organization.* New York: Irwin, 1993.

Marson, Brian. "Building customer focused public organizations." *Public Administration Quarterly* 17:1 (Spring 1993): 30–41.

—. "Leading strategic change in the public sector." *The Public Manager* 26:4 (Winter 1997–8): 26–30.

—. "1998–99 deputy ministers' issues survey." *Public Sector Management* 10:1 (Spring 1999): 5–10.

—. "Report on the IPAC 1996–97 Deputy Ministers' Issues Survey – Public Service Renewal Agenda," *Public Sector Management* 7:4 (Winter 1997): 11–17

—, and Geoff Dinsdale. *Effective Public Service Leadership: Results of EL Participants Survey of Senior Managers.* Ottawa: Canadian Centre for Management Development, 1999.

McCall, Morgan. *Developing Executives through Work Experience.* Greensboro, N.C.: Centre for Creative Leadership, 1988.

McDavid, James, and Brian Marson. *The Well-Performing Government Organization.* Toronto: Institute of Public Administration of Canada, 1991.

McInnes, Craig. "Victoria data site pulled off Internet." *The Globe and Mail* (Toronto) 27 September 1996, p. A6.

McKenna, Barrie. "Your life on a chip." *The Globe and Mail* (Toronto) 23 November 1995, p. B7.

—. "A deal way off course." *The Globe and Mail* (Toronto) 13 May 1995, pp. B1, B5.

—. "Cancelled contracts cost Ottawa millions." *The Globe and Mail* (Toronto) 4 September 1996, pp. B1, B23.

Mechling, Jerry. "Leadership and the knowledge gap." *Governing* 9:12 (December 1995).

Metcalfe, Les. "International policy coordination and public management reform." *International Review of Administrative Sciences* 60:2 (June 1994): 271–90.

Milakovich, Michael E. "Total quality management in the public sector." *National Productivity Review* 15:2 (Spring 1991): 195–213.

Miller, Danny. *The Icarus Paradox: How Exceptional Companies Bring About their Own Downfall.* New York: HarperCollins, 1990.

Miller, Thomas. *Citizen Surveys.* Washington, D.C.: International City/County Management Association, 1991.

Milward, H. Brinton. "Implications of Contracting Out: New Roles for the Hollow State." In Patricia W. Ingraham, Barbara S. Romsek and Assocs., ed. *New Paradigms for Government.* San Francisco: Jossey-Bass, 1994.

Mintzberg, Henry. *The Rise and Fall of Strategic Planning: Reconceiving Roles for Planning, Plans, and Planners.* New York: Free Press, 1994.

Morley, David. "Team building: changing managerial attitudes and behaviour in a quality environment." *Optimum* 22:3 (1991–92): 17–24.

Mumford, Alan. *Management Development: Strategies for Action.* London: Institute of Personnel Management, 1989.

n.a. [Institute of Public Administration of Canada]. "Alberta Workers' Compensation Board Rehabilitation Centre." *Public Sector Management* 4:1 (Spring 1993): 8.

—. "B.C. Ministry of Finance and Corporate Relations: Personal Property Registration." *Public Sector Management* 4:1 (Spring 1993): 4, 6.

—. "City of Vancouver: Neighbourhood Integrated Service Teams." *Public Sector Management* 8:2 (Summer 1997): 8.

—. "Clinical Research and Treatment Institute, Addiction Research Foundation of Ontario." *Public Sector Management* 5:1 (Spring 1994): 14–15.

—. "Government Services Canada, Open Bidding Service (OBS)." *Public Sector Management* 4:1 (Spring 1993): 13.

—. "Human Resources Development Canada: a collaborative approach to change management: re-engineering the Record of Employment (ROE)." *Public Sector Management* 8:2 (Summer 1997): 11, 16.

—. "Ontario Ministry of Consumer and Commercial Relations: Clearing the Path for Business Success." *Public Sector Management* 7:2 (Summer 1996): 12–14.

—. "Re-shaping government: a case study of the Office of Registrar General, Thunder Bay, Ontario." *Public Sector Management* 5:1 (Spring 1994): 4–7.

Niskanen, William. *Bureaucracy and Representative Government*. Chicago: Aldine Atherton, 1971.

O'Grady, Dennis, and Keon Chi. "The Origins of Innovation in State Government." Paper presented at the conference of the American Society of Public Administration, Washington, D.C., March 1991. Cited in James Iain Gow. *Learning from Others: Administrative Innovations Among Canadian Governments*. Monographs on Canadian Public Administration – No. 16. Toronto: Institute of Public Administration of Canada, 1994.

Ontario. Cabinet Office. *The Ontario Cabinet Decision-Making System: Procedures Guide*. Toronto: Queen's Printer, 1997.

—. Executive Development Committee. *Human Resources Plan for the Senior Management Group*. Toronto: Cabinet Office, 1997.

—. Management Board of Cabinet. *Best Value for Tax Dollars: Improving Service Quality in the Ontario Government*. Toronto: Management Board, 1992.

—. Office of the Lieutenant Governor. "The Honourable Hilary M. Weston, Lieutenant Governor of Ontario, Concerned about Erroneous Message on Bill 160." *Press Release*, 17 November 1997. Toronto: Queen's Printer, 1997.

—. Transportation Capital Corporation. "Highway, 407 Info Brochure II." Toronto: Corporation, 1995.

Organisation for Economic Co-operation and Development. *Building Policy Coherence: Tools and Tensions*. Paris: OECD, 1996.

—. *Globalisation: What Challenges and Opportunities for Governments?* Paris: OECD, 1996.

Osborne, David, and Ted Gaebler. *Reinventing Government: How the Entrepreneurial Spirit is Transforming the Public Sector From Schoolhouse to State House, City Hall to Pentagon*. Reading, Mass.: Addison-Wesley, 1992.

—, and Peter Plastrik. *Banishing Bureaucracy: The Five Strategies for Reinventing Government*. Reading, Mass.: Addison-Wesley, 1997.

Overman, Sam, and Kathy Boyd. "Best practices research and postbureaucratic reform." *Journal of Public Administration Research and Theory* 4:1 (January 1994): 67–83.

Palermo, Richard, and Gregory Watson. *A World of Quality: the Timeless Passport*. Milwaukee: ASQC Press, 1993.

Parisotto, Richard, chief administrative officer. Town of Ajax. Interview, August 1998.

Parker, Glenn M. *Cross-Functional Teams: Working with Allies, Enemies, and Other Strangers*. San Francisco: Jossey-Bass, 1994.

Pedlar, Mike. *Action Learning in Theory and Practice*. Aldershot, U.K.: Gower Publishing, 1991.

Peters, Guy. *Managing Horizontal Government: The Politics of Coordination*. Ottawa: Canadian Centre for Management Development, 1998.

—. *Policy and Operations*. Ottawa: Canadian Centre for Management Development, 1997.

—, and Donald J. Savoie. *Governance in a Changing Environment*. Montreal and Kingston: McGill-Queen's University Press, 1995.

Peters, Thomas. "Excellence in government? I'm all for it! Maybe." *The Bureaucrat* 20:1 (Spring 1991): 3–8.

—, and Robert H. Waterman. *In Search of Excellence: Lessons from America's Best-Run Companies*. New York: Harper & Row, 1982.

Pfeiffer, J. William, Leonard D. Goodstein and Timothy Nolan. *Shaping Strategic Planning*. Glenview, Ill.: Scott, Foresman, 1989.

Phillips, Susan D. "How Ottawa Blends: Shifting Government Relationships with Interest Groups. " In Frances Abele, ed. *How Ottawa Spends. 1991–92: The Politics of Fragmentation*. Carleton Public Policy Series # 13. Ottawa: Carleton University Press, 1991.

Philp, Margaret. "Metro to debate welfare ID technology." *The Globe and Mail* (Toronto) 30 April 1996, p. A6.

—. "Toronto planning welfare ID card." *The Globe and Mail* (Toronto) 26 March 1996, pp. A1–A2.

Plunkett, Lorne C., and Robert Fournier. *Participative Management: Implementing Empowerment*. New York: John Wiley, 1991.

Poister, Theodore, and Gary Henry. "Citizen ratings of public and private service quality: a comparative perspective." *Public Administration Review* 54:2 (March/April 1994): 155–160.

Posner, Barry Z., James M. Kouzes and Warren H. Schmidt. "Shared values make a difference: an empirical test of culture." *Human Resource Management* 24:3 (Fall 1985): 293–309.

Public Management Research Centre. *Federal Executive Compensation and Retention: Perspectives from the Private Sector*. Ottawa: Public Management Research Centre, 1997.

—. *Final Report: Executive Consultations on Issues Related to Organizational Retention and Compensation*. Ottawa: Public Management Research Centre, 1997.

Rawson, Bruce. "Public Service 2000 Service to the Public Task Force: findings and implications." CANADIAN PUBLIC ADMINISTRATION 34:3 (Fall 1991): 490–500.

Reguly, E. "Quebec-led group wins bidding war for Highway 407." *The Globe and Mail* (Toronto) 10 April 1999, pp. B1, B4.

Reich, Robert. *The Work of Nations*. New York: Vintage Books, 1992.

Reschenthaler, G.B., and Fred Thompson. "The information revolution and the new public management." *Journal of Public Administration and Theory* 6:1 (January 1996): 125–43.

Revans, R.W. *Action Learning*. London: Blond and Briggs, 1980.

Roberts, Alasdair. "Worrying about misconduct: the control lobby and the PS 2000 reforms." CANADIAN PUBLIC ADMINISTRATION 39:4 (Winter 1996): 489–523.

Roberts, David. "Ottawa adds $55 million to venture." *The Globe and Mail* (Toronto) 9 June 1998, p. A5.

Roberts, Nancy, and Paula King. *Transforming Public Policy: Dynamics of Policy Entrepreneurship and Innovation*. San Francisco: Jossey-Bass, 1996.

Rocine, Victor. "Total quality management: excellence by design." *Public Sector Management* 2:1 (Spring 1991): 18–21.

Rodal, Alti. *Special Operating Agencies – Issues for Parent Departments and Central Agencies*. Ottawa: Canadian Centre for Management Development, 1996.

—, and Nick Mulder. "Partnerships, devolution and power-sharing: issues and implications for management." *Optimum* 23:1 (1992–93): 29–45.

Rokeach, Milton. *The Nature of Human Values*. New York: Free Press, 1973.

Rosell, Steven A. *Governing in an Information Society*. Halifax: Institute for Research on Public Policy, 1992.

Sarick, Lila, and Gay Abbate. "Fingerprint plan approved for Metro welfare recipients." *The Globe and Mail* (Toronto) 20 June 1996, p. A7.

Sathe, Vijay. "Implications of corporate culture: a manager's guide to action." *Organizational Dynamics* (Autumn 1983): 5–23.

Savoie, Donald J. "Central Agencies: A Government of Canada Perspective." In J.M. Bourgault, M. Demers and C. Williams, eds. *Public Administration and Public Management: Experiences in Canada*. Quebec City: Les Publications du Québec, 1997.

—. *Thatcher, Reagan, Mulroney: In Search of a New Bureaucracy*. Toronto: University of Toronto Press, 1994.

—. What's wrong with the new public management?" CANADIAN PUBLIC ADMINISTRATION 38:1 (Spring 1995): 112–21.

Schmidt, Faye, and Teresa Strickland. *Client Satisfaction Surveying: A Manager's Guide*. Ottawa: Canadian Centre for Management Development, 1998.

Schon, D.A. "Deutero-learning in organizations: learning for increased effectiveness." *Organizational Dynamics* 4:1 (Summer 1995): 2–16.

Séguin, Francine. "Service to the public: a major strategic change." CANADIAN PUBLIC ADMINISTRATION 34:3 (Fall 1991): 465–73.

Seidle, Leslie. *Rethinking the Delivery of Public Services to Citizens*. Montreal: Institute for Research on Public Policy, 1995.

Sellers, Phillip. "New Information Highway almost ready as finishing touches put on the 407." *Computing Canada* (6 January 1997): 1, 4.

Selznick, Phillip. *Leadership in Administration: A Sociological Interpretation*. New York: Harper and Row, 1957.

Senge, Peter. *The Fifth Discipline: The Art and Practice of the Learning Organization*. New York: Doubleday/Currency, 1990.

Shepherd, Robert P. "The citizens' forum: a case study in public consultation." *Optimum* 23:4 (Spring 1993): 18–27.

Silverman, Art. Cited in n.a. [Institute of Public Administration of Canada]. "Fisheries and Oceans Canada: management strategy shift produces increased efficiency and effectiveness of DFO's science fleet." *Public Sector Management* 4:1 (Spring 1993): 10–12.

Simpson, Richard. "Making government a 'model user' of the Information Highway – Canada's progress to date." *Public Administration and Development* 17:1 (February 1997): 103–107.

—. "The Information Highway: An Update on Canada." Paper presented to the second biennial conference of the Commonwealth Association for Public Administration and Management, San Gorg, Malta, April 1996.

Skinner, Murray. "Building on heritage: CCG and St. Joseph Corporation." *The Focus Report* 6:4 (August 1997): 10–15.

Stemshorn, Barry. "The Canadian Food Inspection Agency – A Work in Progress." Paper presented to the B.C. Federal Regional Council ASD Workshop, 1998.

Sterne, Peter, and Sandra Zagon. *Public Consultation Guide.* Canadian Centre for Management Development, Management Practices # 19. Ottawa: Supply and Services Canada, 1997.

Sutherland, S.A. "The Al-Mashat affair: administrative accountability in parliamentary institutions." CANADIAN PUBLIC ADMINISTRATION 34:4 (Winter 1991): 573–603.

Sutherland, Allen, and John Knubley. *Case Studies in Federal – Provincial Analysis and Policy Making: Lessons and Conclusions.* Ottawa: Intergovernmental Affairs Secretariat, Privy Council Office, 1995.

Swift, Frank. *Strategic Management in the Public Service: The Changing Role of the Deputy Minister.* Ottawa: Supply and Services Canada for the Canadian Centre for Management Development, 1993.

Swiss, James. "Adapting total quality management (TQM) to government." *Public Administration Review* 52:4 (July/August 1992): 356–62.

Tandem Computers. *Tandem Value System.* Tandem Computers, 1990.

Thomas, Paul G. "Coping with Change: How Public and Private Organizations Read and Respond to Turbulent External Environments." In F. Leslie Seidle, ed. *Rethinking Government: Reform or Reinvention?* Montreal: Institute for Research on Public Policy, 1993.

—. "The politics of performance measurement." *Public Sector Management* 8:2 (Summer 1997): 17–19.

VanNijnatten, Debora L., and Sheila Wray Gregoire. "Bureaucracy and consultation: the Correctional Service of Canada and the requirements of being democratic." CANADIAN PUBLIC ADMINISTRATION 38:2 (Summer 1995): 204–21.

Vantour, Jim, ed. *Our Story: Organizational Renewal in Federal Corrections.* Ottawa: Canadian Centre for Management Development, 1991.

Varette, Sharon. "Consultation in the public service: a question of skills." *Optimum* 24:4 (Spring 1993): 28–39.

Verespej, Michael. "When you put the team in charge." *Industry Week,* no. 239 (3 December 1990): 30–2.

Versteeg, Hajo. *A Case Study in Multi-Stakeholder Consultation: The Corporate History of the Federal Pesticide Registration Review or How We Got From There to Here. Volume 1 – General Principles for Decision Makers. Volume 2 – Practical Considerations for Process Managers and Participants.* Ottawa: Canadian Centre for Management Development, 1992.

Vogt, Judith, and Kenneth Murrell. *Empowerment in Organizations.* San Diego, Calif.: University Associates, 1990.

Wilkins, Alan L., and William G. Ouchi. "Efficient cultures: exploring the relationship between culture and organizational performance." *Administrative Science Quarterly* 28:4 (December 1983): 468–81.

Wilson, James Q. "Innovation in Organization: Notes toward a Theory." In J.D. Thompson, ed. *Approaches in Organization Design*. Pittsburgh: University of Pittsburgh Press, 1966.

Winsor, Hugh. "Salvaged computers teach valuable lessons." *The Globe and Mail* (Toronto) 24 December 1997, p. A4.

Wolfson, Judith. "The MCCR Story: A New Approach to Governance." Notes for a speech at the University of Toronto, 16 February 1995.

Won, Shirley. "How to sew up government work." *The Globe and Mail* (Toronto) 4 September 1995, p. B5.

Wright, David. *Special Operating Agencies – Autonomy, Accountability and Performance Measurement*. Ottawa: Canadian Centre for Management Development, 1995.

—. "Structural innovation in government organizations." *Optimum* 23:1 (1992–93): 27–36.

Young, Bruce, manager, Team Effectiveness. B.C. Hydro. Interview, 27 August 1991.

Zeithaml, Valarie., A. Parasuraman and Leonard Berry, *Delivering Quality Service: Balancing Customer Perceptions and Expectations*. New York: Free Press, 1990.

Zenger, John H., Ed Musselwhite, Kathleen Hurson and Craig Perrin. *Leading Teams: Mastering the New Role*. New York: Irwin, 1994.

Zussman, David. "Developing Policy Capacity for Government: The Canadian Experience." Paper presented to the third international conference of the International Institute of Administrative Sciences, Beijing, October 1996.

—. "Government's new style." *Public Sector Management* 8:2 (Summer 1997): 21–3.

—, and Jak Jabes. *The Vertical Solitude: Managing in the Public Service*. Halifax: Institute for Research on Public Policy, 1989.

### SELECTED WEB SITES

Canada, Treasury Board Secretariat. http://www.tbs-sct.gc.ca

Merseyside Education On-Line. www.icl.com

Policy Research Initiative. http://policyresearch.schoolnet.ca

Public–Private Partnering. http://www.ppp.beyondgov.ca

South Bristol Learning Network. www.sbln.org.uk

Standards Council of Canada. http://www.scc.ca/iso9000/ques9000.html

Standish Group International. www.standishgroup.com

# About the Authors

**Kenneth Kernaghan** is professor of political science and management at Brock University. He received his honours BA in economics and political science from McMaster University and his MA and PhD in political science from Duke University. He is the author or editor of many books, monographs and articles on public administration and public policy, including the co-authored text, *Public Administration in Canada*, which is in its fourth edition. He has served as president of the Institute of Public Administration of Canada and editor of the journal *Canadian Public Administration*. He was the founding director of the Case Program in Canadian Public Administration and the chair of the Academic Advisory Committee of the Ontario Council on University Affairs. Since 1989, he has been editor of the International Review of Administrative Sciences. He is senior research fellow of the Canadian Centre for Management Development, a recipient of the Vanier Gold Medal for excellence in public administration, and a fellow of the Royal Society of Canada. He has served as an adviser to governments in Canada and elsewhere.

**Brian Marson** is senior adviser, Service and Innovation, Treasury Board of Canada Secretariat. He received his graduate degrees in public administration and economics from the University of British Columbia and from Harvard University, where he also served as fellow of the Center for International Affairs. He has served as comptroller general of British Columbia, chair of Service Quality British Columbia, and vice-president of the Canadian Centre for Management Development. His academic experience includes teaching appointments at Harvard, the University of Victoria and Queens University. He is the co-author of *The Well Performing Government Organization*, *Public Financial Management in Canada*, *Good Practices in Citizen-Centred Service* and *Innovations and Good Practices in Single-*

*Window Service*, as well as numerous articles on innovative public-sector management in professional publications. He is past president of the Institute of Public Administration of Canada.

**Sandford Borins** is professor of public management in the Rotman School of Management, University of Toronto, and chair of the Division of Management, University of Toronto at Scarborough. He received his BA from Harvard University, his master's degree in public policy from the Kennedy School of Government and his PhD in economics from Harvard University. He is the author of numerous articles on public management, as well as of four books, the most recent being *Political Management in Canada*, co-authored with Allan Blakeney, former premier of Saskatchewan, and *Innovating with Integrity: How Local Heroes are Transforming American Government*. Professor Borins has been a member of the selection panel for the Institute of Public Administration of Canada Award for Innovative Management, the Commonwealth Association for Public Administration and Management international innovations award, and the Amethyst Award for excellence in the Ontario Public Service. He was a director of the Ontario Transportation Capital Corporation (Highway 407). He is adviser and conference rapporteur to the Commonwealth Association for Public Administration and Management.

# Index

## Monographs on Canadian Public Administration/
## Monographies sur l'administration publique canadienne

1. *Shaping the Canadian City: Essays on Urban Politics and Policy, 1890–1920* – John C. Weaver
2. *Structural Changes in Local Government: Government for Urban Regions* – C.R. Tindal
3. *The Politics of Urban Development: Canadian Urban Expressway Disputes* – Christopher Leo
4. *Quebec's Health System: A Decade of Change, 1967–1977* – Sidney S. Lee
5. *An Approach to Manpower Planning and Management Development in Canadian Municipal Government* – Anne B. McAllister
6. *Le côté humain des systèmes d'information: une vue pratique* – Rolland Hurtubise et Pierre Voyer
7. *The Effects of Transition to Confederation on Public Administration in Newfoundland* – J.G. Channing, C.M.
8. *Coordination in Canadian Governments: A Case Study of Aging Policy* – Kenneth Kernaghan and Olivia Kuper
9. *Public Non-Profit Budgeting: The Evolution and Application of Zero-Base Budgeting* – James Cutt and Richard Ritter
10. *Institutions and Influence Groups in Canadian Farm and Food Policy* – J.D. Forbes
11. *Budgeting in the Provinces: Leadership and the Premiers* – Allan M. Maslove (editor)
12. *Getting the Pink Slip: Severances and Firings in the Senior Public Service* – W.A.W. Neilson (editor)
13. *City Management in Canada: The Role of the Chief Administrative Officer (CAO)* – T.J. Plunkett
14. *Taking Power: Managing Government Transitions/Prendre le pouvoir: La gestion des transitions gouvernementales* – Donald J. Savoie (editor / directeur)
15. *Agencies, Boards, and Commissions in Canadian Local Government* – Dale Richmond and David Siegel (editors)
16. *Learning from Others: Administrative Innovations Among Canadian Governments* – James Iain Gove
17. *Hard Choices or No Choices: Assessing Program Review / L'heure des choix difficiles: L'évaluation de l'Examen des programmes* – Amelita Armit and Jacques Bourgault (editors / directeurs)
18. *So-Called Experts: How American Consultants Remade the Canadian Civil Service 1918–21* – Alasdair Roberts
19. *Genesis, Termination and Succession in the Life Cycle of Organizations: The Case of the Maritime Resource Management Service* – M. Paul Brown
20. *New Public Management and Public Administration in Canada/Nouveau management public et administration publique au Canada* – Mohamed Charih and Arthur Daniels (editors/directeurs)

# MONOGRAPHS ON CANADIAN PUBLIC ADMINISTRATION

# MONOGRAPHIES SUR L'ADMINISTRATION PUBLIQUE CANADIENNE

Peter Aucoin, Vincent Lemieux
Co-directeurs / Co-editors

This monograph series is sponsored by the Institute of Public Administration of Canada as part of its continuing endeavour to stimulate and publish writing in the field of Canadian public administration. It is intended to be a complement to other publications sponsored by the Institute such as the Canadian Public Administration Series, the magazine *Public Sector Management*, the journal *Canadian Public Administration* and the Case Program in Canadian Public Administration, as well as the proceedings of its public policy seminars. By launching the monograph series for medium-length manuscripts and those of a more specialized nature, the Institute ensures that there is a wide variety of publication formats for authors in public administration. While the first titles were in the area of urban local government, the series is intended to cover the broad public administration field and is under the guidance of the co-editors and of the Research Committee of the Institute.

Cette collection de monographies est parrainée par l'Institut d'administration publique du Canada et témoigne de l'effort suivi de l'Institut pour promouvoir et publier des écrits dans le domaine de l'administration publique canadienne. Elle a été conçue comme un complément aux autres publications parrainées par l'Institut telles la Collection administration publique canadienne, le magazine *Management et secteur public*, la revue *Administration publique du Canada* et le Programme de cas en administration publique canadienne, de même que les comptes rendus de ses colloques sur des questions de politique publique. En lançant la collection de monographies pour les ouvrages de longueur moyenne et ceux de nature plus spécialisée, l'Institut s'assure que les auteurs dans le domaine de l'administration publique disposent d'une grande diversité de formats de publications. Bien que les premiers titres traitaient du gouvernement local urbain, la collection s'étend à l'ensemble du domaine de l'administration publique et est sous la direction des co-directeurs de même que du Comité de recherche de l'Institut.

IPAC
The Institute of
Public Administration of Canada

IAPC
L'Institut d'administration
publique du Canada